Skills of Supervision and Staff Management

LAWRENCE SHULMAN
University of British Columbia

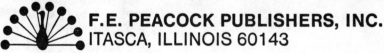

F.E. PEACOCK PUBLISHERS, INC.
ITASCA, ILLINOIS 60143

To My Sons David and Stuart

Copyright © 1982
F. E. Peacock Publishers, Inc.
All rights reserved
Library of Congress
Catalog Card No. 81-83338
ISBN 0-87581-278-3
Printed in the U.S.A.

Contents

Acknowledgments

I would like to acknowledge the contribution of the P.A. Woodward's Foundation, of Vancouver, British Columbia, and the Welfare Grants Directorate of Health and Welfare Canada for their support of the research project cited extensively in this book. From the P.A. Woodward's Foundation, the late Dr. Jack McCreary was most helpful in encouraging my early preparatory work which led to the project grant provided by the Welfare Grants Directorate. From the Directorate, I am particulary indebted to J. Evariste Theriault who provided advice and encouragement for this project, as well as for the social work practice study which preceeded it. However, the views expressed in this book are solely the responsibility of my research colleagues and myself.

I owe a great debt to William Schwartz. While he never was one of my teachers, he nevertheless taught me a great deal. His theoretical model has given direction to my study of social work practice and supervision, and his published and unpublished works have helped to develop the ideas set forth in this text.

In pursuing this line of research into supervision, I was joined by two colleagues, Elizabeth Robinson and Anna Luckjy. Ms. Robinson worked under my supervision on developing and testing one of the questionnaires used in the study as part of her research requirements for the Masters of Social Work degree at the School of Social Work, The University of British Columbia. Her research instructor, my colleague John Crane, provided important consultation on methodology to her. Another colleague, Anne Furness, provided assistance as a member of Ms. Robinson's major paper committee. Ms. Luckyj played a major role in the implementation of the design and the initial analysis of the data. Special mention must be made of the contribution of April Hamilton, my secretary and research assistant. She supervised production and distribution of the questionnaires, maintenance of data files, coding, and organization of findings. We were also fortunate to have the assistance of Elizabeth Harmer, who advised on data preparation, wrote our computer programs, and executed most of the computer analyses.

The project was dependent on the cooperation of supervisors, workers, and the administrators of the agencies and hospitals involved. Particularly helpful were John Noble, Deputy Minister, the Executive Committee, and Brian Taylor, Manager of Staff Development, of the Ministry of Human Resources of British Columbia, and Joseph Messner, Executive Director, and Mary Sinclair, Director of Training, of the Children's Aid Society of Ottawa.

I would also like to thank the many supervisors, workers, and students whose recorded accounts of their practice have been included. Their material gives life to the theory and provides practical illustrations which aid understanding of the complex processes involved. In my supervision contacts, consultations, and workshops for supervisors, I have been taught a great deal about supervision. My colleague, Kloh-Ann Amacher, read portions of the manuscript and made many helpful suggestions. Preliminary editing assistance from Chris Burridge was invaluable. The manuscript was skillfully typed by April Hamilton and Mrs. M. Visentin. Finally, I would like to thank the staff at Peacock Publishers—Ted Peacock, Tom La-Marre, Joyce Usher, and Gloria Reardon—for once again providing their competent assistance.

Introduction

This is a book about skill. It focuses on the skills in communications, relationship, teaching, and group leadership that supervisors and administrators in the helping professions need so they can direct the work of their staffs more effectively. Although administrators and supervisors have an essential impact on the effective provision of services, they receive surprisingly little training in the necessary key skill areas. Training programs often concentrate on the management aspects of the job (e.g., budgeting, time management, report writing, setting objectives) and give little attention to the interactional skills required for implementing supervisory and administrative functions.

These training programs seem to be based on the proposition that professionals who can do their jobs well as social workers, nurses, psychologists, child care workers, and so on should be able to make the transition to supervisory positions on their own. While there is some truth to the idea that direct practice experience with clients, patients, and others can be useful (as will be illustrated in this text), it is a myth that this parallel will be apparent to the neophyte supervisor. There is a need for clear, simple models of supervision practice that will help new supervisors learn how to implement their complex human relations tasks and help experienced supervisors understand why some staff contacts go well and others do not. The development of such models is the task to which this book is directed.

Much of the content is drawn from my own practice experience and discussions I have conducted in scores of workshops and training sessions for supervisors and administrators in a number of the helping professions. The issues selected are those that workshop participants have repeatedly identified as central problems. This enhances the book's practical value and relates it to day-to-day problems experienced by supervisors in the real world. In attempting to understand the dynamics of the problems as well as to develop an approach for dealing with the issues, I have applied a practice theory developed by my colleague William Schwartz, who devised a model of practice for the social work professional (Schwartz, 1961, 1971, 1976, 1977). Early in his work he suggested that this powerful practice theory could have applications to other helping relationships, such as supervision, administration, and teaching (Schwartz, 1960, 1968). While the approach described in this book is rooted in the seminal work of Schwartz and draws on his written and verbally communicated ideas, the content reflects my own elaboration and thus is my responsibility.

There are three assumptions underlying this presentation. First is the belief that there are a number of common dynamics and core skills which are central to all supervision processes. While the examples draw on a range of setting (e.g., social welfare agencies, hospitals, residential treatment centers) and include the work of many different types of professionals (social work supervisors, hospital administrators, nursing supervisors, consultants, child care supervisors), all of whom may be involved in offering different forms of services, the common elements of the practice are stressed. This focus recognizes that there are also aspects which may be specific to the particular setting and actors involved. The goal is to develop a *generic* model for the helping professions. Although many of the examples will be familiar to supervisors in other areas, such as business or government, these supervisors are not the primary audience for this book.

A second assumption is that the core dynamics and skills which underlie effective supervision can be related to the many different contexts and modalities within which these supervisors operate. Many key skills, for example, are equally relevant to working with staff individually or in groups. There are, of course, important differences in group sessions, and these are identified. There are also similarities in working with staff members within a formal conference structure and in providing the more informal type of supervision in short, focused discussions on specific issues. In addition to being responsible for formal group meetings (e.g., staff or team conferences), supervisors are responsibile for coordinating the work of staff members in the informal system. This part of their task is often the most frustrating and difficult, for interpersonal and professional conflicts can lead to a lack of cooperation. These same skills and dynamics can also be applied to the work of the supervisor in relation to other systems, such as representing staff concerns to the administration, dealing with other supervisors (department heads, etc.) on issues of conflict between units, or relating to outside agencies. Examples will illustrate the skills involved in working with individual staff members, the staff as a group, and the system as a whole, and they will deal with both the formal and informal contexts of this work.

The third assumption is that there are similarities in the processes that take place in the supervisory relationship and in any helping relationship. The central dynamics and key skills that are important in direct practice are also important to the supervisory relationship. The similarities have been identified by a number of authors (Arlow, 1960; Schwartz, 1968; Doerhrman, 1972). I do not suggest, however, that supervision should become a therapeutic relationship, in the sense that the staff member is regarded as a client of the supervisor. Indeed, it is absolutely essential that this does not happen, and the work of supervision remain focused on helping staff members carry out their work-related tasks. Nevertheless, much of what we know about effective communication and relationship skills can be very useful in implementing diverse aspects of the supervisory function, such as coordination, education, and evaluation.

Inevitably, the way the supervisor demonstrates the helping relationship will influence the manner in which the staff relates to clients. For example, when supervisors attempts to help staff members develop a greater capacity for expressing empathy with difficult clients, they ought to demonstrate their own empathy for these learning struggles. Supervisors can draw on a number of similar ideas from the field of human relations. Many of the techniques and dynamics to be described in this text are discussed by authors on social work, and several were introduced in my text on practice, *The Skills of Helping Individuals and Groups* (Shulman, 1979). While the problems and examples in the following chapters will relate directly to the supervision function, because of these parallels even a supervisor who has recently moved from the ranks of practitioner will already know a great deal about the communication and relationship skills needed for effective supervision. This text will demonstrate how drawing on relevant practice experiences can enhance understanding of the skills of supervision.

Organization

The opening chapter which describes an interactional approach to supervision, lays the conceptual groundwork and provides an overview of my sense of the purpose of supervision and the supervisor's function. There is no discussion of the history or theory of supervision because this has been dealt with thoroughly in other texts (see, for example, Kadushin, 1976, for the social work field; Kutzik, 1977, for both social work and medicine; and Munson, 1979). Instead, this text focusses on the relationship between supervisor and supervisee, the tasks of the supervisor, and some major assumptions about the process.

Several chapters employ time as an organizing principle, borrowing the framework of the phases of work from Schwartz's practice theory (1976). Skills needed for the preparatory and beginning phases of supervisory work are examined in Chapter 2, starting with the skill of tuning in, or developing empathy with the staff's feelings about the new relationship. The underlying assumption of the beginning phase is the importance of developing a clear working contract at the start. Both the problems of beginning as a new supervisor from outside the system and those of the new supervisor who is promoted from within are examined. Another section discribes the contracting and preparatory work needed to incorporate a new staff member into the working unit.

In Chapter 3 the focus is on the work phase in individual supervision. The core interactional and communication skills required in ongoing work with staff regardless of the particular issue or problem under discussion, are reviewed. The skills of empathic response, sharing one's own feelings, providing data, and making what Schwartz has called a "demand for work" are among those described and illustrated in this context. A number of common situations in the work phase are used to illustrate the theory, such as the problem of authority and how it affects the supervisory relationship, and the obstacles encountered in trying to relate to a defensive staff member who has little trust in the supervisor. Resistance is also explored, both the active kind, which supervisors experience as an open challenge to their authority, and the passive kind, which in some ways is even more difficult to handle. An example is the staff member who consistently avoids changing, though often exppressing such attitude as: "You are absolutely right about that, and I am definitely going to do something about it".

Chapter 4 examines the educational function of the supervisor in helping the staff to develop the skills needed for carrying out its work. While unique issues connected with student supervision are included in this chapter, the general purpose is to identify core issues involved whenever one person attempts to help another master new skills.

Group variations in supervision are considered in Chapter 5, which explores the skills needed for effective leadership of both the formal and informal staff systems. This includes such diverse tasks as directing staff meetings and helping staff members deal with conflicts.

The role played by the supervisor in the middle position, between the staff group and the external systems that powerfully affect its work, is examined in Chapter 6. Examples include how to relate to staff when introducing changes in policy or procedures which may generate resistance, and how to provide feedback to higher authorities on the feelings and concerns of staff members. The mediation function suggested by Schwartz (1969) provides a framework for discussion of this critical and difficult supervisory task. This chapter also addresses the unique aspects of the role of the administrator, who is often one or more levels removed from the work of the staff. Many of the dynamics and skills described in the preceding chapters are directly relevant to this work, and these connections are stressed.

Chapter 7 deals with one of the most difficult aspects of supervision—the task of holding staff members accountable for their work through ongoing feedback and evaluation. Evaluation is presented as a potentially effective tool for helping staff members grow in the work situation. A discussion of the dynamics and skills involved in the ending phase of the supervisory function is included in this chapter.

As this brief overview suggests, there are two types of content in this book. The first is a discussion of the dynamics of supervision in the helping professions and the model of interactional skills, and the second examines how these skills are applied in practice by giving examples of specific problems. To make it easier to refer to the text discussion of particular problems or issues, such as dealing with defensive staff members or how a new supervisor promoted from the ranks adjusts to the position, these illustrations are referenced by topic in the index.

Research Findings

Each of the seven chapters of this text has a section on research findings which is used primarily to share the findings of a study of the supervision process which was directed by the author, Lawrence Shulman, with the aid of his associates, Elizabeth Robinson and Anna Luckyj. For this study of supervisors and their staffs, instruments were developed to measure variables associated with the context, content, and process of supervision and to relate these variables to effectiveness. The findings were then used to analyze the practice approach critically. These findings, which should be viewed as tentative because of the limitations of the study, are reported throughout the text, and other research findings related to supervision are also discussed.

The design of the study has been described in detail elsewhere (Shulman, Robinson, and Luckyj, 1981). Notes on the research methodology, ranging from instrument development and examples of questionnaire items to data analysis are given in Appendix A at the back of the book. A brief summary of the design and its limitations is provided here, however, to help put the findings discussed in the text in proper perspective.

The central line of inquiry in this study was to examine the communication, relationship, and problem solving skills in supervision and to explore how what supervisors do with workers is related to the development of a positive working relationship and enhanced helpfulness. This project was similar to an earlier study into social work practice skill with clients (Shulman, 1978, 1981). In fact, many of the same skills were examined in both projects, and these skills were found to be important for both workers and supervisors (see Appendix A).

In addition to the process skills, the study explored the effects of the context of supervision (e.g., availability of the supervisor, frequency of individual and group sessions) and the content of supervision (e.g., case planning, administration). Demographic factors for both supervisors and workers (e.g., training, age, experience), the supervisor's time investment in various roles (e.g., teacher, manager), satisfaction with the role demands, job stress and job manageability, and provisions for ongoing training and emotional support were also studied.

One of the two principal instruments developed in the study was the *Supervision Questionnaire: Worker's Version.* This questionnaire was designed to be completed by workers as a report on their supervisors' use of skills, as well as a number of other variables in the study. For example, the skill of articulating the worker's feelings was phrased as follows: "My supervisor can sense my feelings without my having to put them into words." The worker would choose a response from the following: "(1) None of the time; (2) A little of the time; (3) Sometimes; (4) A good part of the time; (5) Most or all of the time; (9) Undecided." Another item, dealing with supervisor's availability, was phrased "My supervisor is available when I need him or her." The response scale was the same.

The workers also were asked to comment on their perceptions of their relationship with the supervisor ("In general, how satisfied are you with your working relationship with your supervisor?") and the supervisor's helpfulness ("In general, how helpful is your supervisor?"). Four-point scales were provided for these responses. These two key items were used as separate dependent variables and combined into a relationship and helpfulness scale.

A second questionnaire, the *Supervision Questionnaire: Supervisor's Version,* was developed to obtain information from the supervisors themselves. Items on this instrument dealt with preparation and ongoing training for supervision, access to ongoing emotional support, job stress and job manageability, and time allocation for various tasks.

In the instrument development stage of the research process, both questionnaires were tested for reliability and validity. The results of these tests were positive as reported in Appendix A. However, these instruments should be considered as in an embryonic stage, requiring further testing and refinement.

The study involved mailing questionnaires to 120 supervisors who had indicated an interest in participating and all their professional workers (nonclerical staff). Among the supervisors, 109 (91%) returned the questionnaires. The final sample included 55 social work supervisors from child welfare offices in British Columbia (Ministry of Human Resources), 2 from the Manitoba Children's Aid Society, and 14 from the Ottawa Children's Aid Society. Thus, 71 (65%) of the participating supervisors were involved in child welfare settings, 15 (13.8%) of the participants were nursing supervisors, 13 (11.9%) were residential treatment center supervisors, and 10 (9.2%) were social work supervisors from other settings (e.g., hospitals, schools).

It is important to note that all these supervisors volunteered to participate in this study. In addition, many of them had been participants in workshops I had provided on the skills of supervision. The inclusion of supervisors from a number of fields, different areas of Canada, different agencies, different settings (e.g., rural, urban, suburban), and the different professional functions (social workers, child care workers, and nurses) increases the generalizability of the findings. Nevertheless, the factor of self-selection, prior training experience with the researcher, and the heavy child welfare weighting of the group (65%) must be considered as biasing the sample.

Of the 1,078 workers who were sent questionnaires, 671 (62.2%) responded. Of this group, 270 (40.2%) identified themselves as in the child welfare field, 102 (15.2%) in financial assistance, 59 (8.8%) in residential treatment work, 138 (20.6%) in nursing, 98 (14.6%) in other social work settings, and 4 (0.6%) did not answer this question. Though this sample also is a diverse one, the factor of self-selection must be taken into account.

Average scores were computed from the workers' returns for each supervisor, and these were added to the supervisor's own responses. A number of forms of data analysis were employed. Simple correlations were computed between all variables and the outcome measures of working relationship and supervisor helpfulness. Composite scales were created by averaging scores on a number of related variables, and these were correlated with outcome measure scales. In addition, a partial correlation procedure allowed for interesting inferences about which variables contributed to relationship building, which ones contributed to helpfulness, and which ones contributed to both. Other analyses were conducted to compare contrasting groups of supervisors (e.g., the top 25% and the bottom 25% on the relationship skills scales), and regression analysis was also employed.

The findings of this study must be considered in light of the limitations of the study design. A number of these have been identifed, and a review of Appendix A would also help place the findings in perspective. It shall be borne in mind that the study was essentially of supervisor and worker perceptions. Although testing of the questionnaires tended to support their reliability and validity, further work is needed to increase confidence in the findings. The fact that they indicated that the same core skills that are important in social work practice are also important in supervision adds some weight to the results. However, the limitations of the study suggest the findings should be considered as tentative, although useful for developing theoretical constructs for further testing.

The wording of the nondemographic items on both questionnaires, as well as the correlations between these items, and supervisor helpfulness, can be found in Tables 1 and 2 in Appendix A. Tables 3 and 4 in this appendix provide detailed data on the supervisor sample and the worker sample, respectively. Table 5 gives the findings of the third-variable analysis (partial correlations) described in the text.

Chapter 1

An Interactional Approach to Supervision

This chapter sets out some of the central ideas of the approach to supervision and staff management presented in this book. It describes a model for understanding the supervisee as interacting with a number of key systems (e.g., the client, agency, colleagues), and includes a statement of the supervisor's functional role in respect to that interaction. These ideas form the basis of the interactional approach to supervision.

It is important to note that the ideas presented in this book are tentative and still evolving. They represent a form of practice wisdom that has been derived from analysis of hundreds of anecdotes prepared by supervisors and administrators. In analyzing these examples and theorizing about the supervision process, I have employed the major elements of the practice theory developed by a colleague, William Schwartz (as noted in the Introduction), as well as a number of other theoretical constructs and models from the behavioral and social sciences. These are not presented as dogma but rather as helpful tools which can be of use in studying the dynamics of supervision. My own research findings and those of others are described, but it must be acknowledged that the scientific basis of our understanding of supervision is still tentative and undeveloped. The ideas presented in this text, therefore, should always be considered in the light of personal experiences. The final test of the value of each idea must be whether or not it can help supervisors deal with specific concerns more effectively or can explain why their current approach to supervision does or does not work.

Terminology

In developing the framework for his model of practice for the social work professional, Schwartz (1962) defined a practice theory as:

> . . .a system of concepts integrating three conceptual subsystems: one which organizes the appropriate aspects of social reality, as drawn from the findings of science; one which defines and conceptualizes specific values and goals, which we might call the problems of policy; and one which deals with the formulation of interrelated principles of action. (p. 270)

In this view, a practice theory of the supervision process needs to identify underlying assumptions (which would correspond to present knowledge) about human behavior and social organization. It needs to set out specific practice goals based on these assumptions. And finally, it should describe the supervisory behaviors that might achieve these goals.

Accordingly, this book first identifies what is known about the supervision relationship, drawing on such sources as group dynamics and organizational theory. For example, in examining the way in which a new supervisor begins to relate to staff, some of the principles which guide people's behavior in new situations, especially when dealing with people in authority, are examined. On the basis of these assumptions, specific goals for the beginning phase of supervision are suggested, and the skills (such as contracting behaviors) designed to achieve these goals are identified and discussed. As another example, what is known about organizational theory and the process of change provides the theoretical basis for exploring the dynamics involved when a supervisor attempts to introduce a new policy or procedure to a resistant staff group. Based on this knowledge, particular goals for the staff meeting that are designed to lower defenses and to encourage open communications are identified, together with the skills needed to achieve them.

Taken as a whole, the book represents an initial effort to develop a practice theory of supervision designed to assist supervisors in facing day-to-day problems with a clear idea of what we know, what we might hope to achieve, and what skills are required. This is the sense in which the term *practice theory* is employed in this book.

The term *model* is used to describe a representation of reality. A number of such models are presented in order to simplify the presentation of the complex process of supervision. For example, models are used to describe the relationship between a supervisor and supervisee, the operations of staff groups, the organizational dynamics of the work setting,and the process through which supervisors have an impact on their staffs.

The term *skill* describes behaviors used by supervisors in the execution of their professional tasks. Many of these skills have been identified as the core relationship, communication, and problem-solving skills that are important in all human contacts, such as empathy and listening. The focus in this book, however, is on their use in the context of supervision and management.

The terms *worker* and *agency* are frequently used in describing the supervisee and the setting of supervision, since social work practice encompasses a wide range of settings in the helping professions. Moreover, the study of supervision which forms the research basis for this text is an extension of my study of social work practice. Often the terms *worker* and *agency* have broader meanings in this book, however, and they can be interpreted as synonymous with *staff member* and *the institutional setting.*

Task Definition

Almost 50 years ago, Robinson (1936) defined supervision in the context of social work as "an educational process in which a person with a certain equipment of knowledge and skill takes responsibility for training a person with less equipment" (p. 53). This emphasis on the educational aspect of supervision has been combined over the years with a second emphasis on the administrative aspect of the work, such as efforts to control and coordinate workers in order to get the job done. In a more recent definition of supervision, Kadushin (1976, p. 20) added to these two sets of tasks the "expressive-supportive leadership function" which focuses on the problem of sustaining workers by offering emotional support and making efforts to assist them when they have "job-related discouragements and discontents." This, Kadushin says, gives supervisees a sense of worth as professionals, a sense of belonging in the agency, a sense of security in their performance."

Combining these three major functions, Kadushin (1976) provides a definition of supervision which serves well for the purposes of this book:

> . . .a social work supervisor is an agency administrative staff member to whom authority is delegated to direct, coordinate, enhance, and evaluate on-the-job performance of the supervisees for whose work he is held accountable. In implementing this responsiblity the supervisor performs administrative, educational, and supportive functions in interaction with the supervisee in the context of a positive relationship. The supervisor's ultimate objective is to deliver to agency clients the best possible service, both quantitative and qualitatively, in accordance with agency policies and procedures. (p. 21)

A crucial aspect of this definition is the emphasis on carrying out these tasks in interaction with the supervisee "in the context of a positive relationship." An important assumption throughout this book is that the supervisees have a key part to play in the supervision process, and the supervisor will be unable to implement his or her functions without their active involvement.

Schwartz stressed this interactional nature of supervision in describing his ideas about working with staff. After pointing out that the final effectiveness of an agency is determined by the skills with which the practitioners implement its services, he describes supervisory tasks as "designed to enrich these skills, increase the efficiency with which each worker manages his job, and coordinate many workers and their functions into a smoothly articulated whole" (1968, p. 358). Thus, he identifies supervisory tasks as concerned with skill, efficiency, and coordination.

Schwartz also highlights the supervisor's limitations in implementing these functions:

> The interesting thing about these administrative tasks is that they cannot be accomplished by administrators, that is, they cannot be "legislated" or "administrated" from on high, but depend almost entirely on the interest and energy that the staff members themselves are able and willing to throw into them. Thus, the quality of staff education is determined by the extent to which workers feel free to reveal their problems, share their mistakes, and use the wisdom and experience of both their supervisors and their peers. So too, morale is a group product, involving a sense of group support, a feeling of being "in the same boat," and an atmosphere in which workers can draw strength from each other as they face common problems. (p. 358).

From the supervisors' viewpoint, Schwartz says that organizing human beings into a harmonious and effective work group is dependent on the ability of the workers to lend themselves wholeheartedly (privately as well as publicly) to their task, which essentially is "making policies and procedures come alive in action." He suggests that the old saying that leading a horse to water is not the same as making it drink is demonstrated in "the complexities of an agency culture, where the subtle operation of hostilities, confusions, and simple ignorance can so effectively undercut policies on which everybody is in apparent agreement" (p. 358).

As all supervisors soon find out, the process of carrying out the administrative, educational, and supportive aspects of the job is complicated by the inherent necessity of involving staff along the way. Many supervisors experience a sinking feeling as they attempt to educate a low-performance staff member who sits passively at the conference, arms folded, nonverbally signaling, "Go ahead, change me!" A similar feeling is the panic before a meeting where supervisors must deal with a hot administrative issue which they know will be greeted by active or passive resistance. This fear often leads them to place the item last on the agenda and then subtly conspire with the staff to ensure that there is no time left for discussion. Such an effort to move quickly past the issue, or, conversely, to act heavy-handedly and demand conformity, is usually met by direct or indirect forms of resistance. Moments such as these lead supervisors to wonder why they ever left direct practice for the often frustrating job of helping others work effectively.

While the interactional work generates the most difficulty in implementing the supervision function, it is also the part that can prove most challenging and satisfying. The fact is that supervision is not a mechanical process; it requires a positive working relationship with staff. Supervisors must develop their communications and relationship skills, harnessing those they already have to the new situation and learning new ones to fit the unique aspects of their jobs. The very qualities of work which initially attracted the supervisor to work with people can be rediscovered in the ongoing relationships with staff. The satisfactions derived from direct practice, such as positive feedback from clients or the excitement of observing, growth and change and feeling a part of the process, can be realized in supervision as well.

The goal of this book is to suggest new ways of looking at situations which supervisors have reported as being most difficult for them. An essential feature is identification and discussion of the communications and relationship skills which are helpful in dealing with these problems. As a first step, a model for conceptualizing worker-systems relationships relevant to supervision and the functional role of the supervisor in these interactions is presented in the following section.

Staff-System Interaction

The way supervisors view the supervision process is necessarily influenced by their perception of those they supervise. In the helping professions, a useful model of supervision conceptualizes staff members as constantly interacting with a number of systems that are directly related to their work. A social worker in a child welfare agency, for example, must deal with numerous systems, including clients, foster parents, the agency administrators, the supervisor, professional colleagues, and clerical staff, and other agencies or institutions, such as the schools. These relationships are illustrated in Figure 1.1.

At any moment in their workday, child care workers could be called on to negotiate with one or more of these systems. This interactional model can be applied to helping professionals in any setting, though the particular systems differ; for a hospital-based nurse, for example, the work would be with patients, other health disciplines, housekeeping, and so on. The point is that it is possible to conceptualize any worker as being involved in interaction with a number of work-related systems. The relationship with each system places unique demands on the worker and requires specific knowledge and skills if the worker is to negotiate it effectively.

Effective agency service requires that child welfare workers, for example, understand the dynamics of worker-client interaction and develop relationship and communication skills. In addition, a specific worker's knowledge of the unique problems facing specific clients, the research findings related to effective child welfare practice, and the systems of community support available to clients will affect the success of his or her work. Many of the communications and relationship skills are also important in dealing with other agencies

FIGURE 1.1
Worker-System Interaction in a Child Welfare Agency

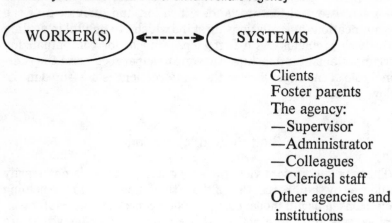

Clients
Foster parents
The agency:
—Supervisor
—Administrator
—Colleagues
—Clerical staff
Other agencies and
  institutions

or systems which are important to clients. An unskilled or heavy-handed worker who intervenes in the school system on behalf of a foster adolescent, for example, can create problems for both the client and the agency.

The worker's relationship to the agency can be broken down into a number of components. First, there is the question of job management. A worker must be able to work within the structure of the agency in terms of time (e.g., being on time for work and meetings, meeting deadlines on reports, and timely recording and development of the skills needed for effective management of case loads). A second important area is the worker's ability to relate effectively to agency policy and procedures. Workers must implement policies and follow established procedures while they are developing the skills necessary to influence them. Effective practice also requires workers to develop skills in dealing with professional colleagues, support staff, and supervisors. As workers attempt to deliver a service, their efforts must be coordinated with those of other staff members. Harmonious work relationships are required to help staff members relate to each other effectively in providing help to clients. When breakdowns occur in team relationships, the outcome is almost inevitably a deterioration of client service. In addition, workers must deal with supervisors, a symbol of authority, and learn how to use this relationship to their advantage.

Even this brief analysis reveals how complicated the systems facing a worker can be. Fortunately, all these systems are not operating at every moment, and some are more urgent than others. By viewing the worker's function as dynamic and interacting with systems, supervisors can partialize the tasks and begin to develop the supervisory agenda with specific workers or the work group as a whole. In addition, this way of conceptualizing the tasks helps to take the focus off of analyzing the worker and places it on the worker's activities. It is better for the supervisor to deal with the way a worker relates to various authorities in the agency, for example, than to try to help with the worker's "problem with authority." The approach of analyzing the worker's personality, which is rooted in some early misconceptions of helping processes with clients, can lead to resistance by workers and complaints they are being "social worked" by a supervisor.

Obstacles to worker-system interactions

The interactions between workers and the systems they deal with do not always go well. In fact, it is because of the many ways in which the relationships can break down that the supervisor's function is required. These obstacles emerge from a number of sources. For example, the complexity of the process or the system may lead to difficulties. Giving and receiving help is one of the most complex human relationships, and there are a number of ways in which the process can go wrong. The worker may be the source of the difficulty, or the client, or, as in most cases, both. An agency, for example, is a complex system, and it is easy for workers to feel overwhelmed by the bureaucracy or for administrators to lose track of the realities of workers' experiences.

The difficulty of maintaining accurate communications is another major source of trouble in a work situation. People often hear and remember only what they want or expect to hear. Misinterpretation of messages based on the stereotypes that workers and clients or supervisors and workers hold about one another is the rule rather than the exception. Some subjects, such as authority and dependency, cannot be openly discussed easily in our society. A staff angry at a supervisor for something said, done, or not done may express that anger in a number of indirect ways such as passivity at staff meetings, lateness, or the silent treatment. Even more powerful may be the norms which govern communications between peers. Normal work-related strains, which are to be expected in any working relationship, may lead to antagonisms which remain beneath the surface. These emerge indirectly to block effective collaborative efforts, but they are rarely discussed openly because of general injunctions against direct confrontations.

A third area of potential problems in interactions results from the difficulty the staff may have in understanding and acting on the common ground they hold with the various systems with which they interact. For example, an agency administration's stake in the positive morale of staff can have a profound impact on the achievement of agency goals. In turn, staff members need an administration which operates effectively, is in tune with the realities of practice, and is able to make the work situation more supportive. Supervisors depend on staff in order to carry out their tasks; workers need supervisors who are knowledgeable and supportive and whose expectations of them will help them undertake their work. In addition, staff members need peers who can offer mutual support as they tackle their common tasks.

These examples suggest lines of mutual dependence in the staff-system interaction which can easily be obscured by the pressures of self-interest. There are some areas where the needs of the staff and the needs of the administration may not overlap or, in fact, may be clearly divergent. It is easy to understand, for instance, why members of a nursing staff would not want to work nights and weekends, but the realities of hospital staffing requirements make this necessary.

The problems inherent in a conceptualization of the staff as in interaction with key systems will be expanded on throughout this book. This interactive model is used to begin the analysis in each example, and the ability to identify the people or systems that are on the right side of the interaction is a powerful aid in theorizing about supervision practice. The breakdowns described are often normal and to be expected in the staff-system relationship; indeed, all of these problems, and others, could be encountered in any complex system. In fact, it is the existence of the obstacles and the difficulty workers have in negotiating these demands which establishes the need for the supervisor's functional role, which is described in the next section.

The Supervision Function

The definition of the term *supervision* and description of the general supervisory tasks of administration, education, and support in a preceding section are helpful in clarifying the responsibilities of a supervisor. But they are too general to be of assistance in the many instances of staff-system interaction described in this chapter. For example, how does a supervisor execute administrative and coordinating tasks when faced with a serious conflict between workers which is blocking effective service? Or how is the educational role implemented when a worker is struggling to deal with an angry and defensive client—and the worker is angry and defensive as well? Or, in an even more common example, what is the functional role of the supervisor when caught in the middle between a staff angry at a new hospital administration policy and an administration which expects the supervisor to "sell" the idea? Both the staff group and the administration expect the supervisor to identify with them rather than the other side in the dispute.

It could be argued that there is no one supervisory function which holds true for each of these cases, and the function varies according to the supervisor's style or the circumstances (e.g., whether or not the supervisor agrees with the policy). This is an attractive argument, since there is some truth to it. Nevertheless, it would be helpful if some statement of function could be developed which is widely applicable to many of the circumstances encountered by supervisors. If this statement were activity oriented, that is, if it said something about the supervisor's part in the proceedings (what he or she actually does), it could provide a framework for making sense out of complicated situations and for developing a strategy for action.

While I recognize some important limitations in employing the functional statement developed for social work practice by Schwartz (1960, 1968, 1977), I will borrow it and test it in analyzing the many practical supervisory situations described in this text. He described the client-system interaction in terms similar to those I have used to describe staff-system relationships. He then proposed that the general function of the social work profession is to "mediate the process through which the individual and society reach out for each other through a mutual need for self-fulfillment" (1961, p. 15). This *mediation,* or "third force," function is central to Schwartz's practice-theory. Its application to the supervision model is illustrated in Figure 1.2.

To the two elements in the model of a worker negotiating the various systems of demand shown earlier in Figure 1.1, this figure adds a third element, the supervisor. It suggests that the functional role of the supervisor may be best explained as mediating the engagement between the worker and the systems to be dealt with. This idea may be more true of some situations than others, however. For example, if there were two workers interacting with each other it would be easy to argue that the supervisor needs to help them talk to and listen to each other and discuss their differences, without losing sight of their common interest. In other situations, such as at the point of conflict between staff members and the agency itself, more doubts might be raised. These would be particularly strong if mediation is interpreted as simply reducing or covering up conflict, or not taking sides on an issue—being neutral—or in some way trying to avoid or smooth over conflict. But as later chapters will show, none of these commonly expressed criticisms of mediation

FIGURE 1.2
The Mediation Function in the Supervision Model

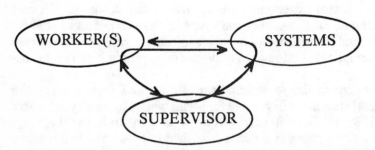

Source: Adapted from William Schwartz, "Social Group Work: The Interactional Approach," in John B. Turner (ed.), *Encyclopedia of Social Work,* vol. 2 (New York: National Association of Social Workers, 1977).

applies to my view (or Schwartz's) of the process. In fact, the opposite is often true, because supervisors utilizing mediation bring issues out in the open rather than leaving them, and the accompanying feelings, hidden and festering. Another reservation has to do with those situations where the supervisor must exercise authority, ranging from demanding work be produced by a certain date to the extreme of recommending dismissal of a nonproductive employee. What does mediation have to do with these functions?

These doubts are important, and they will be examined as examples are presented in the chapters to follow. In some cases it will be clear that other functional responsibilities, in addition to those suggested by the mediation idea, are carried by supervisors. In other cases, implementing this "third force" function will appear to be the only way to help—for example, the only way to identify with the staff and the administration at exactly the same time. In all of this discussion I argue that the power of this theoretical idea, indeed of any theory, rests in its ability to help us understand a situation in a new way and to provide alternatives for action. If a theory cannot do that, then it is not useful, no matter how elegantly it may be stated. In the last analysis, this is a crucial criterion for testing the validity of any set of new ideas.

Research Findings

The findings on the role of the supervisor, the context of supervision, and job stress and manageability presented in this section were principally derived from the study on supervision described in the Introduction and in Appendix A (Shulman, Robinson, & Luckyj, 1981). The description of this study, particularly the section on limitations, should be read to help place the findings in proper perspective. Although the discussion in this section is related to social work supervision (the focus of this research), many of the findings are adaptable to other areas of human services. Other research, particularly a study of sources of satisfaction for workers and supervisors by Kadushin (1973), is also reported.

Role of the supervisor

The 109 supervisors in one study (Shulman, Robinson, and Luckyj, 1981) were asked to consider their role as supervisors and indicate the percentage of time they allocated to various tasks. They were then asked to indicate the percentage of time they would *like* to allocate to these tasks. The results are reported in Table 1.1.

The largest difference between preferred and actual time spent on tasks was a desire for more concentration on supervision-consulting. The respondents in this study were offered the opportunity to add comments to the questionnaire, and the following selected comments provide a sense of the supervisors' concerns:

> I feel I am fighting the trend to have us become more managerial.

> The current issue is, shall we be supervisors-managers or casework consultants? The two roles do clash at times, especially in large offices.

> I find the emphasis switches from being a supervisor to a manager constantly. This creates difficulty as to my focus. I do not necessarily meet staff expectations.

This interest in increasing the supervising-consulting role fits with a finding in a study of social work supervision by Kadushin (1973), in which he reported the responses of 469 supervisors and 384 social workers. When supervisors were asked to rate factors which were strong sources of job satisfaction, two of the top three factors were helping supervisees grow and develop as professionals (88% of the supervisors checked this item as a strong source of satisfaction) and sharing social work knowledge and skills (63%).

In our own study the workers also appeared to prefer that more time be invested in supervision-consulting and teaching. The 671

TABLE 1.1
SUPERVISORS' REPORT ON ACTUAL AND PREFERRED TASKS

Tasks	Percentage of Time—Actual	Percentage of Time—Preferred
Supervision and consultation	39.4%	45.0%
Management	19.8	17.8
Personnel	10.9	10.3
Coordinating	17.8	19.4
Other	10.2	7.3
Total	98.1%*	99.8%

*Responses of some supervisors did not total 100%.

workers who responded were asked to indicate the percentage of their time they had devoted to categories of content in their supervision contacts and then to indicate their preferences for content. These findings are reported in Table 1.2.

The content area with the largest increase of preferred to actual time spent was teaching practice skills, followed by discussing information from research which would be helpful on the job, and, third, providing feedback on ongoing job performance. The major reductions were in discussing administrative requirements, other tasks, and planning on individual cases. The shift in preference for planning on individual cases may be a reflection of the workers' feelings about the type of supervision and consultation received. The focus on this type of consultation is usually the case, with very little attention paid to the worker's performance, such as the skills employed in interviews.

In Kadushin's study, when workers were asked to indicate their sources of satisfaction with their supervisors, 27% indicated that the stimulation provided by supervisors for their thinking about social work theory and practice was a strong source of satisfaction. When asked to indicate their major source of dissatisfaction with supervisors, 25% indicated that the supervisors' failure to provide real help in dealing with the problems they faced with their clients was a strong reason to be dissatisfied.

TABLE 1.2
WORKERS' REPORT ON ACTUAL AND PREFERRED CONTENT OF
SUPERVISION CONTACTS

Content	Percentage of Time—Actual	Percentage of Time—Preferred
Planning on individual cases	42.6%	37.8%
Teaching practice skills	11.8	18.7
Discussing research information	8.7	13.6
Providing feedback on job performance	11.5	13.5
Discussing administrative requirements	15.0	11.8
Other	9.1	4.0
Total	98.7%*	99.4%*

*Responses of some workers did not total 100%.

Thus, both supervisors and workers appeared to agree on a desire to see an increase in their investment in the supervision-consultation and teaching aspects of their work.

An additional analysis in our study examined the correlations among all variables. When two variables have little or no apparent association with each other, the correlation (expressed in the statistic Pearson's r) is equal to or close to 0.00. The maximum positive correlation is +1.00, and the maximum negative correlation is -1.00. All correlations reported in this study were significant at the $p \leq .05$ level (5 chances or less, out of 100, that the correlation could have occurred by chance). Since a large number of correlations were computed in the analysis of this data, the level of significance employed suggests that five correlations out of each 100 identified may indeed have been generated by chance.

To increase confidence in these results, we will only report correlations of 0.24 or stronger. Even at that, correlations of less than 0.29 should be considered as accounting for only a small portion of the variation; at 0.29, the amount of variation accounted for would be approximately 8.5%. It should be borne in mind that a correlation between variables is not an indication of the *direction* of influence. Thus, although in our study a good working relationship strongly correlated with supervisor helpfulness, we are not sure if the working relationship caused the supervisor to be helpful, or being helpful led to a good relationship, or, perhaps, each affected the other.

When the variables discussed above were examined for significant correlations over 0.24, we found a negative correlation (-0.24) between involvement in management, as reported by the supervisor, and supervision content focusing on the development of practice skills, as reported by workers. In addition, there was a positive correlation (0.25) between supervisors indicating a preference for more supervision and consultation time and workers reporting an emphasis on practice skill teaching.

We were also interested in exploring the part worker variables might play in the results. For example, did worker education or experience affect how the supervisors saw their role or the content of supervision? Our findings were that workers with higher levels of professional education reported that their supervisors implemented more of a consulting function ($r = 0.26$) and less of a teaching function ($r = 0.29$). In addition, workers with more experience in their particular practice area also reported more discussion of relevant research ($r = 0.34$).

The workers' own preferences may also have had some impact, since the correlation between the workers' preference for planning on individual cases and the actual amount of time spent on this task was high ($r = 0.52$). Thus, the role played by the supervisor and the content of the supervision may be somewhat dependent on the influence of both the supervisor and supervisee, with supervisors taking education and experience into account. The setting of work also seemed to have had some impact, since planning for individual cases correlated positively with the supervisor being in a child welfare setting ($r = 0.52$) in which such planning is an almost daily necessity.

For another type of analysis we created scales using two or more variables and then assigned scores to each supervisor. The supervisors were then ranked in order of scores on the scales, and the top 25% (approximately) and the bottom 25% of the supervisors were identified. These two contrasting groups were then compared on the scores they received from their workers on a scale which combined relationship ("In general, how satisfied are you with your working relationship with your supervisor?") and helpfulness ("In general, how helpful is your supervisor?"). Comparisons were implemented using the analysis of variance technique. (See Appendix A for the statistics for most comparisons noted in these findings.)

One of the scales developed was an index of supervisors' satisfaction with their role. We simply subtracted the percentage of time they reported they would like to invest in each task from the percentage they indicated they actually did invest (see Table 1.1). The absolute differences (disregarding positive or negative signs) for each task were summed to produce the index of role satisfaction. When the group of 18 highly satisfied supervisors was compared with the group of 21 who indicated low satisfaction, there was no difference in their workers' responses on the relationship-helpfulness scale. Thus, the supervisors' satisfaction with their roles did not seem to affect how their workers judged their working relationship and their helpfulness.

The findings were different when we examined worker satisfaction with supervision content. Employing a similar procedure, we summed the absolute differences between the actual content of supervision and preferred content and computed an index of worker content satisfaction. Then we ordered the supervisors from those with the least satisfied workers to those with the most satisfied. When the 25 supervisors with the most satisfied workers were compared with the 28 with the least satisfied, a significant difference was found on the relationship-helpfulness scale in favor of the supervisors with more satisfied workers (p = .02).

Thus the data appeared to support the argument that the workers' satisfaction with the content of supervision was a factor in how they judged their supervisors, while the supervisors' role satisfaction did not seem to have any impact. Since the theoretical model guiding the study assumed that factors associated with the content, context, and process of supervision would be important contributors to supervision effectiveness, these findings offer some support for the model.

The context of supervision

A number of items on the Supervision Questionnaire: Worker's Version explored the context of the contact between supervisor and worker. The scale used on these items contained six responses: "(1) None of the time; (2) A little of the time: (3) Sometimes; (4) A good part of the time; (5) Most or all of the time; (6) Undecided."

The average supervisor in this study sets aside regularly scheduled time for individual supervision "a little of the time" to "sometimes," and these sessions are, on average, held monthly. Group sessions are "sometimes" regularly scheduled, with an average of twice a month reported. On a related question, when workers were asked to report on their supervisors' availability when needed, the mean reply was "a good part of the time." The following worker comments on the questionnaire give a flavor of the most frequent statements:

> I feel regular individual supervision would be helpful.

> Peer group supervision can be very helpful. Most of my concern centers on not getting enough scheduled time for myself.

> My supervisor stresses the team approach and encourages his staff to give input on almost all aspects of our work.

> Supervision at the start of the job should be more frequent, and as the worker progresses, he should have the option to request it when needed.

> My greatest frustration is the low priority on direct supervision.

In the Kadushin study, 86% of the supervisors and supervisees reported that individual conferences were the most frequent context for supervision. In addition, 21% of the workers identified failure to provide enough regularly scheduled, uninterrupted office conference time as a strong source of dissatisfaction with supervisors.

In the correlation analysis of our study data, the supervisors' expression of preference for personnel work correlated negatively with holding regularly scheduled individual sessions (0.28), while a preference for coordinating work correlated positively with individual sessions (0.25). In what appears to be a contradiction in the findings, a preference for coordinating work, which included holding team meetings, correlated negatively with holding regularly scheduled group sessions (-0.25). This may be one of the examples where the preferred and the actual had to be different.

Workers were also asked to describe their supervisors' investment of time in different tasks. Supervisors who regularly scheduled individual sessions were described as filling the consultant role ($r = 0.29$) and the teacher role ($r = 0.33$). Holding regularly scheduled individual conferences correlated negatively with the role of manager (0.39). Similar correlations occurred between these three roles and the frequency of individual sessions. Setting was again important, with child welfare the only setting (compared to nursing, residential treatment, and other social work settings) to correlate positively with regular individual sessions (0.39) and frequency of individual sessions (0.47).

There were some interesting findings in respect to the issue of holding regularly scheduled group sessions. Holding more group sessions correlated positively with the working relationship between worker and supervisor (0.34), the supervisor's role as teacher (0.36), and the supervisor's skill in helping workers discuss taboo subjects (0.29). These findings are discussed more fully in the chapters on the educational function of supervision and the group work skills of the supervisor.

The question of supervisor availability was an important one in this analysis, correlating with a large number of other variables. For example, availability correlated positively with working relationship (0.40), ability of the worker to talk openly with the supervisor (0.41), the provision of a supportive atmosphere (0.35), and the supervisor's helpfulness (0.47). In addition, supervisors who were available were also seen as demonstrating an ability to: clarify the role of the supervisor ($r = 0.26$); help the worker discuss taboo subjects (0.31); understand the worker's feelings (0.39); articulate the worker's feelings (0.25); partialize the worker's concerns (0.28); and provide relevant data (0.33). These skills are discussed in more detail in the next two chapters.

In considering the meaning of these correlations, the problem of not being able to determine the direction of influence must be recognized. Are supervisors who are available able to demonstrate their capacity for empathy, for example, while those who are not available cannot do so? Or do supervisors who are more empathic make themselves more available? My own experience suggests that both statements are partially true. These findings raise a question as to how the workers actually interpreted the phrase "available when I need him/her." While the question was meant to get at the supervisors' allocation of time, for some workers it may have meant being emotionally available when needed.

Whatever the inferences—and different ones are possible and very reasonable—the findings suggest that the context of supervision does have some impact on supervisor effectiveness, although it may not be simply a question of how much regularly scheduled time is provided. While regularly scheduled individual and group time appears to be important, no specific pattern is identified as the right one. I can imagine a supervisor holding regularly scheduled individual conferences with a worker, but because of the worker's lack of satisfaction with content or the supervisor's lack of skill, the worker might still say: "My supervisor was not there when I needed him/her." Another supervisor might meet on a less regular schedule and yet always be there when needed.

The procedure of comparing groups of supervisors on context factors added evidence to these inferences. For example, a scale on contact regularity was computed by combining a worker's responses to the questions on the regularity of individual and group sessions. The 26 supervisors with the lowest scores on regularity were compared with the 26 supervisors with the highest levels. There was a significant difference in their scores on the relationship-helpfulness scale, favoring the supervisors with the higher levels of regularity ($p = .000$). A second scale on supervisor availability was constructed by combining the contact regularity items with the item specifically asking if the supervisor was available when needed. This scale also produced significant differences between the 26 supervisors with the lowest scores and the 26 with the highest, also favoring those who were considered the most available ($p = .000$).

Job stress and job manageability

The issues of job stress and job manageability are crucial ones in supervision. While the emphasis may vary in different settings, in all of my workshops the theme most commonly stressed by supervisors has been the difficulty of the job. In a workshop for child welfare supervisors, one supervisor put it this way:

> The public just doesn't understand the stress we are under. They don't realize that some days, when I drive to work, I feel physically sick thinking about the decisions I am going to have to make that day; whether to leave a child in a home, or take the child away. When you have a child killed by a client on your case load, the feeling is simply terrible. You always wonder, could I have done something different.

Similar comments have been voiced by nursing supervisors dealing with the pressures of emergency or operating room procedures, or those concerned about patients receiving the proper medication. Child care supervisors describe the pressure of feeling they are often a child's last resort, and they fear the not-uncommon teenage suicide.

In addition to the stress of the decisions to be made, supervisors also cite work-load stress. They often feel stretched too thin, with too much management and coordinating responsibility and not enough time for consultation and supervision. Some of the supervisors' written comments on our questionnaire addressed these problems:

> The number and kinds of service that the agency provides—the standard of service expected versus the level of service possible—the span of control is currently too wide.

> Often I feel I'm not as available to workers as perhaps I should be because of many other meetings, high-risk case involvement, and policy and planning projects.

> The amount of paperwork and heavy demands on social work staff detract from time available for effective case consultation.

Supervisors usually raise these issues when explaining why they cannot be available to their workers as much as they would like, why they can't provide regularly scheduled conferences, or why they can't focus on the consultation and teaching roles. For many supervisors, this is clearly a serious problem. In order to obtain data in this area, we asked supervisors to respond to two statements: "My job as a supervisor is stressful," and "My job as a supervisor is manageable." The scaling was the same as described earlier, ranging from "(1) None of the time" to "(5) Most or all of the time." The two questions resulted from key-informant interviews in which supervisors indicated that their jobs could be both stressful and manageable at the same time.

The average score on stress indicated that the job was considered stressful between "sometimes" and "a good part of the time" by most of the supervisors. The average score on manageability indicated they considered the job manageable "a good part of the time."

These findings must be considered in light of the self-selection of supervisors in this study. As pointed out in Appendix A, there is some reason to believe that some of the supervisors contacted who felt most under stress and who had low job manageability simply did not participate. We believe the sample was biased in this way. However, even with this biased group, there were variations on both items and some supervisors could be placed at both extremes on the scores. Another explanation for these scores may be that the moments when the job is very stressful and very unmanageable are those that have an extremely hard impact on the supervisor. As one supervisor put it, "It's not always hard, but when it is hard, it's *hard!*"

Other studies have also pointed to stress and job manageability as problem areas. In one study of work loads for supervisors in a public welfare agency, Galm (1972) found that supervisors simply did not have enough time to supervise. In the Kadushin (1973) study of 469 supervisors, 53% indicated that not having time to supervise was one of the strongest sources of their dissatisfaction with the job. For 27%, having to make decisions without clear guidelines was a strong source of dissatisfaction.

In spite of the clear data on the reality of job stress and job manageability difficulties, in my opinion some supervisors use the stress and manageability issues to explain their lack of involvement in certain areas of supervision when other factors, such as lack of confidence or skills, are also blocking them. When I have pressed supervisors in workshops, many (though not all) of them admitted that they could provide more help, even within the limitations of the job. This experience led me to assume that stress and manageability, by themselves, would not be crucial factors affecting supervision effectiveness for most supervisors. For some supervisors, they might be the *only* factors but on the whole other factors would be more crucial. Some stressed supervisors with jobs they often found unmanageable could nevertheless provide significant help to their workers, while some unstressed supervisors with manageable jobs might provide very little help.

The data, in part, tended to support these assumptions. Stress did not correlate with any other item in the study. Job manageability, however, was positively correlated with the workers' perception of the supervisors' availability ($r = 0.25$). The importance of the supervisors' availability (discussed earlier) suggests a causal chain in which a more manageable job leads to more availability, which, in turn, leads to more effective supervision. This is not a particularly strong correlation, however, and therefore it supports the idea that job manageability has some influence on effectiveness, but not necessarily the major influence. For some overwhelmed supervisors, however, it may be the *only* factor.

Responding to the key-informant supervisors' comments about the job being stressful but still manageable, we computed a stress-manageability index which tried to take both factors into account. By combining these scores, we were able to rank supervisors along a continuum, at one end of which were supervisors with high stress and low manageability and, at the other, supervisors with low stress and high manageability. Comparing the group of 19 supervisors reporting the most difficult stress-manageability problems with the group of 30 reporting the least difficult, we found no differences in their workers' responses on the relationship-helpfulness scale ($p = .82$).

I do not infer from this finding that stress and manageability do not matter, and therefore administrators can feel free to increase their supervisors' work loads. They *do* matter, and supervisors with more time can give more help. However, supervisors do not necessarily give that help just because they have more time. Other factors are crucial to the process, and content and context variables are important contributors to the outcome. As these questions are explored in the research sections of the following chapters, the process of supervision and the skills of the supervisor will emerge as the most potent influences on their effectiveness.

Summary

This chapter sets out some of the central ideas of the approach to supervision presented in this book, starting with Kadushin's definition of the supervisor as "an agency administrative staff member to whom authority is delegated to direct, coordinate, enhance and evaluate the on-the-job performance of the supervisees for whose work he is held accountable." The supervisor's general tasks include administrative, educational, and supportive functions. Especially important is the interactional nature of the process; the supervisor is dependent on the active involvement of the staff, just as the staff is dependent on the supervisor,

In the model for viewing staff-system interactions described here, the staff member interacts with certain key systems according to his or her professional function and the setting. Examples of such systems or people are clients, patients, the agency or organizational setting, the supervisor, colleagues, and professionals from other disciplines or settings. A number of obstacles can complicate the interactions between staff members and these important systems, including problems associated with complexity (e.g., the inherent problems found in large organizations), difficulties in maintaining accurate communications, and the ease of overlooking the common ground between workers and their relevant systems.

The mediation practice theory first developed by Schwartz for the social work profession has been adapted to the supervision context. It is proposed as a useful framework for analyzing many of the complicated situations supervisors find difficult to handle.

Chapter 2

Preparatory and Beginning Skills in Supervision

As in any interactional system, the beginning phase of a supervisory relationship is critical. Many of the problems supervisors encounter can be traced back to issues which arose in the beginning phase and were ignored or not handled well. The difficulties in this phase are compounded by the fact that these issues must be dealt with at precisely the time when both supervisors and staff are most tense and uncertain in their relationships. One supervisor who had been faced with a group of resistant and angry staff members at her first unit meeting agreed that an alternative strategy developed at a workshop might have helped her deal with the problem directly, but, she asked, "How can you say something like that when all you feel is scared spitless?"

Her point is well taken. The feelings of new supervisors have a great deal to do with how well they can deal with a particular problem, and their skill may be demonstrated in efforts to catch and correct a mistake an hour, a day, a week, or even months later. Preparatory work, an understanding of the dynamics of new relationships, and clarity about the core skills required can help speed up the process of arriving at satisfactory supervisory relationships.

This chapter explores the dynamics and skills of preparing for and beginning a supervisory relationship. It addresses the problems of starting as a new supervisor as well as those of helping new staff members begin. It also examines a number of common variations on the themes, including the unique dynamics involved when a new supervisor is brought in from outside the system or a staff member is promoted from within.

Supervision and the Phases of Work

Supervision of staff and work with clients are both helping relationships, and there are significant parallels between work with clients and work with staff members. While many of the dynamics and skills involved are similar in the two helping contexts, there are also important differences. The purpose of supervision is to get the work of the agency or other institutional setting accomplished, and the functions of a supervisor, as described in Chapter 1, differ in important ways from those of a social worker, nurse, counselor, or other staff members. It would not be appropriate, for example, for a nursing supervisor to provide counseling for a nurse who has a personal problem, but listening, understanding, and trying to help her obtain any necessary assistance from an appropriate source would be supportive. In the work of supervision, helping staff members examine how personal problems are affecting their ability to work is a legitimate function. The supervisor's ability to be empathic and yet set expectations which can aid a staff member's performance are extremely important. These are the same skills that are important for the worker's effective practice with clients.

The parallels between work with clients and work with staff suggest that the complex skills of supervision and staff management can be approached in the same framework as the skills of direct practice. The approach I will take is similar to the one used in *The Skills of Helping Individuals and Groups,* my earlier text on social work practice (Shulman, 1979). Generally, it employs time as an organizing structure, an idea Jessie Taft (1949) first applied to helping theory. In this structure, the work is divided into consecutive segments, so the process can be traced through a series of phases from beginning to end. William Schwartz (1961) described the phases of social work as (1) preliminary, (2) beginning, (3) work, and (4) transition or ending.

This chapter is concerned with the unique dynamics and skills involved in the first two phases. But the framework is also useful for analyzing each brief supervisory encounter with staff, every staff meeting and individual conference, whenever they might occur. In the work phase (see Chapter 3), when skills of the other phases are called for, they are described as *sessional skills*. Throughout the book, the model of the phases of work provides an introduction to explicit examples of how the skills of the various phases of supervisory work can be developed and applied.

The Preliminary Phase of Supervision: Tuning In

The work of the preliminary phase, as the term suggests, takes place before the initial encounter between supervisor and staff. For a new supervisor entering a system, preliminary phase work involves personal preparation for the first individual or group sessions. One of the key skills of the preliminary phase is described by Schwartz (1976) as *tuning in*, or trying to develop some preliminary empathy by putting oneself in the place of the other party. The goal is to sensitize oneself to the concerns, feelings, and issues that may be present in a relationship but are not easily communicated. When supervisors begin this process by tuning in to their own feelings, they often find parallels between their fears and concerns and those that are probably troubling staff members.

The importance of tuning in is emphasized by the indirect nature of many of the communications that staff members have with supervisors. Human communication can be difficult under any circumstances. The process of encoding ideas into words (or gestures, facial expressions, or other nonverbal behaviors) is complex in even the simplest of situations. The many obstacles to direct communications that can arise in an engagement between a supervisor and a supervisee often lead staff members to employ indirect means of sending their signals. Most people learn in childhood that there are certain risks involved in being honest with people in authority—especially when negative feedback is possible.

An example of tuning in: The new child care supervisor

The experience of Eleanor, a supervisor of child care workers who was beginning work at a residential treatment center, provides an example of how tuning in works. During the first staff meeting, one of the members had asked her if she had had much experience working with acting-out adolescents such as those in the residence.

At a workshop for supervisors, I asked Eleanor how she felt when the question was asked. She replied that she was embarrassed and uncomfortable; the worker apparently was challenging her competency, since her only experience had been in residential centers for younger children. She felt she had been put on the spot. In response, she said, "I told them I had not worked in this specific area, but that I had lots of experience in residential centers for younger children and I didn't think it was that different. I also told them I had taken a number of courses on work with adolescents while completing my child care degree."

Other members of the workshop group were then asked how they would have reacted to this anwer if they had been the workers in the group. They all said they felt put off by the response, as if Eleanor were trying to impress them. They thought her reply began to create a barrier between the workers and herself, the new supervisor who "obviously didn't understand." Eleanor said she had sensed that the answer did not go over well, but the issue seemed to be dropped.

It was easy to understand why this supervisor had responded as she did. She had been extremely nervous about beginning, and the question about her past experiences with adolescents struck right at the heart of her own fears, doubts, and questions of competency. Had she tuned in to her own fears and concerns before her first encounters she would have been less vulnerable when the question was raised.

This supervisor could also have tuned into the concerns that the staff might be expected to have, such as whether or not, as a new supervisor, she would understand how they felt working with very difficult kids. Possibly they had experienced other supervisors who were harsh and judgmental, who did not seem to appreciate how difficult the work was, how easy it was for them to lose their tempers, or how worn out they could be after particularly tough emotional encounters.

Given such circumstances, the question "Have you had much experience with acting-out teenagers?" might not be an attack of Eleanor's competence but rather an indirect way of raising this concern. A supervisor who was tuned in to the possible meaning of this comment could have avoided making a defensive comment. Instead, a skill described by Schwartz (1976) as *responding directly to an indirect cue* could be employed. The exact form of this response would vary according to the particular style of the supervisor. One version might be to say: "No, I haven't had much experience in treatment centers for adolescents. Why do you ask? Are you concerned that I might not understand what it's really like to work here, how hard it is, and how it feels for you? Because frankly, I am concerned about that as well."

When this alternative response was role-played in the supervision workshop, the participants felt more responsive to the supervisor, liked her honesty, appreciated that she understood what they were concerned about, and, most importantly, felt they might be able to "train her." The direct response to the indirect cue, based on the supervisor's tuning in during her preliminary phase preparation, would give the staff members permission to discuss an important but difficult area. Her message would be that it was all right with her to deal with even this tough issue. Her honesty could help to open up the relationship rather than closing it off through responses that the staff might immediately interpret as defensive.

Some reservations about tuning in

It is not easy to tune in to the feelings of staff members or to have the courage to open up a potentially touchy subject early in a new relationship. This is why it is also important for the supervisor to tune in to his or her own feelings as well. All too often supervisors are thrust into their positions without preparation. Department heads or administrators can be insensitive to the many fears or doubts a supervisor might have. Because the supervisor does not want to appear unsure or incompetent these fears may be withheld in discussions with the administrator. A later illustration will show how new supervisors can be helped to develop some comfort and skill in becoming aware of their own feelings.

There is also the possibility of tuning in to the wrong issues. The classic example is of the supervisor who anticipates that the staff is going to be upset and angry because he has been selected for the job rather than a popular staff member. He tunes in to this anger, and at the first hint of an indirect cue says: "I realize you must be angry at my selection." His staff members look blank and say: "No, we're really not upset about that." He replies: "Look, I can appreciate that you would be upset that I got the job instead of Frank." One of the members quickly reassures him, but the supervisor stubbornly persists, insisting that they must be angry at him. Finally, one of the staff members says: "Damn it, now I *am* mad!"

The important idea about tuning in is that it is tentative: the supervisor must be ready to abandon preconceived notions and respond to the reality of the present. There may be other issues that are more important to the staff members, or the supervisor may be projecting feelings which do not really exist. If the subject is in a particularly taboo area, such as authority, and the supervisor is fairly certain the concerns or feelings are present, it would be appropriate to reach for them a second time, gently, and without making the staff members feel defensive about having refused the first offer. For example: "I know you all like Frank quite a bit, and it would not surprise me if you were disappointed when he didn't get the job." By reaching a second time, the supervisor sends the message that it really is all right to discuss their feelings in this manner. Staff members will often accept a second invitation so long as it is not phrased as an accusation. If they do not, then the supervisor must drop the issue and not engage in a battle of wills with the staff which may provoke angry feelings. Staff members have heard the invitation to discuss the matter, and if it is a real concern that needs to be discussed, they may take the supervisor up later when they have developed greater trust.

Another potential problem with tuning in is that if purpose and function are not clear, the supervisor will be seen as trying to employ therapeutic techniques with the staff. A worker's reaction is likely to be, "Don't social work me!" When staff members say this, I believe they are referring to poorly applied social work skills which can cause clients to view workers' intellectual interpretations as mechanical or artificial. If the supervisor is genuinely tuned in to the staff members' feelings, the staff will not resent the interaction. Intellectual interpretations or statements about the staff's supposed feelings that really disguise the supervisor's own fears or hostility will always meet resistance. The classic case is the defensive supervisor who responds to an angry staff member with the punishing accusation that he or she "seems to have a problem with authority."

Advantages of tuning in

One of the most important arguments for tuning in and acknowledging workers' feelings is that the staff can learn a great deal about a supervisor's view of the helping process from the way the supervisor deals with them. For the staff working with Eleanor, the new child care supervisor in the example above, for instance, tuning in and responding directly is a critical skill they must develop in their work with residents. Acting-out teenagers constantly send indirect cues of their real feelings, and if these are missed by the workers they will lose an opportunity to be helpful and often end up in unnecessary battles with residents. The supervisor can be helpful by modeling an alternative way of responding to indirect cues.

Although tuning in and responding directly to indirect cues are critical skills for a supervisor who is new to a setting and in the preliminary phase, these skills are also essential for encouraging honest communications in all situations and in every phase of supervision. A supervisor who is introducing a new and somewhat controversial agency policy at a staff meeting, for example, could benefit from tuning in to potential staff reactions and considering some of the indirect ways these may emerge. Planning how to reach for an honest expression of negative responses, rather than leaving them to fester beneath the surface, can give the supervisor a beginning handle for work. Of course, this is not always easy to do. As one workshop participant commented: "First, I have to decide just how much honesty I really want." Facing this question is the first step in developing the courage to risk.

The Beginning Phase of Supervision: Contracting

A staff anticipating the appearance of a new supervisor wonders what kind of person she or he will be. They also wonder about the new supervisor's sense of the purpose of supervision and the role of the supervisor and how the supervisor's authority will be implemented, though they probably would not express these concerns in those words.

The supervisor's idea of the purpose of supervision determines the content of supervisory contacts. Staff members may wonder, for example, what kind of questions can be brought up in conferences or staff meetings. They may wonder what areas of work this new supervisor will want to deal with and what kinds of expectations will be placed on them. Even though they have had prior experiences with supervisors, they know that each one has personal ideas about the purpose of the work. And since the supervisor has such an important impact on their work life, they are anxious to know how this one will operate.

The staff also has to figure out how this particular supervisor will play his or her role in the relationship as they deal with the content. This raises the question of function. The purpose of supervision and the role carried out by the supervisor are separate matters, since it is entirely possible for supervisors to implement different functional roles in relation to the same supervisory purposes. For example, one purpose of supervisory conferences may be case management discussions, but for one supervisor this can mean: "Tell me what is going on and I will tell you what to do," while for another it means: "Tell me what is going on and I will help you figure out what you are going to do." Much of what happens in supervision will be affected by the supervisor's and the staff's sense of purpose and function, as derived from past experiences.

Another major area of concern for the staff is the supervisor's authority and how it will be implemented. Supervisors are powerful factors in a worker's life, and how their power will be employed is of central concern at the start of a relationship. Supervisors can evaluate a worker and recommend promotions, merit raises, dismissals, or changes in assignments. As in all new relationships with people in authority, tension is inevitable until the questions are answered and the uncertainties resolved.

The questions of purpose, role, and authority are the crucial areas cited by Schwartz in his analysis of the importance of the *contracting* process in social work practice, whereby worker and client develop a mutual understanding that provides a structure for the work. This structure is essential in giving both of them the freedom necessary to carry out their parts in the proceedings. Although these are central questions of the beginning phase, however, often they are not dealt with directly by either worker or client (Shulman, 1979).

The same is true in the supervisory relationship. I have found that there is often little direct conversation on the issues, and the result is a prolonged period of testing during which the staff members have to figure out what the supervisor is going to do. Lack of clarity in these areas causes heightened anxiety for the staff and frustrations in the development of the early working relationship. In addition, supervisees will find it difficult to use the supervisor's help effectively unless they are clear about what that help can be. Thus the supervisory relationship may be haunted by unanswered, underlying questions as long as it lasts.

This section explores some of the reasons why the issues of purpose, role, and authority are often ignored by supervisors and are raised only indirectly by the staff. The specific skills that help a supervisor deal with these critical areas are described and illustrated with the example of a new nursing supervisor in a hospital.

Contracting skills

Four key skills of contracting in the beginning phase of work call for the supervisor to share his or her sense of purpose, explore the supervisor's role, reach for feedback from the workers on their perceptions, and discuss the mutual obligations and expectations related to the supervisor's authority. These tasks may sound simple, but the process is actually very complex.

In workshops for supervisors I often role-play a naive new worker and ask the assembled supervisors to describe their role to me and explain the kind of help I can get from them. A long silence usually follows before one of them asks: "What kind of help do you want from me?" In response I point out that my question has been answered with a question, and if I understood what kind of help there was to offer I might have a better idea of what kind of help I needed. Another supervisor will then usually suggest, "I'm going to help you do your job better." When I ask "How exactly will you do that?" it is obvious that this supervisor's answer to my question was provided in terms of her own expectations for the outcome of our work together, rather than as a description of what our work would actually be. A third group member may then say something like: "I'm going to discuss your work with you, and, through a mutual learning process in which you will have an opportunity for individual inquiry, I will facilitate your growth as a worker, enhance your job performance, and enable you to work more effectively with clients." I would credit this supervisor for mentioning that we would discuss the work together (the first hint of the purpose of supervision) but I would point out that the statement was so full of jargon that a worker probably wouldn't have understood a word.

It *is* difficult to describe the purpose of supervision and the supervisor's role in simple phrases that do not use overworked terms like *enhance, enable,* or *facilitate.* This is not surprising, because supervisors are often given unclear, if not mixed, messages from administrators about what it is they are supposed to do. In one study of supervisors, Olyan (1972) found that most describe learning how to do the job from role models, without any specific directions. If the purpose of supervision and the role of the supervisor are not clearly defined by these role models or by the administration which hired the supervisor, then lack of clarity will persist. The supervisor's uncertainty here can lead to hesitancy in discussing purpose and role.

Staff members seldom raise such questions directly. The discussion of authority issues, in fact, is generally taboo in our society, so such concerns are usually raised indirectly. A worker who says: "One of the things we really liked about our old supervisor was that she let you make some of your own decisions," may be asking: "Will that be the way you will supervise?" The worker's lack of directness allows the supervisor to avoid open discussion in this area.

Supervisors also may feel uncomfortable about discussing the authority aspects of their work. A new supervisor wants to be liked by the staff and may fear that raising authority-related issues casts him or her as a heavy. Staff members in turn, may be wary of being direct in this area or may have found it convenient not to be direct. They may think that if they do not ask questions about what they can do on their own, then they won't hear the answers they don't want to hear. Thus, both the supervisor and the staff members may have a stake in avoiding direct discussions.

Some supervisors hesitate to be direct in contracting with the staff in certain areas because they are afraid the members might take them up on their offer. One purpose for, example, could be helping workers develop their practice skills in relation to work with clients. Stated simply, as part of a contracting statement of purpose by a supervisor, this could be: "I will go over the specifics of your work with clients and try to help you develop your skills for dealing with the tough parts of the work." Supervisors may be concerned that the worker will ask for help and they won't be able to give it. This concern stems from the idea of a supervisor as the one with all the answers, an unrealistic expectation supervisors often assume for themselves.

Thus, lack of clarity about role and purpose, the taboo nature of authority issues, the possibility of avoiding direct discussion by employing professional jargon, the discomfort experienced in direct discussion of authority, and the fear of making an offer one cannot back up are all reasons why the working contract can remain vague and unclear. As in work with clients, however, the lack of a clear contract will frustrate efforts at almost every turn. Workers will end up seeing the supervisor as a stereotyped personality, based on their own past experiences with a range of people in authority and past supervisors in a particular setting.

An example of contracting: The new nursing supervisor

There are many variations in the way contracting proceeds, depending on the context within which the work takes place, the definition of the supervision role provided by the administration, the particular style of the supervisor and the specific needs of the staff. In the following example Leta, a new nursing supervisor, reported her attempts to clarify the purpose of supervision, her role, and the authority issues at an early staff meeting with the nurses on her ward:

> I started by saying: "I thought it would help us to get off to a good start if I took a few minutes to describe how I approach supervision. You probably have some of your own ideas about supervisors, so I would like to get your comments as well. The way I see it, it's my job to try to help the rest of you provide a good quality service on the ward. In order to do this, I will meet with you regularly, both individually and as a group, to discuss our work. I'll let you know if I have any ideas about how you can improve the quality of your work, and I'll want to know your ideas about what we can do around here to make your work easier and more satisfying. I also see it as my job to help you work well with each other, so if there are problems and you need help in sorting them out, you can come to me about them.
>
> "If you have specific questions about patients or procedures, I'll try to answer them or find out where you can get your answers. If you have any feedback you want to see passed along to the administration, I'll do my best to see that they hear what you have to say. Finally, nursing can be very demanding, and there may be some days when you feel you have had it and want a chance to unload—I'll try to be available to listen if it's any help. That's about it, as I see it. Now, it's your turn. How does that sound, any questions, any reactions? Is that what supervision has been like around here before?"

There was a short silence as they seemed to be taking it all in. I waited, and finally Rita responded by saying it sounded all right and would be a nice change. I asked what she meant, and she proceeded to describe how the last supervisor was really a "snoopervisor." I asked her to explain what she meant by that, and she described how my predecessor had always hovered over them, constantly complaining if they were talking to each other or taking a few extra minutes on coffee breaks. I said I thought I could understand what she meant and that perhaps I should say something about my approach in this area. I didn't think it helped to have someone always on your back, and so I try to treat my staff as responsible adults. However, if a pattern of a problem exists, that is, a staff member is always late, or not taking her share of the responsibility, or sluffing off, then it *was* my business, and I would raise it directly with the staff member. It was part of my responsibility to evaluate job performance, and I took that part seriously. I thought, however, that it could be done in a constructive and helpful way. If they ever felt it wasn't being handled well, that I seemed to be "snoopervising," then I'd like to hear about it from them.

They nodded and Rita laughed and said: "Don't worry, you'll know." I laughed with them and asked if there were any other comments or reactions. There were none, so we moved on to the next question on our agenda.

Just because these words were spoken by the supervisor does not mean that they were heard, understood, or will be remembered. Probably each nurse on that ward heard something a little different, depending upon her own circumstances, background, and prior experiences with people in authority. In addition, the nurses might not believe that Leta really means what she has said. Perhaps other supervisors have invited feedback and then shot them down when they provided it. They will have to test this new one to see what she really is like in action.

Rita, who may be an internal leader for the staff group (see Chapter 5) begins the testing process when she raises the issue of "snoopervision." Leta passed the first test of supervision by opening up the discussion and relating it directly to herself. In addition, she did not pretend she did not have responsibility for their work or would not be holding them accountable. Instead, she described under what circumstances she would have to call them to task and in what way she would try to do it.

The contracting process is not begun and finished in the same session, or even in the beginning phase of work. Clarification of purpose, role, and authority will come in the day-to-day operations of the ward, in the sessional phases of work described in Chapter 3. As the implications of the process take on meaning in the daily routine, Leta will have to discuss again the role she has described. But at least she has stated her views, and her staff can watch how she implements them. They can also take her up on problems with which she has offered help.

Of particular importance in this example were Leta's comments about being available to support the staff when the going got rough. One of the major contributions supervisors can make comes through their ability to empathize with the feelings of staff. This skill, which will be discussed in more detail in Chapter 3, can be briefly described as the capacity to genuinely feel, as closely as possible, what the staff member may be experiencing and to communicate that understanding through words, expressions, touch, respectful silence, or other appropriate means.

Most staff members have experienced so many different responses to their emotions from people in positions of authority that they are reluctant to reveal their vulnerability. They have been taught that dependency is a sign of weakness and that one should be able to handle problems and feelings on one's own. When their ambivalence meets the ambivalence of the supervisor, the result may well be a supervision process that deals with the symptoms of the underlying feelings but provides little in the way of support for the worker or satisfaction for the supervisor. By directly mentioning her availability to the staff when things are difficult, Leta issued a clear invitation which the members needed to hear. As with other aspects of the contract, it is likely that they will test her in this area by limited sharing of a concern. They may raise what is called in the literature a "near problem" and wait to see how the supervisor handles it. If she picks up the hint, takes the time to listen, is supportive and nonjudgmental, and appears to be genuinely trying to understand, then the staff will get the message that she meant her original offer.

Supervisors in my workshops often ask themselves whether they really want their staffs to take them up on the offer to share feelings. They are afraid they will not know what to do once feelings are raised, or that feelings will be about personal problems, or that they will hear their own feelings coming back to them from the staff.

While the supportive function of supervision and particularly the skills of dealing with feelings in pursuit of purpose are discussed in a later chapter, the point here is that, one way or another, a supervisor has to deal with feelings. A television advertisement for an autombile repair service makes the point directly: "You can pay me now, or you can pay me later." The feelings of staff have a powerful impact on the operations of a service, and the supervisor simply chooses whether to deal with the problems themselves or to struggle over the results of having ignored them. Lowered staff morale, sharp drops in levels of performance, conflicts between staff members that prevent them from working together, increased use of sick leave, and complaints of poor service from consumers are all possible results of the powerful forces operating in the emotional underlife of the work situation.

The New Supervisor: Some Variations on the Theme

The examples of the new child care supervisor and nursing supervisor illustrate the importance of tuning in and responding directly to indirect cues, and the contracting skills of dealing with purpose, role, and authority and inviting staff feedback. Each situation has unique characteristics, however. The following examples will illustrate the same dynamics and skills in a number of different contexts. The problems discussed have been raised often in supervision workshops, an indication that they involve universal issues. They include a new supervisor who is promoted from within the ranks and has to deal with a staff with whom she has had a social relationship, an office manager who began to work at the agency in the year the supervisor was born, and a colleague who thought he should have gotten the job. In two other examples the supervisors are brought into the job for the express purpose of straightening out a problem with a poorly performing staff.

From practitioner to supervisor

The point at which the helping professional makes the role shift from direct practice to supervision is both an exciting and a trying time. Even under the best of circumstances the transition can be difficult. Schwartz (1968) describes a training group of assistant supervisors in a welfare department who reported feeling "shaky about role-switch from social investigator to supervisor, teacher and —most frightening—'boss' " (p. 360). Even though they may have actively sought their jobs, new supervisors inevitably face doubts about competency as they try out a new role.

The beginning period is complicated by the experiences supervisors have had as supervisees. They know the usual feelings toward supervisors, having felt them themselves. They also have participated in after-work discussions, when a supervisor's most minute faults can be the topic for hours. Inevitably, the first time they enter a staff room and the conversation falls suddenly silent, they wonder what is being said about them. While the supervisor's judgment of the staff member is powerful, so is the combined judgment of the staff on the supervisor. Kadushin (1976) notes the dependency of the supervisor on the supervisees for some kinds of psychic rewards: "Approbation from supervisees, expressions of commendation, and appreciation from supervisees are a source of intrinsic job satisfaction for the supervisor" (p. 107).

The problem can be even more complicated if a staff member is promoted from within. In one workshop, Fran, a recently promoted supervisor in a child welfare agency, reported being faced with the problems of a strain in her social relationships with former colleagues, a much older office manager, and a more-experienced colleague who had applied for the same job and had been passed over. When the workshop members were asked to help her with these issues, one of them laughed and suggested: "Given that situation, have you considered quitting?" Fran replied, "Actually, I have given serious thought to telling them I have changed my mind." The consultant suggested taking a look at the problems one at a time to see if the members could come up with any alternatives for Fran; she could always quit later.

Social Relationships with Staff. Fran began with the social relationships, the most painful area for her. She described having been part of a small group of staff members who had lunch regularly, went for drinks after work on Fridays, and had out-of-work contacts such as going to movies. This all had changed in the past few weeks, and the invitations had stopped. She had missed some lunches to catch up on all of the manual reading she had to do, and suddenly she found herself going for lunch on her own. She said she felt miserable about this change in her relationships: "Actually, I'm finding myself feeling all alone in the office, and it's just not as much fun." She indicated that she had made some joking comments to her colleagues about cutting her out, and they had joked back about her being the "boss" now, but they had not really discussed the issue. She was just too uncomfortable and did not want to seem as if she was forcing herself on them.

All of the supervisors in the workshop group could identify with the poignancy of the problem. A middle-range supervisor is half in and half out of the group, close enough to be able to identify with the staff and yet removed enough to feel that a significant change had occurred in the relationship. Such problems are not easy to sort out clearly, particularly the dilemma of still wanting to be a friend while understanding the need to also be the boss. The group did some tuning in to how the staff might feel, and it was soon obvious that they were probably just as uncomfortable in knowing how to relate to Fran. Using the tuning-in as a basis, members role-played how Fran might use the next opportunity to open up the direct discussion of the role change by sharing her own feelings and asking the staff to share theirs. The role play went this way:

Fran: I wanted to take a few minutes to talk about something on my mind since I switched jobs and became a supervisor. I have always felt close to all of you and thought we had a good friendship going, but recently it seems to have been strained. I have been trying to figure out how to still be friends with you while carrying out this supervisor job—and it has not been easy. I just know I value your relationship too much to lose it. How about you? Has it been on your mind too?

Louise: We felt things were more uncomfortable, but we figured you were just cutting yourself off now that you were a supervisor—you know, not wanting to have as much to do with us.

Terry: Frankly, it's not as easy to talk in front of you anymore. I mean, we used to be able to share all the dirt about what was going on—you know, the gossip about who was doing what or goofing off. Now, it would feel like squealing. It's hard enough already, knowing what you know about what we do around here.

Fran: You know, that's my problem too. Those same conversations would have a different meaning for me now since I'm responsible for that stuff.

Louise: Maybe we just have to sort out what we can talk about with you and what is so work related we need to separate it from the social part. Just knowing that you still want our friendship is important to me, because I felt a loss as well.

After the role play, Fran said she realized she had been avoiding an uncomfortable issue, and she felt that with the help of the group she might be able to handle it. The group gave her a great deal of support, and when she reported back at the next session, she indicated that her friends had been relieved that she had brought up the problem. She said she felt much better because she realized that although the friendships might make some aspects of the work more difficult, such as setting limits if staff got out of line, it was not necessary to give up the personal relationships completely.

Avoiding Stereotypes. The work on the other two parts of her problem moved quickly as the same analysis was applied, using the tuning-in and role-playing skills to practice a more direct response. Fran's written notes of her conversation with Ellen, the long-term office manager who "began to work at the agency the year I was born," were presented at a follow-up workshop. This office manager had had ongoing problems with the professional staff, who always seemed to be in conflict with her clerical workers. Her relationship with the previous supervisor had not been good. He had handled the strains by attempting to appease her at some times and at others by doing an end run around her and setting policies or procedures which stripped her of some of her authority.

Fran's previous relationship with Ellen had been reasonably cordial, if not close. Shortly after becoming supervisor, though, Fran had noticed that Ellen was becoming more reserved in her contacts. Employing the tuning-in and role-playing skills practiced in the workshop, Fran attacked the problem head on:

> I had asked Ellen in to discuss how we would work together now that I was the supervisor. I told her I realized that there were tensions in the office between the clerical staff and the professional staff and that she often found herself in the middle, having to protect her workers. I told her I hoped we could find a way to work together on the problems, because I felt I genuinely needed her help and support if I were to do my job properly. I continued by saying I realized she had been part of the office a long time and had seen lots of young supervisors like me come along, some of whom made her job more difficult. I didn't want that to happen with us. I asked her what she thought about this. She replied that it would certainly be a change from the way supervisors had worked with her in the past. I asked her to fill me in on the details, since I only heard one side of the story.

She described with great feeling how she had continually been rebuffed by my predecessor whenever she tried to bring up problems between the professional and clerical staffs. He would attempt to smooth things over, and sometimes he didn't even listen to her. She finally gave up and decided she would just have to protect her staff as best she could. She went on to describe, with bitterness, the ways in which he had reduced her responsibility in a number of important areas, often without talking to her about it. I told her that after having worked so long in the job it must have felt like he was wiping out her contribution to the office. She said that was exactly what it felt like.

I told her I wanted to try to deal with these problems in the hope we might clear some of them up, but that, frankly, I was a bit wary of jumping in too fast, since I was just starting. I said I certainly couldn't see how I could have any impact unless I had her help and support. I wanted to see if we could change the feelings of battle lines, and the we-versus-they thing going on in the office. But, first, I thought we had to make sure we had sorted things out between ourselves. I asked her how she felt about it. She told me anything would be better than the way it was now. I suggested she make a list of the issues she thought we should tackle and that we could meet again the next day to see where to go from there. She smiled and said that was fine with her, and that she hoped my good intentions were not just part of being a new supervisor. I said I realized that she wondered if I would change after a while, and, frankly, I was worried about that as well. I told her I would count on her to keep me honest.

The key factor in this first interview is that Fran did not treat this office manager as if she fit the stereotype that everyone else had accepted. She avoided the trap of treating Ellen as if she had a "personality problem" and instead dealt with her behavior as a symptom of a problem in the system, and the result of previous interactions with supervisors. Thus Fran was able to reach for a different response.

"Deviant behavior" by a staff member (see Chapter 5) is often misunderstood as a communication, and the kind of work that follows a beginning effort to deal with long-term office conflicts such as those between clerical and professional staffs is examined in later chapters. The point is that by not treating Ellen as a stereotypical defensive, hostile staff member, Fran made it impossible for Ellen to simply dismiss her as a stereotypical new supervisor. Each had to deal with the other as a complex rather than one-dimensional personality.

This example reflects a serious mistake that new supervisors often make: They believe the "grapevine's" description of a problem staff member. In many ways, doing so is a convenient defense for not dealing with a problem ("Everyone else has problems with Ellen too.") By tuning in and addressing the problem directly, it is often (but not always) possible to break the patterns of miscommunication which can create a vicious cycle and inspire a self-fulfilling prophecy.

Skillful intervention by a supervisor will not always produce a positive response. It is important to recognize the interactional nature of the supervision process; the supervisor has a part in the proceedings, but so does the person being supervised. Therefore, although the skills and strategies suggested in this book can achieve effective results, it is entirely possible to conceive of situations where, for any number of reasons, the supervisee does not respond as expected. A worker might not find it possible, for instance, to lower defenses, to admit to vulnerability, or to trust the supervisor's intentions. This is why it is sometimes necessary to give up on an employee and recommend dismissal or other job action. The focus of this discussion is on how the supervisor can do his or her part as skillfully as possible, in the belief that effective supervision will bring out the strength in most, if not all, workers.

Continued Resistance. The dynamic of continued resistance was illustrated when Fran reported back to the workshop group on her efforts to deal with John, the colleague with seniority who was angry when he did not get the supervisory job. Fran described verbal and nonverbal communications from this worker which bordered on outright hostility. She had been hurt by his reaction but again had kept her feelings inside and had not confronted him. Her written report of her efforts to engage him directly on this sensitive issue, after she had tuned in and role-played the interview in the workshop, follows:

I had asked John to meet with me to review his current case load so I could be in touch with any problems he felt I should know about. He missed the first appointment, apologizing later and telling me he had forgotten. He was ten minutes late for the second appointment and had not brought his files with him, even though that was the usual procedure for reviewing cases. I was getting the distinct feeling that he was not too happy about meeting with me. Taking my courage in hand, and strengthened by my other experiences, I decided to try to get at the problem directly.

I told him I had the feeling he was not too anxious to talk with me about the cases—at least he certainly didn't seem enthusiastic. He said he didn't really see the need for the discussion because, as he told me before, there were no problems on his case load that he needed help with right now. I told him I could appreciate that he had his case load in order, but I felt, as a new supervisor, it was important for me to get a feel for the work that all of the staff was doing. He told me that Sam (the previous supervisor) had respected his competence and left him to do his work alone.

At this point I felt stuck and frustrated, as if we were going around in circles. I finally leveled with him and told him that I felt there was more to this than just a change in procedures. I told him I had felt some tension from him since I had received the promotion, and, particularly since I knew he had applied for the same job, I was worried about what it meant. I told him I had felt uncomfortable about the whole situation. I had even avoided raising it with him—which was a mistake. I realized he was an experienced caseworker and had even been at the agency longer than I, and yet I got the job. I was frankly afraid he would be mad at me, and that was what I was sensing.

He told me he didn't understand what I was talking about. He was not angry at me, although he didn't feel he had received completely fair treatment in the selection process. I asked him what he meant by that, and he responded by saying he did not want to talk about it, it was all over. I told him that I was feeling upset about them having to make the choice between us, and I got the job. Therefore, I wouldn't have been surprised if he had some feelings as well.

He got angry at me and said: "Look, if you feel people are angry at you for getting the job, that's your problem, not mine. Maybe you feel guilty about having gotten it in the first place." I told him I wasn't feeling guilty, just worried about how we would get along in these circumstances. He told me that if I left him alone, there should be no problems. I told him I couldn't do that and feel comfortable about the job, so we had just better work out what we could expect from each other. I told him I would expect to be informed about his work, as I would with all staff. He could, however, expect that I would respect his competency and give him a good deal of leeway in the way he handled cases. In those situations where I differed with him, and I thought they would be few, I would have to take responsibility for the final decision, since that came with the job. I asked if he would make another appointment, and, this time, I would like him to bring the folders. He said he would do that and our conference ended. I was glad, because by this time, my knees were shaking so hard I was sure he must be able to hear them.

Although the session was a difficult one, and Fran did not think she was much further along with John, some important things had happened. First, she had declared the formally taboo subject as legitimate for discussion. Second, John actually had gotten quite angry at Fran, while simultaneously denying he felt any anger at all. It is quite possible that John was not in touch with how he felt in the situation and meant the denial. At any rate, the quarrel was out in the open, and it might get picked up at a later date when John felt more free to discuss it. Even if it was not raised again, simply pointing out the obstacle in this way might effectively diminish its effect.

Fran had confronted the issue of their working relationship and made it clear that she would not be intimidated by John into pretending she was not his supervisor. This was important for John to hear, since now that she had made it clear she would not just disappear, he was going to have to deal with her in one way or another. At the same time she made this part of the contract clear, she offered recognition of her respect for his experience and competency, which he also needed to hear—although his feelings may have made it hard for him to understand this at this point.

The workshop group offered support to Fran for her courage in the exchange. It was important that she did not close the door because of John's first response. Often a staff member needs time to think things over before being able to engage in a dialogue. It would be a mistake to assume that the question was closed forever or that John would not become more responsive as the work progressed. Fran would have to achieve the delicate balance of remaining sensitive to his feelings while simultaneously not letting up on her demands and expectations.

The group members also tuned in to the problem of gender, since this would be the first time John was supervised by a woman. They agreed that Fran should keep this in mind until a better working relationship was established; it would not be wise at this point to raise yet another potential obstacle. Fran ended the discussion by saying that although it had been rough going in this case, and she still saw problems ahead, she felt strengthened by having at least confronted the problem and finding that the whole world did not collapse.

This is an important observation, and it recurs in the examples given throughout this book. It is often true that the problems we fear the most turn out to be less potent the moment we start to face them.

The Hired-Gun Syndrome

Another common variation on the theme of the new supervisor appears when the supervisor is brought in from outside the unit for the express purpose of straightening out perceived problems. I call this the *hired-gun syndrome,* because that is the way the staff often sees this type of new supervisor. This is the most extreme version of the problem of a new authority person, an outsider, entering any system. The discussion in this section, therefore, is relevant even in situations where serious problems are not apparent.

When a new supervisor enters an established system, staff members are concerned about how this authority figure will judge them. All helping professionals have some concern about their effectiveness, and any system, even the best, will have unresolved problems in its operations. Staff members are well aware of the blemishes in the program and its weaknesses, and this awareness heightens their concern about how the new supervisor will judge them.

If a staff group has been formally or informally identified as operating poorly, or it presents some other type of problem for the system, its concerns and defensiveness are usually heightened. Most helping systems have subgroups of staff members which are so identified: the regional office to which all of the "losers" have been transferred; the ward in the hospital which contains the "negative" staff; the department in the agency whose staff members are the "sweathogs" of the system; the residential treatment center in which the staff seems to have lost any sense of control over residents; or the transition house which has been recently incorporated into the formal welfare system but is rebelling against any forms of accountability. In a discussion on administration skills in Chapter 6, the functional role often played by such staff groups in the system as a whole is considered. Here the concern is only with the problems such a group presents for the new supervisor in the beginning phase.

A common mistake made by new supervisors in this kind of situation is to try to lay down the law at the very beginning. This is often the result of poor preparation, in which the supervisor may be charged by an administrator with "cleaning up the mess." The supervisor is made to feel that early progress is required, and the sole reason for his or her involvement in the situation is to bring about change. Another factor which leads the supervisor to come on heavy in the beginning is her or his own anxiety about the situation. Because resistance and anger are expected, the supervisor moves in a way which brings them about quickly. Still a third reason is the supervisor's feelings about having been selected for this "choice" role. One supervisor was transferred from an extremely well-run hospital ward to the trouble spot in the system. Because of the poor way the assignment was discussed with her, she experienced it as a punishment rather than a recognition of her superior abilities. She directed her anger at the administration toward her new staff.

In another case, where the assignment was handled well, the supervisor really did not want to leave her unit in a child welfare agency, even though she recognized the validity of the administrator's appeal and clearly understood it as a demonstration of faith in her competence. At a workshop, when I challenged her on her real feelings about beginning with this new group of staff and pointed out that it sounded as if she were really upset about leaving her old staff, she broke into tears, revealing the depths of her feelings about the endings. It is often true that beginnings are infused with many unresolved feelings about endings.

Whatever the reasons for coming on strong in the beginning, it is usually a mistake, as is illustrated in the following example from a child care treatment home. A problem in the home had received public notice through a story in the press. A teenager had been acting out in the community, and the police had charged that the staff in the home were not providing enough structure and the kids were being allowed to run free. This precipitated an agency investigation into the home, some confirmation of the problems, the transfer of the child care supervisor to a new position, and his replacement on a temporary basis (for a few months) by a supervisor from another home which had a reputation for strong discipline. Will, the new supervisor, described his first staff meeting as tense. When he walked into the meeting room he could see that many of the staff were angry or upset. Some were sitting with their arms folded in a posture which seemed to say : "Go ahead, change me!" Will had prepared himself for the tough job, however, so he just put his head down and ploughed ahead:

> I told them I realized things had been rather lax around here and that they should realize this was not the way I wanted to see the house run. I pointed out they had run into all kinds of problems which we were not experiencing at my other home, and that I thought lack of proper

discipline was at the bottom of the troubles. I told them I thought we could straighten that out fairly quickly, making the place better for the kids and for them.

The response he received was a sullen silence. He quickly changed the subject and raised some questions about staff rotations and other policy issues. Things went "miserably" after that, Will said: "They hardly even talk to me, and I feel it's like going uphill all the way."

This new supervisor had made the classic mistake of attacking the staff at a time when they were most vulnerable. He would have been helped by Hollander's (1961) analysis of how leaders build up "idiosyncratic credits" through a process of conforming to the group's norms before initiating any challenges to them. In a modified version, this would mean that any new supervisor would be wise to spend some time with the staff, learning to understand the problems through the eyes of its members before attempting to initiate changes.

It is important to develop a working relationship, based on understanding, to draw on when the time comes to *make a demand for work* (Schwartz, 1961). The same holds true in any new staff contact. Since this staff seemed to feel so vulnerable, what they needed at this point was not a lecture on how to straighten out their house but rather some understanding of how tough the past few weeks must have been for all of them. Without such a relationship, defenses are heightened by an attack. The results might have been different if Will had begun another way, perhaps as follows:

> I know you have all been going through a rough time in the past few weeks, what with the publicity, a change of supervisors, and everyone coming down hard on you. I also realize you're probably worried about my being transferred in here to make some changes. I wanted you to know I realize I need to find out a great deal from you about what goes on around here, what parts of the program you value, and where you see the problems. So don't worry. Although I was asked to help you examine the program, I'm clear that I can't do a thing without your cooperation and involvement—and so I won't try. Now it's your turn to speak, and I'll listen.

It is important for the supervisor to be genuine in such comments. If the staff finds out it is really a con job; that is, that he is setting them up and doesn't really mean what he is saying, the reaction will be very negative. In reality, it is impossible to make serious changes in a program without the cooperation of the staff. And if the staff has been having difficulty in the area of setting limits, then exploring the issues involved and trying to understand why it is hard for them is the first step in helping them to make changes. A supervisor who simply makes demands without providing support will be experienced by the staff as harsh and uncaring.

In the case of Will, the child care supervisor who had made the mistake of coming on too strongly, members of the workshop role-played how he might go back to the staff and admit his mistake, asking for a chance to start over. They suggested Will might say:

> I wanted to talk to you about the way I began at this place. Frankly, I was nervous about starting under pressure to bring about changes. As a result, I came on heavy and probably put you all off just at the time you were already reeling from everyone coming down on your backs. It certainly didn't help our working relationship, which I feel is not in great shape right now. I would like a chance to start over. How about it?

The workshop participants felt this might help. They thought the staff members would appreciate the honesty and the admission of a mistake. It is interesting that this particular approach—admitting a mistake—usually provokes an important discussion among supervisors. Many say they have felt that to be effective, they should not admit to faults. They view it as exposing a weakness which would lower their status in the eyes of their workers. But when asked to think about important authority figures in their lives, most realize that this kind of honesty made these people seem more real, less like cardboard figures, more vulnerable, and less threatening. In fact, workers are relieved when supervisors make and admit mistakes. Indeed, it is the supervisor who always seems to be perfect, in control, and never flustered who is very hard to live with.

There is another important reason for dealing with staff with more honesty and understanding. Staff members often relate to their clients in a parallel manner to the way the supervisor relates to them. Two interesting studies have highlighted this phenomenon. In a study of the training of a psychotherapist, Doerhrman (1972) found that therapists act out with patients the effects of the conflicts engendered in them by their supervisors. And, in a study of social work student training, Mayer and Rosenblatt (1974) found that the students' security with their clients was directly associated with how secure they themselves felt with their supervisors.

Thus, the supervisor in this child care setting has an opportunity to demonstrate to the staff, through his work with them, a way of dealing with residents. With acting-out teenagers in a residential setting, who are there because other forms of help such as foster homes have not worked, it is critical that the staff begins with support and understanding. This can develop the kind of working relationship that allows the youngsters to accept the limitations the staff must set for them. The ability of the staff to understand deviant behavior by residents as a form of communication and to reach for the underlying feelings is crucial.

In addition, the staff should feel free to admit to mistakes they may make with residents. This is an essential skill when working with youngsters, who will respond with a battle of wills to any adult they perceive as arbitrary and unfair. To carry the parallel further, it is precisely the ability to admit to mistakes and to take responsibility for one's own actions that the staff wishes to develop in the youngsters. Thus, the modeling of adult behavior really begins with the supervisor, continues with the staff, and gets picked up by the clients. The importance of such modeling in the setting as a whole is described in Chapter 4.

Another example of the hired-gun syndrome concerns a new supervisor who took responsibility for a transition house for women in crisis which had recently been incorporated into a large government agency. It had operated independently on grants and had constantly been in money trouble until, after a campaign for public recognition of the service, it was accepted into the agency's structure. This house had operated without a supervisor, through a form of group democracy which had been popularized as an alternative leadership approach involving colleagual decision making and shared authority. Thus a supervisor was being sent in from the outside to take responsibility for a setting that had been independent and without a supervisor for its first year of operation. The issues and problems involved with leaderless groups or teams are described in Chapter 5.

This example was presented in a supervision workshop before Betty, the new supervisor, joined the group, so the members were able to anticipate a number of problems and develop a strategy for dealing with them. As in all situations, the tuning in began with the supervisor, who was feeling very concerned about rejection and hostility. Betty was pleased about the assignment because she felt a strong commitment to the type of service provided, but she was worried that she would not be accepted and would always be viewed as the "agency's person."

In the tuning-in exercise the workshop group focused mostly on the negatives in the situation. They were quite skillful at anticipating the problems but did not tune in at all to the possibility that some staff members might feel pleased at the arrival of the supervisor. This is a common mistake; when I point it out in workshops, many participants admit that the problems scare them so much that they simply cannot respond to the strengths in the situation.

People's feelings, in most situations, are ambivalent. Staff members in the transition house might be worried about their freedom, concerned about being co-opted by the system, and fearful of the new supervisor's efforts to direct them. But they might also feel relieved at the end of their funding problems, pleased to be recognized as an important service, and hopeful that a new supervisor could help them with some of the difficulties of the job.

Whenever there is a leaderless team, I have found, a number of serious problems are created in the work situation, and these problems are not dealt with. There are complex reasons for this, having to do with the difficulty peers have in confronting one another and the problems in trying to organize cooperative efforts without a clearly recognized leadership role. In addition, while staff members can be supportive and helpful to each other on the technical issues associated with the work (that is, in this example, the skills of working effectively with women in crisis), there are some forms of help which require a supervisory function that they will not provide for each other, such as making demands in difficult areas. These dynamics are discussed later in the book. The important point is that a new supervisor should also tune in to positive feelings.

The following extract describes Betty's beginning contracting efforts as she attempted to deal with purpose and function, while opening up the issue of authority:

> I began by telling the staff I was pleased to get this job. I told them
> I had a strong commitment to their service to women and was pleased
> to have the opportunity to work with them. I told them I realized they

had mixed feelings about the agency takeover and my being there. I wanted to tell them my views on the matter, which I had given a great deal of thought to, and then hear some of theirs.

I told them I felt the takeover was a tribute to their efforts during the past year to establish this kind of service as meeting a real and persistent need. At least they would not have to worry about whether they are going to exist beyond the end of the month. At this point, Lill interrupted me and said: "*Now* we have to worry about whether we are still going to be operating in the same way at the end of the month." I asked her what she meant, and she [replied] that integration was a mixed blessing, and they were worried about what the agency had in mind for them. I said I could appreciate that, since I realized they had had fairly free reign. I told them that, as far as I knew, there were no plans for changing the service as they had established it. I explained that I saw my function as partly being in the middle between them and the agency, and if there was anything they wanted me to communicate to the administration I would try to do that, as well as keep them informed on what was in the works on the administration's part.

I then told them that I realized that the biggest change they had to face was my involvement and that they probably had mixed feelings about that. They had operated without a supervisor for one and one-half years, had done a fine job in establishing an important new service, and now they had to take me along with the money. I was worried about their feelings at having an outsider move into this role.

Hazel spoke up and indicated they were not too happy about it at all. I asked what they were worried about, specifically. Rhoda said that most of them had been attracted to this job partly because of the kind of work it was, but, also, to get out from under authoritarian supervisors who were on power trips. I asked if they were concerned about me going on a power trip. They nodded in agreement.

I told them I was new to this setting, and so I would have to learn a lot about their work from them. I did not come in with all kinds of preconceived ideas and changes in mind. I told them I did not feel I could operate effectively without their cooperation [and so] how I planned my role would, in part, depend on our discussions. I saw my job as carrying out some of the coordinating functions, which meant I would pay attention to how they worked together to deliver this service. Whenever it seemed helpful, [I would] draw their attention to issues or questions that needed to be addressed in order to maintain its effectiveness or improve it. As I had already explained, I also saw this coordinating function in relation to the agency, for example, in making sure we get our resources or [in] improving communications with referring agencies. I couldn't do this work myself but, rather, would coordinate our joint efforts in these areas or others that they identified as troublesome.

They agreed that it might be helpful to have someone pay attention to these areas, since they sometimes fell between the cracks. I asked what they meant, and they described some of the administrative foul-ups with other agencies, and even some of the internal communications problems.

Zoey, who had been looking most closed during the discussion, said with some force: "All of this sounds terrific, but why don't we cut the bullshit and get to the real issue? If you're the supervisor, you're the boss, and what is that going to mean?" I said I guessed we had all been trying to avoid getting to the toughest part. I knew it was the part I had lost sleep over for the last few nights. As I saw it, I was responsible to the agency for the operations of this house, and that included supervision of staff, seeing that the house conformed to general policies, and evaluating general and individual work performances. However, I was free to develop the way I carried out these jobs , and, as I [had] said earlier, I didn't think I could do them alone without their active involvement.

Zoey said that at least I was straight about it. I told her I did not think power-tripping was the answer, and that if I did get out of line in that way, I would want to know about it. Hazel said: "Don't worry, with this group you would hear about it fast enough." She laughed, as did the rest of us, breaking the tension a bit. I continued by [telling them] that while [I was] new to the house itself, I did bring some experience to the situation which they might find helpful. Part of my job, as I saw it, was to help them strengthen their work skills. I knew they did lots of group work in the house, and I thought I could be helpful in that area by providing a sounding board for examinig the dynamics of the groups and [suggesting] ideas about how to work with them.

I also [said I] thought it would be my job to try to give them some emotional support when they needed it. I realized they gave a great deal to the women and the kids, and that having to deal with broken and battered families took a toll on them. I knew they helped each other during the tough times, but, as a supervisor, I would see that as my job as well. I [asked them] what they thought about that. There was silence for a while, and Hazel said: "I hope you're prepared for calls at two A.M. from the hospital emergency ward." I told them I guessed since they had to be ready for those calls, I should be [too.] They were quiet for a while and then began to talk about the impact of all of the brutality on them. I just listened.

Our meeting time was almost over when I asked them what they thought. Zoey said she still didn't think they needed a supervisor, but she really had no choice. I said I guessed we were stuck with each other now. I asked them to give me a fair chance, since I very much wanted things to work out and realized it was not possible without their support. The meeting ended on that note.

This discussion did not resolve the issues, but it did establish a beginning working relationship. Betty won the respect of the staff, if not their acceptance. It would be in future weeks, as she demonstrated her sense of her function and purpose, that the relationship would have a chance to deepen. A critical factor in this beginning was her honesty, as well as her direct recognition of the pain involved in carrying out this kind of work. These attributes gave the staff a glimpse of what might be available for them if they could bring themselves to trust and accept her.

Supervisory Beginnings with New Workers

Another type of beginning is necessary when the supervisor is already established in a system and the staff member is new. Supervisory skills in the preliminary and beginning phases are examined in four different situations in this section. The first involves beginning work with a new and inexperienced worker or staff member. In the second situation, the new worker has had some prior experience. In the third, the worker is new to the fields but has just completed professional training and wants everyone to realize just how "professional" he really is. The fourth is an example of beginning with a student placed for a practicum experience by a school of social work.

The inexperienced new worker

In some settings, it is not unusual for a staff member to begin to fill a position with little or no prior experience. This lack of experience can accent the difficulties in adjustment which, in turn, can significantly delay effective integration into the service. New workers in child welfare settings, for example, have described a beginning at an agency that consisted of an orientation to policies, procedures, and forms that left them completely overwhelmed and bewildered.

This was followed by a traumatic entry into the system in which a harried supervisor merely handed them files of cases to be seen. Often there was very little preparation. If there was discussion, it was usually on case management issues, rarely on practice skill questions (such as how to handle the first contact with a client). Very little attention, if any, was paid to the reactions and feelings of the worker. Workers have described how they ended their first day on the job in a daze, close to tears, or ready to quit—or all three.

While this is admittedly an extreme example, some elements of it are often part of the beginning process. One of the serious implications of such a beginning is what it says to a new social worker about the way in which new relationships are handled in the agency. This can have an impact on the worker's future practices with clients. In many ways, the worker's beginning at the agency offers an excellent teaching opportunity to make the worker sensitive to the parallel relationship with a client.

Although the beginnings described in this section are often expressed in terms of workers and agencies, many of the ideas are applicable to assisting new employees to integrate into any system in the helping professions. And while they are expressed in terms of new, inexperienced workers, they also are applicable to all new workers, regardless of their experience.

The Beginning Phase for Inexperienced Social Workers. In the supervision model illustrated in Figure 1.2 in Chapter 1, the worker is viewed as interacting with a number of significant systems, and the supervisor is seen as mediating these interactions. In the beginning phase of the supervision process with a new social worker, for example, which is illustrated in Figure 2.1, the key areas for attention are the agency and its policies and procedures, including personnel practices and physical facilities; the staff unit or department in which the worker and others will do most of their work; the larger staff system which relates to this unit; the supervisor; and the client or receiver of services. It is easy to see how a new worker can feel anxious and uncertain about so many unknowns, and how confusing the beginning process can be. An established supervisor can forget just how complicated the system must appear at the beginning.

This is especially true when early efforts at orienting new workers consist of providing a deluge of information that is impossible to integrate, particularly when they have other concerns about the job. A two-week orientation that attempts to teach the whole policy

FIGURE 2.1
The Supervision Model in the Beginning Phase

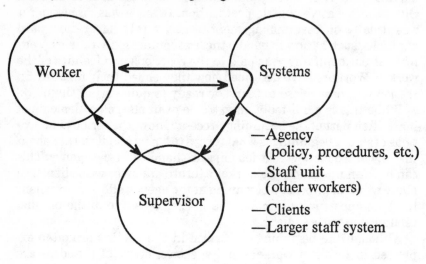

manual to a worker who has no idea how to use the information, for example, will usually engender more anxiety than it relieves.

With a little advance planning, the supervisor should be able to partialize the beginning problem into its component pieces and help new workers tackle each one, a step at a time. In relation to the agency, going over personnel questions such as payroll procedures and benefits can answer some urgent personal questions. Location is also important; having a desk ready provides some reassurance that the supervisor has thought about making the worker comfortable. If the supervisor simply is free on the first morning to take the new worker around, introduce colleagues, and point out key spots such as the cafeteria or local eating places this helps begin the orientation process. In each case the supervisor should resist the temptation to tell new workers everything they need to know the entire first year and should instead concentrate on helping them get through the first day and the first week.

Orientation to agency policies and procedures should be designed to make workers aware of the availability of manuals and how to use them, rather than expecting them to memorize their contents. A supervisor who watches the eyes of a new worker during orientation will quickly notice when the worker has had enough. Simply acknowledging that there is a lot to learn, but it does not have to be learned all at once, can help a great deal.

In addition to such orientation, a worker who is new to the area may have a number of important personal questions about housing, schools for children, and so on which the supervisor can help with or suggest sources of help for. The more quickly new workers get settled in their personal lives, the faster they will have the energy available to make the necessary adaptation to the agency.

Orientation to the staff group is also important on the first day. Workers have reported the sinking feeling they experienced on their first day at work as noon approached and they did not know if they should go to lunch on their own, wait for someone to ask them to join them, or initiate a contact themselves. Some thoughtfulness on such simple matters on a first day is most helpful. The supervisor can appreciate the importance of the way in which a worker begins with the peer group if the staff group is considered as an informal as well as formal system. The informal system (which is described in more detail in Chapter 5), is characterized by a well-developed set of rules of behavior, certain norms which its members subscribe to, taboo subject areas which members agree not to discuss, and subgroups. In many ways, the operation of the informal system can have a much more powerful effect on the effectiveness of services than the formal, recognized system can. In the beginning phase, a new worker is making a start at integrating into this informal system.

Schwartz (1961) describes the anxieties about beginning a new relationship as part of the *authority theme.* He uses the term *intimacy theme* to refer to the dynamics which take place between members of a peer group (a theme which is explored in some detail in later chapters). A supervisor who is conscious of this aspect of the beginning process may help to ease this integration. Sometimes this can be accomplished by calling attention to the arrival of a new staff member and asking the staff group to take some responsibility for the beginning phase. A simple question such as, "Any ideas on how we can make it comfortable for Frank on his first day here?" can set the process in motion.

The smaller staff unit is usually set within the context of a larger system (for example, the hospital ward in relation to the hospital or the unmarried parents' department in relation to the child welfare agency). Because it is not possible to provide services to clients within the smaller unit without taking into account relationships with staff in the larger system, it is helpful in the beginning phase if the supervisor identifies key individuals in related systems and helps the new worker make the initial contacts. The first weeks might involve learning about the system, the people in it who help to make it work, and some of the formal and informal ways it operates. This information should be shared in manageable doses, and it should be related to the worker's current tasks.

In some settings, the new worker may have to take some time to learn about the community in which the work takes place. A new child care worker who visits the local school attended by the children in a group care home can make personal contacts which later will be invaluable. A community health nurse who stops in to meet the staff at a family service agency may be able to make more effective referrals as they become necessary. Attendance at an interprofessional committee meeting can serve to attach a face to a name that will become important as service is delivered. While the specifics of this aspect of orientation differ depending on the setting and the helping professional's role, the general idea of orientation to the larger system within which the working system is set is an important one in any beginning.

The process of orienting the new worker to the supervisor was described in the section on contracting skills. As soon as possible, time should be set aside for a discussion of the purpose of supervision and the role of the supervisor. This provides an opportunity for the supervisor to answer questions as well as to explore how the worker is feeling about the beginning. Simply acknowledging the strain of so much new information in such a short time means a great deal to the new worker. In addition, the supervisor can open up the question of client contact and recognize the worker's probable concerns about being thrown into first interviews without some preparation. A discussion of the possible early case load might help, and any efforts to lessen the pressure would be reassuring.

Helping a new worker prepare for work with clients is one of the educational functions of supervision (see Chapter 4), but some consideration of questions and concerns in this area is important in the beginning. In a hospital setting, for example, it is reassuring to let a new nurse know that the supervisor will provide some direct help with patients for the first few days. In the social work or counseling setting, supervisors might invite new workers to sit in on their own interviews as observers in order to get some ideas on how to begin. Workers usually appreciate the willingness of supervisors to share their work in this way. The workers not only get a chance to begin to relate with clients without the pressure of responsibility, but they also can observe the supervisors' own style of work.

Integrating New Staff Members. The techniques for helping new social workers begin can be applied by supervisors to ease the integration of new staff members in all the helping professions. It may seem that devoting so much attention to this phase simply takes too much time, and the pressures facing both new staff members and supervisors are not recognized. Sometimes supervisors have had to carry workers' case loads or perform staff services in addition to their own responsibilities for months while awaiting the arrival of new staff members. By the time a new employee arrives they are under great pressure, both to put the worker to work quickly and to deal with their own piled-up tasks. This opens up the question of how to attempt to influence policy on the handling of short-term vacancies and orientation procedures for new staff. (Providing feedback on the implications of policy for practice is discussed in Chapter 6.)

While the time available for effective beginning work may be affected by factors beyond the supervisor's control, being conscious of the possibilities could help many supervisors provide more effective orientations for their staffs. Supervisors often orient beginners in precisely the same way they themselves were oriented, even though they know that the process did not meet their own needs. Time spent in a more careful orientation process can save time later because the new member will be able to move more quickly into the staff system. In the beginning phase, as in all the others, good practice saves time in the long run. Key issues overlooked always come back to haunt the supervisor.

A supervisor may be able to tap the resources of the staff group to provide much of the help described in this section. Experienced staff members often are glad to help with the orientation of new members, if they are asked, and they may appreciate recognition of their abilities. An office manager or ward clerk also can provide some of the most important information needed by new employees.

Asking the staff to reflect on their own beginnings at the setting and then to share in developing an effective orientation program for new staff members might help distribute the labor. Even more important, it could make the orientation process more effective.

The experienced new worker

When new staff members are experienced, there are some unique variations in the orientation process. Experienced staff members may have even more concerns about beginning a new job than those who are inexperienced. If their past encounters with supervisors have been unsatisfactory, they may have a stereotyped idea of supervision that is not helpful.

Additions to the staff may also be concerned that the skills and understandings they have acquired in their previous jobs may not be relevant in the new setting. The normal questions of competency are heightened as they prepare to test themselves in a new context. Adding to the stress may be concerns about what will be expected of them *because* of their experience. They may feel more reluctant to ask for help or to reveal their ignorance because they believe they are supposed to understand already.

Two examples of this kind of relationship are given here. In the first example, a nursing supervisor for an emergency unit was engaged in dialogue with a new nurse. The supervisor attempted to develop the proper balance between recognition of the nurse's prior experience, while allowing her to feel free to be a learner:

Supervisor: First of all, welcome to the unit. I want to tell you about the unit, and how we work around here. But before that, I want to find out a bit more about your prior work experience. I realize you have had four years on a general ward, and I'm really pleased to get someone with that kind of background. At the same time, you probably have a lot of questions about how to fit in on emergency, how it will be the same, and what will be different. Maybe we can start there.

Nurse: Actually, I was kind of worried about that. You know I took training on emergency, but that was a long time ago. I'm sure things have changed now. I wasn't even sure I wanted emergency, but as you know, that was the only opening.

Supervisor: It's always a lot easier if you can find a place on a service you're already comfortable with. Also, there are a lot of advantages for us to have an experienced emergency room nurse. However, up here in the boondocks you don't have any other hospitals to choose from, and we don't get applicants with exactly the experience we want. We're really pleased to have gotten you, though. What are some of the things you're worried about?

Nurse: Things can happen fast on emergency—maybe too fast for someone learning on the job.

Supervisor: I'm not going to expect you to be able to handle situations on your own for a while. Until you feel more comfortable, you will work along with me or another nurse on serious situations. On the other hand, you have a lot of experience that will be helpful, so you should be able to pick up independently on much of the routine stuff. I will make a point of checking with you as we go along, and when you feel OK about handling something, just do it. If you're not sure, or I'm not sure, then we will do it together. The important thing is that I don't expect you to simply jump in and act like you have worked here for years. How does that sound?

Nurse: That's a relief. You know, I was really scared about reporting this morning. It felt just like my first day on a ward back at nursing school.

Supervisor: Let me show you around and introduce you to the other staff. That will help you feel a little more at home.

The second example concerns an experienced social worker who joins a community mental health team after having worked for years on a similar team in another part of town. In this case, the worker is less concerned about the setting and the job than about the type of supervision he will be receiving. Close supervision of practice skill development is important in the early years of practice, but workers with substantial experience are usually ready to take a more active responsibility for setting the continued learning agenda. They need a supervisor who can serve as a practice consultant, and the supervisor should recognize this and avoid relating to these workers as if they were inexperienced. In the following report the supervisor described how she tuned into this issue and raised it directly:

> I told Frank I though we were particularly lucky to have gotten him on staff. I said I was looking forward to working with him and thought it would help if we discussed our relationship. I explained that I was responsible for monitoring his cases with him and also wanted to provide whatever help I could on the tough ones. [But] I felt he was experienced enough to work independently and have a say in which areas I might need to become involved. I saw myself somewhat as a practice consultant for him, with him taking responsibility for devel-

oping his own agenda and deciding how best to use me. I asked him how that sounded to him.

Frank smiled and told me he was glad to hear what I had just said. He had been concerned about that, having changed jobs from one where he did have a good deal of professional autonomy and independence. I asked if he had worried that I might not recognize that. He replied that he had been somewhat concerned about what my approach would be. He described other supervisors he had known who seemed to feel that a worker never got past the dependent stage. He felt this was a serious problem in social work, which had a strong tradition of smothering workers.

I laughed and told him I knew what he meant, having experienced some of that in my own early practice. I [said] we would have to develop a balance between my being involved and knowing what is going on and, at the same time, giving him some freedom of action. Most important, I wanted him to feel free to use any help I might be able to give, even if [I acted] only as a sounding board for his own thinking. I might like to use him in a similar way [I said.] He agreed it would be helpful to talk with someone about the practice.

The abrasive new worker

In a supervisors' workshop, Jim, a supervisor in a child welfare agency in a rural area, described a first conference with a new worker who had just graduated from a social work professional program. Most of the staff, including Jim, had not had professional training. In the midst of the conference, the new worker asked whether he would be able to use his professional training in that agency. He said he had really enjoyed the "reality therapy" approach, combined with an "ecological view" of the client and the relevant systems. Jim said he felt like telling the worker that a few weeks in the agency would be a real "reality therapy" for him, and what he really wanted to suggest was what the worker could do with his ecological approach.

Others in the workshop shared incidents when graduates of professional schools had immediately attacked the agency on the first day of work. One supervisor described how a new worker made it clear that he thought the government-run agency was simply a "tool of the oppressor class" and the social workers were being used to "suppress dissent."

These incidents precipitated a more general attack on professional training by the workshop group members, who said they thought it often was far removed from the reality of the field. These supervisors, and others I have worked with in related fields such as nursing, education, and counseling, have strong feelings about professional training programs that seem to turn new graduates into "agency haters." That they have some valid arguments is evident in the literature of the profession, much of which attacks helping systems without appreciating their strengths as well as their weaknesses. Since agency staff supervisors often judge their own services harshly, these attacks are felt even more strongly.

In the workshop, I pointed out that when recent graduates articulate highly theoretical positions or arguments which tend to negate the services of the agency, they put the supervisor on the defensive, and this often leads to an initial battle of wills. Jim, the supervisor with the new worker who wanted to combine reality therapy and an ecological approach, said he had expressed his anger by letting the worker know in no uncertain terms that they didn't operate with fancy theories in that agency; while that might have been OK at school, here he would really have to deal with reality. This led Jim and the worker to undertake an hour-long argument on the questions of the relationship between theory and practice, the professionalism of the agency, and the freedom of action available to workers. It became clear that the supervisors felt put on the spot by such staff members and responded angrily and defensively. Since, in this example, Jim also had worked up through the ranks and lacked professional training, it was little wonder that the new worker was able to get to him so quickly.

Similar examples have been presented by nurse supervisors who had had new staff members who wanted to instigate a "team nursing approach" on their second day at the hospital, or residential treatment home supervisors who had encountered recent graduates who claimed to have found "the answer" in their training—behavior modification, reality therapy, or remotivation theory, for example—and were prepared to educate the rest of the staff at the first staff meeting they attended. In such cases, it is helpful to think of the worker's pattern of behavior as a form of indirect communications to the supervisor. Such "deviant" beginnings may be a signal of the new worker's concerns about his or her own effectiveness in the system, but the manner in which they raise their feelings makes it difficult for them to be understood. When the supervisor's own feelings of anger and defensiveness are so strong, it is difficult to understand the staff member's behavior as a call for help. A parallel exists in practice; clients feeling pressure from the agency often handle their anxiety about the new contact by appearing hostile and defensive. A worker who responds only to the anger will often miss the clients' concerns that lie just below the surface.

In the case described above, if Jim had understood how such "deviant" communications from the new worker might be such a signal, then instead of responding quickly with an angry remark, the conversation might have gone like this:

New worker: I really enjoyed using reality therapy and an ecological approach in working with my clients in my previous job.

Supervisor (Jim): Sounds like you developed some ideas about what you can do with clients, and you feel comfortable with them. Are you worried that you won't be able to use what you know in this setting, that is, that the demands will be so much different?

There is at least a chance that the conversation might have taken a different turn had the supervisor been able to understand and reach further for the worker's concerns. It is not at all unusual for students graduating from a professional school to be very anxious about their ability to put theory into practice. New workers who sound terribly sure of themselves may actually be sending a signal of opposite feelings. The supervisory skill involves taking some time to find out what the workers are really saying before jumping in to respond or try to provide an answer. (This skill is described in Chapter 3 as *sessional contracting.*)

Many new workers have misconceptions about the service, fear becoming stereotyped social workers, or worry about being co-opted by the system. They may even be anxious about all three. An abrasive new worker who is critical of the agency may be simply expressing the same concerns felt by all new workers fresh out of school, but doing it in a way which makes it hard for the supervisor to understand. Since the worker will be facing many clients who handle their anxiety in new situations in precisely the same manner, it is all the more important for the supervisor to model an effective response that reaches behind the facade for the real person.

The student as new worker

For social work students placed in a field practicum experience the receptivity of the setting can be a particular problem. A decision to accept a student is sometimes reached between an administrator and the school, with only a superficial involvement of agency staff. If the situation has not been handled well by the supervisor, the student may not be received positively by the staff and, in fact, may be frozen out of the system. The signals of such a rejection are often subtle. A common one is that repeated requests by the student's supervisor for appropriate referrals to the student's case load result in many promises but no cases. The problem is often rooted in the fact that the staff agreed to accept the student without openly expressing their reservations.

A student must be seen as the responsibility of the whole staff, not the exclusive problem of the agency supervisor. Thus, a supervisor anticipating this relationship would be wise to explore the feelings of other staff members in some detail before agreeing to accept a student. In the following report, Susan, an agency field instructor for a social work student, described the staff meeting at which she raised the possibility of taking a student for the first time:

> After I had explained what would be involved if we took a student I asked if there were any questions. Lou asked me if I thought I would have enough time for a student on top of everything else. I said I thought I could fit it into my schedule. There was a brief silence, and then someone suggested that there didn't seem to be a problem and we should move onto the next item on the agenda.

There *was* a problem, but it was lurking just beneath the surface, and the prospective student supervisor did not want to reach for it. In a workshop for school field instructors, she admitted that she had sensed the lack of enthusiasm, but she felt it would change after the student had arrived. It didn't, and that was why she was raising the problem. The student was a real outsider at the agency, no referrals had been made, and Susan did not know what to do about it.

The problem really began in that silence when she sensed their ambivalence but did not reach for it. She could have said something like: "You all don't seem that enthusiastic about the idea of a student, and since I am going to need your help if we decide to take one, maybe we should have your doubts out in the open." Schwartz describes this skill as *looking for trouble when everything is going your way.*

This skill is important because people often have difficulty talking to each other directly in controversial areas. It is easier to hold back negative comments than to risk disagreeing with a colleague. (This issue is dealt with in relation to the culture of the staff group in Chapter 5.) Because of this general tendency to withhold honest communications, Susan needed to give permission to her colleagues to open up, so they would say what they really felt rather than what they thought she wanted them to say. Otherwise, the negative feelings beneath the surface would be more powerful in their effect on the student than those that were brought out in the open. By inviting honest discussion, she could genuinely involve the staff in weighing the pros and cons of a student at the agency. If they then agreed to the placement, it would be *their* student and not just the supervisor's responsibility.

Schwartz (1968) noted this dynamic of the *illusion of work* in his work with supervisors, many of whose presentations, he said, illustrated

> ... the problem of the "false consensus," in which staff workers "agree" on a course of action, only to fail repeatedly to implement it. Here the supervisor's frustration is born of the fact that he can raise neither disagreement nor compliance, but only acceptance of the logic of the official position and an implacable inability to do anything about it. In most of the meetings reported—on instituting new forms, keeping dictation up to date, carrying out new service decisions and others—it was not open, or even conscious, defiance that held up the action. Rather, it was a kind of blind passivity that muffled the feelings and immobilized the energy either for or against the move. What had happened was that the "rightness" of the decision had been so incontrovertibly established—by both supervisor and workers—that one would require great courage to mention any of the lurking negatives, even though they were there, and would thereafter proceed to work underground. In this climate, the staff had made what we came to call a "New Year's resolution," in which the will is registered, but the work necessary to make it function has been left out. (p. 359)

The task for the supervisor is to reach past this artificial agreement and to make a *demand,* that the conversation be real. When

Susan returned to the agency, she opened up the issue directly with the staff in the following manner:

> I told the staff I had sensed some resistance toward having the student. I quickly pointed out that I thought it had been there right from the beginning, but that I had been so anxious to get a student that I had ignored it. I didn't think it was too late to talk about it, even though I had pushed ahead, and I wanted to hear their real feelings on the matter.
>
> There was a silence, and then Lou began by saying he had wondered if they were in good enough shape as a unit to carry a student. He then went on to describe some of the problems we were experiencing, since we were only recently formed, and made a case for us needing to straighten out our own work before we taught others.
>
> This opened up a flood of comments, and it became clear that I had missed a lot of negatives. We discussed some of the pros and cons of having a student. I had to resist the temptation to jump in all the time with "yes, buts . . ." As the conversation continued, I was surprised to find other staff arguing the positive aspects of a student's involvement —bringing in new ideas from the university and a fresh perspective on practice, asking questions which forced them to think more clearly about our work, and so on. June pointed out that we all have a responsibility to train new workers, just as we had been taken on by agencies for our training.
>
> After the discussion had proceeded for a period I asked them where we stood now. I realized it was rather late, but if they felt it really wasn't go for this year, maybe I should raise the question at the school and we could consider a transfer. I would be disappointed, but that was a reality. Lou felt we could handle the situation this year, but that we should evaluate it at the end of the year before we decided about going ahead again. I laughed and said, "Don't worry, I won't make that mistake again."
>
> I then told them that if we were going to keep the student, I wanted her to be their student as well. I would need their help in thinking about her program, I would need referrals, I would need their active involvement. They nodded their heads in agreement, and we discussed the specifics of how we could proceed.

Susan reported a marked change in attitudes toward the student after the meeting. She said that she had initially not really wanted them to discuss having a student because she had been afraid they would say no. She now realized how important it was to negotiate the contract with the staff system, as well as with the student, so that the acceptance of a student was a real one. To do this, the hidden negative and ambivalent feelings had to be honestly explored, or they would trouble both her and her student throughout the year.

Research Findings

This section examines research on variables related to the supervisor and the worker which can affect the relationship between them. It considers such factors as the supervisor's and the worker's education, and whether the supervisor's access to ongoing support has any impact on ability to relate to workers. Research on supervisory skills directly related to the beginning phase of work—tuning in, clarifying purpose (contracting), dealing with the authority theme, and developing a relationship based on mutual trust—is also presented.

Supervisor-related variables

Complete data on the supervisor and worker samples in our study (Shulman, Robinson, and Luckyj, 1981) are given in Tables 3 and 4 in Appendix A. One important observation concerns the distribution of genders for the supervisors and workers. There were 66 (61%) males and 43 (39%) females in the supervisory group surveyed. All 15 of the nursing supervisors were female, however, and when they were removed from the sample, it had only 28 (30%) female supervisors; while 66 (70%) of the supervisors were males. This proportion is particularly significant compared to the worker distribution. After the nurses were eliminated from the sample, 312 (60%) of the workers were females, and 210 (40%) were males. Thus, a worker group with 60% females was being supervised by a supervisory group with 70% males. This suggests some systematic selection process is operating, but we do not know what it is. Self-selection, administrative bias in selecting supervisors, or some other factors may be at work.

Supervisors were asked to indicate their level of agreement with a number of statements related to their preparation and support.

The scale was as follows: "(1) Strongly agree; (2) Agree; (3) Uncertain; (4) Disagree; (5) Strongly disagree." In response to the statement, "I received adequate preparation for the tasks and problems I faced as a beginning supervisor," the average reply was between "uncertain" and "disagree." This finding was amplified in written comments, a few of which were:

> I'm expected to carry out my jobs with minimal support and no training.

> I had very little preparation for the transition from social work to the supervisory role.

> I had inadequate training in the actual process of supervision.

When asked to comment on the following statement: "I have opportunities for ongoing training to deal with the tasks and problems I face as a supervisor," the average response from supervisors was between "agree" and "uncertain." Another statement on the supervisors' questionnaire read as follows: "I have access to ongoing emotional support from other staff in the agency which helps me to carry out my job as a supervisor." The average response to this item was close to "agree." Supervisors who did not indicate they received support used written comments to indicate how difficult they considered the job to be:

> I'd like to see a closer sharing of information between supervisors—I feel so isolated in my own office.
> I would like more support from management for our individual concerns.
> It's been a lonely experience—with being in the middle, I don't truly feel a part of the overall agency.

When the correlation analysis was conducted with the supervisor's demographic variables, we found a number of expected correlations, such as age and experience (these will not be reported here). It was of interest that none of the demographic variables (age, sex, education, experience as a supervisor, or experience in the setting), by itself, correlated with worker perceptions of supervisory skill, development of a positive working relationship, or helpfulness. This parallels the finding in my study of social work practice skill in which these variables were not, by themselves, associated with worker effectiveness (Shulman, 1981).

In an additional analysis of the impact of education, the supervisors were divided into three groups: those with M.S.W. degrees, those with B.S.W. degrees, and those with other degrees. When these groups were compared in terms of their scores on all other variables using crosstabulation with a chi-square test of significance, no significant differences were found.

It would be a mistake to infer from these findings that education and experience do not contribute to supervisory effectiveness. A number of factors need to be taken into account. First, these studies were not designed to examine the impact of education or experience. Second, examining education and experience as if all training and experience are equal is naive. Educational programs, even those within the same school, produce strikingly different skills in their graduates. Therefore, the terms *education* and *training* are not well defined, and the impact of educational programs and experience may be lost in the analysis. I believe the effects of education and experience, when combined with effective skills in supervision, do have an impact on the supervisor's effectiveness. These findings suggest that there is a need for further study of the question, and we cannot take for granted that training and experience automatically lead to greater effectiveness.

Correlation analysis of the variables dealing with adequate preparation, opportunities for ongoing training, and access to emotional support from other staff in the agency yielded only one correlation which met our requirements. Opportunities for ongoing training associated positively with supervisory content dealing with planning for individual cases ($r = 0.27$). This was an interesting finding, corresponding to what supervisors have told me: "If I'm going to be able to help my workers in their practice, who is going to help me?"

In another effort to examine the impact of these variables, a support-training scale was developed by combining preparation, ongoing training, access to ongoing emotional support, and the supervisor's ability to talk to fellow supervisors about job-related concerns. When the 20 supervisors with the more positive reports of support and training were compared with the 23 with the least positive scores, there was no significant difference on the relationship-helpfulness scale. In summary, factors associated with the supervisor, by themselves, do not seem to contribute to supervisory effectiveness as judged by workers.

Worker-related variables

The worker sample in this study was relatively young, with 43% under 30 years of age (see Table 4, Appendix A, for a more complete description of the worker sample). Experience in the field was higher than was expected; over half the sample (52%) had six or more years of experience, and only 20% had two years or less. This changes, however, when experience in present setting is examined. Over 50% of the workers had been in the setting for two years or less, and only 20% for six or more years. The distribution in terms of area of work favored child welfare (40%), with nursing (21%), financial aid (15%), other social work (15%), and residential treatment (9%) following in that order. Child welfare supervisors were the original target sample, and the other groups were added as the project developed. All participants received their questionnaires within the same two-month period, however.

Several expected correlations were found, such as an association between the worker's age and experience ($r = 0.73$). These will not be reported here. Others raised interesting possibilities about the contribution of worker variables. For example, there was a positive correlation between the age of the worker and the ability of the supervisor to articulate the worker's feelings ($r = 0.33$); older workers reported their supervisors were more tuned in. In addition, older workers reported that they were able to talk openly to their supervisors ($r = 0.24$) and that their supervisors were more helpful ($r = 0.27$).

This suggests that the individual worker plays at least some part in the process, perhaps by being more amenable to the supervisor's empathic responses, more willing to risk, and better able to use the supervisor's help. This is another area where further research might be profitable, as a more precise analysis of the interaction of worker and supervisor factors may reveal ways in which the unique qualities of the worker affect the actions of the supervisor.

Preliminary and beginning skills

This section examines the impact of skills that are particularly important in the preliminary and beginning phases of supervision. They include putting the worker's feelings into words, clarifying role, encouraging the worker to raise concerns, developing a supportive atmosphere, and providing the freedom for workers to make their own mistakes. A number of these skills are discussed further in Chapter 3, which deals with the work phase.

Putting the Worker's Feelings into Words. The ability of supervisors to put themselves in the shoes of workers and to develop a preliminary empathy with them is an important skill in the first stages of supervision. By developing this sensitivity to the indirect cues of the worker, the supervisor is better able to respond directly to indirect cues. In our study there was no way to determine the supervisor's use of the tuning-in skill, but it was possible to measure a skill which should be enhanced by tuning in: the skill of putting the worker's feelings into words. The item on the workers' questionnaire designed to measure this skill was worded as follows: "My supervisor can sense my feelings without my having to put them into words." The worker could select a response from among the following: "(1) None of the time; (2) A little of the time; (3) Sometimes; (4) A good part of the time; (5) Most or all of the time; (6) Undecided." The same response categories were employed to measure most of the skill items.

The average supervisor in this study was judged by his or her workers as demonstrating this skill "sometimes," the average score on the six-point response scale. A number of workers underlined the importance of this skill with comments such as, "It is important that the qualities of empathy for both client and worker are in a supervisor." Other workers commented on their supervisors' lack of being tuned in: for example: "Many times I have the feeling that my supervisor is not really interested in what I have to say—is preoccupied." When the correlation between this skill and supervisory helpfulness was examined ($r = 0.77$), it proved to be one of the three most important variables in the study. This paralleled the findings in my social work practice study (Shulman, 1978, 1981).

Since our supervision study was essentially an examination of a theory of supervision practice, another line of analysis was introduced to deepen our understanding of exactly how these skills contribute to the outcomes. This approach, called third-variable analysis, was borrowed from a sociological research procedure suggested by Rosenberg (1968). The technique is discussed in detail in Shulman, 1981. Most theoretical formulations of practice suggest that the helping person's skills contribute to the development of a positive working relationship with the person being helped, which is a precondition for helpfulness. The working relationship could be considered an intervening variable in that the use of the skill actually develops the relationship. The relationship, in turn, has an impact on the supervisor's helpfulness.

The methodology is briefly described in Appendix A, and details of the correlations are given in Table 5. Essentially, third-variable analysis involves employing partial correlation to account for the impact of the third variable and then making inferences about the changes or lack of changes in the correlations. Such findings must be considered tentative, and since they are based on the inferences of the researchers, other interpretations might be just as valid. Viewed in the spirit with which the technique was employed by the researchers, as a tool for helping us theorize about supervision, it can be both interesting and useful.

The third-variable analysis of the impact of the supervisor's skill in putting the worker's feelings into words indicated that it apparently contributed equally to developing a working relationship and to the supervisor's helpfulness. This paralleled the findings in my social work practice study, but in this case it appeared that the contribution of this skill to developing a working relationship was strongly affected by the worker's perception of the supervisor's helpfulness. Put another way, social workers employing this skill appeared to be able to develop a positive working relationship with clients, even in those cases where the clients indicated the workers were not especially helpful. This was not found to be true with supervisors. The conclusion was that in order to develop a working relationship, a supervisor needs to be empathic and helpful.

A major assumption of the interactional model of supervision is the parallels between the supervisor-worker relationship and the worker-client interaction, or the existence of a common core of dynamics and skills. Differences in the relationships are also acknowledged, however. Thus, we were interested not only in how the dynamics are similar but in how they are different. An unexpected finding, such as the one just described, offers an opportunity to think more deeply about the processes and to speculate on their meaning. This is the cyclical way in which theory building should proceed, with theory guiding empirical research, and the results of the research returning to influence the theory.

One interpretation of these findings may be related to the differences in expectations of clients and workers. Many of the clients in my social work practice study were dealing with extremely difficult problems in their personal and family lives, as well as having to cope with social factors like low income or poor housing. Analysis of their comments led to the inference that they seemed to be able to appreciate their workers' understanding, even in cases where the worker could not provide specific help. For a number of clients, their previous experiences with helping professionals had been poor, and they were pleased to have a worker who at least seemed to care for them. Some clients believed that their problems were of their own making and realized that they needed to take responsibility for changes.

Workers, in contrast, expect supervisors to be able to help. When faced with concrete problems in carrying out the job, support is not enough. Workers do not just accept stressful conditions such as high case loads as part of life; they expect their supervisors to do something about them. A high level of skill in tuning in to a worker's feelings may be a necessary condition for a good working relationship, but apparently it is not a sufficient condition. In fact, a supervisor's helpfulness may be the crucial factor in developing the working relationship. The results of analysis with other skills appear to support the importance of being helpful.

Clarifying Role. The skill of clarifying role is another crucial contracting skill in the early stages of a relationship. For our study, this skill was operationalized on the workers' questionnaire as follows: "My supervisor has explained how we might work together, and has described the kind of help he/she can provide to me." The five-point scale from which workers chose responses ranged from "has not explained at all" to "has explained well." The average for supervisors in the study was slightly better than "partly explained," the center of the scale. The correlation ($r = 0.62$) with helpfulness was strong. The results of the third-variable analysis were similar to those for the skill of articulating worker feelings, suggesting that the skill contributed both to developing a working relationship and helpfulness, but helpfulness was crucial to its impact. One interpretation is that clarifying what a supervisor can offer will speed up the development of a working relationship, but only if the supervisor actually provides the help offered.

Encouraging the Worker to Raise Concerns. This skill, which is crucial for the development of trust in the supervisor-worker relationship, was phrased on the workers' questionnaire as follows: "I can talk openly to my supervisor about job-related concerns." The five-point scale ranging from "none of the time" to "most or all of the time" was used. The average score was positive on this item, with workers reporting they could talk openly slightly better than "a good part of the time." One characteristic positive comment described the supervisor as "open and straightforward and very approachable." In contrast, some supervisors were described as "very critical and hard to approach," or simply "too defensive."

The correlation analysis revealed that this was the strongest variable associated with helpfulness in the study ($r = 0.78$). However, in the third-variable analysis, the correlation with helpfulness almost disappeared when the nature of the working relationship was taken into account (controlled). The impact of helpfulness on this skills contribution to relationship was not large. The interpretation of this finding was that the essential contribution of this skill is in developing the working relationship. If a supervisor does not create such an atmosphere, it is not possible for workers to bring their concerns to the fore, and thus the supervisor cannot be helpful. Since workers will often be ambivalent about asking for help, this factor is of crucial importance to the success of supervision.

Developing a Supportive Atmosphere. This factor was borrowed from the Kadushin (1974) study of supervisors and supervisees and was worded on the workers' questionnaire as follows: "My supervisor creates the kind of emotional atmosphere in which I feel free to discuss my mistakes and failures as well as my successes." On average, supervisors in the study were rated positively on this factor, with a rating close to "a good part of the time." The following comments give a flavor of the reactions of those workers who thought they had a supportive supervisor, as well as those who felt they did not:

> He backs me up!
>
> I get moral support in times of stress.
>
> My supervisor works with me, providing the help and information as I ask—gives me a real feeling of accomplishment.
>
> ... a genuine concern for his workers' well-being.
>
> I feel free to share my inadequacies and to ask for help when I need it.
>
> My supervisor's emotional support and praise of my efforts is really what keeps me going.

Workers really need to feel appreciated by their supervisors.

My supervisor is inclined to favor one worker and spend more time with that person than the rest of staff.

I would like my supervisor to discuss my mistakes and failures more frequently than once a year at evaluation.

There is a lack of support in all areas from my supervisor and upper management.

The correlation analysis indicated that this was one of the more important skill areas ($r = 0.74$) associated with helpfulness. Third-variable analysis indicated the impact was strongest on the development of a working relationship, which was to be expected. Some degree of helpfulness was nevertheless required for its impact to be seen, though not as strong as the skills in clarifying role and putting feelings into words described earlier.

Providing Freedom for Mistakes. Dealing with authority issues in the supervisor-client relationship is important to the success of supervision. Particularly difficult is working out an understanding of the worker's limits of authority, ability to take responsibility, and so on, in a way which allows the worker some freedom while still maintaining the supervisor's accountability. Using another item borrowed from the Kadushin (1974) questionnaire, workers were asked to comment on the following: "My supervisor permits me to make my own mistakes (in those areas where I have discretion within the boundaries of policies and procedures)." The average supervisor in our study was rated as being able to do this "a good part of the time."

The correlation between this item and helpfulness was lower than the ones which preceded it ($r = 0.42$) but was still high enough to be important. The third-variable analysis indicated it had an equal impact on both the relationship and helpfulness factors. A good relationship was needed for it to be helpful, and its impact on the relationship was somewhat dependent on the supervisor's helpfulness. In Kadushin's (1973) study, lack of such permission was cited by 20% of the workers as their strongest source of dissatisfaction with supervision.

The Trust Scale. In another form of analysis, a trust scale was developed by combining and averaging the scores the supervisor received on providing a supportive atmosphere, permitting mistakes, and encouraging open expression of concerns with three other skills: supporting workers in discussing taboo subjects, sharing his or her own thoughts and feelings, and encouraging workers to deal openly with the theme of authority (e.g., giving feedback when the worker was upset with the supervisor). When the 25 supervisors with the lowest scores on this scale were compared to those with the highest scores, in terms of their scores on the relationship-helpfulness scale, there was a strong significant difference (p = .000).

In testing for significant differences, a statistic known as an F score is computed. In general, a larger F score indicates greater differences. The F score in this comparison was 83.00. In the earlier examples of comparisons of this type, differences were found to be at a significant level between the high- and low-score groups of workers on the following scales: contact regularity (F = 13.61); supervisor availability (F = 20.68); and content satisfaction (F = 5.81). Since the size of the F score is one measure of the magnitude of that difference, the trust scale emerged as a powerful factor in predicting supervisor effectiveness.

The skills important in the preliminary and beginning phases of the supervision relationship, therefore, appear to be associated with the supervisors' helpfulness—either directly or through their influence in developing a positive working relationship, or through both. The workers' comments indicate that their feelings toward their supervisors often were quite strong. One general comment of a positive nature was: "I rate my supervisor as really first class." One of the strongest negative comments was expressed by a worker who said: "My supervisor is a narrow-minded bureaucrat who has little or no feeling for social work and would be better suited for a position in the post office."

Summary

In the preliminary and beginning phases of supervisory work in the helping professions, preparatory empathy (tuning in) can help a supervisor get ready to enter a new system as well as to integrate a new worker into the system. The contracting skills help the supervisor to clarify the purpose of supervision and his or her sense of function, to reach for feedback from staff members, and to deal with issues arising from authority.

New supervisors face particular problems in moving from practitioner to supervisor within an agency, or in being brought in from outside the system to deal with staff problems. Other problems are involved in integrating new workers into a setting, including inexperienced workers, experienced workers, abrasive workers, and students in a field practicum.

The next chapter examines the work phase in supervision, combining presentation of a skills model of the work phase with examples illustrating a number of problems common in this phase.

Chapter 3

Work Phase Skills in Supervision

The work phase in supervision, which begins after the working contract has been clarified, can be even more difficult than the beginning phase. One reason is that anxiety over beginning a new relationship directs the supervisor's attention to the supervision process. As the working relationship settles down during the long haul of the work phase it is easier to take the process for granted, and less energy may be invested in it. Routine aspects of the work are handled superficially, as indeed they must be in some cases. Existing problems may not be picked up precisely because of the supervisor's tendency to be lulled by the commonplace activity of the work phase.

In addition, as other priorities call for the supervisor's attention, the temptation to ignore the more subtle cues of supervision problems is increased. A lower performance level by a staff member could signal a serious personal problem, but it may not be low enough to attract the attention of the supervisor or indicate the need for dealing with it. The policy of leaving it alone and hoping it will go away is tempting to supervisors who have to deal with the many other realities of their jobs. It is not uncommon for a supervisor to avoid confronting a difficult staff member, particularly one who is not too much of a problem, and then have to raise troublesome issues for the first time during a formal evaluation conference (see Chapter 7).

Another problem complicating the work phase of supervision is that staff members often express their concerns in indirect ways, so it is hard for supervisors to know what really may be troubling them. The illusion of work described in the preceding chapter can cause both staff members and supervisors to ignore serious problems, while maintaining the misleading perception that the work is proceeding well when they encounter one another during individual conferences and staff meetings. The combination of indirect communications and the ability of staff and supervisor to tolerate the illusion in place of real work can frustrate the growth and movement needed in any supervisory situation.

With these problems in mind, this chapter examines the unique dynamics of the work phase. A model of communications, relationship, and problem-solving skills for the work phase of supervision is diagrammed and described. Then examples are presented of how the various skills can be applied in common work phase problem situations drawn from supervision practice. The dynamics of the problems are explicated, and the application (or nonapplication) of appropriate skills is discussed in each case.

A Model of the Work Phase

The skills of the work phase in supervision described in this chapter have been grouped into general categories called *skill factors.* Each skill factor consists of a set of closely related behaviors, in which the common element is the general intent of the supervisor using the skill. In the model of the work phase of supervision shown in Figure 3.1, all behaviors associated with the supervisor's efforts to deal with the worker's affect, or emotional responses, for example, are grouped in the empathy work skill factor.

The skill factors in this work phase model include adaptations of the tuning-in and contracting skills from the preliminary and beginning phases described in Chapter 2, as well as the ending skills to be considered at the end of this chapter. Because these skills are associated here with single sessions during which much of the work of supervision proceeds, they are described as *sessional skills.* With the other supervisory work skill factors listed in the model, they give the supervisor an array of techniques for dealing with day-to-day problems in staff supervision.

Prior to an individual conference or team meeting, the supervisor considers or tunes in to potential themes that may emerge during the work. This involves sessional tuning in developing a preliminary, basic empathy with the staff's feelings in preparation for indirect

FIGURE 3.1
Model of the Work Phase of Supervision

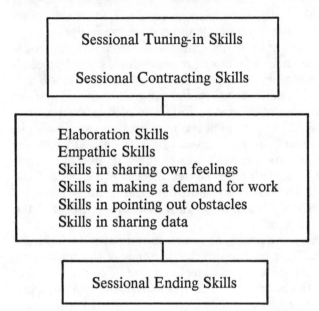

communication of the issues. Then a direct response to the indirect cues is planned.

In the beginning sector of each session, one of the supervisor's central tasks is to determine the concerns of the staff members. Sessional contracting skills are used to clarify the immediate work at hand. For many conference or staff meeting sessions, the supervisor prepares an agenda in advance. Sessional contracting deters the supervisor from moving too quickly into the set agenda before determining the staff member's sense of urgency about a problem or from too precipitately proposing a solution for the problem before it has been completely understood from all points of view. The work skill factors, elaboration and empathy, are often applied in this phase to encourage staff members to reveal their concerns.

When the sessional contract has been tentatively identified, other skill factors facilitate the supervisory work of the session. Important in achieving results is the supervisor's use of empathic skills and readiness to share his or her own feelings spontaneously.

As the work progresses, it is not unusual to encounter some resistance from staff members, who often are of two minds about proceeding in difficult areas of work. In part they reach out for growth and change, while at the same time they want to pull back and hold on to what is known and comfortable. Evidence of this ambivalence often emerges just as the session starts to go well. It can be seen in the staff's evasive reactions (e.g., jumping from one issue to another) or defensiveness, or expressions of hopelessness, or in other forms. Resistance is both normal and to be expected. It is a sign that the work is going well. The supervisor must have the ability to read this resistance and make a demand for work that will help the staff take the important next steps.

Throughout the work phase, obstacles may emerge to frustrate the staff's efforts. Their reaction to the demands of the supervisor, for example, can generate negative feelings that affect the working relationship. As the supervisor and the staff deal with the *task* facing them, reactions to the *process* (the way in which they approach the task) may become important. The supervisor must be able to point out obstacles such as the authority theme and be prepared to discuss them openly.

The staff must have access to the supervisor's "relevant data"—facts, beliefs, and values, as well as information on policies and practices. Sharing such knowledge and judgments is an important part of the supervision process, and how it is shared can have far-reaching effects on its usefulness to the staff.

The dynamics of endings of sessions must be considered by the supervisor. Issues that may only have been hinted at during a session can emerge when the staff is about to leave the office (as in the classic "doorknob therapy" in direct practice). Attention is also due to the transitions involved in each ending. If, for example, an agreement has been reached to undertake a course of action at the end of a team meeting, then it must be established who will implement the next steps.

Although this complex model of the work phase of supervision has been discussed in terms of formal individual conferences or group staff meetings, the same skills can be applied in brief contacts, informal talks, and hallway meetings between supervisors and staff members. The description has been oversimplified, of course; the work session seldom proceeds simply or directly, from skill factor to skill factor, and the factors are not mutually exclusive. During the sessional contracting, for example, the supervisor will often employ both the empathic and elaborating skills, as noted above.

Because of the interactional nature of supervision, how well supervisors use the skills in this model of the work phase of supervision will affect not only their own efforts but the effectiveness of their staffs in direct practice. By modeling how the skills can be used in supervising workers, they teach workers how to use the same skills in their work with clients. Additional examples of applications of the skills of supervision are given in the topics on supervision approaches to teaching workers' skills in Chapter 4, which examines the educational function of supervision.

Sessional Tuning-in Skills

The principles of tuning in during the preliminary phase of supervision described in Chapter 2 are equally applicable to every session or encounter with the staff. In sessional tuning in, the supervisor anticipates concerns and feelings of the staff that may emerge during the session, as well as his or her own feelings about the encounter that could affect the work.

Consider, for instance, the problems supervisors face in reporting unpopular policy decisions to their staffs (see Chapter 6). Supervisors often dread such a session, feeling caught in the middle between their staffs and the administration. As a result, they place the crucial issue at the end of the agenda, so there will be little time available for discussion or adverse reactions. This is a mistake, because the staff's real reactions and feelings will emerge later in indirect forms such as absenteeism, apathy, or less commitment to work.

Instead of avoiding the problem, the supervisor could concentrate on the particular meaning the decision will have for the staff. One way is to tune in, not only to the staff's probable anger at the policy but also to the underlying feelings staff members often have but do not always express. They may feel that the administration does not appreciate them or understand staff problems. In one hospital, for example, staff shortages and the opening of a new wing meant that some of the most experienced nurses were going to have to take weekend supervisory shifts, which they had not had to do for some 18 months. In the opinion of these nurses, going back to weekend shift work represented a drop in hard-won status, and they felt less valued. In addition, the changes involved major complications in their family situations. But tuning in to these reasons for their anger, the supervisor was able to help the staff discuss the effects of the changes on them, the reality of the situation which necessitated the change, and the measures they might take to minimize its impact.

While this discussion by itself would have been helpful, the supervisor also tuned in to another key issue, one that could well have gone unnoticed. The change also meant that these nursing supervisors would have to master some unfamiliar, difficult practices, and they would be called on to learn and demonstrate new techniques. Therefore they also felt professionally threatened. Through her tuning-in preparation, the supervisor was able to reach for this reaction. The ensuing discussion helped the nurses by letting them discover they were not alone, and others were in the same boat. The staff group then discussed training that would help the nurses feel more comfortable with these new demands.

The staff's perceived need to maintain a professional image often causes them to mask fears about new procedures by the expression of strong feelings about other real, but relatively less important, issues. Social workers in a child welfare agency, for example, expressed strong objections to being asked to approach parents of teen-aged children who had been taken into care about their ability to make support payments. They raised a number of ethical objections and insisted that this would turn their jobs into collection agents, and it would turn natural parents away from the children and the agency. Although there was an element of truth to these objections, the agency's position that maintaining a reasonable financial involvement was an important way of keeping families connected to their children was also valid. When supervisors reached past the initial objections, they found that some workers were embarrassed and concerned about how to handle the interview with the parents. Money is often a taboo subject in our society, and the staff needed help to deal with their own feelings about the interview. Once this was given and a number of interviews had been attempted, members became more inclined to accept the new procedure. Their fears would never have been discussed in a staff meeting had the supervisor not tuned in.

In both the nursing and child-care staff examples, the first step was for the supervisors to tune in to their own mixed feelings about the policy in question and the effects it would have on their efforts to help their staffs. It soon became clear that they had many of the same feelings their staff members did, so they could easily identify with the staff's opposition to the administration and the policy. This identification might have prevented them from dealing with key staff issues, but their tuning-in skill made their affective identification with the staff an important tool rather than a potentially serious impediment to their effectiveness.

In addition to tuning in to specific reactions to events, a supervisor can use the skill to understand a staff member's pattern of behavior. For example, supervisors often report workers who appear to be suffering from *burnout,* a new addition to the professional jargon referring to the worker's development of apathy as a response to undue conflict and strain. Some agencies offer burnout workshops where workers are able to discuss these feelings and become remotivated and rejuvenated. I have found that burnout usually results when a worker feels ineffective with a range of clients and, in particular, with a specific current client. A supervisor who can tune in to this reason for burnout can plan to reach for the particular causes of the syndrome. The supervisor might identify the current tough cases and try to help the worker see them in a new way and then develop some sense of a next step to be taken. In many cases I have observed, the practice problem was that the worker needed to make more demands on the client (see Shulman, 1979). As in all cases, the first step is for the supervisor to tune in to her or his own feelings, which often mirror the feelings of the worker.

Tuning in also can help a supervisor deal with the staff's reaction to a specific traumatic event. For example, a nurse in a psychiatric setting had a profound reaction to the suicide of a patient for whom she had carried major responsibility. By tuning in to the feelings involved, the supervisor was able to help the nurse deal with her sense of guilt and to gain a clearer perspective on the situation. While such discussions usually do not resolve these feelings, since the effects of such traumatic events endure for a long time, at least this nurse had someone to talk to who understood what she was going through.

In the midst of a busy schedule, finding time to tune in can be difficult. At supervisory workships, some group members express a great deal of guilt at having missed the boat in this respect. Often, however, tuning in is only possible at certain times or after certain events have taken place. It is impossible for a supervisor to always be tuned in to the meaning of all indirect cues. Fortunately, the staff will often give the supervisor a second or third opportunity to pick up the cues, or it will simply keep sending the signals until they are heard. If the feelings are important enough, the supervisor may find that dealing with the results of the problem takes more time and effort than anticipating it would have. Most supervisors agree with this point, but many of them say that the real question is whether they want to deal with these feelings. Given the complexity of the work and the many demands on the supervisor's time, the question is understandable. But the very asking of this question can be the first step toward expanding a supervisor's capacity for effective tuning in.

Sessional Contracting Skills

Sessional contracting differs from contracting in the beginning phase, as described in Chapter 2, in that it identifies the specific agenda for the immediate encounter, individual conference, or group meeting. In its simplest form, the beginning of the session is used by the supervisor to introduce the agenda items he or she proposes, while inquiring what the staff would like to discuss. By leaving some room at the beginning of each formal session for this agenda-setting operation, the supervisor allows the staff to place urgent questions on the table. The mere act of paying attention to these concerns may encourage staff members to overcome their ambivalence. It sends a message to staff members that the time belongs to them as well.

Allowing staff members to voice their concerns at the beginning of the session has the added value of freeing them to invest themselves in the total agenda. A worker at a staff meeting who is obsessed by certain issues or anxieties is unlikely to be able to hear or respond to the topics under discussion. This is one of the common evidences of the illusion of work: conversation takes place, but nothing really happens. The real agenda is just below the surface of the session, and all of the worker's energy is committed there. Simply recognizing the concerns and placing them on the agenda may be all that is necessary to free the worker for the task at hand. At other times, the issues may need to be discussed, the feelings shared, and, if it is not possible to deal fully with them then, an appropriate time must be set aside for a follow-up. A supervisor who ignores the staff's concerns in the interests of covering the agenda may find that the original agenda is not covered at all.

The importance of sessional contracting is underlined by the fact that the staff's sense of urgency may change according to current circumstances. If, for example, agreement was reached at a prior conference to discuss a particular case or work problem, but the worker experiences a stressful interview on the morning of the conference, then this particular interview may require immediate attention. If sessional contracting is ignored, the issue often is raised either directly or indirectly at the end of the meeting, as the staff member leaves. At this point, it may be too late to deal with the issue.

Another reason sessional contracting skills are required is the staff's indirect ways of communicating its concerns. In some situations the agenda appears to be set and the work begins, but the real agenda is not on the table, perhaps because the worker is ambivalent about raising it, or fearful of the supervisor's response, or not even clear what the agenda is. The worker may then simply hint at the agenda. Until the sessional contract is clear, the supervisor is wise to be tentative in the beginning phase of each encounter.

An example is the following report of a brief conversation between a worker responsible for financial aid in a public welfare agency and his supervisor:

> Frank came into my office appearing agitated and somewhat upset. He asked if I had a minute for an interruption of a policy question. I said, "Sure, what is it?" He described the problem, which related to eligibility for special funds. I interpreted the policy as I understood it, and he nodded his head vigorously, agreeing with me.
>
> I said he really seemed agitated by this question, and I wondered why. He then went on to describe an interview he had just had with a client who had been abusive when he had explained the policy. The client had verbally attacked him, a new experience for this worker. I said I thought that was upsetting and wondered if he wanted to spend a minute talking about it. He said he did, because he hadn't really known how to handle it and wasn't feeling too good about what had happened.

While this worker had raised the policy question, his nonverbal cues and evidence of strong emotions indicated another agenda for the supervisor. In some ways, Frank may have simply been waiting to see if the supervisor would be willing to deal with the issue. Had the supervisor been hard pressed for time, he could have at least identified the issue, acknowledged the feelings, and set another time to discuss it. If the supervisor had simply ignored the underlying message, Frank would have understood that he could not get help in this area from this supervisor.

The indirect raising of concerns in the beginning phase of any session or meeting is quite common. Through verbal or nonverbal methods, the staff alerts the supervisor to important issues. Sometimes these issues will emerge slowly, because the workers themselves are not sure of their feelings. It is helpful if the supervisor can maintain a tentative attitude in the beginning stage until the sessional contract is fully understood. In moment-by-moment encounters with staff members, the supevisor should resist the temptation to offer immediate answers to their questions until he or she knows exactly what the questions are. The skills for determining the sessional themes often involve the supervisory work skill factor of elaboration, which is the topic of the next section.

Elaborating Skills

When workers begin to share a particular concern, they often present the problem in a fragmentary way. These initial offerings provide a handle the supervisor can use to deepen the work. The elaboration skills are important in this stage, for they help the staff tell its own story. The focus of the supervisor's questions and comments is on helping the staff to elaborate and clarify specific concerns. Some examples of the elaboration skills which are explored in this section include moving from the general to the specific, containment, focused listening, questioning, and reaching inside silences.

Moving from the general to the specific

When staff members raise a general concern that is related to a specific event, their statement is best seen as a first offering. It may be presented in universal terms because the worker experiences it that way at the moment. Its general expression may also represent the worker's ambivalence to dealing with it in depth.

In one of the most common situations where this skill is crucial, a worker brings a practice problem to the supervisor's attention. Note how the issue is expressed in general terms in the following report of a supervisory conference, in which a psychiatric social worker raised a problem she was having with a "defensive client":

> Louise began the conference by saying she would like to discuss the problem of defensiveness. When I asked her what she meant, she explained she needed help on how to get clients to admit they have problems, and not just blame the problems on their wives or kids. I told her that defensiveness was quite normal if people felt threatened, and she shouldn't be discouraged by it. I felt that after clients got to know her better, they might let down their defenses.
>
> She looked doubtful, and I asked her if she disagreed with me. She said that some people don't want to change, and no matter what a worker did, they would not own up to having problems. I agreed that there were unmotivated clients and it was tough to give up on them, but sometimes it was necessary. She pointed out that it was easy to say that, but hard to do, especially if there were kids involved. I agreed that workers often felt guilty if they couln't bring about changes, and then pointed out that the client had responsibilities as well. She agreed.

When a concern is presented generally, it is easy for the supervisor to enter into a general discussion of the problem. Unfortunately, at the end of this conversation the worker is no better off, in terms of ideas for what to do next, than at the beginning. Consider the following contrasting example, where a supervisor of a family support worker responded to a similar opening comment by employing the skill of moving from the general to the specific:

> **Worker:** You know, some people are just impossible to work with. They don't want to change.
>
> **Supervisor:** Did you have a tough interview?
>
> **Worker:** It's the Gruber family. I don't think they will ever admit they have any problems. As far as Mr. Gruber is concerned, I should just straighten out their teenage daughter, make her listen to them, and everything will be okay.

Supervisor: Sounds like you hit a bit of a stone wall. Give me some details of the interview, and maybe we can discuss this whole business of defensiveness. At what point did you sense the wall go up?

Worker: He seemed a little distant right from the beginning, the first session, but he really closed up this time. I wanted to get at his parenting skills, but he kept saying that kids had no respect for their parents any more.

Supervisor: How had you tried to get at this parenting skills? What did you actually say?

Worker: Well, he described how his daughter was a tramp, didn't listen to him, stayed out late at night, the whole business. He was coming down heavy on her, and I could see that she was close to tears.

Supervisor: Were you feeling upset for her and angry at him for not understanding her feelings?

Worker: Exactly! I was thinking that if he handles her that way all the time, no wonder she doesn't listen to him.

Supervisor: It's easy to understand how you would feel that way. Probably at that moment you identified strongly with his daughter. I wonder, if you were with his daughter, who was with him?

Worker (after a brief silence): I guess he was alone.

Supervisor: You know, he probably already feels pretty guilty and defensive about his part in the problem. He may figure that everyone else, you included, is against him and siding with his daughter. If he is going to let the barriers down, he needs to know that you understand his feelings and that you don't judge him too harshly. After all, if he could handle his daughter differently, he wouldn't need your help. What did you say to him?

Worker: I'm embarrassed to say that I told him that things were different here and that kids had more freedom than they did in the old country. Wow! I guess he really knew then whose side I was on.

Supervisor: Exactly! The interesting part is that if you want him to have more understanding for his daughter, you are probably going to have to model what you mean by having more understanding for him. You can't ask him to be empathic with her while at precisely the same time you won't empathize with him.

Not only did the supervisor begin this interview by asking if the worker had had a tough session, she also persisted in getting the specific details of the interaction between this worker and the defensive client. The general discussion of defensiveness turned into a much more productive discussion of one specific defensive client and the worker's part in the proceedings. The supervisor was able to be helpful only after she had used the skill of moving from the general to the specific. After some work on this example, she could then generalize with the worker about the problem of defensiveness and how to deal with it. As in this case, supervision work often moves from the general to the specific and back to the general, then again to the specific, and so on.

By handling the discussion in this way, the supervisor also modeled the very same skill the worker needs to employ. The next time Mr. Gruber makes a comment about how hard it is to raise teenagers these days, instead of engaging in a general discussion of cultural differences between countries the worker might ask: "Did you and your daughter have an argument this week?" Thus, in the same way the supervisor helped focus on the discussion of the details of the interview, the worker can help focus on the discussion of the details of the family encounter. Another good example of modeling this skill for workers is given in Chapter 4.

In workshops for supervisors, a comment such as the following is common: "If I reach for the specifics in the case, then the worker is going to expect me to have some ideas on how to help. In a lot of situations, I don't have the foggiest idea about what to do." This raises the important issue of the supervisor's ability to understand practice issues, to be able to conceptualize the dynamics and skills, and to be able to teach them effectively. It is indeed hard to teach while one is still learning. In addition, some skills have been learned from experience but never articulated in a way which makes them teachable.

Even if supervisors do not have all the answers, it is helpful for them to explore practice problems with their staffs. Specific discussions often lead both staff and supervisors to clarify and develop their ideas. The professional literature, which is giving more and more attention to method—that is, what helping professionals actually do—can also be helpful to both. It is possible to find clearly articulated descriptions of skills and dynamics which can be shared and reports of findings from practice and empirical research which help develop keener insights into how to do the job.

By being specific, supervisors sometimes learn as much (perhaps more) from their teaching as those they try to teach. I found, for example, that teaching the concepts of my own supervisory practice forced me to sharpen my ability to articulate what I did in a way that was easily understandable. In turn, this helped me to be more consistent in my practice.

Containment

As the staff describes its concerns, a supervisor may be tempted to begin to help before the whole story has been told. New supervisors, who very much want to be helpful, find this a special problem. They often rush in with suggestions that are not in fact helpful, since they are not directed at the staff's actual concerns. The elaboration skill of containment, that is, refraining from action, is an active skill.

The following example is a nursing supervisor's record of her discussion of a new recording system with a nurse who had been on the staff for 15 years. The supervisor, new to the hospital, had found some general resistance to the introduction of this system, which includes daily dictation of notes by the nursing staff. The supervisor tried to overcome the initial resistance by providing a "solution" to the problem:

> I mentioned that I was concerned that Janice had not started to use the new system. I told her she was the only one on the ward who had not begun. She said it was hard to find the time to do the dictation. I told her that was no problem; I would arrange for her relief to pick up a few minutes earlier so she could have a few minutes to herself. She then pointed out that there was a rush for the equipment at 4 P.M., with everyone wanting to get their notes done at the same time. I told her I could easily arrange for another machine on the ward. She agreed that would help and promised to get her recordings started.

This is an example of a "New Year's resolution"; both the supervisor and the nurse knew that the agreement would not be implemented. After tuning in, the supervisor reopened the conversation on an occasion when the records had not been prepared. This time, instead of rushing in with solutions, she contained herself and reached for the real concerns:

> When I mentioned I was still not getting [her recordings], Janice apologized and said she had had a hard time getting the recording machine to work. She had tried to dictate but found she had not pressed the record button. I resisted the temptation to show her how to operate the machine and instead asked if there was something about this whole recording business that was bothering her. I told her I realized it was new to most of the staff, and she might have some feelings about it.

There was a period of silence, and then Janice told me that she had never recorded on a dictating machine before. She froze up when she tried and couldn't think of a thing to say. She always [had] had this problem; [she] couldn't even leave a message on a telephone answering machine when she encountered one. She just hung up. I also asked her if knowing what to say and being able to compose her ideas as she spoke was a part of the problem. She agreed that it was and said she was too embarrassed to [bring it up].

I then proposed to work with her on how to put an oral report together and on how to dictate on the machine. She said she thought that would help a great deal.

Focused listening

While listening is something everyone does all the time, focused listening concentrates on a specific part of the staff's message. Even the simplest of communications can be complex. Particularly in sensitive areas, the staff may send many messages all at once, so the key concern is buried in the words. A simple analogy suggests the difficulty. In the evening it sometimes is possible to hear two radio stations with close frequencies simultaneously. In order to hear either one clearly, the listener has to fine tune the set, tuning one station out and the other one in more clearly. In a similar way, the supervisor must tune in to the central concerns and eliminate the "noise."

A worker beginning a conference on a specific practice problem, for example, might begin with an apparently personal story. At first the supervisor may put this down as idle chatter, preliminary to getting down to work, but if he or she listens with awareness of the purpose of the conference, the connection to the work may become clear. It is often the case that the introductory story is related to the content of the meeting or conference.

Questioning

Questioning, in the elaboration skill factor sense, means requesting more information on the nature of the problem. In moving from the general to the specific, the supervisor uses questioning to help the worker elaborate the details of the interview: "And what did you say at that point?" or "Can you tell me more about what was bothering you?" The questions are designed to help the worker elaborate on the content of the presentation so that the supervisor has a clearer idea of the details.

Questioning is particularly important when the worker raises an issue or states a concern that puts the supervisor on the spot. The natural reaction is defensive, but often a question is a better response: "Why are you asking that question?" or "You seem really angry at me; how come?"

Questions designed to encourage a clearer definition of the concern at the start of an exchange can be very useful, particularly because the use of jargon in the helping professions can be confusing. If, for example, a worker asks about handling *transference* in working with a client, the supervisor should determine exactly what the worker means by that term before replying.

Reaching inside silences

Silence can be an important form of communication during a conference or meeting. The difficulty is that exactly what the staff is "saying" with such a response is often unclear. A worker may be reflecting on the implications of the conversation or be dealing with powerful emotions that have been released by the discussion. Silence can indicate a moment of uncertainty as the worker pauses, deciding whether to plunge headlong and risk a difficult area of work. Silence can also indicate that the supervisor's previous response was off base to the worker's concerns. Or it can indicate that the worker has not understood the supervisor; these silences are usually accompanied by a glassy-eyed look. Frequent silences in a conference can be a systematic attempt to express anger passively.

Since silences mean many things, the supervisor's response must be equally flexible. The supervisor's own feelings during the silence are important. If, for example, the silence represents the emergence of difficult feelings, such as when staff members share personal tragedies, their nonverbal communications of posture, facial expression, and body tension can speak loudly to the observing supervisor and can trigger empathic responses. At times like these, the supervisor can respond to the silence with silence or with some nonverbal expression of support, sometimes through physical contact. All of these responses offer support to the staff members while allowing them time to experience the feelings.

If the supervisor believes staff members are silent because they are thinking about a key point, then silence in response gives them room to think and demonstrates respect for their work. A long period of silence can turn into a battle of wills over who will speak first, however.

One of the main reasons supervisors have trouble with silences, like the deadly silence at a staff meeting after asking a question, is that they often interpret them as negative feedback. They feel they must have done or said something wrong. This interpretation of silence may lead the supervisor to respond by changing the subject, which could cut off an important communication. The message sent to the staff might be, "I don't really want to hear what you have to say."

The skill of reaching inside the silence involves exploring its meaning. Thus, the supervisor who responds to a silence by saying, "You've grown quiet in the last few moments. What are you thinking about?" is encouraging the staff to share its thoughts. Alternatively, a supervisor could try to articulate what the silence may be saying. To a worker who hesitates as he describes a particularly difficult experience, the supervisor might say: "I can see this is hard for you to talk about." Or, in the face of silence at a staff meeting which apparently is a negative reaction, the supervisor might say: "I get the feeling you're not too happy about what I just said, but you're not sure you can let me know. Is that what you're thinking?" The supervisor's own feelings should guide attempts to explore the silence, although she or he must be open to the possibility that the guess is wrong and should encourage the staff to feel free to say so.

The importance of dealing with silences was brought home to me in a research project on social work practice with child welfare clients (Shulman, 1977, 1978). The skill of reaching inside silences was one of the five skills used least often of the 27 studied (1977, p. 273), although another analysis showed it to be one of the most significant. The 15 workers with the most positive overall skill scores had more positive working relationships and were more helpful than those with negative scores. When the practice skill profiles of these two groups of workers was compared according to their scores on the 27 skills, the skill of reaching inside silences was one of the three most important in which the positive skill group of workers differed from the negative skill group. The limitations of this study make all findings tentative, and it cannot be inferred that the same skill would be as important for supervision relationships as it was in practice. Nevertheless, these findings suggest that there are important communications within silences which can lead to more effective work.

Empathic Skills

The assumption that the emotions of the staff members have profound consequences for their ability to work effectively is the basis for the empathy skill factor in supervision. It is important that a supervisor pays attention to the staff's feelings as well as to the facts involved in any situation. In an excellent chapter on supportive supervision, Alfred Kadushin (1976) introduces the issue of empathy by pointing out that both staff and supervisors face a variety of job-related stresses. Some resource must be available to help them deal with these stresses, or their work will suffer and agency effectiveness will be adversely affected. This resource, he suggests, is empathy for the other person's position in the supervisory relationship:

> The supervisor is responsible for helping the supervisees adjust to job-related stress. Higher administrators are usually responsible for support to first-line supervisors. The ultimate objective of this component of supervision is to enable the workers, and the agency through the workers, to offer the client the most effective and efficient service. (p. 198)

Kadushin (pp. 205–21) lists a number of sources of job-related tension for a staff member. They include:
1. Administrative pressures—requirements for work assessment and evaluation; demands of agency policies and procedures.
2. Educational supervision—challenges to long-held positions; situations which cause the worker to be uncertain.
3. The supervisor-supervisee relationship—the intimate, personal, and demanding relationship with a person in authority leading to elements of transference; the acting out of problems encountered with clients within the supervision relationship.

4. Client relationship pressures—the raw emotions expressed by many clients under strain and in crisis; hostile and resistant clients.
5. The nature and context of the task—the work setting itself; constant changes in directions; the particular problems facing clients.

The power of affect on all aspects of clients' or consumers' lives is generally acknowledged in the helping professions. Jessie Taft was one of the early theorists to stress the importance of feelings:

> There is no factor of personality which is so expressive of individuality as emotion. . . . The personality is impoverished as feeling is denied, and the penalty for sitting on the lid of angry feelings or feelings of fear is the inevitable blunting of capacity to feel love and desire. For to feel is to live, but to reject feeling through fear is to reject the life process itself. (1933, p. 105)

Carl Rogers directed the helping person to listen for the affective component of a communication and try to understand rather than evaluate or judge a message. According to Rogers,

> Real communication occurs when the evaluative tendency is avoided, when we listen with understanding. . . . It means to see the expressed idea and attitude from the other person's point of view, to sense how it feels to him, to achieve his frame of reference in regard to the thing he is talking about. (1961, pp. 331–32)

Research evidence on the relevance of the empathic skills to work with people has been cited in studies in a number of the helping professions. These skills have been found to be important, for example, in teaching (Flanders, 1970), psychotherapy (Truax, 1966; Berenson and Carkhuff, 1967), social work (Shulman, 1978), and medicine (Charney, 1967).

Obstacles to empathic responses

In spite of a growing emphasis on the importance of empathy in work with clients, use of these skills is often lacking in work with staff in the supervision process. There are a number of reasons for this. One is that the capacity of supervisors to be in touch with the feelings of the staff is related to the supervisors' ability to acknowledge their own feelings. Supervisors also may have difficulty in expressing empathy with feelings of the staff that are similar to their own. Being only human, they face the same stresses and strains experienced by workers. They must receive support from administrators or colleagues, or both, if their capacity for empathy is not to be blunted.

Another major obstacle to empathy may be the supervisor's authority over the staff. Many supervisors accept the myth that it is unprofessional to get too close to workers. They feel they must "remain objective" in order to implement the part of their role that sets expectations and makes demands on the staff. Because they are afraid of becoming "too buddy buddy" with individual workers they try to maintain a detached, clinical, cold front. As a result, when they must make demands on a worker, as in raising questions about performance, they may withhold their empathic responses. At such times when a worker may need support most, it is not forthcoming.

For effective supervision, it is necessary to develop the capacity to be both supportive and demanding at the same time, rather than separating the two functions. As later examples in this section show, it is precisely this ability to integrate support and demand which is the hallmark of effective practice, both in work with staff and in work with clients. This synthesis of two apparent opposites is one of the more difficult skills for supervisors to master in their professional and personal activities.

Another obstacle to the use of empathic skills by supervisors is the notion that these are "therapeutic techniques," and employing them is akin to turning the staff into clients. Some supervisors with extensive counseling experience and a well-developed ability to express empathy, therefore, are nevertheless reluctant to empathize with their workers. They do not want a staff member to be able to say, "Don't social work me!" (see Chapter 2).

The major reason for this kind of staff reaction is that the supervisor is employing a mechanical empathic technique, such as automatically reflecting back everything as staff members says without really understanding what she or he is experiencing. Consider, for example, the child care worker who says: "I don't know if I can take any more of Jimmy's bugging—he has me really angry now." A supervisor who responds by saying: "So, Jimmy's bugging has you really angry now" is asking for a negative response from the worker. The worker probably will experience this kind of automatic reflection, which Schwartz termed *echoing,* as a therapeutic technique and will resent it. It would also be resented by a client, who would have every reason to respond angrily by saying to the worker: "I just *told* you I was really angry."

The key issue is whether or not the supervisor's expressed empathy is genuine. There are so many technique-focused training approaches that it is easy to understand how empathy could become a ritual. Phrases such as "I hear you saying that . . .," followed by the supervisor's interpretation of the worker's feelings can easily lead to the perception that one is being "social worked." To avoid this the supervisor must try to actually experience, as fully as possible, the underlying feelings of the staff member and acknowledge them by putting these unstated feelings into words. In response to the child care worker's expression of anger at Jimmy's annoyance, the supervisor might reach for the worker's accompanying feelings by saying, "You really sound frustrated and at the end of your rope." The worker has named the angry feeling, and the supervisor has articulated the frustration and feelings of hopelessness that may also be present. This specific skill will be discussed in more detail in the next section, but in whatever ways the supervisor expresses empathy, the worker must experience it as genuine.

Another reason why supervisors with clinical experience may avoid employing their empathic skills in work with staff is their lack of clarity about function and purpose. When a staff member raises, directly or indirectly, a personal problem affecting job performance, some supervisors do not like suddenly discovering themselves in the role of counselor. This can be avoided if the supervisor is clear that the purpose of supervision is to get a job done, and supervision is not a therapeutic experience. If the functional differences between supervision and counseling are clearly recognized, the supervisor is free to empathize with the staff member's feelings and also to discuss the implications of the problem for job performance.

Supervisors who are clear on these issues can help staff members find other appropriate sources of help for their impersonal problems. They deal with *feelings in pursuit of purpose,* a phrase suggested by Schwartz to indicate that all feelings are not appropriate for work, and empathy must be employed in relation to functional role and the working contract. Three empathic skills which meet these qualifications—reaching for feelings, acknowledging workers' feelings, and articulating workers' feelings, or putting them into words—are discussed in this section.

Reaching for feelings

By reaching for feelings, the supervisor asks the staff to share the affective portion of the message. As pointed out earlier, this request must not be handled in a routine manner, such as asking "How do you feel about that?" without being prepared to experience the other person's feelings.

An example involves the way a nursing supervisor dealt with a nurse on a hospital ward whose work performance was being affected by a marital crisis. After two years of satisfactory performance, Jan, the nurse, had started coming in late and missing work, and while on the job she seemed to be in a daze. The staff was aware of her personal problems, which included physical violence by her husband, and had tried to cover up for her poor performance. Eventually the supervisor had seemed to become part of the conspiracy to ignore the work problems; she did not want to mention the personal problems for fear of invading the nurse's privacy. As the problems increased they became impossible to ignore, however, since patient safety could be involved.

Once a personal problem affects performance on the job, it is no longer just personal. A staff member facing great personal strain may be sending an indirect message to colleagues by diminished work performance. In this case, with Jan's personal life in a shambles, it was very little help to her to allow her professional life to go to pieces also. It would be better to confront the problem in a supportive manner, so she would be helped to keep in control of the work world. Being able to maintain herself effectively in the work situation could be the very thing Jan needed to strengthen her ability to deal with her personal problems.

At a supervisors' workshop, the supervisor in this situation admitted that her embarrassment at raising personal concerns was really protecting herself, not the worker. At the same time, she and the other nurses were starting to feel guilty about the problems on the ward and a bit angry at Jan for not carrying her load. The group role-played how the supervisor might handle a conference with this staff member, honestly reaching for the problems and the associated feelings. Here is her report of the conference with Jan, presented at a follow-up workshop:

Supervisor: I wanted to talk to you about your work performance. There have been a lot of problems with being on time, missing days, and generally seeming out of it.

Nurse (Jan): I know things have been going badly, but I have been under some strain. I'll be able to handle it.

Supervisor: I've heard you've been having troubles at home, and I figured that must have been making it tough for you here as well. I didn't raise the issue because I felt it was your personal business, and it *is* personal. However I wanted you to know that I have been concerned for you. Has it been very rough for you?

Jan (starting to cry): It's been the toughest time of my life.

This example is continued in the discussion of the other empathic skills in this section. The key point here is that the supervisor has given Jan permission to discuss the feelings that are affecting her ability to work. The question, "Has it been very rough for you?" both reaches for these feelings and communicates her acceptance of Jan.

Although this example concerns a personal problem, the same skill could be employed in asking a worker for an affective response while discussing a practice problem. When a worker describes a hostile or aggressive client, the supervisor might enquire: "What were your feelings while he was coming on so strong?" Or when a child care worker describes how a teenager cried while talking about the recent death of his father, the supervisor could ask: "How did it hit you while John was telling you all this?"

Acknowledging feelings

The skill of acknowledging the staff's feelings involves indicating —through words, gestures, expression, physical posture, or touch— the supervisor's understanding of the workers' expressed affect. Supervisors must attempt to understand how workers feel about experiences, even if they believe that a situation does not warrant such a reaction or that the workers are being too harsh on themselves or are taking too much responsibility for the problem. They may think the workers should not have such feelings, but the important point is that the workers do have them.

A common mistake is to rush in with reassurances, to tell the worker "not to feel so bad." All this does is indicate to the worker that the supervisor has failed to understand. We have all had moments when we felt like saying to friends or loved ones, "If you really understood how bad I felt, you wouldn't be trying to cheer me up."

In the example of Jan, the nurse whose marriage is in crisis, the supervisor attempted to display her understanding of the feelings involved this way:

> **Jan** (starting to cry): It's been the toughest time of my life.
> **Supervisor** (sitting quietly for a few moments and then putting her hand on Jan's shoulder): This has really hit you hard, hasn't it?

Thus, through words, expression, and physical touch, the supervisor maintained closeness with the nurse, indicating her understanding of the feelings involved.

This is the true meaning of support: to share another's feelings as much as possible. Jan responded to this invitation by describing her current crisis with her husband. She described how he had recently beaten her during an argument. The supervisor listened for a while as she unloaded her problems. But the supervisor displayed her clarity of purpose and role by refraining from starting to explore the problem in an effort to offer counseling. Even if the staff member requests this help from a supervisor, providing it is a subversion of the supervision process. Supervisors who feel more comfortable counseling than supervising can easily be drawn into this more familiar role, and they may turn the worker into a client. This is not the purpose of supervision. The supervisor who makes this mistake and begins to "treat" the worker often will neglect those aspects of supervision that *are* the supervisor's responsibility.

In this case, the supervisor tried first to discuss sources of help that might be available for the worker:

> **Supervisor:** It sounds like you've been going through a very stressful time. Have you had anyone to talk to?
> **Jan:** I've been too ashamed to tell people. I mean, I'm not the kind of person who gets beaten up by a man. That happens to other people. I didn't come in for four days until my black eye could be covered up by makeup.
> **Supervisor:** So you have been all alone during this.
> **Jan:** That's right.
> **Supervisor:** I think you are going through a tough time, and no one should have to do that by themself. Have you considered seeing someone

about this—for example, the family services agency, or perhaps the staff at the women's center? You're not the only one to go through this kind of experience. Just talking about it may give you some relief.

Two elements of the supervisor's response are particularly important. First, she encouraged Jan to seek out help for the personal problem. In some cases the staff members may not be aware of such services; in others, such as this one, they may be ashamed to talk to other people and need some support in order to do so. When the nurse in the example was able to break the ice with the supervisor, who did not make her feel less of a person for having a problem but, rather, understood it, seeking help elsewhere became easier. In some large agencies or settings specific staff members may be available for those seeking help with personal problems. They provide alcohol and drug counseling, for example, or psychiatric aid. Whether or not staff members actually follow up on this course of action is their responsibility. They must make the decisions related to their own lives.

The second crucial element of the supervisor's response is that she began to explore the implications of this crisis for the nurse's ability to do the job. This task, which is part of the purpose of supervision and well within the supervisor's function, is illustrated in the next section.

Putting workers' feelings into words

There are times when a staff member comes close to expressing emotions but stops just short of it. The individual might not fully understand the feeling and thus be unable to articulate it, or might not be sure that it is all right either to have such a feeling or to share it with a supervisor. The use of this supervisory skill involves articulating the worker's affect just before the worker does so. The stage is set when the supervisor's tuning in and intense efforts to empathize during the session result in associations to his or her own experiences as the worker elaborates a concern.

In the example of Jan, the nurse with a personal problem, when the supervisor suggested that she consider some sources of help, she hesitated and did not respond. The supervisor sensed her reluctance and tried to articulate the feelings:

Supervisor: You seem thoughtful right now. Are you feeling you would be too ashamed to go for help?

Jan: I'm a professional myself; I shouldn't have this happening to me.

Supervisor: Look, this is your life and your problem. I can't tell you what to do about it. However, this can happen to anyone, and it's nothing to be ashamed about. The important thing is getting the kind of help [you need] so you don't have to go through this alone.

The only reason I raised this [issue] is that I thought it might be part of what was making things so rough for you here at the hospital. Now that *is* my business. Can we talk about what's been going on?

It is at this point in the interview that the supervisor's clear sense of function and purpose takes her to the question of job performance. Rather than being seduced into helping the nurse to deal with the problem, she must deal with how the problem is affecting the nurse's work. While Jan must make her own decision about how to handle her personal life—whether, for example, to seek help or not—it is the supervisor's responsibility to hold her accountable for her work performance. Had the supervisor begun this discussion of accountability without first exploring the family crisis, the discussion would have had a quite different and, I believe, less productive effect. Note how the supervisor continued to articulate the nurse's feelings:

Jan: This thing has hit me so hard I find myself thinking about it all the time. Some mornings I just don't want to get out of bed.

Supervisor: I can understand how bad you must feel and how that would make it difficult to work. However, I'm getting worried, particularly about the safety of [our] patients. In addition, I can't believe you feel too good about being late, being absent, and having the rest of staff cover for you. It's bad enough having problems at home; it must make it worse when the job goes badly as well.

I'd like to try to help you pull yourself together on the work side. I realize it will be hard, and we may have to work things out to make it a bit easier, but I know you're a good nurse, and I think we can deal with this thing. What do you think?

Jan: I could tell people were giving me funny looks on the ward.

Supervisor: That must have made you feel even worse, and more like staying home. I think at first everyone, including me, just felt sorry for you, and [they] were afraid to say anything. We all just hoped it would go away. That really wasn't very helpful, and that is why I'm [talking about] it today. Can you tell me how you see it affecting your job and what we can do to help?

The ensuing discussion explored some of the specific responsibilities carried by the nurse, and an arrangement was made to modify her duties for a time until she felt better able to cope. The supervisor said she would make some time available for Jan to see a counselor. They agreed to see how things worked out for a week and to check with each other then. At the end of the session, Jan thanked the supervisor for raising the issue directly with her and for giving her a chance to do something about it.

Skills in Sharing Own Feelings

The supervisory skill factor of sharing one's feelings is another method supervisors can use to present themselves to the staff as real human beings. In some theories of supervision, the model of a supervisor is that of an objective, clinical, detached, knowledgeable professional. In such an approach, direct expression of a supervisor's real feelings—anger, fear, ambivalence, caring—is viewed as "unprofessional." Many staff members hold parallel view of their work with clients. This narrow concept of professionalism forces both staff and supervisor to choose between being personal or being professional.

Research on sharing of feelings has been undertaken recently in a number of helping professions. There are indications that this skill factor, sometimes called *self-disclosure,* plays as important a part in the helping process as the empathic skills (Carkuff, 1969, p. 38). The key characteristic is that the helping person appears to have a congruent personality, in which a person's external actions and expressions coincide with her or his real inner feelings. In my study of social work practice, the worker's ability to share personal thoughts and feelings ranked first as a powerful correlate to both developing working relationships and being helpful (Shulman, 1978, p. 278).

In the supervisory relationship, the staff does not need a cool, unruffled supervisor, one who has already worked out every professional problem, but rather a real human being like themselves, who cares deeply about their success at work, expresses a sense of urgency about it and openly acknowledges feelings. A supervisor who appears to be always under self-control, who has everything all worked out, and who is never at a loss or flustered would be an impossible person to relate to in any way.

Showing vulnerability

Some feelings are particularly difficult to show, of course. Supervisors describe vulnerability as one of these. In one example, a residential treatment supervisor was strongly attacked by his staff members at a unit meeting for failing to stand up strongly enough to the agency on a policy issue. This supervisor had had a good relationship with the staff, and he felt deeply hurt at their anger and unwillingness to understand his position. He shared none of this at the meeting, however, and instead sat passively, in stony silence, taking the punishment. Later he said he didn't think it was right to let the staff know they had hurt him. He held back so he could think about it later and deal with it in a more rational way.

This supervisor encouraged his staff to share their feelings with him, but when they took him up on that offer, he was not willing to share his own feelings with them. He seemed to be saying: "You should take risks with me and allow yourself to be vulnerable, but don't expect me to do the same." His staff must have sensed his discomfort and the discrepancy between the way he felt and the way he acted. Supervisors agree that it is hard to level with staff in such circumstances. Observation of their own supervisors often has taught them not to be honest with their feelings. Many report they have trouble leveling with others in all relationships, not just professional ones.

One of the most important reasons for more honest, spontaneous expression of feeling by the supervisor is the consequent release of energy needed to empathize with the worker. In the example cited, there was important work to be done with the staff members on their feelings and the policy decision, but the supervisor could not begin to empathize with the staff while he was sitting there unhappily, trying to control his own feelings. At his next staff meeting, the supervisor caught his mistake nicely, reopening the issue as follows:

> I wanted to talk about how I felt last week when you all attacked me. I didn't level with you then, because I felt I couldn't—that I had to keep my cool. Now I think that was a mistake. You should know how I really feel. At that meeting I felt lousy and disappointed. I know you had every right to be upset because I couldn't get that decision changed, but I thought you owed me a little understanding of the bind

I have been in, and a little more concern for my feelings. You can get angry at me, and sometimes I will deserve it, but last week, you just dumped all over me.

This opening was followed by a long silence, and then the discussion began. It turned out that the staff had felt guilty about jumping on him. They went on to explain how upset and frustrated they had felt, how the agency didn't seem to appreciate how tough it was for them, and how they had probably taken it all out on him. After acknowledging their feelings, they discussed what possibilities remained for further action on the issue with the agency.

It is interesting to examine the nature of the feelings described by the workers; in many ways, they were similar to those felt by the supervisor at the time of the attack. This similarity is meaningful since one way staff people communicate their own feelings is by making their supervisor feel the same way. Bion (1961) identified this process in practice with clients as *projective identification*. Rather than simply describing their feelings, the workers may act in a way which evokes a similar response by the supervisor. When the supervisor can respond with an expression of his or her own feelings, it is easier to acknowledge the staff's feelings. The supervisor's affect thus becomes an indicator of the affect of the staff. When a supervisor is made to feel cornered and insecure, for example, the cause may be the staff's own insecurity.

Showing anger

Another feeling supervisors find very hard to express is anger; rather, they find it hard to express anger openly and directly. They express anger all the time, but usually through indirect, "professional" means. A supervisor who is angry at a worker who presses negative feedback too strongly is clearly expressing that anger by questioning the worker about an apparent "problem with authority." The difficulty with this kind of expression of anger is that it cuts off communications and intensifies the worker's negative feelings. The difficulty of openly expressing anger is common in our society, where we are taught early in life that it isn't polite to be angry. We also learn that open expressions of anger can be dangerous, especially if they are directed at people in authority. If we are openly angry at another person, we may get an angry response.

The problem with this suppression of anger, both personally and professionally, is that the feelings are nevertheless there. If left unexpressed, they work under the surface and can have a powerful underground effect on a relationship. When anger is suppressed, the result often is apathy, depression, or transference of the anger onto a safer object.

Anger is as much a part of any relationship between supervisor and staff as is caring. There are times when a supervisor's legitimate demands will make the staff angry. In fact, the effectiveness of supervisors whose workers are never angry at them might well be questioned. (In workshops, some supervisors greet this observation with expressions such as: "Great! Then I must be doing something right, because my staff sure gets angry at me.") There are also times when a supervisor has every right to be angry at a staff member, and honest expression of this anger can have a positive effect.

The following example concerns Marge, a staff member nearing retirement (in two years) who was obviously slacking off in her work in a child welfare agency. She was often late or absent, complained of constant medical problems, and was becoming a general nuisance in the agency. Other staff members were covering for her. Until recently, Marge had been a very effective contributor to the work of the agency and had a great deal to offer younger workers. In effect, the staff had prematurely retired her, saying: "We might as well wait until she quits." The supervisor had made the same decision but felt very uncomfortable about it.

At a workshop session, members tuned in to Marge's feelings about retirement and ending her work life. Then the supervisor could see that she had avoided discussing this area. In role play, she practised how she could reach for discussion, exploring the work-related issues facing Marge. The workshop participant who role-played Marge's position presented an image of a woman overwhelmed by the situation. The supervisor responded with a proposal to rework her job description to include more opportunities to train other staff. She suggested that this might help make the last few years more interesting and productive for Marge, and it would give the agency a chance to draw on her years of experience. The worker in the role play kept coming up with excuses why she could not accept the suggestions, however, and it became a classic "Yes, but . . ." encounter.

When the supervisor was asked how she felt as the worker stubbornly insisted on her helplessness to change or to try something new, she replied: "I feel like wringing her neck!" I pointed out that she could have fooled us: none of that had come through. I argued that feelings respond to feelings, and Marge might perceive a direct, honest expression of her anger as really caring. The cycle might be broken if the supervisor could be honest. In response to a suggestion that she go back into the role play and say exactly what was on her mind, instead of censoring it until it sounded professional, her first line was: "Damn it, no matter what I suggest, you find another reason why you can't do it. I'm really angry because you already have one foot out the door, and I think you have so much to give here at the agency. I don't want just to give up on you." The participant role-playing the worker sat in stunned silence. She said that she wasn't sure how she would feel just then, but the supervisor sure had her attention.

Quite possibly the supervisor might be honest with Marge and still get no response. This depends on Marge's ability to respond to the demand and the caring. In this case, the anger came from the supervisor's real caring for Marge. I believe Marge would sense that, which might make it easier for her to respond. The supervisor is saying: "You have something to offer, and I think you can do it!" That could be just what Marge needs to hear.

Concerns about showing feelings

In addition to sharing vulnerability or anger or other emotions, many supervisors have great difficulty demonstrating their underlying feelings of warmth and caring. This is most clearly evident in the ending phase, when it is time to say goodbye because either the supervisor or a staff member is leaving. Often, as will be pointed out later, endings are dealt with too hastily, without an honest discussion of mutual feelings. We are as embarrassed by good feelings as by others, if not more so. Yet it is important for supervisors to let staff members know that they do care about them, and, in turn, to let staff members tell them of their feelings.

The genuine concerns of supervisors about sharing their own feelings should not be dismissed lightly. They worry about disclosing personal feelings that might change the nature of the relationship. This is a valid concern if the supervisor shifts the focus of the work to examining his or her own difficulties—a form of asking the staff for counseling that is certainly inappropriate. The feelings shared should be relevant to the staff's own agenda and the purposes of supervision.

Supervisors also worry about expressing the "correct" feelings. If they were to be more spontaneous, they fear, there might be times when they would "blow up" at a staff member simply because they are having a bad day. Without doubt, spontaneous responses will be inappropriate at times, but it is always possible to apologize in such situations. An apology may be all the staff member wants to hear. Workers do not expect supervisors to be perfect; in fact, they may be relieved if the supervisor occasionally "blows it." This makes it a little less difficult when they fall short in their work with clients. The supervisor's apology also provides a model of how they can deal with such mistakes.

At any rate, if supervisors monitor every expression to make sure they never say anything wrong, it is likely that they will rarely say anything right.

Skills in Making a Demand for Work

The model of the work phase of supervision developed in this chapter stresses dealing with feelings. It starts with tuning in and focuses on the supervisory work skill factors of empathy and sharing one's feelings. The model is also based on the development of a clear contract, using the work skill factors of elaboration to identify the staff's agenda and reach an understanding of its concerns.

Despite efforts to ensure that both the staff and the supervisor understand the interactional nature of the supervisory relationship, and both invest the work with feelings, there is a point in the supervision process at which the staff reaction will be marked by ambivalence and possible resistance. At this point, the work phase skill factor of making a demand for work enters the model-building process.

As the work proceeds, supervisors often find that the staff is of two minds about taking direction. In part, as an expression of the need for growth, they want to move toward understanding, and they would willingly risk new endeavors. But in another part, as an expression of resistance, they pull back from tackling a difficult new procedure. Effective work requires staff members to deal with troublesome subjects and feelings, to recognize their own contributions to a problem, to take responsibility for their own actions, and to lower their established defenses. In response to such difficult demands, many of them demonstrate some ambivalence.

Understanding the change process

Kurt Lewin (1951) described a model for change which incorporates this idea and can be applied on a number of levels—individual, group, family, or organization. His view, stated simply, is that the individual personality develops some form of balance with the environment, or a "quasi-stationary social equilibrium," and change requires breaking this balance. For a defensive staff member, for example, denial may work as a way of dealing with painful feelings of insecurity about practice competency, but although an equilibrium could be maintained, it would not allow for growth. This comes only from facing reality.

According to Lewin (p. 224) the three steps in change are "unfreezing" this equilibrium, moving into a state of "disequilibrium," and then "freezing" at a new quasi-stationary equilibrium. The process will probably be familiar to anyone who has learned a second language. There often is an initial burst of learning when words and phrases are memorized, but before they can be used in conversation it is necessary to mentally translate each one. After an initial period of such learning, particularly in an intensive immersion situation, learners will often wake up one morning and find they have apparently lost all ability to speak or understand the new language. This is experienced as a severe and painful regression. Actually, it may be the period of disequilibrium when the mind is making an important shift. After days, hours or sometimes weeks, they discover that the language skills have come back, but now the words and phrases come naturally, without the need for a mental translation. This is the new quasi-stationary equilibrium. It is still "quasi" because it too is a stop along the way.

Since the defenses maintaining the initial equilibrium are valuable to the individual, expecting the unfreezing process to be easy is to ignore the essence of the dynamics. The more serious the issue and the more deeply an individual feels it as a challenge to the self, the more rigid will be her or his defenses, and the greater will be the ambivalence about change.

Lewin's ideas have several implications for the supervision process. The first is recognition that expressions of ambivalence, defensiveness, and resistance are normal, and they can be dealt with more easily if they are understood that way. A supervisor who is aware of this may be less threatened by the signals of resistance. To take the argument a step further, a supervisor who never encounters resistance or defensiveness may not be making strong enough demands on the staff. Most supervisors experience staff resistance, defensiveness, or evasiveness as a sign they are doing something wrong. In fact, they may all be signals that the supervisor is doing something right.

Second, if the staff is to abandon the safety of a quasi-stationary equilibrium and accept the disruption of the disequilibrium required for change, members must feel safe and supported throughout the process. This is the reason for the emphasis on the empathic skills, honesty in sharing feelings, and the importance of relationships in the supervision model presented in this book. I suggest that a "fund" of nonjudgmental acceptance can be established by the supervisor, to be drawn on when the time comes to make demands. If the supervisor can understand a worker's feelings which lead to anger or defensiveness– the resistance side of the ambivalence—then the supervisor can reach for the growth side of the ambivalence in a way that is less threatening to the worker.

Third, the ambivalence about change may make it necessary for the supervisor to exercise more power to facilitate the process of growth. Although many changes can be made by workers on their own, those that are more difficult may require the additional energy that is transmitted when the supervisor makes a demand for work. This notion of the demand for work is one of Schwartz's most important contributions to our understanding of the helping process. As he describes it in the context of workers' relations to clients:

> The worker also represents what might be called the demand for work, in which role he tries to enforce not only the substantive aspects of the contract—what we are here for—but the conditions of work as well. This demand is, in fact, the only one the worker makes—not for certain perceived results, or approved attitudes, or learned behaviors, but for the work itself. That is, he is continually challenging the client to address himself resolutely and with energy to what he came to do (Schwartz and Zalba 1971, p. 11).

The demand for work in the supervision process

When the notion of the demand for work is applied to the supervisor-worker relationship, the supervisor's expectations of the worker can be a key element in helping the worker to respond with strength. This is one of the most difficult ideas for supervisors to accept, particularly when they are uncertain and ambivalent about their own role. If their own self-confidence is fragile, they may back off from important supervisory work at the first sign of the staff's defensiveness or unwillingness to deal with a tough problem. They read the subtle clues of the resistance side of the message of ambivalence from the staff but fail to understand or have faith in the growth side.

The staff's communication of ambivalence about a difficult area can be interpreted as indirectly asking the supervisor, "Are you really prepared to tackle this with me?" It is one of those situations in which a person is saying no but hoping the other person won't really believe the message. The surface message may be "Leave me alone in this area," but the real message is, "Don't let me put you off."

The example of Marge, the worker about to retire which was described in the preceding section, illustrates this point. The work problems may signal the area where help is needed but simultaneously the resistance to help seems to say, "Leave me alone." Another example would be a worker who brings up a particularly tough case at the beginning of a conference, but who changes the subject or digresses into generalities whenever the supervisor tries to get at the specifics of the problem. Yet another example concerns Janice, the nurse who dealt with a performance problem raised by her supervisor by agreeing fully with the supervisor and offering assurances that whe would stop stalling and adopt the change in record keeping. This was a form of passive resistance because both knew, even during the interview, that the change would not occur.

In each of these examples (and the many others to follow), the supervisor must understand this process of change and his or her part in it, must develop the courage needed to deal with it, and must refuse to be put off by signs that the going will be rough. It is at exactly these moments that the worker needs the supervisor's help the most and the skills in making the demand for work are most effective.

The skill factor of making a demand for work is not limited to a single action or even a single group of skills. Rather, it pervades all supervisory work. The process of contracting described in Chapter 2, for example, is a form of demand for work: the supervisor communicates early in the relationship that he or she means business. The attempts of the supervisor to bring the worker's feelings into the discussion are another form of demand for work. Thus, when a worker says a client "was really being hit hard in that interview by her father's rejection," and the supervisor asks, "And how did that hit you?" this is a form of demand for work. Note that the demand can be gentle and coupled with support; it is not necessarily confrontative.

Supervisors who are able to empathize with staff members can develop a positive relationship, as noted in the preceding sections of this chapter, but they are not necessarily helpful in getting the work done. Supervisors who only make demands on the staff, while ignoring the empathy and the working relationship, often seem harsh, judgmental, and unhelpful. The most effective help is offered by supervisors who are able to synthesize caring and demand, each in her or his own way. This is not easy to do, in either helping relationships or life in general. There is a tendency to dichotomize these two aspects of a relationship. First, we may care about someone and express it through empathy. If we get nowhere, our frustration leads to anger and demand, and there is an associated lessening of empathic response. But it is precisely at this point, when crucial demands are made, that the capacity for empathy is most important. The next sections describe demand-for-work skills and give examples common to supervision practice.

Facilitative confrontation

The term *facilitative confrontation,* drawn from psychoanalysis, refers to the efforts of the helping person to confront the client with reality in a supportive manner. Research has suggested that this is a crucial skill in provoking movement (Carkhuff, 1969). An example of a facilitative confrontation was the supervisor's final remarks to Marge, the staff member about to retire, as described above. Such a confrontation requires the supervisor to overcome social norms of behavior he or she has internalized over the years. As was noted in the preceding section, we have been taught that confrontation is not polite and have learned to fear its potential impact on a relationship.

In many of the examples given in the following chapters, confrontation is the key to movement in a situation. A common problem to which the skill can be applied arises in job management: dealing with a worker who is not functioning up to par. In one example, the worker was a new nurse's aide who had just completed her six-month probation period in an extended care facility for geriatric patients. Linda had begun serving at the setting as a volunteer and then worked part time at night, under minimal supervision. She had appeared to be functioning well, but immediately after her probation period ended she began to come in late and take extended coffee breaks. She needed to be continually prodded to handle her assignments. The supervisory staff was very upset with Linda and angry because they felt she had taken them in during her probationary period.

When this interaction was examined in a workshop, the three supervisors involved indicated they had not confronted Linda directly with her pattern of behavior. Each had dealt with individual incidents as they arose, but none of them had actually sat down with her and detailed the overall job management difficulties. Further exploration revealed that Linda had hoped to get into a special activity program in the setting, a job which was more interesting and stimulating than general ward care. She had been disappointed at not getting this job, but none of the supervisors had discussed the decision with her.

The workshop participants, who were supervisory members of the staff, suggested a number of reasons why they had not confronted her. First, they said they generally felt uncomfortable confronting a staff member with poor performance. It increased their sense of being a boss rather than a helper, and they found this uncomfortable. Second, in a setting such as an extended care hospital for geriatric patients, it can be difficult to get and to keep staff, so they were often willing to overlook the first signs of trouble, hoping it would go away by itself or the staff member would get the message through specific comments on job performance. Third, the supervisors admitted that they often felt guilty about their own job management and organization skills, and questioning their own efficiency made it difficult to demand greater efficiency from the staff. Finally, in Linda's case the supervisors felt guilty about not having given her more help in the beginning. They were as angry at themselves for having ducked the confrontation as they were at this aide for having provoked it.

It would be helpful to view this young worker, in her first full-time employment, in terms of her stage of life development. In many ways it was unreasonable to expect her to be able to handle responsible job management without significant help from her supervisor. She was moving out of a period of life when she was dependent and in many ways not required to be responsible, and she needed time to learn the needed skills and develop work maturity. Helping her to do this was part of the supervisor's function. Linda's job management problems, rather then being simply provocation aimed at the supervisors, might represent her own agenda items for learning.

Understanding this young aide's life situation was as important as tuning in to the concerns and feelings of the worker about to retire in the earlier example. In each case, the supervisor could use the understanding to help the worker deal with the job tasks related to the life tasks. Learning to take responsibility and to live with disappointments such as not getting the activity center position are normal elements in a new worker's development.

With this sense of the importance of facilitative confrontation as a normal part of supervision and of the potential help the supervisors could provide this new staff member, the workshop participants role-played an interview. They pointed out Linda's poor work pattern, reached for her feelings about the job (including her disappointments), and then set clear expectations for job performance. During the role play, the supervisor admitted her part in perpetuating the problem, acknowledging that she should have dealt directly with Linda about these questions earlier.

It was clear from the workshop discussion that the supervisors would expect changes in Linda's work pattern, or she would receive a negative evaluation with consequences which could affect her employment. Her immediate supervisor felt she could make these strong demands more easily if she believed she had done the best supervisory job possible with Linda. After the supervisor's efforts, the results depended on how well the young aide could respond to the demands. That was her part in the proceedings.

Partializing the worker's concerns

Staff members often experience their concerns as overwhelming. A worker may present a number of complex issues, each with some impact on the others. His or her feeling of helplessness is as much related to the apparent difficulty of tackling so many problems as it is to the nature of the problems themselves. The worker may feel immobilized and not know where to begin. Furthermore, it is not unusual for such multiple problems to be presented to the supervisor at the last minute, such as 4 P.M. on a Friday afternoon, when the worker spots the supervisor and says: "Have you got a minute?" Very quickly the supervisor can feel as overwhelmed as the worker.

Partializing is essentially a problem-solving skill. The only way to tackle complex problems is to break them down into their component parts and address them one at a time. The way to move past feelings of immobilization is to begin by taking one small step toward solving one part of the problem. This is where the supervisor can make a demand for work on the worker. While listening to the worker's concerns and attempting to understand and acknowledge the worker's feelings of being overwhelmed, the supervisor begins the task of helping the worker to reduce the problem to smaller, more manageable portions.

The skill of partializing concerns' for the worker is illustrated in the following report of a supervisor's interview with a crisis worker in a child welfare agency who is himself in crisis.al Although this worker, Tad, had had some practice experience in the child welfare field, it had been in adoptions. He had recently been transferred to a downtown office to handle calls which often involved coming into contact with clients in crisis situations. This kind of work was new to him and a bit threatening.

Tad had come into the supervisor's office out of breath, looking disheveled and upset. When the supervisor asked him what was up and acknowledged his different distress, be began:

Worker*(Tad):* This new Johnson case is a doozy! I don't know what to do with it or where to go next. Maybe we should consider apprehending the child.

Supervisor: Slow down a bit and let me have the details. What has you so concerned?

Tad: When I went to visit Mrs. Johnson after that telephone call about possible abuse she broke down and told me her husband had threatened her with a knife. She was afraid he would lose his temper and beat her up. While we were talking the two-year-old was pulling at her dress and getting into her sewing things, and she grabbed him and shook him right in front of me.

Supervisor: That must have been upsetting!

Tad: In addition to the knife-wielding husband and her shaking the kid, then she tells me she has just received an eviction notice from the landlord —and she really starts to cry. She told me her sister said she would take the kid for a while, but her sister's husband hates her and she is afraid to go there. She was really at a loss.

Supervisor: You must have felt that way too. What did you do?

Tad: I sympathized with her and told her I would think things over and see if I can come up with an answer. What I was really feeling was that it was quite a mess, and I wondered if I should be leaving the kid there tonight.

Supervisor: You probably also wished you were back in adoption.

Tad: (smiling for the first time): That's exactly what I thought!

The parallel processes of supervisor-worker and worker-client relationships are helpful in analyzing an illustration such as this one. The client feels overwhelmed by the problems and conveys this anxiety to the worker. The worker, in turn, feels overwhelmed and projects these feelings onto the supervisor. By not getting overwhelmed, the supervisor will model the skills needed for dealing with the client's concerns. He has already begun to do this by recognizing the worker's feelings about the interview. The next step is to partialize the concerns so that the worker can begin to get a handle on some next steps.

Supervisor: So you really have a number of things to deal with, just like the client. You're concerned about the possibility of violence with the husband, there is the abuse potential with mom under so much stress, and the eviction notice hanging over her head. Which one should we start with?

Tad: It's the husband who has me really scared.

Supervisor: Okay. Have you had any contact with him yet?

Although partializing does not alone solve a problem, and each of these concerns is a bit overwhelming in itself, it at least provides the possibility of tackling them one at a time. Breaking large, overwhelming problems into their smaller components is a first step and an important beginning in the problem-solving process. In addition to helping to ease the worker's obvious anxiety, the supervisor conveys the message that there is some possible next step and that, together, they will try to find out what the alternatives are.

Holding to focus

As the worker begins to deal with each issue, its connections with other related concerns can often cause a rambling presentation, a difficulty in concentrating on one issue at a time. Asking the worker to stay focused on one question only is using a problem-solving skill incorporating a demand for work. Moving from one concern to another can be evasion of work—that is, not staying on one issue means not having to deal with the associated feelings. Holding to focus sends the message to the worker that the supervisor intends to deal with the tough issues and feelings.

In Tad's case, after the supervisor had partialized the issues and they had begun to focus on the knife-wielding father, Tad switched the conversation back to his concern about the child. The supervisor attempted to hold the focus by saying: "Could we stay on what to do about Mr. Johnson for a minute, and then get back to your concern about the child?"

It became obvious from the discussion that Tad needed to contact the father, since up to this point he had only the mother's perception of what was going on. Even a telephone call might help to get a sense of how agitated the father actually was. The supervisor then discussed resources available to the mother and child which could provide immediate protection until Tad was clearer on what was going on for Mr. Johnson. He suggested contacting a particular transition house for possible acceptance of the mother.

Checking for underlying ambivalence

One of the dangers in any helping situation is that the staff may appear to go along with the supervisor, expressing agreement with an idea or proposed change, while nevertheless feeling very ambivalent about it. Members may not want to upset the supervisor by voicing doubts, or they may simply be unaware of their true feelings. The supervisor may even sense this "lurking ambivalence" but fail to reach for it, for fear of exposing and thus reinforcing their doubts.

As a result, both the staff and the supervisor may participate in the illusion of work. The supervisor may prefer to stress the positive aspects of the strategy or try to further convince or sell the staff on the idea, in the belief that bringing the doubts to light could frustrate the required action. Actually, the reverse is often true. Only after ambivalent feelings are fully discussed and dealt with do they lose their power and leave the staff free to act. Whatever the reasons for the staff's reluctance to act, the supervisor helps most effectively by listening, understanding the ambivalence, and then making the demand that the staff act in spite of its mixed feelings.

Supervisors therefore need to guard against the temptation to accept a worker's facile agreement and must instead *reach for doubts*. In the example of Tad, the child welfare worker, the supervisor discussed next steps concerning possible child abuse and how to handle the landlord and the eviction notice. Then he asked the worker to review the agreed-on strategies. Tad seemed to have forgotten the agreement to contact the father, although when the supervisor reminded him he quickly added that step to the list. The supervisor sensed his reluctance to contact the father and reached for it directly:

Supervisor: You don't sound too excited about calling Mr. Johnson. What is it? Are you afraid of him?

Tad: Well, now that I think about it, talking to an angry father with a knife doesn't sound like my idea of a pleasant afternoon.

Supervisor: I can appreciate your concern. Would it help if you made first contact by phone and then asked to see him here in the office?

Tad: I think I would feel better about that. Also, I'm not sure what to say to him. Do I ask him if he really pulled a knife on his wife? He might not appreciate that.

Supervisor: Let's take some time and see if you can find a way of carrying on this conversation without creating additional problems. It won't be easy under any circumstances, but with a little planning, maybe we can improve your ability to handle it. Why not start by tuning in to him to imagine what he will be feeling when you call him?

By reaching for the underlying ambivalence the supervisor opened up an important area of work—the feelings of a worker faced with potentially violent clients and the technical aspects of how to deal with such clients. If the supervisor had not opened this up and had then tried to help through discussion and a brief role play, there was a good chance that the worker would report back that he had been unable to contact the father or that the father was resistant. If Mr. Johnson felt strongly enough in this case, both Tad and the supervisor would be hearing from him soon enough, for he would really be angry at the way he was being left out.

The modeling by the supervisor of how to proceed is important, since the worker is likely to be faced with the same kind of illusion of agreement from the client. Mrs. Johnson, for example, might agree to move out of her home if she feels threatened and stay at a transition house for women and children. Tad would be surprised to find that she did not go there when she said she would, or that she quickly moved back to live with her husband. If the interview with the mother were examined closely enough, he could probably find many clues signaling the mother's ambivalence about following his advice and leaving her husband. These clues might be ignored by a worker determined to get the client to implement his "solutions" to the problem. This tendency of workers to agree to an artificial consensus is explored further in the next section.

Challenging the illusion of work

One of the greatest threats to effective supervision lies in the ability of the worker to create what Schwartz termed the *illusion of work*. The capacity to engage in conversations which have no meaning is easily developed, and the ability to talk a great deal and not say anything meaningful can quickly become a part of the supervision process. For staff members this can often be a subtle form of resistance, because by creating the illusion that work is proceeding, they do not have to really tackle the tough issues. The empathic skills which encourage the staff to share feelings as well as facts in the supervision process are one way whereby the supervisor tries to encourage work of substance. In addition it is often necessary for the supervisor to call attention to the illusion of work. By exposing it to view, he or she can begin the process of returning the staff to effective work.

In discussing the illusion of work in the group context, Schwartz (1968) provides an example drawn from his work with middle-level public welfare supervisors. He was leading a workshop on group methods in supervision and he detected a pattern of resistance among the participants which in many ways paralleled the resistance they had experienced in their own staff group meetings. Schwartz noted how this resistance affected the workshop proceedings:

The effect was to produce a sporadic way of working, alternating periods of apathy and inertia with flashes of feeling and creative work. But it also produced before your eyes many of the very conditions that troubled them, and about which they were trying to learn. About midway in the consultation period, I confronted each group with its way of working and asked them to come to grips with how they were using the consultation. They made a thoughtful and serious response and it was at this point that they were able to crystallize many of their deepest feelings and ideas about their work. (p. 363)

Most supervisors fail to make this direct challenge to the illusion, partly because they fear that the problems they sense are of their own making. Schwartz challenges this reluctance, confident that resistance is an essential part of the work and that its appearance in fact signals proximity to the "deepest feelings and ideas about their work." The challenge is difficult for a less experienced supervisor to make, because the same set of norms and taboos which cause staff members to be reluctant to speak directly about their feelings are operating for the supervisor.

In Schwartz's workshop, he found that the confrontation sessions in each group marked a turning point for the supervisors: "... it was thus in the context of their own groups that they could see how fuzziness and fear could hinder creative work among people and how a direct and honest attempt to deal with the feelings could trigger deeper work and some hope for future possibilities." A number of participants brought in examples of how they had confronted their own staffs in the same manner Schwartz had confronted them. They realized that as a result of his confrontation they had opened up honestly, and so they believed the tactic might work in the same way with their own staffs.

The role of the supervisor as model is crucially important in presenting this skill to the staff. The supervisor who challenges the illusion of work with a staff member is demonstrating its importance to the staff member's own work with clients.

Another example of challenging the illusion of work, this time in the individual supervision context, concerns how to deal with a staff member who employs a form of passive resistance in responding to the demands of the supervisor. This is the example of Janice, the nurse who always agreed with the supervisor's criticisms and suggestions but never implemented any changes which was described in the section on containment. After noting this pattern of resistance, the supervisor decided to challenge it:

Janice: You're right about my problem with getting those forms in on time—and I'm really sorry. I'm going to get organized this week. I'll check those statistics and get them in to the office manager by Friday.

Supervisor: You know, you have said that the last two times I have raised this issue, and nothing has happened. I get the feeling you find it easier to put me off this way than to really deal with what's going on. Am I right about this?

Janice (with anger): I don't know why you have to make interpretations all the time. I've just been late, that's all.

Supervisor: Look, I'm not attacking you for this. I just have the feeling you are not leveling with me about these forms. What's important to me is that we talk straight about things like this.

Janice: Well, frankly, I'm so busy right now I don't have time to breathe —and even less time to fill in these ridiculous forms that no one will read anyway.

Supervisor: That's better! Now let's talk about what's happening to your work load and let's look at exactly what these forms are all about.

In pointing out the pattern of resistance, the supervisor gave a signal to Janice that this form of evasion of work was no longer acceptable. At the same time Janice was encouraged to start saying what she really felt, rather than what she thought the supervisor wanted to hear. If this resistant behavior reoccurred with another issue, the supervisor could then discuss the general pattern to be followed in handling disagreements. Such incidents could be the springboard for a discussion of the worker's way of relating to supervisors, a way she had developed over years of learning to deal with people in authority.

The worker's pattern of dealing with authority is not the subject of supervision. Rather, it is a way of understanding how this worker deals with this supervisor, so a new process of relating can be developed. This dealing with the authority theme is more fully presented in the next section of this chapter. The mere identifying of the illusion of work, however, may be the critical step in helping staff members develop a new culture for work with norms of behavior that encourage rather than hinder productive, honest work (see Chapter 5).

Skills in Pointing out Obstacles

The model of the work phase of supervision presented in Figure 3.1 at the beginning of this chapter is admittedly an oversimplification. The various supervisory work skill factors are not so well defined as to be completely independent of one another. The skill of challenging the illusion of work, for example, which was associated with the factor of making a demand for work, could also be considered part of the factor of pointing out obstacles. Certainly, identifying a pattern of passive resistance by a worker and challenging it could also be used as an example in this section.

In examining the skill factor of pointing out obstacles, however, certain obstacles emerge which require specific attention. Two of these will be discussed in this section: staff methods for dealing with taboo subjects such as sexuality, and the issues involved in the authority theme (also a taboo subject).

Supporting workers in taboo areas

The culture of the society in which we live imposes taboos against open discussion in certain sensitive areas. From childhood on, direct questions and discussions about sex, for instance, are frowned on. Other areas in which we are subtly encouraged not to acknowledge our true feelings include dependency, authority, money, death, and anger. What's more, we are taught how we *should* feel in these sensitive areas. Boys, for example, are traditionally taught that to be a "real man" means to be independent; dependency is equated with weakness. Girls are traditionally taught to be passive and submissive. The real world is so complex, however, that everyone is interdependent with others. Both men and women, therefore, may feel independent or submissive, consciously or not, but think they should feel the other way. Cultural norms include taboos which make honest discussion in these areas difficult.

Both helping professionals and the clients have difficulty overcoming their reluctance to discuss issues in taboo areas. Staff members cannot help others feel comfortable in such discussions if they themselves are uncomfortable. If they are to be able to help clients deal with feelings, they must first examine their own feelings and learn to accept them. This skill has been identified as one of three that help to distinguish more effective workers from those who are less effective (Shulman, 1979, p. 79). It also correlates strongly with clients' perceptions of workers' helpfulness.

The supervisor must create a culture for work with staff in which taboo subjects are seen as acceptable for discussion and all relevant feelings can be freely shared. One example of this comes from my work on sexuality with a group of child care workers. Jon, a handsome 22-year-old staff member, was working in a residence which included teenage girls. In the course of a workshop discussion, he made a joke about the attractiveness and seductiveness of a girl whose problems were being discussed, and the other staff members laughed. I decided to reach for the serious issue I felt was lurking just behind the joking. I told them I realized they all had had some humorous experiences of this type with the youngsters, but I wondered if this whole question of sexual attraction wasn't a serious one. They all had to work closely with young, attractive teenagers of the opposite sex, many of whom did come on strong to them. I wondered how it made them feel.

Jon, who had introduced the subject with the joke, said he felt very uncomfortable. I asked if he found himself being turned on by the kids and then felt guilty about these feelings. He nodded vigorously and others, male and female, gave similar examples. After some discussion of the naturalness of these feelings, I asked the group how this made it difficult for them in their work. Jon described how the teenaged girl they were discussing sent him notes and made comments which made him feel she had a crush on him. He was just ignoring her. When I asked if it was harder to deal with her because he felt attracted to her, he acknowledged that it was.

I told the staff that being in touch with their own feelings was a start in dealing with this issue. The next step was to see how they could turn this interaction with the youngster into effective practice. By reaching directly for the work beneath the joking hint, I gave a signal to the staff that I was ready to work in this taboo area. Opening the door to this discussion simultaneously moved us into some important work and affected our group's culture for work. The ability of the staff to share their feelings and the comfort of finding others in the same boat are important helping factors in supervision. It would have been inappropriate to turn the session into a discussion of their sexual concerns and feelings.

I disagree strongly with approaches to helping the staff discuss such matters which are centered on an active exploration of the members' own sexuality. A staff member's fantasies, fears, or early experiences in the sexual area are not the business of the supervisor or trainer; in fact, exploration of these areas is counterproductive to work. It can easily become an invasion of privacy, a form of therapy for the staff, or a seductive distraction from the actual work of supervision. Once the staff has recognized the difficulty of talking about this subject, and they understand that their own feelings in relation to the work are important, the discussion must be clearly connected to their practice. The questions is: "What is it about your feelings that makes it hard for you to deal with the clients?" When workers see that the discussions will be bounded by the working contract, and the supervisor will actively guard that contract against attempts to subvert it (if, for example, the staff asks for help with their sexual hangups), they will feel more comfortable in such discussions and will be freed by the structure.

As the workshop discussion contined, we examined the practice implications of the staff member's feelings. I suggested we could start by tuning in to the teenaged girl's feelings in this this area. Given her past experiences, they should consider what it must be like to be 15. Could they sensitize themselves to her fears, concerns, and questions? Among the issues that emerged in this work was a concern about what it was that made a "real woman": what qualities were needed for the gender role? Another was what qualities made a young woman attractive to men. Most of these girls had been taught that sexuality is a central tool in relating to men, and their value is related to their attractiveness as sexual objects.

Returning to the incidents Jon had described I acknowledged the reality of the "crush" part of the message but suggested that the youngster was also saying she needed to talk to an adult, specifically a male adult, about these concerns. Rather than just viewing her notes and comments as a come-on and ignoring them, if Jon were able to find a way of responding to them they could become handles for work. Jon was excited about this; it offered him an opportunity to work with this girl rather than constantly trying to hide from her. We role-played how we might open this topic up without crushing her feelings. Jon needed to let her know he appreciated her interest, to make it clear that he could not become involved in any way, and to indicate that he had heard the concerns she was expressing. One of the staff members got the point and said: "You mean reaching for the real message, just like you did here this morning?"

In another example of dealing with staff feelings about taboo subjects I was impressed with how strong the taboos can be and how even the worker may be unaware of his or her own feelings. In this case, I was supervising male workers, the first group leaders for mutual aid groups being established for men who had battered their wives or women they lived with. Formation of these groups had been requested by staff members at the women's shelter, whose anger at these men was understandable. They wanted to "straighten them out," even suggesting that films of battered women be shown to help them see the results of their behavior. It was clear that the shelter staff had great difficulty in seeing these men as clients in their own rights. They were mad at them, and they only wanted the service offered because, in spite of their efforts, the battered women kept returning home.

It was agreed that the men's groups needed to be mutual aid groups in which they could help each other with feelings that made it difficult for them to relate to women. Essentially, the groups had to relate to the concerns raised by their members. The male workers who were to lead these groups strongly supported the need to accept the men as they were and to treat them as clients in their own right. In the early sessions they were quick to disassociate themselves from the harsh and judgmental attitudes that had been expressed by the female shelter workers. As they began their pregroup interviews with these men, however, their practice began to reveal their real feelings. In subtle ways they were communicating the attitude they had appeared to reject.

When I pointed this out to them as we reviewed the records of the interviews, I asked them to describe how they really felt in key moments of the interaction. Faced with the reality of their actions, they began to admit their real anger at the men. I credited them with their admissions, pointing out how easy it would be for them to deny, even to themselves, these "unprofessional" feelings. With the taboo challenged, the door was open for discussion of their strongest feelings in relation to the work. It went as follows:

Consultant: Do you have any ideas about what it is about these men that makes you so angry at them—so angry, you have a hard time even admitting it to yourselves?

Terry: You know, when I see their anger at women it really scares me, because I think I feel some of that anger as well.

Frank: There have been lots of times when I felt mad enough to belt my lady—but the difference between me and them is that I don't do it.

Consultant: It's a bit scarey though, isn't it, seeing how similar your feelings can be to theirs?

This discussion, and others which followed, began a process of helping the workers be less judgmental of their own feelings, and thus less judgmental of the clients' feelings. It was a difficult admission under the circumstances, but once they were able to face their own anger at the men and to identify in part the source of these feelings, they were in much better shape to provide help.

In many ways, professionals must deal with both the general societal taboos against certain feelings and a strong sense of professional taboos. The perception is that people should not have certain feelings, and a professional person *certainly* should not feel that way. This double burden makes it especially difficult for workers to discuss their fears, anxieties, and feelings, particularly in taboo areas, without the support and encouragement of their supervisors.

Dealing with the authority theme

The authority theme was described by Schwartz (1971) in the worker-client context as "the familiar struggle to resolve the relationship with a nurturing and demanding figure who is both a personal symbol and a representative of a powerful institution" (p.11). In a similar manner, as the worker deals with a supervisor, both positive and negative effect will be generated. There will be times when the supervisor will appear to be a caring and supportive figure. At other times, the supervisor will make demands on the worker. Each of these processes will generate some affective response. Even the most skilled supervisor operates under many pressures and cannot be "perfect." Supervisors miss signals, overreact, are not supportive enough, fail to represent staff feelings to administration, and so on in the natural course of events in the agency or other setting.

Stresses related to the authority theme should be anticipated as a normal part of the work of supervision. In fact, the energy flow caused by the affect between a supervisor and worker can be an important part of the driving force of supervision. Because supervisors who feel inadequate often interpret problems of authority as a negative judgment of their abilities, however, they may be reluctant to create a setting where such feelings and reactions can be openly discussed and dealt with.

In my view it is the supervisor's task to teach the staff that supervisors are to be treated as real persons not as a symbol of authority. This is an ongoing process which never ends. The goal of the work is not to create a situation in which all negative affect is resolved, and supervisor and staff "live happily ever after." Rather, it is to create a climate where both the positive and negative feelings inherent in the work can be freely expressed. If this is not done, these feelings will go beneath the surface and emerge later to haunt the supervisor in such forms as staff passivity, defensiveness, the illusion of work, low productivity, or even sabotage.

The authority theme includes elements of transference and countertransference which are familiar in the context of work with clients. Strean (1978) describes their effects on the worker-client relationship, drawing on the psychoanalytic theory of Freud. Simply substituting *supervisor* for *worker* and *worker* for *client* makes the following discussion clearly relevant:

> This relationship has many facets: subtle and overt, conscious and unconscious, progressive and regressive, positive and negative. Both client and worker experience themselves and each other not only in terms of objective reality, but in terms of how each wishes the other to be and fears he might be. The phenomena of "transference" and "countertransference" exists in every relationship between two or more people, professional and nonprofessional, and must be taken into account in every social-worker-client encounter. By "transference" is meant the feelings, wishes, fears, and defenses of the client from reactions to significant persons in the past (parents, siblings, extended family, teachers) that influence his current perceptions of the social worker. "Countertransference" similarly refers to aspects of the social worker's history of feelings, wishes, fears and so on, all of which influence his perceptions of the client. (p. 193)

The powerful influences of transference and countertransference make it quite possible that the supervisor and the staff will relate to each other as stereotypes rather than real people. Inevitably, in such a situation, real communications break down; both parties hear what they expect to hear, misinterpret what they hear to fit their stereotype of the other, and remember selectively. The key to breaking this cycle is to build into the ongoing working relationship a mechanism for bringing differences out into the open. The supervisor must change the norms by which his or her staff have learned to relate to people in authority and develop a new norm which rejects the commonly accepted taboo against straight talk in this sensitive and fearful area.

The process can start in the beginning phase of work if the new supervisor (or the supervisor with a new staff member) includes in the contract discussion an expectation of honesty on issues of the authority theme. One new child care supervisor in a residential setting issued the invitation in the form of the following statement in an early staff meeting: "I want to encourage you all to level with me about your feelings in terms of how I do my job. I'm sure there will be times you get angry with me, or want something from me I'm not giving. It would help a great deal if you could level, because I need to really know what you're feeling."

Although the staff members nodded in approval of the comment, it would be naive to think they really believed this supervisor. They heard her and appreciated the invitation, but many of them had heard the same words before, only to find that the first time they gave negative feedback they were "clobbered" by the supervisor. Therefore the staff will usually wait and see whether the supervisor really means the invitation. One way of testing the supervisor is to provide a relatively safe bit of negative feedback and see how it is handled. If the supervisor accepts it without cutting down the staff member, the signal will encourage more feedback.

Make no mistake about it, all staff members watch closely how the first encounters are handled as the "internal leaders" in the staff (see Chapter 5) begin the testing process. Staff members have a powerful stake in the outcome, and, since they feel vulnerable, they have learned to be particularly sensitive to early cues in this area.

The testing of the child care supervisor whose introductory remarks were quoted above was carried out by the grapevine—the first time a decision that was resented by the staff was made, the negative reaction was voiced informally. Conversations over lunch, in the staff lounge, and at the Friday afternoon unwinding sessions in the local pub were the mediums for expression of these feelings. One staff member, acting in a crucial role, passed along the presence of the negative feelings to the supervisor. The stage was set for an important encounter, the outcome of which would set the tone for further work on the authority theme.

At the next staff meeting, the supervisor began by indicating her knowledge of the staff's negative feelings on the issue (a change in staff rotations and weekend coverage) and opened the question for discussion. It was important that the supervisor begin with the substantive issue (the task focus) and try to deal with that effectively. She was able to accept some of their objections and, at the same time, to clarify some of her reasons for maintaining some aspects of the change in rotation. The staff was not fully satisfied with her position, but they agreed that a compromise was the best solution. At the end of this discussion, the supervisor turned her attention to the authority theme (the process focus) and began the work on effecting changes in the norms of the work group. The dialogue went as follows:

Supervisor: I want to talk a bit about how this issue was raised. You know, even though I invited you to level with me if you were not happy with how things were going here, I had to find out about how mad you were through the grapevine. Let's talk about that for a minute. How come you didn't raise this directly?

Ted: I can only talk for myself, but I didn't think you were going to appreciate us taking you on so early. In fact, I really wasn't sure I wanted to take you on so early.

Supervisor: You weren't sure how I would handle it?

Louise: Look, I have had bosses tell me to level with them before. What they really meant was: "Be honest when you agree with me."

Supervisor: I'm sure you all have had experiences with supervisors and others who have invited the feedback, then acted like the king who killed the messenger. It's understandable that you are a bit wary of me and not sure I mean what I say. I can't guarantee that I will always be able to handle your feedback. There will be times when I will blow it, too—I'm only human. But I want you to know that I really mean the invitation, [and] I will do my best to make you feel safe when you have something to say. I can't do my job correctly unless you agree to be honest. I know it's a tough demand I'm making, but I think it's worth it. How about it?

Ted: I have to admit you were open to our feedback on the rotations— even though you didn't buy all of our arguments. I sure as hell would like to be able to level. (Other staff members nod in agreement.)

Supervisor: Great! I think this is a good start. I know it won't be easy to maintain this openness, so on occasion I'm going to raise it again to see how we are doing. You can raise it as well, if you think it's necessary.

By addressing the question of norms in relation to the authority theme, the supervisor was working on the structure of the work group. She also acknowledged the importance of maintaining this structure when she pointed out that they would have to return to this theme later. This is the sense in which the work on the authority theme never ends. Periodic attention is needed to make sure the structure is sound. An analogy from space technology may be helpful. When a rocket is sent to another planet, the specific orbit is preprogrammed into the computer. Scientists recognize the need to make periodic adjustments in direction as the rocket proceeds in its flight, however, so they build in self-correcting mechanisms. Another self-correcting feedback mechanism is the home thermostat, which reads the house temperature and automatically adjusts the heating system to maintain the required temperature range.

Similar maintenance mechanisms are needed in human relationships of all kinds. In the supervisor-staff relationship, where power can suppress real communications, it is absolutely essential that a structure for honest communications not only be developed, but that it be systematically maintained to ensure it is working well.

An example of this maintenance work comes from the work of another supervisor in a child welfare agency, one who had had a positive relationship with his workers for over two years. Nevertheless, a number of seemingly casual comments by staff members had struck him as indirect signals of authority theme issues. Determined to do some "maintenance work" on the authority theme, he invited the staff to discuss how they worked together, pointing out that the comments indicated attention was necessary. Staff members evaded his direct question in the early part of the session, probably because they were unsure that he really meant it and so were afraid to begin. When he pointed this out, they opened up a discussion that touched on each of the major subthemes of the authority theme. These include the supervisor's: (1) role, (2) position as an outsider, (3) supportive function, (4) limitations, and (5) demand function. In the course of a working relationship, all these subthemes must be considered. They are described and the first four are illustrated with summarized excerpts from the videotaped staff meeting in the topics below. Some further examples of how specific issues of group leadership fit into these subthemes are given in the section on the authority theme in Chapter 5.

The Supervisor's Role. The question of role, which was discussed in some detail in Chapter 2, came up in respect to how the supervisor offered help on cases. One staff member said: "When I come to you asking for advice on a case that's really giving me trouble, you usually start with a lot of good ideas about what I can do. But I can't hear any of them because I'm sitting there churning away inside with my feelings. I'm saying to myself, 'Okay, run that by me again and maybe I can hear it this time.'" The supervisor asked why the worker didn't let him know how he was feeling. The worker replied: "I know you're interested in us, and in the last few years you have given me a lot of support. But I'm not sure if these feelings really belong—like I'm not sure I'm supposed to be telling you how shook up I'm feeling. You once said supervision doesn't get into our personal lives, and I'm not sure if this isn't personal." When the supervisor checked and found others with similar concerns, he explained that he felt these feelings *were* related to their work, and he needed to hear them.

The Supervisor as Outsider. Even if this supervisor had been a staff member and had experienced the problems of being a worker, he is now something of an outsider. Although prior experiences can help supervisors understand what the staff is experiencing, they are no longer in the same situation. Recognition of this reality can help.

In an excerpt from the same staff meeting, another member pointed this out: "Do you remember when I had that kid I couldn't place, and I was at the end of the day, with no place to put him? I was feeling complete frustration and completely alone. You tried to tell me that other staff members were in a similar bind." The supervisor responded that he had felt how upset the worker was and wanted to let her know she was not alone. The worker replied: "Well when you said that, I figured that you just didn't understand what was happening. I mean for you, as a supervisor, you can treat this more objectively. I mean, you're not out there with the kid." The supervisor acknowledged that his comments had not really helped. He went on to say: "You know, it's hard for me to really remember, in my gut, what it feels like to be in some of the binds you experience. I sense your discomfort, and try to pick you up, but you're right, I'm not really in your shoes any more."

The Supervisor's Supportive Function. I believe most workers want the support of their supervisors. They may have trouble admitting it, partly because of societal norms about dependency and fears of vulnerability. Their ambivalence may lead them to send mixed messages to their supervisors about their feelings. This is why it is helpful, during the course of the working relationship, to pay some direct attention to this issue.

In the example, the worker who described not being able to hear the supervisor's suggestions when he was anxious about a case expressed this need in this way: "It's not that the solutions aren't helpful. It's just that it would be better if you let me unload a bit, get all those feelings off my chest. After I clear that up, then I think I might be able to listen better to your ideas about the problem." The supervisor said: "I think I sense that you are upset, and sometimes I jump in with answers before I let you tell me what the real problem is. What you're telling me is that you need more in the way of support." Another worker quickly made a balancing comment, reassuring the supervisor that the staff felt they had received a lot of support from him, especially in the last few years. When they were in a real panic though, they sometimes felt cut off.

The Supervisor's Limitations. In addition to discussing the mutual expectations inherent in the authority theme, it is also important to recognize the limitations in the relationship. The supervisor is human, will have feelings, and is often overwhelmed. Workers need to discuss and come to grips with the differences between their wishes and hopes and the supervisor's reality.

To continue with the example, the supervisor leveled in response to their feedback: "You know, to be honest, there are times when you come to me and I feel I don't have it to give you. I really sense what you're feeling, but a big part of me doesn't really want to hear it." Another worker asked: "Do you ever say that?" The supervisor indicated that he probably didn't, he probably just listened and pretended to be there. The worker replied: "I can always tell when you're not with me." Another worker interjected: "Maybe he can't always be with us. Maybe we are going to have to find ways to support ourselves and not always depend upon him."

The Supervisor's Demand Function. This aspect of the authority theme concerns the feelings generated in the staff members by the supervisor's demands on them. Even if the demands are clearly appropriate and the workers understand them as being in their own best interest, the very process of making the demand must generate some negative feelings. Recognizing these feelings and understanding that they are part of the work process is crucial. The supervisor must acknowledge and validate these feelings, resisting the initial temptation to run from them or perhaps to share his or her "hurt" at not being liked. Running from them only drives them beneath the surface where they become more powerful deterrents to effective work. Supervisors who are constantly "wounded" by them may end up generating guilt on the part of the staff, which also drives the feelings underground.

In most situations the problem has two sides and the supervisor has every reason for being angry at the workers as well. An open exchange of this quarrel is the healthiest way to deal with it. The following example comes from another supervisory context. In a discussion of the authority theme, a nurse in a staff group said: "Even though I knew it was right, and you had to do it, I was really —and I still am—angry at you for pushing me around that way." The supervisor responded by saying: "Sure you're angry, and I don't blame you. But, I'm not exactly happy that I have to push you on something like this. Why don't you take some responsibility so I don't always have to feel I need to be on your back?" Another staff member, speaking to the first, said: "You know, she's got a point there. We really dragged our heels on this one."

Discussion of the authority theme is a two-way process. Supervisors also have rights, can have expectations of the staff, and do not have to allow themselves to be pushed around. If a supervisor is really hiding feelings, sitting there and apparently empathizing with the staff's complaints while basically not agreeing, the artificiality will not help in the development of honest communications. Just as the staff members are free to accept the supervisor's invitation to level with their feelings, so the supervisor must have the same right. Staff members should feel free to say what they feel, but they also need to listen and be willing to take responsibility for their own part in the proceedings.

Skills in Sharing Data

In describing sharing-data skills in the practice context, Schwartz (1961) defined data as facts, ideas, values, and beliefs which the worker makes available to the client. The skill is also central to supervision; in fact, a major part of supervision involves passing along information. The supervisor has access to agency policies, information about clients, research knowledge about practice, and a fund of information comprising a form of practice wisdom which comes from experience in the field. It is important for supervisors to share information because of its potential in building a working relationship. But also, because the staff looks to the supervisor as a source of help in difficult areas, withholding of data, for whatever reason, can be experienced as a form of rejection.

Most supervisors identify sharing data as a central part of their function. The problems arise in relation to the way in which the information is shared. There are many misconceptions about the process. Sharing data is essentially one of the teaching skills which are examined in Chapter 4. This section defines three of the skills in this supervisory skill factor: providing relevant data, monitoring the learning process, and providing data in a way that is open to examination.

Providing relevant data

The skill of providing relevant data calls for direct sharing of the supervisor's knowledge and information as they become relevant to the staff's task at hand. Workers usually will not learn something the supervisor thinks may be needed at some future time unless they find it useful in handling their immediate concerns. Careful monitoring of what the staff is working on, so as to be ready to provide needed information as it becomes relevant, is a necessary part of the process of supervision.

Many agencies make the classic mistake of designing an orientation program for new workers which consists of studying the agency manual of policies and procedures. Most of these can only have meaning in the context of the practice, however. Some of the material can be learned in advance, but workers may well be overwhelmed by information which is irrelevant to their immediate tasks. They may go through the motions of learning but then need to refer to the manual in order to be able to apply a policy when a case actually requires it.

When the supervisory skill of providing relevant data is applied to the orientation program, the staff's learning needs are considered and the program is organized to match their immediate requirements. Beginners are better off learning how to use a manual, perhaps with some common case examples, rather than attempting to learn all the data in the manual. Supervisors tend to forget how complicated the data can be. It may have taken them many years to understand the information they wish to share, and it is because of those years of effort that it now seems so simple.

Sharing data is also critical in the ongoing work. In order to really learn new facts or ideas, that is, to integrate them, the staff must have practice using them. This integration takes place during the implementation of an idea. Therefore it is wise to teach a new skill or concept close to the time it will be needed. The tendency to present everything one knows can create only the illusion of teaching.

As in the orientation program, the staff's ongoing learning agenda should be developed by monitoring the demands of the job. The first time questions about an area of policy come up in a case, an opportunity is provided to start exploring the policy implications of that portion of the manual. Similarly, the first time a worker runs into a resistant client may be the best time to explore the meaning of resistance and to discuss those skills that help to deal with it. In both cases, the teaching to immediate concerns gives the staff members practical experience which provides a framework for the data.

Monitoring the learning process

A supervisor imparting data, in both group and individual settings, must be able to monitor the nonverbal cues of the staff members which indicate how they are responding to the presentation. Educational practice sometimes seems to suggest that the mere statement of an idea by a teacher is enough for it to be heard, understood, and remembered by the learner. The learning process is interactional in nature, however, and requires the active involvement of the learner. A supervisor may be doing an excellent job of sharing information, but the worker may be getting none of it. This leads to the frustrating problem of the staff asking questions about the very issue the supervisor is sure has already been "covered."

Monitoring the cues may involve simply watching the staff members' eyes and noticing when they seem to glaze over—a common response when the learning is incomplete or stops. In staff meetings, other signals that communication is breaking down are sent when members stare out the window or even fall asleep. Supervisors who read such signals as signs that they themselves are ineffective may even keep their heads down while speaking to make sure they do not see them.

Supervisors should anticipate that the teaching-learning process will break down many times during the sharing of data. Rather than ignoring the signs of this breakdown, they can use them to deepen the work. They must recognize, however, that these signals have many different meanings, and the first step in using a signal is to call attention to it and determine its message.

One message may be that the supervisor has overloaded the learners or gone too fast. Years of educational experience have trained them to sit quietly and continue to nod in agreement, even if they have lost all threads of comprehension, so the supervisor has to monitor the process. In the following example, the supervisor had been presenting the organizational chart of the agency to a new worker at an early conference, mentioning all the names of the people he would have to work with. The worker was nodding, but his eyes seemed slightly glazed. Noticing this reaction, the supervisor stopped and explored the reason:

Supervisor: You look like I may have gone too fast and lost you. I am throwing an awful lot at you at one time, so I'd better check it out.

Worker: (looking relieved): I'm still not clear about the very first part of the description of our own department. I'm still trying to figure *that* out.

Supervisor: (laughing): Of course you have questions about that. Here I am trying to explain the whole agency structure in five minutes when it took me months to figure it out myself. Let's go back; ask your questions. I'll take it slower. By the way, if I go too fast again, if you don't understand, feel free to stop me. That way I'll know if we are connecting or not.

Not only did this supervisor monitor the process of learning and adjust the speed of the presentation, but her comments also began to set an important norm for their working relationship. Workers sometimes refrain from interrupting or asking questions because they are afraid they ought to understand, and it is a sign of being dumb if they do not. This supervisor indicated that she was going too fast, recognized how complicated the subject was, and gave the worker permission to not understand. She also indicated that it was important to her that the worker did understand.

Another reason for such signals may be the staff's feelings about learning. Many people are convinced that they cannot learn or understand certain data. In most cases the real problem is with poor teaching, but they have internalized the idea that the problem is with them: They are just poor learners. When they begin to hear something they are afraid they will not understand, as if in a self-fulfilling prophecy they do not understand. Presenting statistics is a good example of this dynamic. The minute a supervisor starts to deal with data in a research finding, a worker's eyes may glaze over in anticipation of not understanding.

Working with a computer is another technological area which can generate fear in staff members. The following example shows how a supervisor helped a staff member who was overwhelmed by her belief that she would not be able to understand a new computer case-tracking system recently installed in the agency. She knew she would never be able to get the hang of how to use a terminal to enter data.

Supervisor: Let's begin by going over how you sign on with this terminal and how you would enter your data. Then we can look at the printout you will get in return. Is that okay?

Worker (jumpy): What! What did you say?

Supervisor: Just a minute—you look a little pale. What's wrong?

Worker: Nothing, really, I was just off somewhere else.

Supervisor: You really don't look happy about this whole thing. Has the computer got you worried?

Worker: Well, I have never used one of those things, and it scares the hell out of me. I'm not too mechanically inclined—I even have trouble filling out those damn cards where you have to fill in the spaces.

Supervisor: Let's talk about this for a minute. You know it's not unusual to be a bit put off by this stuff. We weren't raised with it, and the way the computer people talk, it's enough to make you think it's a whole other language—in fact, a whole other world. I found it a bit intimidating as well, at the start. But after I got into it, I found I really only had to understand a little about the computer, not the whole thing, how it works and so on. I discovered the part I needed to know wasn't really as complicated as I thought it would be.

How about if I take it one step at a time, and I stop each step along the way to make sure I've made it clear?

Worker: That would help a great deal.

In addition to the supervisor's moving too fast, or the staff members' affective reactions to the process of learning, a third major reason for blockage in the learning process is the feelings that may be generated in the staff by the data presentation. As the supervisor is speaking, the members may have associations with data that generate strong affective reactions. While their stares may make it appear that they have lost interest, they also can be a sign that the supervisor is really hitting home.

A good example involves group supervision of students on an issue of practice skill. One student, Lou, made a case presentation which clearly showed he had identified with a teenaged son against a rather strong, domineering father. Lou's tape recording of the interview provided ample evidence he was not feeling with the father and this was cutting him off from any chance of helping that client. When the supervisor suggested that the father was all alone in the family session, he noticed that some of the students in the group seemed to be turning off from the discussion, their eyes glazing over. He pointed this out:

Supervisor: There is something going on in your eyes, but I'm not sure what it means. Some of you seem to be off somewhere, not with Lou and me on this example. What happened?

Ted: Maybe it's just the heavy lunch I had before the session.

Supervisor: I'm sure that [would have] an impact. But, actually, I was wondering if you weren't thinking of your own cases, families you are or have been working with. Maybe you have found yourself in the same situation and did exactly the same thing.

Frank: That's what I was thinking about. My God, how many times I have blown it in that kind of situation! I get so mad at the parents I could wring their necks.

The ensuing discussion dealt with the student workers' feelings of guilt about their poor practice. The supervisor tried to reassure them by pointing out that they could only give what they had at the time, and they needed to work, as they were doing just then, at improving their ability to give more. The glazed looks were important signals of the feelings that had been evoked by the practice example. If they had been ignored, further discussion of Lou's case would have been less fruitful. With their affect acknowledged, they were able to discuss their feelings towards parents in similar situations, and the supervisor could introduce the concept of countertransference or the tendency of the students to draw on their own past experiences with people in authority and so view the parents in stereotypical ways.

In this case it was helpful to explore the students' nonverbal reactions because it was apparent that the discussion was hitting them hard, and if the supervisor reached for the underlying feelings they would be related to the work. The skill of monitoring the process of work for clues while simultaneously paying attention to the content is one which must be developed over time. With practice, a supervisor can integrate attention to both. The more confident supervisors are of their own grasp of the content and their abilities to present it, the more effective they will be in monitoring the process of learning. This is a skill which comes with time and practice.

Presenting data in a way open to challenge

This skill enables the supervisor to share information in a way which makes workers feel free to dispute ideas. This is another area in which educational theory and practice have often led to misunderstanding of an important learning dynamic. New supervisors often are advised by colleagues and administrators to try to impress their staffs with their expertise, so the staffs will be more willing to accept the supervisors' ideas. As a result, supervisors who are somewhat insecure about their positions may become defensive when staff members challenge their ideas. Evidence of this reaction can cause the staff to accept ideas shared by the supervisor in an uncritical manner, or the way in which the ideas are presented can produce resentment and defensiveness, even a battle of wills. In neither case is learning taking place.

Supervisors must sort out the differences between their own view of reality and reality. In some areas supervisors can share facts, that is data that are exact and indisputable. More often, however, they are sharing opinions, beliefs, or values, either their own or those of the experts in the field. A supervisor who confuses the difference between facts and opinion may present data as fact rather than one more source of information the staff can use in developing their own sense of reality. Simple phrases such as, "there are differences of opinion on this, but in my view, I believe . . .," can help workers begin to sort out the difference. If workers sense that a supervisor is presenting a viewpoint dogmatically, then a battle of wills may ensue which prevents learning from taking place.

Supervisors also must recognize that acceptance of these viewpoints, without challenge, can constitute an illusion of work. The staff may be agreeing when they really disagree. In some situations, the staff may simply be allowing the supervisor to do their work for them, by substituting the supervisor's view of reality for their own. Rather than fearing challenge and dispute of their ideas, supervisors should be worried about too quick an acceptance. Right from the start of the relationship, the supervisor should invite critical reaction with such observations as: "I'm going to share my own views on this with you, but I want you to feel free to take on my ideas if they don't make sense in relation to your experiences."

There are some areas where the supervisor may believe that his or her views ought to be accepted in practice, and these should be made clear at the start. Nevertheless, effective supervisors want to encourage their staffs to share their real feelings in respect to the information being shared. If workers agree too easily with an idea, a skill described by Schwartz as "looking for trouble when everything is going your way," or reaching for underlying doubts or ambivalence, should be employed. If a supervisor has suggested an approach to a problem and the staff does not really agree or has unvoiced doubts or concerns, the supervisor must elicit these feelings, or they will reappear as the staff's failure to implement the idea. It is a natural tendency to sell harder when we encounter doubts or resistance to our views. I think, however, that the most effective teaching takes place when we resist that tendency and instead accept and explore the reasons behind the doubt or resistance.

I also believe that the more a staff member resists or challenges an idea presented by the supervisor, the more likely it is that real learning is taking place. The meaning of resistance was explored in the section dealing with the skills of making a demand for work. If an idea is really hitting hard, perhaps at the core of many beliefs held by a staff member, then resistance to a change of thinking is natural and a signal that the work is going well. If resistance is never encountered, it is likely that the staff member is not being challenged enough.

The supervisor's first reaction may be that the resistance is a challenge to supervisory authority. This may sometimes be the case but more often it is a signal that the staff is feeling challenged. The staff member who attacks the idea most strongly will often be the one who is working on the question with most energy and who already has doubts and questions in the area.

In the following two brief excerpts, both supervisors were working with staff on the issue of developing a greater capacity to empathize with clients. In the first one, the supervisor responded defensively to the staff member's angry challenge.

Worker: That sounds good, but in reality, clients don't always appreciate being "social worked."

Supervisor (responding to the sarcastic tone of the comment): I'm afraid I have to differ with you. There is a lot of research that supports how important it is to empathize with clients.

Worker: You can get research to support whatever you believe. It's what really happens in practice that is important.

Supervisor: I think that after you have had a little more practice experience yourself, then you will be able to understand my point.

The supervisor's last comment, which was also said with some sarcasm, effectively cut off the negative feedback and the worker simply sulked for the rest of the group session. If the worker persisted in this behavior, some supervisors would see it as a signal that it was time to talk to him about his "problem with authority."

A strikingly different response was made to almost the same comment in the following example. In this case, the worker is not seen as an obstructor of learning but rather as one who could help take it further. The supervisor viewed this worker not as an enemy but as a potential ally.

Worker: I'm not sure all that feeling stuff really helps. It makes me sick to think of social work do-gooders who ask you how you feel all the time.

Supervisor: You seem to feel this very strongly. How come?

Worker: I went in for counseling once, and I felt social worked to death. Every time I said anything the guy repeated my comments, just like a machine. I caught on to what he was doing right away and started to play games with him.

Supervisor: That's what's gotten you all worked up—the idea of being mechanical, not being honest, putting the client on.

Worker: Exactly!

Supervisor: What about the rest of you (speaking to other staff members)? Have you had similar experiences?

In the ensuing discussion, many workers echoed the concerns of the worker. Would they be mechanical? Would they be seen by their clients as phony? This allowed the supervisor to discuss the differences between genuine empathy and automatic responses, a very critical discussion at this stage in the workers' development. The key to opening up this discussion was reaching for the meaning behind the resistant worker's comments. The supervisor experienced the challenge to her ideas as an attempt to work, rather than as an attack on her expertise and authority. In order to stand up to such strong indirect communications, however, she had to have some confidence in both her expertise and her authority.

Sessional Ending Skills

As with beginnings and ongoing work, endings have unique dynamics and special requirements for supervisory skills. This is the resolution stage, in which the supervisor concentrates on how the work of the session will be resolved. But resolution of work does not suggest that each session or encounter ends neatly, with all issues fully discussed, ambivalences cleared up, and next steps carefully planned. A sign of advanced skill is a supervisor's ability to tolerate the ambiguity and uncertainness which may accompany the end of a session dealing with difficult work. If uncertainty is present, or the supervisor and the staff group have not agreed how to resolve a conflict, then the resolution stage might consist of identifying the status of the discussion.

A number of skills are useful in this phase: summarizing, generalizing, identifying next steps, rehearsal, and identifying "doorknob" communications. Some of these have already been mentioned in this chapter. The ending phase in groups is discussed in Chapter 5, and Chapter 7 considers endings when a worker leaves a job and when a supervisor terminates association with a staff.

In the skill of summarizing, a few minutes at the end of an individual conference or group session are utilized to review the encounter. This might involve identifying agreements which have been reached by a staff group, reviewing understandings in relation to a case, identifying areas for further discussion, or identifying ideas which have been important to the session. The process of summarizing can help a worker to grasp the learning more effectively or it can identify areas in which the supervisor may have thought there was agreement when none really existed. Summarizing is not required in all sessions; this is not an automatic ritual, but rather a skill to be employed at key moments.

The skill of generalizing involves moving from the specific discussion to the general principle. It is the reverse of the skill of moving from the general to the specific which is a part of the elaboration skill factor. After the staff has worked on specific issues in a staff meeting or a worker has worked on how to handle a particular client problem, it is often possible for the supervisor to generalize on the experience in a way which increases the learning to be derived from it. For example, the supervisor might point out the similarity between a specific case and others discussed previously. This helps the worker begin to develop an idea about the general principles to be employed in dealing with like examples.

If the skill of identifying next steps is omitted, much frustration can result. Suppose a staff group has agreed that an analysis of how staff time is used is crucial in order to make a case for more additions to the staff. Unless the supervisor addresses the question to who is going to do the analysis, it is likely that everyone will leave the meeting being certain that someone else is going to do it. Asking a worker to focus on specific next steps in relation to a client can also reveal an underlying ambivalence which is essential for discussion.

In the skill of rehearsal, discussed in more detail in Chapters 4 and 5, the focus is on helping the staff members to practice handling a difficult encounter with a client or someone in the system. A worker may agree that a confrontation with a client is crucial, but the ability to find the right words is another matter. Providing a form of mini role play, with the supervisor taking the role of the other person, gives the worker an opportunity to practice in a safe situation. The supervisor also can change roles, try his or her hand at solving the problem, and then switch back again to give the worker an opportunity to offer solutions. This is a powerful device for aiding workers to find the right words which can help them feel more confident about tackling tough encounters.

The skill of identifying "doorknob" communications refers to the phenomenon that staff members often share a potent concern when they already have one hand on the doorknob in preparation for leaving. When such a pattern becomes apparent, it is helpful for the supervisor to point it out and to discuss why it is difficult to bring such things up directly at the start of the session. Usually this discussion makes the workers aware of the pattern, and this helps them to be more direct.

Research Findings

A number of the skills described in this chapter were incorporated into the workers' questionnaire for our study of supervision skill (Shulman, Robinson, and Luckyj, 1981). These skills include putting the worker's feelings into words, supporting the worker in taboo areas, understanding the worker's feelings, sharing thoughts and feelings, partializing the worker's concerns, dealing with the theme of authority, providing data, and demonstrating a knowledge of policy and procedures. The skill of putting the worker's feelings into words, considered to be one indication of the supervisor's tuning-in skill (as well as a demonstration of empathic skills), was discussed in the research section of Chapter 2, where it was described as having one of the strongest correlations with supervisor helpfulness (r = 0.77). The other skills are discussed in this section.

Supporting workers in taboo areas

The item measuring this skill appeared on the workers' questionnaire as follows: "My supervisor helps me to talk about subjects that are not comfortable to discuss (e.g., my reactions to working with clients around sexual issues)." On average, the workers gave supervisors in the study a score of "(3) sometimes." The skill was positively correlated with supervisor helpfulness (r = 0.70). Findings from the third-variable analysis suggested that a good working relationship was necessary for a supervisor to be able to help a worker explore such areas. (For the actual results of the third-variable analysis, see Table 4 in Appendix A.) The analysis also indicated that this skill contributed most strongly to the supervisor's helpfulness.

These findings parallel those in my social work practice research (Shulman, 1978, 1981). For a worker to feel free enough to discuss uncomfortable areas, a good relationship with the supervisor is crucial. Since many of the most difficult aspects of practice are associated with taboo areas (e.g., sex, death, money), and since help cannot be offered if the areas are not directly discussed, this is a crucial supervision skill.

Understanding workers' feelings

This skill was phrased on the questionnaire as follows: "When I tell my supervisor how I feel, she/he understands (e.g., my own frustrations with a client)." The average supervisor score indicated that supervisors were able to understand "a good part of the time." The positive correlation of this skill with helpfulness was also one of the stronger findings ($r = 0.70$). This is similar to the importance attached to this skill in a number of areas of research in the helping professions, such as social work, psychoanalysis, nursing, medicine, and teaching.

In supervision research, Kadushin (1973) found that receiving emotional support was described by 21% of the workers surveyed as the strongest source of satisfaction with their supervision. Another study by Olmstead and Christenson (1973) used a standardized leadership opinion questionnaire to study 228 social work supervisors in three settings. Scales used in this study made it possible to rate supervisors in social work on consideration (mutual trust, respect for ideas, consideration of feelings, and warmth in the relationship). These supervisors could then be compared with supervisors in other fields. Social work supervisors were among the highest rated supervisors on the consideration scale, and providing support was described as what social work supervisors did best. Another finding of the Olmstead and Christenson study was that satisfaction with supervision itself is positively associated with satisfaction with the agency, positive individual performance, less absenteeism, agency competence, and agency performance.

On the issue of keeping the supervisory function clear in relation to discussion of personnel problems, workers in Kadushin's study indicated that supervisors were not too involved in dealing with their personal problems. Supervisors, more often than workers, viewed the legitimate source of help for job-related personal problems as outside of the supervisory relationship. Among the workers 48% agreed with the statement that they would want the supervisor to help them if personal problems came up in their work with clients, while only 30% of the supervisors supported that idea.

In the third-variable analysis in our own study, understanding workers' feelings appeared to be associated with helpfulness for the most part because of its positive impact on the working relationship. This finding paralleled those in my social work practice study.

Sharing thoughts and feelings

This item was worded on the questionnaire as follows: "My supervisor shares his/her thoughts and feelings (e.g., sharing frustrations around a work situation)." The average score indicated that supervisors were able to do this between "sometimes" and "a good part of the time." The positive correlation with helpfulness was lower on this item (r = 0.53) than on most of the other skills examined, although it was the highest positively correlating skill in my social work practice study (r = 0.47). The third-variable analysis indicated that it contributed to both the supervisor's working relationship and helpfulness, with each important to the other.

The difference in the relative importance of this skill in the supervision study compared to its standing in the social work practice study provides an opportunity to further the theorizing about this process. One possible interpretation that would fit with practice observations is that workers feel more strongly about the importance of maintaining a "professional" mask than supervisors do. While supervisors have some need to appear professional, they are dealing with fellow employees as opposed to clients. Their contacts may be on a regular and at times sustained basis, and they often get involved in social activities (e.g., lunches, office parties) with workers. Therefore presentation of the human side of the supervisor may not have as great an impact on the worker as the worker's appearing more human would have on clients. Other interpretations are also possible.

Partializing workers' concerns

This skill was worded on the questionnaire as follows: "My supervisor helps me sort out my concerns in a situation and look at them one at a time." Supervisors were rated as demonstrating this skill between "sometimes" and "a good part of the time." Its positive correlation with helpfulness was one of the highest of the study (r = 0.77). The third-variable analysis, as expected, indicated the skill made a contribution to the helpfulness factor, although it also made some contribution to developing the working relationship when a supervisor was also helpful. Given the workers' large case loads and the overwhelming problems faced by many of their clients, it was expected that partializing would be an important skill. Its strength was somewhat surprising, however, because the correlation was one of the lower ones in my social work practice study. This may represent a difference between supervision and work with clients, in which the ability to help a worker manage the issues to be dealt with plays a larger part.

Dealing with the theme of authority

The item on the workers' questionnaire dealing with this issue attempted to measure the supervisor's efforts to encourage feedback, particularly negative feedback, on the part of the worker. It was worded as follows: "When I am upset about something my supervisor says or does, he/she encourages me to talk about it." The supervisors in this study also fared well on this item, with an average score halfway between "sometimes" and "a good part of the time." The positive correlation for this skill with helpfulness was also quite high ($r = 0.75$).

Workers in this study made most of their comments in respect to the issue of authority. Some examples were:

My supervisor has a strong authoritarian role.

My supervisor should feel secure enough in his self not to feel threatened by a question or a suggestion.

My supervisor has a good sense of fair play.

My supervisor has an excellent capacity to give workers independence yet keep track of what they are doing.

I especially appreciate the flexibility with which he deals with different employees' needs and his responsiveness to personal work styles.

My present supervisor is the best I've ever had . . . what has impressed me the most is the willingness to look at his own shortcomings and to work on them.

In the third-variable analysis, while there was evidence that this skill contributed to both the working relationship and helpfulness, the findings suggested that being helpful is important as a precondition for it to have an impact on the relationship.

Other research on the issue of authority has suggested that it plays an important part in the supervision process. For example, Mayer and Rosenblatt (1974) found that workers who felt secure with supervisors also felt less anxious with their clients, while those who felt insecure with their supervisors felt more anxious with their clients. In the Olmstead and Christenson (1973) study, when social work supervisors were rated on a scale measuring structure (exercise of control and authority), they were found to be the lowest in the exercise of authority of the 36 groups examined. This conforms to Kadushin's (1973) finding that the exercise of authority is one reason for supervisors' strong dissatisfaction with the job. These findings offer evidence in support of the idea that the integration of support and demand is difficult for the human service supervisors.

Providing data

Our study attempted to get at the issue of providing data through two items. In the first, we asked workers to assess their supervisors' knowledge of policy and procedure with the following item: "My supervisor has a detailed and accurate grasp of policy and procedures." In the second, we asked if the supervisor shared his or her views: "My supervisor shares his/her suggestions about the subjects we discuss for my consideration." On the first question, supervisors in the study received very positive scores and were rated as being knowledgeable between "a good part of the time" and "most or all of the time." The positive correlation of this item with helpfulness was $r = 0.61$. As for the second item, supervisors shared their views "a good part of the time," and the correlation of this item with helpfulness was $r = .65$.

These findings were as expected. In Kadushin's (1973) study, both supervisors and workers rated "expert power" as the main source of influence of a supervisor. In the Olmstead and Christenson (1973) study, "expert power" was the first source of influence when ranked by workers, with "positional power" second, "referent (relationship) power" third, and "reward and coercive power" last.

Workers' comments in our own study also dealt with the supervisors' knowledge and sharing of information. Some examples of these comments were:

> My supervisor has difficulty making dicisions regarding a particular case. My supervisor has never carried a case load and therefore is not knowledgeable.

> The supervisor should ask what a worker feels she wants to do with a case before giving his suggestions of what he would do.

In the third-variable analysis, the contribution of being knowledgeable and sharing data appeared to be important to both the working relationship and a supervisor's helpfulness. The contribution to helpfulness is easy to explain, since information on policy and procedures, as well as suggestions, can be crucial to effective practice. As for relationship, I believe a worker who feels his or her supervisor is withholding, even with the best of intentions (e.g., "Let them learn it for themselves"), is viewed as uncaring. Sharing whatever might help, in a way in which the worker feels free to use the ideas as a resource to his or her own thinking, is an important gift a supervisor can make to a worker.

Summary

The model of the work phase in supervision presented in this chapter is based on a number of skill factors, including the following: sessional tuning in, sessional contracting, elaborating, empathizing, sharing supervisor's feelings, making a demand for work, pointing out obstacles, and sharing data. Common supervisory methods employed to apply the skills within each factor are concerned with finding solutions to such problems or the poorly performing worker, the worker with personal problems, and the worker who resists supervision, actively or passively.

Chapter 4

The Educational Function
of Supervision

The focus in this chapter is on the dynamics and skills of the educational function of supervision. Educational supervision was described by Kadushin (1976) as a more specific kind of staff development, in which "training is directed to the needs of a particular worker carrying a particular case load, encountering particular problems and needing some individualized program of education" (p. 126). His research (1976, 1974) suggests that educational supervision provides two of the main sources of satisfaction for both supervisors and staff members.

To explore the educational function of supervision, this chapter first sets out some underlying assumptions about the teaching-learning process. Then it examines how the teaching function is implemented in supervision. The main part of the chapter is a section on teaching core practice skills which deals with the process of helping a beginning professional develop the skills needed for practice with clients. These skills are the same as those that have been identified and described in the chapters on the preliminary, beginning, and work phases of supervision. Each skill is illustrated with process recording excerpts from practice with clients. Methods supervisors can use to help workers develop the skill are discussed and illustrated with process recording excerpts from supervision practice. This gives a clear picture of the parallel process in which the supervisor models the same skills the worker needs to develop. The chapter also provides a standard for skill development for beginners in the field which supervisors can use to evaluate their progress and some notes on supervising experienced workers. Although much of the discussion is presented in terms of workers and agencies, it is also applicable to other helping professionals and, in large part, to students in a field practicum.

The focus is on interactional skills, but of course these represent only a part of the total learning the staff requires. Supervision can include work on human growth and behavior theory, research findings of importance to practice, skills of assessment, and other such areas, but interactional skills are both least often addressed in the literature and most likely to cause supervisors difficulty. Even highly skilled supervisors find it hard to articulate what it is they do with clients and to develop techniques for teaching their views on method. Many supervisors experience this area as threatening and often prefer instead to discuss the client, or values or underlying knowledge base. These discussions are indeed important, but when they become a substitute for dealing with specific skill development, an important gap is left in the educational process.

Underlying Assumptions about Teaching and Learning

The teaching and learning process in supervision, as in educational settings, has been profoundly affected by acceptance of the myth that teaching essentially involves transmitting existing ideas to learners who somehow absorb them and make the ideas their own. This myth suggests that all that is necessary for teaching is to have a good grasp of the knowledge and to be able to transmit it clearly by organizing ideas well, articulating them systematically, and illustrating them.

As with most myths, there is an element of truth in this one. A study of college teaching (Shulman, 1972) found that these two skills —having knowledge and the ability to transmit it—were associated most highly with effective instruction. The next most important variable, however, was the instructor's ability to empathize with students, and the fourth was the ability to present ideas so that they are open to challenge. These findings suggest that there may be more to teaching than just knowing a subject and putting it across. In fact, they support what we usually experience as consumers of teaching:

we have had teachers who were very knowledgeable and clear pre-
senters from whom we learned very little, and other teachers who
were less certain of their grasp of the subject and more hesitant in
their presentation from whom we learned a great deal.

In short, experience should suggest that the teaching and learning process is a complex one which is affected by many variables in
the subject and the context of learning and in the teacher, the
learner, and the interaction between the two. The learner is not
simply a passive object onto which the teacher can project already
developed ideas. Rather, the learner is actively involved in the learning process. This view, proposed by William James and elaborated
by John Dewey, maintains that "The organism is not simply receiving impressions and then answering them. The organism is doing
something; it is actively seeking and selecting certain stimuli"
(Dewey, 1916, p. 46).

William Schwartz (1979) in discussing education in the classroom,
also commented on the importance of the active involvement of the
learner. Citing the contribution of an 18th-century historian and
philosopher, Biambiattista Vico, he argued that "this is the true
process by which students learn: they cannot own their knowledge
until they have 'made' it, worked it over, put their mark on the data,
imposed their own order upon it, and altered it to fit with what they
already have."

This is the central assumption of this chapter on the educational
function of supervision. The staff members are active participants in
the learning process, and the supervisor's job is as much to present
ideas as to monitor the ways in which they relate to these ideas. This
may range from simply monitoring the workers' eyes to make sure
they are following directions for filling out a complex form, to having
regard for the workers' feelings while trying to help them tackle a
difficult practice issue. It can also mean being sensitive to the subtle
interplay which takes place between the supervisor and the staff
which has been described as the authority theme; the feelings resulting from this relationship can generate major obstacles to the integration of new ideas.

Knowing the subject and transmitting the ideas clearly is an
important precondition to teaching, but these skills should not be
confused with the entire process. Schwartz (1979) put it nicely:

> In this light, the problem of the transmitting function is not that it is
> "unprogressive" or even unproductive, but simply that it does not go

far enough into the educational process. When the facts are told, the notes taken down, the "truth" laid out, the work is only just begun. The hardest part remains (p. 19).

The following section discusses some of the requirements for effective teaching and learning and identifies some of the obstacles which can frustrate the endeavor and make it the "hardest part."

Requirements for effective learning

A first requirement for effective learning is that the learner must have a stake in the outcome. A worker who is to learn new skills or procedures must be willing to invest some affect or feeling in the process, and this will only take place when, as Dewey put it, the learner is allowed to "share in the social use to which his action is put." In effect, he suggests that workers should become co-partners with supervisors so that by engaging in the activity together, they can have the same interest in its accomplishment and share in the ideas and emotions that result.

This may seem a rather obvious idea, but its implications for teaching are often ignored. The supervisor must be clear about the usefulness of the content for the staff, or the connection will not be made. Orientation programs with extensive content on the structure of the setting, for example, may have little meaning in the day-to-day operations of a worker, and they can become illusions of work in which little real learning occurs.

In many situations, the connection between the content to be learned and the staff's present sense of urgency may be only partial or hard to perceive without extensive experience. Then, beginning supervisory efforts must search out this connection and help the members understand clearly why the information is important, before the ideas are presented. This is a form of contracting at the start of a supervision session: the supervisor concentrates on helping the staff members to connect the data to be learned with their own felt needs.

A second key requirement for effective learning is that the staff members must be actively involved in the investigation of ideas, building their own models of reality. No matter how much the supervisor may want to impart understanding to a worker or to share quickly the results of her or his own years or learning, it cannot be done. John Holt (1969) put it well:

> We teachers—perhaps all human beings—are in the grip of an aston-
> ishing delusion. We think that we can take a picture, a structure, a
> working model of something, constructed in our own minds out of long
> experience and familiarity, and by turning that model into a string of
> words, transplant it whole into the mind of someone else. (p. 39)

Many educators seem to persist in believing that by speaking the
words they can transmit an idea, even though their own educational
experience has taught them differently. If we think back to how we
learned something new, we know that the ideas did not exist until
we created them for ourselves. Real learning requires the active
creation of knowledge by the learner, using all the resources available. The teacher can be one central resource among others, but the
construction of the idea, fact, or theory, and so on, must be undertaken by the learner.

Complete comprehension of the idea that knowledge does not
exist for the learner until he or she creates it would lead to major
changes in thinking about the teaching-learning process. Teaching
cannot be conceived of as simply handing over knowledge or covering the agenda. Instead, the teacher must concentrate on the interaction between the learner and the ideas to be learned, placing
a priority on continuous monitoring of the learning interaction and
keeping in touch with the learner's progress in constructing the
ideas.

This emphasis is especially important in teaching complex skills
that may have taken years to develop. Supervisors are apt to forget
the steps they followed to deepen their own insights into the content.
Ideas that have become rather obvious to them are not the least bit
simple or obvious to their staffs. For example, learning to contract
with clients (by clarifying purpose, clarifying role, and reaching for
client feedback) may seem an obvious process to supervisors. As
workers or students, they may have had to struggle to develop ways
of doing this quickly, however. Perhaps they thought they understood the idea of contracting in the first semester, only to find that
in the second semester, as they got bogged down in the work phase,
they had no more than a superficial understanding of the power of
the idea. As they moved to a new setting, changed their practicum,
or started practice with a different category of clients or using a new
modality such as group or family work, each new situation helped
to deepen their grasp of the contracting notion.

Unless supervisors work hard at it, they can forget about how they had to construct, bit by bit, their understanding of an idea such as contracting. They think they can simply hand over the years of learning and are surprised to discover that a staff member is having great difficulty constructing even a simple version of the idea. As learners who themselves have ventured into this subject area, who have discovered some of the shortcuts and are aware of some of the pitfalls, supervisors can guide their staffs and make their trips more certain and quicker, but they cannot take the trip for them.

Another requirement for effective learning is that the learners must have structured opportunities for using the information presented. A theory about social behavior, for example, will become meaningful when a worker employs the ideas in order to understand a real client who must be dealt with. The doing part, the application of theory, strengthens the worker's understanding of its structure. Knowing and doing are closely related.

Practice skill development is another area where this is most obvious. A nurse being taught a new procedure is more likely to learn it if she can practice it while it is being taught. Practitioners developing group leadership skills can only go so far in their understanding of beginning group skills before they will be blocked in their learning by a lack of practical experience. When actual practice experiences are not easily available, laboratory simulations may be useful, but they lack the reality of trying skills out with real clients.

The three essential requirements for effective learning are that the learner perceive an investment in the knowledge, be actively involved in creating the ideas, and have an opportunity to practice the use of the information. Even with these elements present, many obstacles can emerge to block the learning effort. The supervisor helps overcome these obstacles by mediating the learner's mastery of the skills needed for effective work in the helping professions, as described in the following section.

Mediating Learning of the Skills of Professional Performance

In an article on classroom teaching of social work practice, Schwartz (1964, p. 5) identified four categories of professional performance: (1) professional practice; (2) professional impact; (3) job management; and (4) professional learning. Professional practice refers to the work of helping professionals with clients, which calls for skills in communication, relationship, and assessment. Professional impact is defined as the skills required "to implement a course of action designed to make one's professional contribution to the processes of social change—in the agency, in the neighborhood, and in the profession itself." Job management includes the skills required to organize a practice such as the recording of experience, the collection of data, or publication of results. And professional learning includes the skills required to work on professional problems and to incorporate resources such as supervision, the literature, colleagues, and specialists in a personal approach to professional problem solving.

This structure is useful in conceptualizing the broad learning areas involved in professional educational supervision. Some of the issues related to job management have been dealt with in preceding chapters, and this chapter focuses on the teaching of skills for professional practice and professional learning. The category of professional impact is considered in Chapter 6 where supervision is examined in relation to helping workers negotiate the system.

In teaching the skills required in these categories of professional performance, the supervisor's role is that of a mediator between the learner (the subject of the learning process) and the ideas to be learned (the objects). Dewey (1916) was one of the first to recognize the possibilities of such a functional role, noting that "the teacher should be occupied not with the subject matter itself but with its interaction with the pupils' present needs and capacities" (p. 74). Figure 4.1 illustrates the mediation function served by the supervisor in the learning process.

The role of mediator is an essential one in the interactional concept of supervision which is presented in this book. It also is suggested as a useful statement of function of the helping person in my text on practice skills (Shulman, 1979). This practice theory, derived from Schwartz's work, is useful in explaining how the worker tries to help clients negotiate the various systems of demand they encounter, such as school, work, peer groups, or family. In this book the mediation function idea has been applied to the practice of supervision, and the supervisor's role is seen as in the middle, between the workers and the systems with which they must deal—the agency, the client, colleagues, the community, and so on (see Figure 1.1 in Chapter 1).

FIGURE 4.1
Mediation Role of Supervisor in the Learning Process

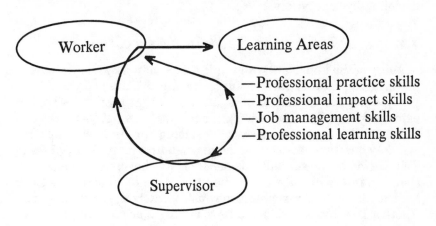

—Professional practice skills
—Professional impact skills
—Job management skills
—Professional learning skills

Teaching Core Practice Skills

The mediation character of the teaching function can be utilized by supervisors to help staff members develop core communication, relationship, and problem-solving skills. Many of these skills have been discussed in earlier chapters in relation to supervision. Here the focus is on the same skills as they are applied by the worker in direct practice, with implications for the educational function of supervision. Each skill is illustrated by a verbatim account describing how a worker has employed it with a client followed by a section on supervision approaches which suggests how supervisors can teach the skill. These supervisory suggestions are also illustrated with verbatim reports, and the ways in which supervisors can model use of the skill for workers are pointed out.

The skills discussed from these viewpoints include tuning in, contracting and dealing with authority (one of the supervisory skills of pointing out obstacles discussed in Chapter 3), and the skill factors of empathy, elaboration, making a demand for work, sharing one's feelings, and sharing data. These are the key skills required by beginning workers in most helping relationships (more complete discussion and illustrations of these skills, and others, can be found in my text on practice, *The Skills of Helping Individuals and Groups).* They are also the skills most adaptable to teaching through modeling by supervisors.

Tuning in and responding directly to indirect cues

Many of the important communications shared by clients, particularly in taboo areas such as authority and sex, are expressed indirectly. Clients will often hint at a concern that they are afraid to express openly. The tuning-in skill helps workers put themselves in the place of the client as a way of developing preliminary empathy.

A key question clients often have when first meeting a worker is "What kind of worker will this person be?" They may be concerned that workers will judge them harshly and not understand their feelings. Parents, for example, may ask workers they have just met whether they are married and have children, as an indirect way of finding out if the worker can understand their concerns. Workers who respond by providing a detailed description of their training can turn these clients off in the first interview. If, however, they are tuned in to the possible meaning of this question, they can use the skill of *responding directly to an indirect cue.* A worker could say, for example "No, I'm not married. Why do you ask? Are you worried that I might not understand what it's like for you to raise kids?" Such an invitation encourages the clients to be more direct about their concerns, and it gives the worker an opportunity to demonstrate an understanding of the difficulty they are experiencing in the encounter. This can help develop a more positive relationship between them.

Workers can tune in to a range of possible feelings and concerns on the client's part and prepare to reach for them. Tuning in is tentative, however, as was noted in Chapter 3, and the worker must be prepared to abandon preconceived ideas about what the client might feel and instead respond to the reality of the interview. The preparation of tuning in gives the worker a better chance of responding to the real meaning of indirect communications rather than reacting defensively.

Supervision approaches. Supervisors can teach the skill of tuning in by providing an exercise to prepare workers for a first interview. The workers should be encouraged to really try to sense the feelings of the clients by remembering a similar instance in their own experience when they sought help from some professional. The exercise becomes a form of role play in which the workers try to attune to the clients' underlying feelings. As they do this, they should also tune in to their own feelings, like nervousness at being new to the job or concern about having enough professional or life experience to be able to help a client.

The supervisor can help by understanding and directly reaching for the workers' feelings as beginners. If supervisors can remember what it was like at the start of their own practice, they are more likely to be supportive of workers. Supervisors who are themselves tuned in and respond directly to the feelings of new workers will thus demonstrate the importance of these two skills for workers. The supervisor's modeling of these skills is an effective way of teaching them, as was noted in Chapter 2.

In the following example, a supervisor tries to respond to a young student's feelings of panic when called by a new client who is herself in a panic. The client, Mrs. C., was extremely upset and had called the student to demand that she find an immediate placement for J., six year-old child. Mrs. C. claimed she was no longer able to handle the child and didn't know what to do if they couldn't get J. off her hands. The student, S., was so upset herself she panicked and told the client she would call her back after she called her supervisor.

The supervisor's account of how *she* tried to tune in to the student's feelings during the telephone conversation and help her develop a strategy for handling the client included the following notes:

S. said she felt overwhelmed by C.'s (the client's) demands and didn't know how she should respond. I went on to explain that it was not S's role to provide solutions, rather that she should work to explore C.'s feelings, the options she could envisage, their possible consequences, etc.

I stopped talking and there was silence on the other end. I told her I was quiet to allow her to raise concerns I might not yet have addressed. She said she was thinking how she would say this to C. She told me she had copied down everything I was saying. I acknowledged her problem in that she had my words but that it is hard to feel good about using someone else's words.

Student: I'd like to be able to tell her something. C. feels that the psych assessment unit and our work with her hasn't done any good because she's still got the problem. I really feel terrible.

Supervisor: Your C. seems to have misunderstood what you, the assessment team, or any other helping person is able to do, and you're feeling bad in recognizing how limited we as helping persons are. We can only help C. work out ways of coping with her problems, we can't come up with *her* answers.

Student: I'll try to think about all these things and get all my "social working" notions put together before I call her this evening.

Supervisor: That's good, but don't let *your* concerns get in the way of being able to hear *her* concerns.

Student: But what if she still wants to put J. in a foster home like she did this morning?

Supervisor: C. was in a panic and was proposing a panic solution and it sounds like you're getting caught in her panic.

Student: That's exactly where I am!

Supervisor: I figured that. Let's look at what panic does. It crowds your mind so you can't think, and there's one idea that gets stuck in your head and you can't think your way past it.

Student: Yes, that's how I feel.

Supervisor: So now we need to figure out a way to help C. past her panic thought of foster placement.

I proceeded to talk about what S. could do to lower C.'s anxiety level and her own, until they were both calm enough to consider a whole range of options and critically explore their respective advantages and disadvantages. She said, "That sounds good."

I went on to suggest to S. that going through this exercise with C. and exploring this process with her is ever so much more helpful to C. than trying to solve her problem for her. Learning how to cope with and overcome panic so that she can deal with the issues in a reasonable way will, in the long run, be much more beneficial to C. than her frantic pursuit of answers.

My impression was that S. was beginning at this point to overcome her own panic and was starting to think constructively how she would deal with this evening's interview or phone contact. S. was told to contact me at home in the evening.

Contracting

In the beginning phase of work the client is probably wondering: "What's this all about?" An important part of the worker's preparation includes planning to clarify the potential working contract with the client during the first interview. As in supervision (see Chapter 2), four critical skills of the worker in contracting are clarifying purpose, clarifying role, reaching for feedback on purpose, and dealing with the authority theme. The first three of these skills are discussed in this section, and the authority of the worker is the topic of the following one.

There is a general problem in the helping professions of *clarifying purpose and role,* or defining precisely what the worker is to do. In the case of family workers, which will be used to illustrate these skills, it is not unusual for workers to be unclear about what they are supposed to offer a family. A first interview will be uncomfortable under the best of circumstances for both the worker and the members of the family, but this discomfort will be increased if there is doubt about the worker's role. To set the client quickly at ease, it is helpful for the worker to prepare a brief opening statement describing the reason for the referral and the services that can be offered.

The following material drawn from an actual interview illustrates the skills of clarifying purpose and role in action. It is an example of a first contact with Mrs. H., a 28-year-old mother of three children. After being introduced by Mrs. H.'s social worker, the family worker attempted to explain her purpose in these words:

> I thought it would help if I took a moment to explain why I have been asked to work with your family. John (the social worker) has told me that things are rough right now for you, with a lot of concerns on your mind. I understand it has been upsetting for you since your husband left, and with your oldest boy having trouble at school, it is easy to understand how these things can pile up. John felt that if I could spend some time with your family, there might be some ways I could take some of the load off of you. For example, I would be glad to talk with you if the going gets rough some days with the kids. I could listen and maybe help you figure out what to do about some of the problems the kids are making for you. If you thought it would be helpful, I would be glad to go down to the school and see what is going on with your boy, Frank. Maybe if I talked to the counselor, and the teacher, and then Frank, I could help get him back in. Does any of this sound like it might be helpful from your point of view?

By beginning this way the worker has been direct about her purpose, as well as providing some "handles" for work—suggestions of ways she might help. These handles partialize the problems and provide some concrete indications of what the worker means by her offer to help. This directness helps the client quickly sort out how the worker might help, and it decreases the client's concern that the worker is there to do something *to* her. Workers are often embarrassed at being direct with clients; they fear coming on too strong and turning the client off, or they begin with a notion of their role as "changing" the client. They have a hidden agenda which explains their reluctance to be direct. Since clients do not lend themselves to being "changed," the sooner the worker gives up this hidden agenda, the quicker a more honest working relationship can develop.

Reaching for *feedback* is important because the client has to accept the offer of service. In this example Mrs. H. may pick up on only one part of the contract: the part she feels urgency about or is willing to risk, often a "near problem," one close to the more difficult concerns. Alternatively, she may be ready to trust the worker and deal with more serious problems instead of near problems. It is important to recognize that the worker can only help in those areas where the client feels some sense of investment and a freedom to risk. Mrs. H. began to take the family worker up on the offer, as the worker reported:

> Mrs. H. said that things had been rough and that the school problem just was the last straw. Frank had been suspended for not doing homework and fighting in the classroom. I told her that I thought that must have come as quite a blow. She said she just didn't know what to do. She was at her wit's end. She found herself getting angry at her son when he hung around the house.

With the feedback from the client the work has begun. Because the worker is willing to listen and to respond with some empathy, an important start is being made on the *working relationship,* a necessity for creating the conditions in which the client will use the worker's help.

Although the specifics of the purpose and the role may differ according to the situations in which help is provided, contracting skills are crucial to all helping situations. In the following example of a first session between a worker and a foster adolescent, it would not be surprising if the client refused an offer put in these terms by the worker:

> Since I'm going to be your new worker, I wanted to meet you to find out how things were going with you, and to see if there was anything I might be able to help with. I know you have been moving around a lot this past year, and that starting in a new foster home, at a new school, and with new friends can be difficult. How about it, how has it been?

In this case there is no working relationship yet, and the client may not trust the worker. In addition, the client may not feel there are any difficulties to discuss. Nevertheless, the worker has made the offer and the client has heard it. If problems emerge later, or if the trust develops, the client may be more ready to use the worker's help.

Clarifying purpose and role is also essential in a brief, limited-focus interview. An example is the following comments by a worker in a medical setting meeting with a patient about to be discharged:

> Your doctor has told me that you are about to be discharged. He was concerned that it might be difficult for you when you return home, since you have been through a tough time here at the hospital. I wanted to see if I might be helpful in any way—perhaps by sending a homemaker or someone to help out with the kids until you get settled back in. Is there anything you are concerned about?

As the client describes the situation, it is often possible to identify other areas where services may be helpful. A worker might pick up the idea, for example, that a single parent is having difficulty dealing with her children and suggest a referral to a family agency.

This discussion is not meant to suggest that contracting is a mechanical process for the worker. Each one approaches first sessions differently, and each must respond to the unique nature of her or his client's responses. A worker might find that the client is eager to talk, and the worker needs to listen first, before stating what he or she has to offer. The important point is that at some time in the first interview, the discussion should focus on the connections between the felt needs of the clients and the service that the agency or other setting can provide.

Supervision Approaches.   One of the best ways for the supervisor to help a new worker get ready to make a first contact with a client is to suggest a role play in which the worker tries out an opening statement of purpose and role. The supervisor can then respond in a number of ways, preparing the worker for possible reactions. The worker's opening statement often reveals a lack of clarity, and the supervisor can help the worker rethink her or his purpose and role. The use of jargon instead of precise terms and meaningful expressions can be pointed out and the worker helped to think of alternatives. The role play will often reveal many of the worker's fears about the encounter, giving the supervisor an opportunity to discuss them.

This exercise can provide workers with the confidence to be more relaxed in the first session and thus less defensive. It may reveal the worker's feelings in the situation, feelings that can have an influence on willingness to offer help to a client. Workers are often reluctant to contract with the client in this way if they foresee the apprehension of a child as a distinct possibility, for example. When the supervisor inquires about the worker's attitude towards the client, it turns out that she is afraid of feeling like a rat if she encourages the client to open up and then has to suggest the removal of the child.

Another way of helping workers is to follow up after an interview and discuss the details of the encounter. The worker could write up notes describing the discussion, or, if time does not permit, recall the dialogue from memory. The supervisor must get some of the details in order to be helpful. If the worker comments on the client's defensiveness, for example, the supervisor should request an account of what both client and worker said. Often even a few moments of discussion will help a worker understand the interaction in a new way. As the worker begins to see the client's actions as responses to his or her intervention, the focus can shift from discussion of the case to discussion of the worker's skills.

There is an interesting parallel between this form of supervision and the work done with clients. For example, when a parent discusses a problem with a teenaged child, the worker, like the supervisor, should ask for the details of the encounter—what the client actually said and how the child responded. The worker can be most helpful by examining the specifics of the interaction, and the same is true for the supervisor.

A process recording can be a very useful teaching device. The worker would write a brief description of the conversation at the start of the session, including some verbatim dialogue. A summary would describe what followed, with expanded detailed descriptions of crucial aspects of the middle of the session. The ending would also be written verbatim, for a total process recording of two pages (see the coda for a discussion of process recording).

Another important way the supervisor teaches the contracting skills is by demonstrating them in the supervision context. In early interviews with a new worker, the supervisor should clarify the purpose of supervision and the role of a supervisor and should attempt to reach for worker feedback, as noted in Chapter 2. The supervisor can also prepare an opening statement to begin the contracting with the worker. The contract will inevitably be broad, since the supervisor has many responsibilities. But the part of the contract concerning the development of practice skills might be stated like this:

> Part of what I will be doing with you is helping you look at the way you work with clients. When you are getting ready to go out on first interviews, I can help you prepare by thinking through what you might say. After an interview, particularly one you feel you had trouble with, I will be glad to listen to what went on and try to help you figure out what you did right and what you might have done differently. In addition, there will be some days when the work gets rough and you're feeling low. If you want someone to talk to, I'll try to be available to listen.

There are a number of reasons why supervisors often ignore the specifics of workers' interactions with their clients. Some may not have experienced this kind of work themselves, or they may have had bad experiences with punitive discussions of their practice. They were not allowed to make mistakes. Others refrain from this work because they sense resistance from the worker. Still others are afraid to make this offer because they feel they will not be able to respond adequately if the worker asks for help. But it is not really necessary for supervisors to have all the answers. What supervisors can provide are ways of working on the questions, some insights from their own experiences, and some support for the worker in the struggle. In a parallel way, this is exactly what the workers will be offering the client.

The problem of limited time is often appropriately cited by supervisors who have many demands placed upon them. In reality, however, they may have to spend a great deal of time dealing with the problems created by lack of worker skill. For example, a placement breakdown of a teenager may have been indirectly hinted at by the client but not picked up by the worker who had contracted poorly with the client. This problem may then demand many hours of time and much energy, all of which could have been avoided. Apprehending an abused child (a situation that might never have arisen had the worker developed more skillfully the initial working relationship with the frightened mother) also takes its toll on both time and emotions.

Dealing with the authority of the worker

Whenever a client first comes into contact with a helping person, the tendency is to perceive that person as an authority figure. This is true even in situations where the client is a voluntary one or does not fear the worker's legal authority. The client transfers to the new encounter feelings and perceptions derived from past experiences with people in authority (parents, teachers, other workers). The worker must be sensitive to how the theme of authority affects the client and be prepared to discuss it directly if it blocks the working relationship. Since authority is a taboo subject, the worker may have to help the client feel comfortable enough to discuss it. The necessity of discussing this relationship periodically should be anticipated. In this sense the authority theme may represent an obstacle to work, as it was described in Chapter 3.

In addition to the possibility of transference of feelings by clients, workers should guard against countertransference of their own feelings and perceptions from past experiences with clients. It is not uncommon for young workers to identify with children in a family conflict situation, for example, because they perceive the parents in a stereotyped fashion. Loss of their sense of function may lead them to take sides, which cuts them off as helpers to the parents.

In cases where the agency does carry clear authority over the life of the client, as in child abuse situations, where it has statutory responsibility for the child, it is essential to deal with the authority theme early in the worker-client relationship. Defensive or hostile clients often have a stereotyped idea of workers, based on past experiences or what they have heard from other clients. A client's underlying fear of a worker as, for example, a "baby snatcher" may be expressed as hostile behavior.

A worker meeting this kind of response should deal with it directly, as a start to contracting. The following report illustrates this:

> I told her I had come because we had had calls from her neighbors who were concerned that she might be having difficulties with her kids. I told her I wanted to see if this was true and to see if there was any way I could help. The client responded angrily and defensively, saying her neighbors were lying and out to get her. She told me that what went on with her kids was none of my business, and she would rather not talk to me about it.
>
> I told her it was obvious that she was upset that I was there. I went

on to say that it wasn't easy for me, either. I asked her if she was worried that we might be thinking of taking her kids from her. She told me in a very angry voice that she wouldn't let me if I tried. I told her that we often get calls from neighbors, and just getting a call did not mean we would remove children from families. I told her we were more interested in helping kids stay in families, and that it was only under serious circumstances when children were being beaten or neglected, and their parents were having problems with the kids which we could not help with, that we considered apprehending children—it was only under those serious circumstances. That was not what we wanted. We would much rather help parents out with their problems so that the kids could stay at home.

I asked her why she was so upset at my being there. Had she had experiences with social workers before? She said she had not, but a neighbor of hers had. She went on to describe an incident in which the worker had apprehended a child. I told her I could understand why she had been so upset and worried when I arrived. I asked her if we could start all over. I told her that we had lots of parents who came to us because the going was rough with the kids. When you're alone with three kids, and they are after you all day, and you can't get out because you have no help, it's easy to understand how you could get angry and lose your temper. There was a long silence. I waited. She was staring at my face, probably trying to decide whether to believe me or not. She finally said it was rough sometimes. I asked if she would like to tell me a bit about the rough times.

There are many clients who will not accept the worker's offer of help, particularly in a stressful situation such as fearing apprehension of a child. It may take a long time for some clients to believe the worker, however, it is important for the worker to make the offer. Unless direct statements of purpose and role are made in the beginning stage of work, the sessions will be constantly hindered by lack of clarity of contract.

Supervision Approaches. The parallels between the supervisor-worker and worker-client relationships are most direct in the authority theme. The authority of the supervisor can have a powerful impact on the working relationship. By monitoring this issue and encouraging the workers to be open with them, supervisors can effectively demonstrate this skill. Early in the working supervisory relationship, they should encourage discussion of how comfortable the workers feel in "taking on" the supervisor, being honest, and so on. After such a discussion it is often helpful to point out to the workers that their clients probably feel the same about them. Supervisors also need to consider the possibility of countertransference of their own feelings to their relations with workers.

This is illustrated in an excerpt from a first interview between a white supervisor and a native Indian student who was a mature woman but new to training. The student described with much feeling a court case she had sat in on where, she felt, a white lawyer had made racist remarks while supposedly defending a native Indian mother who wanted her child returned. The lawyer had asked a witness if she had ever heard of "native Indian time," implying that it was common for Indians to be late. The student described how she had confronted the lawyer during a recess and told him how she felt about the comment. After some discussion about her anger at white professionals who did not "understand," the supervisor opened up the authority theme in their relationship this way:

Supervisor: Can I just stop for a minute? I'm just wondering, just going back to what you were saying about what we should be sensitive to. Let's not leave what you're talking about now, but back there, I'm wondering how that applies to me. How can you help me be sensitive to yourself and native culture so that I can be helpful to you in this situation and also grow myself? Because I have to be helpful to you in this, and obviously you're Indian and I'm white. You have something to teach me in this. Let's do a tuning-in exercise for me. You're saying to me, white people—well, I'm a white social worker, so I'm wondering maybe I should also be addressing that.

Student: I think perhaps you could. These issues aren't raised for me until I see a native Indian in a situation. I would be more apt to stick up for myself. I don't think you have to be as conscious in dealing with it with me.

Supervisor: I'm not sure that I'm saying that. I'm just saying, help me tune in to what I should be aware of—not necessarily in you, but in the clients I deal with, or in the people that I supervise, who by and large are going to be white. I'm probably not going to be supervising that many native Indian social workers, because there's not that many of you around. There's not many in the school, and more's the tragedy for that. What should I be aware of? I think I see racism, [and] when I see it, I pick it up, obviously. But how can I be sensitive to ...

Student: I have an excellent book that you might like to look at, Sue. I'll bring it in next Wednesday. But, I think, more than that—realize that a native Indian, especially an older one ... say, from 30 on, is not too apt to disagree with you, even if you're respecting their rights.

Supervisor: Would you disagree with me?

Student: Yeah, I would. But, very likely, [it would be] like that client when she came up and talked to the family support worker in court, and said, "I don't want you to worry about ... feeling bad about testifying against me." The social worker said, "Now isn't that terrific! I mean, she's a real trooper; she knows that the truth is the truth." Actually, in my view, that client was saying: "Please don't be mad at me; and don't think I'm mad at you and react badly to me." I'm making an awful lot of assumptions, and perhaps I'm completely off base.

Supervisor: You're making your assumptions from your perspective, from your cultural perspective and your personal perspective. And maybe they're right. Most likely, they are right.

Student: My idea is that she wouldn't have had the self-confidence to go up and say: "Look, you bitch, I let you in in my home every day and...." She might hit me on the Indian thing. She might bring it back to, Indians shouldn't treat other Indians this way.

Supervisor: I'm asking you to be sensitive to your assumptions. Let's say you were the client's social worker; you're an Indian social worker dealing with a client. Being sensitive to your assumptions, and to the cultural similarities that you have, how is that going to affect the way you work with her?

Student: I would not take her first answer as being her true feelings.

Supervisor: Okay.

Student: Like, if I said, "How do you feel about me coming in every morning?" and she said, "That's really nice of you to do something for me," I would look at that as it's nice of you to do something for *me*.

Supervisor: Would that be any different for a white client?

Student: I think I would look at it [that way] if it was anybody that I felt was feeling in a one-down position, like badly in a one-down position.

Supervisor: I think that I would ask you to be sensitive to the fact that it's a function of maybe Indianness, if there's such a word, but it's also a function of being one-down anyway. And if you were dealing with a white client, by and large that white client would say back to you, "Oh, I'm feeling fine about you being here," when actually they want to say, "You bitch, get out of my house." I think it's really important for you to remember, the client is one-down, more than the client is Indian, two-down if they're Indian. They still have to deal with an authority thing going on in there, whether the authority is native Indian or white and whether the client is native Indian or white. I think part of your learning is, to really be aware that the client is one-down anyway, and that by and large a white client would say the same thing back.

Student: That is quite possible, but I think an Indian might be better at hiding their true feelings.

Supervisor: Right! And that's probably where your sensitivity to what's going on under there is really good.

Although the worker did not take up the supervisor's offer to explore this area further, perhaps feeling hesitant in a first session, the supervisor did make it clear that this could be an agenda item. The supervisor might also have dropped it, feeling it was too threatening to the worker in a first interview. However, she did point to the issue of the authority theme in terms of the worker's relationship with clients, as a native Indian working with native Indians or white clients. Thus, the sensitive subject was brought out in the open for future work. This excerpt is an example of the parallels between supervision and practice? The discussion goes from the supervisor's concern with the worker smoothly to the worker's concern with clients.

Empathic skills

A central assumption about the use of empathy is that the way people feel is related to how they act, and that the way people act will affect how they feel. For example, a single parent who is feeling lonely, unhappy, and judging herself harshly will often express these feelings in the way she acts toward her children. The mother's tensions can lead the children to act out their feelings through negative behavior which, in turn, causes the mother to be less tolerant. A vicious cycle develops. To take another example, a mother on welfare whose children have grown up feels she would like to go back to work and consults an employment counselor about available opportunities. If she feels inadequate about reentering the work force after so many years at home, however, she may act this out by missing job interviews. Such a client is ambivalent: on the one hand she wants independence and self-respect, and on the other, she is afraid of risking herself. In a similar way, an adolescent who has been rejected by his family and has moved through a number of foster homes no longer believes he can have a stable, close relationship with adults. Because he has been hurt so often, he refuses to risk. He then begins new contacts in a residential treatment home with acting-out behavior, which brings about the rejection he fears. A hospital patient who is anxious about an impending medical procedure also may express the feeling through demanding or hostile behavior. In each of these cases, the clients' feelings affect their actions, and their actions further affect their feelings.

Because of this connection between feeling and doing, there is a need for the workers to be sensitive to the affective portion of a client's message. Unfortunately, in our society the open expression of feelings is somewhat of a taboo, and the norms under which most people operate forbid direct expression of some of their most difficult feelings. Workers need to develop skills that will help clients become more aware of their real feelings and willing to share them. The workers efforts to understand a client's feelings, and to experience them, will strengthen the worker-client relationship. The empathic skills discussed in this section are the same as those that were described in the work phase model of supervision in Chapter 3. They are: reaching for feelings, acknowledging feelings, and articulating the client's feelings or putting them into words.

Reaching for feelings involves listening to the client's description of a problem and asking about the associated feelings. For example, a mother describes a conflict situation with a daughter who had come home at 2 A.M. without having let the mother know where she was. The worker might inquire, "What did you feel when your daughter arrived?" The intent is to encourage the client to express her affect, or feelings. It is important that the empathic efforts be genuine; the worker must be interested in understanding the feelings and not just ask about them in a ritualistic manner. For these skills to be effective, workers must attempt to actually feel, as best as they can, the emotions of the clients. To do this in a meaningful way, they need to become attuned to their own affective responses during interviews.

The skill of *acknowledging feelings* calls for the worker to communicate acceptance and appreciation of the client's affect. This skill is demonstrated in an interview with a client who was fearful during the first interview and had responded defensively. Later, the worker reported:

> Mrs. F. told me that she had been fearful of me in the first interview. She didn't feel she could trust me and tell me what was really on her mind. I told her I could easily understand that if I had been in her shoes, I would have been just as scared and upset.

A more sophisticated skill is *articulating the client's feelings* just before they are expressed by the client. In any relationship, particularly at the beginning, people are reluctant to share their real feelings. Workers who are listening to clients and tuned in may be able to sense how they feel, even before the clients say anything about it.

When the worker articulates these feelings, two objectives are accomplished: Clients are in effect given permission to discuss their feelings and they perceive the worker as someone who understands. Even if clients do not acknowledge a feeling, having heard it expressed may be enough. Here is an example of this skill in action:

> Mr. G. asked me how long his youngsters would be in care. I told him for six months, or longer, if he or his wife wanted to extend the agreement (a voluntary placement). He said it was a long time for the kids. I said, "And for you too." He went on to tell me that his son John was confused and sad. I said, "That must make it hard on you to see him." He said it was, because he was not sure of what to say to him. I said, "You mean when he asks you when he is coming home?" He said, "Well, yeah."

This worker was tuned in to the feelings of natural parents, particularly the guilt involved when a child is placed in care. She understood that parents often feel so bad about the placement that they cannot face the question in the eyes of a child wanting to know when it will be possible to come home. Natural parents often avoid that question by not coming to visit their children who have been placed in care, by appearing to be cold and indifferent, or by getting drunk before a visit. In this case the worker is so tuned in to the client's feelings that she is able to state her affective hunches slightly ahead of him. She does this when she says: "That must make it hard on you to see him" and "You mean when he asks you when he is coming home?" The value of the skill is that the worker's empathic reaction encourages the client to risk the feelings.

In another example, a nurse spoke to a mother in a hospital emergency waiting room about her child, who had had en eye injury, in these terms:

Mother: How long will it take to find out what's wrong? I've been here for almost an hour.

Nurse: I'm sorry it is taking so long. The doctor is examining your daughter right now (pause). It's really hard waiting when you're frightened about your daughter's sight.

Mother (starting to cry): Oh God, if I had been watching her, it wouldn't have happened.

Nurse (after a few moments, putting her hand on the mother's shoulder): It's okay to cry—it's very tough for parents to see their own child hurt and not know how badly. I can't give you any real information, but for what it's worth, she didn't look too bad to me when I took her in. I'll try to find out what's up, and I'll let you know as soon as I can.

In any expression of empathy, the feelings must be genuine. Many workers have had training which has taught them to deal with feelings routinely. When the workers themselves are not actually feeling anything, the clients quickly see these efforts as false. Workers who simply echo a client's response, for example, are not helping. If the client says, "I'm angry at the agency," and the worker responds, "You're angry at the agency," the client has every right to say that he has just told the worker that and can't understand why it is being repeated.

A ritual question such as "How do you feel about that?" also seems unmeaningful. Mechanical responses such as "I hear you saying that ... " often turns clients off rather than helping them discuss their feelings. Workers will develop their own personal styles of empathizing, but the key to the effectiveness of the skill is that, as best they can, they genuinely respond to the feelings of the client.

My research on practice has found that the worker's ability to acknowledge the client's feelings is the second most important skill in encouraging positive working relationships and being helpful to clients (Shulman, 1978). In addition, the ability to articulate the client's feelings before they are expressed appears to contribute to the establishment of a good working relationship. These tentative results support the notion that rather than not risking the feeling for fear of putting a client off or putting words into the client's mouth, workers would do better to err on the side of risking their affective hunches, thereby leaving clients room to reject them.

Supervision Approaches. It is with the empathic skills that supervisors can model the helping process most effectively. It does little good for supervisors to tell workers they are not empathic with their clients if at the same time they are not empathic with their workers. In the beginning phase of supervisory work, the supervisor can demonstrate the importance of empathic responses by tuning in to the worker's feelings and starting to articulate them when they first meet. Before a worker's first interview, the supervisor might ask, "Are you worried about seeing your first client?" and later say something to the effect that "It must be scary wondering if you have anything to offer that client." Workers will appreciate a supervisor's genuine efforts to understand the experience and to support them during the tough times. The supervisor's articulation of these feelings also can free workers to express their doubts and concerns.

Discussion of interviews is another instance when the supervisor's use of the empathic skills is helpful. As a worker reports a client's comments, the supervisor might say, for example, "Do you remember what you were feeling at that moment?" By reaching for feelings, the supervisor indicates an interest in the worker's affect during interviews. It is also helpful to explain that how the worker feels during an interview is important to the supervisor. Feelings affect what workers do and say, just as they influence clients' behaviors. Often what a worker says is not related to what the worker feels.

Such discussions can lead to consideration of what makes it difficult for workers to articulate their own feelings. Because they are affected by the norms and taboos of our society, they may feel uncomfortable and embarrassed about discussing people's feelings. Even though the worker is empathic with the client, therefore, expression of this empathy may be blocked. This is a normal response, and acknowledging the reasonableness of the workers' feelings may free them to deal with their clients more effectively.

Another helpful device is to ask workers how an incident might be handled if it should reoccur. Sometimes simply attempting to express empathy in a role play can assist a worker to find the right words to deal with a situation in practice.

The supervisor can also support workers by pointing out that the ability to express empathy develops slowly and is influenced by age and experience, but it does eventually emerge. A worker's capacity to express empathy for clients will grow with practice. As the supervisor examines cases when the worker was not empathic or seemed distant, it may become apparent that another feeling was interfering with the worker's capacity for empathy. Workers who judge clients harshly because of their actions (e.g., child abuse) must learn to consider the clients as people with needs and problems of their own. In effect, workers learn from their mistakes, and the supervisor's support and understanding will help them risk their feelings and feel more comfortable about learning in this way. There will be times when the worker will not have the energy left to empathize, or will be too rushed, or too upset; the supervisor has to acknowledge this. All these can also be problems for supervisors who need support from their own administrators and peers if they are to be able to help their workers.

The following excerpt shows how a supervisor helped a beginning worker to examine her feelings about working with a father who had been accused of sexual abuse of a child. New workers naturally bring a host of reactions to clients to the relationship, and supervision must show them that they can admit to these feelings and begin to understand them more deeply. Workers must learn to see past the possible pathological behavior of clients and tune in to their real feelings and concerns. The supervisor's report noted:

> Theresa began by presenting me with a case. She went into detail about the case, which involved sexual abuse. She said "That guy was really icky." I asked her what she meant by icky. She said, "Well, when Mr. Brown was standing near Jean, he put his hand on her head and she cringed." I observed she really had some feelings about Mr. Brown. She said emphatically, "I sure do hate him, the son of a bitch." I looked at her—silence. She said, "Whew! That was pretty strong!" I said "Yeah, you sound really angry." She said, "I have angry feelings about abuse. I've seen too much of it. . . ."
>
> I asked her to tune into Mr. Brown and what he might be feeling. She said, "Mad." I asked, "How come?" She said, "Because we social workers were in his house." I asked what else; she said "Maybe he feels icky, too." We talked about why he would feel icky. Later she said, "I really forgot to tune in to him and see him in the system. Another time I'll be more aware."

Each new type of client will generate new reactions in the worker, and the supervisor can help even experienced workers by reaching for these feelings. In another example (described in the topic on supporting workers in taboo areas in Chapter 3), very experienced male workers who were preparing to work with men who batter their wives or the women they live with had to look deeply into their own feelings about women and violence before they could honestly tune in to these clients. When audiotapes of interviews preparing clients for the first group meeting were examined in some detail in a group supervision session, the consultant pointed out that a worker had been lacking in empathy for a client and had seemed harsh and judgmental in a subtle way. This was true, even though the workers had indicated they felt they could accept these men as clients. The conversation continued as follows:

> I asked Frank why he had seemed so angry at the client—if he could put his finger on what he was feeling at the time. He indicated that he really hadn't realized he was feeling angry. I acknowledged that this was sometimes the hardest part—dealing with real feelings which are just beneath the surface. I asked if anyone else had any ideas.
>
> Terry responded that Frank was probably really feeling angry at this guy for having beaten his old lady up that way—and that he knew we felt that way as well, even though we were trying to be nonjudgmental. I said, "Good, that's a start." Frank continued: "It's easy to say we shouldn't judge these guys, and I feel funny feeling this way, but I do get furious at them." I asked if they had any idea why this type of client hit them so hard. I told them I knew they were experienced workers and had learned to handle tough problems, such as parental abuse of children. I wanted to know what was different with these men.
>
> After a long pause, Frank said, "I think they remind me of my own anger towards women." I asked what he meant, and he explained that there were often times when he had felt so angry at his wife that he could have hit her—and that the difference between him and these clients was that he could control his anger and they couldn't. I said: "So when you see your own feelings in these men, it's very tough to face them—because they hit you so hard, and because it's tough to admit you have them." Terry said I had hit the nail on the head. I replied that I thought we were now starting to make a real start on tuning in to these men, because they were being so honest in tuning in to their own feelings.

The concern of supervisors about responding empathically to workers was described in Chapter 3. Even those who have developed strong practice skills in this area and have little hesitation about being empathic with clients may be afraid this could amount to "social working" their workers. They recognize that workers are not clients, and they feel it would be inappropriate to bring up areas of personal concern. Nevertheless, the feelings workers have about their practice are directly related to how they deal with clients, and these feelings must be discussed. As long as the supervisor's sense of function is clear and the work stays within the boundaries of the supervision contract, workers very much appreciate evidence that the supervisor understands their dilemmas, concerns, and feelings. Supervisors appreciate the same sort of understanding.

Sessional contracting

In direct practice as in supervision, sessional contracting involves an attempt at the beginning of each session to determine the central areas of concern. The assumption is that clients will only invest themselves in matters about which they feel a sense of urgency. The skill involves asking clients, at the beginning of each session, what they would like to discuss. Even if the worker has an agenda that must be dealt with during the session, this negotiating process reassures clients that their concerns will also be heard. In addition, because clients often employ indirect communications at the beginning of an interview, it is helpful to be tentative about the agenda so that the real concerns can be explored.

In the following example, a teenaged girl had approached the worker for help in finding a foster home. The worker began the session by negotiating the working contract, but remained tentative about it. Rather than dealing with the first issue raised by the client, the worker used the sessional contracting skill to give the client an opportunity to get to a more difficult issue. The worker noted:

> Jean had opened the interview by telling me she had heard from friends that I would be able to help her get a foster home. She said that she wanted to leave home right away. I told her we often did help youngsters find foster homes, but first we had to be pretty clear that they were unable to live at home. I asked if she could tell me why she wanted to move out.
>
> She presented a long description of a fight she'd been having with her mom, not being able to get enough clothing, hassles over the time she needs to get home in the evening, describing a generally difficult relationship. Although it sounded stressful, it didn't sound serious enough for Jean's sense of urgency. I told her that it sounded like she was having a hard time with her mom, but what she was describing didn't seem to be way out of line with the problems that happen in most families. I wondered if there was something else that was also troubling her. There was a silence, and then she said she doesn't like the men that hang around the house. I asked her if she could tell me a bit more about that. I noticed as she talked that she looked down and seemed embarrassed. She told me there was a lot of activity with men at night in the room next to her. It was a small apartment, and she was very uncomfortable.
>
> I told her I realized it wasn't easy to talk about these matters, but

it would be important for me to know what was happening if I was to be able to help her. Acting on a hunch caused by her embarrassment, I asked if any of the men had been bothering her. She looked up quickly, seemed relieved, and said that her mom's latest boyfriend had been making passes at her.

Had the worker simply responded to the first issue, she might have explored the concern simply as a problem between Jean and her mother. The real concern, an embarrassing one in a taboo area, might not have surfaced for a number of interviews. By being tentative at the beginning of the interview, the worker was able to get at the problem behind the problem.

Supervision Approaches. Supervisors can help workers become more conscious of the importance of sessional contracting by concentrating on the tentative beginnings of their contacts as they discuss their practice. Asking "What was the client working on?" can help workers see that particular interviews or sessions with clients moved on too quickly, without adequate exploration. Often real concerns emerge near the end of the session, in what has been described earlier, in the supervision context, as the doorknob therapy phenomenon. By examining the conversation at the beginning of a session, it is often possible to pick up the cues to concerns which will emerge later.

The supervision process can be an important demonstration of the skill of sessional contracting. Workers will often bring partial or incomplete concerns to the attention of their supervisors, who can employ the same tentativeness in their discussions with the workers. The following excerpt is an example:

Fred came into my office appearing agitated and somewhat upset. He asked if I had a minute for an interpretation of a policy question. I said, "Sure, what is it?" He described the problem, [which was] related to agency policy and eligibility for service in an example of a specific client. I interpreted the policy as I understood it, and he nodded his head vigorously, agreeing with me. He then went on to describe an interview he had just had with a client where the client had been abusive when he had made his interpretation of the policy and had attacked him and the agency. I said I thought that was upsetting and wondered if he wanted to spend a minute talking about it. He said he did because he hadn't really known how to handle it and wasn't feeling too good about what had happened.

Supervisors who are themselves busy and under pressure may find it easiest to deal with only the first issue presented, even though they sense there might be more behind it. Some, as has been noted, are concerned that if they invite workers to explore an issue more deeply, the workers might accept the invitation. Certainly there are times when it is necessary to put off discussion until both the worker and the supervisor can devote adequate attention to a problem. Often it is not possible to pick up details on every issue. In any case if an issue is not dealt with the first time it comes up, it could emerge again and thus provide a second opportunity to deal with it.

Elaboration skills

As in supervision, workers' skills which are helpful in encouraging clients to tell their stories include containment, questioning, focused listening, reaching inside silences, and moving from the general to the specific. In direct practice, *containment* helps the worker resist the tendency to provide a solution or an answer to a client's problem before the client has elaborated it in some detail. The feeling many workers have that they are effective only if they can "solve" their clients' problems can lead them to propose answers before they really understand the questions.

As clients describe their concerns, they should be led to provide details with *questioning,* like "Could you tell me a little more about that?" Often the worker has a hard time understanding why a client has brought up a particular issue; it may seem to be idle chatter, irrelevant to their meeting. *Focused listening* encourages the worker to listen with the working contract in mind, in order to discover clues to the real meaning of a conversation.

Although silences are key moments in practice, it may be difficult for workers to understand their meaning. They could experience discomfort during silence and try to change the subject. Observation of videotapes of the practice of 11 workers indicated that over 60% of the time, the discussion following a silence moved away from the client's concern (Shulman, 1979). If workers understand that silences are a form of conversation, they can wait the silences out and ask why clients have become silent, or, if they have a hunch, *reach inside the silences* and try to articulate the feelings. This often frees the client to make a next move.

The skill of *moving from the general to the specific* is very important in practice in the helping professions. The client may begin an interview by raising a general problem, such as: "It's getting awfully tough these days to raise teenage kids, what with drugs and the way morals are changing." If the worker begins a general discussion of the problems of raising teenagers, the client's real concern may be missed. Underlying most general comments by clients there is very specific concern. Workers have a better chance of getting at the concern by reaching for the specific with a question such as, "Have you had trouble with your daughter this week?" The general problem of raising teenagers may quickly become a specific problem a client is having with her daughter.

Requesting elaboration of the specifics of the problem is also helpful. Note in the following example how the worker helped the client to provide details of the concern:

> Mrs. Fredericks told me she found it very hard dealing with her teenage foster daughter. I asked if there had been a specific example recently. She said there was and described how she had come in at 3:00 A.M. earlier that week and Mrs. Fredericks had no idea where she was. I said I thought that must have been pretty upsetting for her. She said it was. I asked what happened when the daughter came in. She told me that she had gotten very angry and ended up getting into a big fight with her. I asked if she could tell me a bit of the conversation with her daughter. I said we could take a look at what happened and I might be able to help her think through what to do when it happens again.

Supervision Approaches. In modeling the skills of elaboration, supervisors can help workers understand their functional role, as well as how to deal with their feelings about the work. The tendency of workers to try to offer solutions because they believe that that is how a worker helps has been noted; often they see the worker as someone who "has the answers." The model of practice in their minds is that the clients tell them their problems, and they come up with the solutions. Since life is not that simple and solutions are often hard to find, workers are frequently disappointed at not being able to help enough. After warning of the temptation to intervene precipitately, the supervisor can open up a discussion of the worker's sense of the helping role with a question such as, "Exactly *how* do you see yourself giving help?" When workers feel less responsible for providing instant solutions, they can allow clients more time to elaborate.

To help workers develop the skill of dealing with silences, the supervisor can ask about their feelings during a silence. Often workers seem to regard a silence as negative feedback on their work. This is true in some cases, and supervisors need to help workers develop the confidence to reach for such feedback from clients. More often, however, silence is not negative feedback at all. The supervisor can ask workers to speculate on what a silence might mean. As they become more aware of how silences affect them, they will develop self-confidence and begin to reach inside the silences.

The supervisory relationship is a perfect one for demonstrating the skills of elaboration to workers, particularly the skill of moving from the general to the specific. As in client relationships, the most common problem in supervision is the tendency to deal with generalities (see Chapter 3). Behind a general question raised by a worker is often a specific troubling incident. It takes only a few minutes of the supervisor's time to ask the worker to describe what happened, and, when the worker reports what the client said, to ask, "And what did you say back?" The supervisor must let the worker know that the details of the interaction are needed in order to think through the problem. A case conference in which the discussion centers only on the client, focusing on the diagnosis and treatment plan, can leave the worker at a loss. Instead, the discussion should center on the interaction between the worker and the client. It is from the specifics of the interaction that an understanding of the situation and a plan for action will emerge.

The following example is a report of a supervisor's discussion with a worker of her first interviews with a client. The discussion remained at a general level and was of limited help. The worker, Nancy, raises concerns about her interview with a young woman client in a hospital who in considering an abortion. She is also concerned about how to handle procedures with other professionals with whom she has consulted on the case. In this first worker-supervisor conference, the discussion went as follows:

Nancy (Worker): As I was saying, I don't have any great things to say today.

Supervisor: Oh, everything you say is great, Nancy.

Nancy (laughing): Right. I had two sessions with this young girl named Fran in the clinic last week. One each day. And I consultated—is that how you say it?

Supervisor: Consulted.

Nancy (laughs): *Consulted* with Risa and Frank both, about this girl, in between the sessions. She was having an abortion. It was sort of abortion counseling, I suppose you might call it, and seeing if that's what she really wanted.

There were some problems with her family. Her mother was supposedly very much against it. She's living in the home. Her parents are taking on a lot of stuff. Anyway, I guess the only thing I did about that is, I went back the next day. I came back [here] and I was thinking that it was all quite clear. What I had tried to do—although it just kind of emerged out of the interview—was just to try to get it all out and look at it with her and get her to look at what each issue was.

Supervisor: Um, hm.

Nancy: You know, the abortion and what it meant and what was happening at home, I guess. When I came back, I asked Risa a little bit about why the parents were upset, and then Risa got into it about the seriousness of the whole thinking and how important it was and what a big deal it was in a way. It just seemed that that's what she was saying, was that this was a very huge thing for somebody to be doing. And it struck me that I didn't . . . think it was so big, and then I talked to Frank and he said the same thing. I'm beginning to think that there's something wrong with my conception (laughs) of how I see problems. And he was saying there's a lot of dynamics there, and you have to sort out all of these different things.

Supervisor: I guess *I'm* wondering, what stage was she at?

Nancy: I think I sort of look at it quite simply, like I don't want to go into all that stuff right away. She was quite clear about what she wanted to do.

Supervisor: I mean, how far along was she?

Nancy: Oh, seven weeks. She'd been in for an operation and they found out that she was pregnant, too. . . . So there was a . . . there were an awful lot of complications.

Supervisor: Why do you think that their views are so different—Risa's and Frank's and yours?

Nancy: Well, I guess, the negative part of me thinks, "These workers, they just have to be so professional that they really need something to do" (laughing).

Supervisor: You mean, Risa and Frank are creating a mountain out of a molehill?

Nancy: Yeah, exactly. And then the other part of me thinks, "Gee, you know, there must be something I'm missing." I can see that there are some things that have to be ironed out and looked at, but it just didn't strike me as being so . . . such a big deal.

Supervisor: I've worked with some people in this area, and it can be a big thing and it cannot be a big thing. I guess my sense of it is, how does the girl view the abortion? Does she see it as a murder? Which is what some people who are very antiabortion might feel.

Nancy: No, no.

Supervisor: Or does she see it as a birth control kind of a measure, almost?

Nancy: Well, as more like a birth control thing. She just felt that she just wasn't ready to have a child.

The conversation continued in a general vein, moving back and forth between the client's perception of the problem and Nancy's continued concern about the other professionals' opinions. At no point, however, did the supervisor ask her to describe, in some detail, how the interviews with the client had proceeded. Nancy persisted during the conference in emphasizing her inability to see why the abortion would be such a big deal.

Note the differences between this general discussion and the following excerpts from a conference between the same worker and supervisor about another client just one week later. In this situation, Nancy feels that the client, who is in a hospital, is avoiding talking about a number of real issues related to when she returns home. For the worker, the issue is similar to the one with her previous client: What is my role, and how do I reach for possible underlying issues and feelings? This time, quickly moving to reconstruct the interview by employing role play, the supervisor helped Nancy explore the question more productively.

Supervisor: Okay, anything else about Louise?

Nancy: Well, I guess I kind of know what to do with that, but I wonder, because her (the client) thing is that everything's gotta be okay, because she can't face pain very well. And when I'm there, often she'll say, "Everything was really terrible a week ago or a few days ago but everything's just fine now, I'm just living blissed-out. . . . Everything's just great, and it's going to be good when I go home, it's just going to be fine."

Supervisor: And this happens every time you come?

Nancy: Yeah, yeah.

Supervisor: Maybe you ought to talk about that.

Nancy: I said to her this morning, "You probably feel okay now, right at the moment, but there must be a lot of hurt and a lot of pain, or you wouldn't have gone through all that stuff." I was trying to get back to the pain, but I'm just not sure where to go with that.

Supervisor: How does she answer when you say that?

Nancy: She won't get into it.

Supervisor: What are you feeling at the time, when that's happening?

Nancy: I'm feeling like this is getting into a social visit, and I'm just not sure what my role is here. It seems like a nice, cutesy little visit, where you go in and visit somebody that's sick in the hospital. And I just don't know how much I should try to therapize or just listen or.... I don't want to interfere, but I don't want to be completely useless, either.

Supervisor: Your feeling, your gut feeling is that she tried to turn it into a social visit. And I'm wondering what your sense is, going on that feeling, what she might by trying to accomplish.

Nancy: She's just avoiding, I think, and trying to make it all seem nice, when ... and afraid of the real feelings. Afraid of putting it out, afraid of the pain. Breaking down, or whatever. And feeling that she's on the verge of tears.

Supervisor: She has a good pattern of avoidance. Her whole family does that. Do you want to try that interview again with me? I'll play Louise....

Nancy: And you're saying how nice it is now, everything's just fine.

Supervisor (role playing): I really had a bad time, but I'm feeling really good now, and it's going to be okay when I get home.

Nancy: How do you know it's going to be okay when you get home?

Supervisor: Well, I can really feel it's going to be okay. I just know, 'cause it was really bad before and I think I know what to do now. It's really going to be good now.

Nancy: Well, I kind of ...

Supervisor: But I still want to see you.

Nancy: Yeah. I feel, I guess I should just say, "I don't think we're getting anywhere the way we're talking. Because it's all just surface niceties and I can feel that there's a lot of pain in you—you're almost crying right now, and you're saying everything's just great. And I just don't believe it. How are you really feeling?"

Supervisor: You know what that does for me. I feel really scared.

Nancy: How?

Supervisor: Like I really feel, wham, you hit me.

Nancy: Oh dear, oh dear.

Supervisor: No, it's good.

Nancy: Is it?

Supervisor: Yeah.

Nancy: I thought it was too heavy.

Supervisor: No, I mean, it was heavy, but I'm not sure what I'm going to do with it, being Louise. I don't know Louise that well, but I feel you really connected with me. Have you talked to Louise that way?

Nancy: I came close to it today and I just didn't think.... I wanted to talk to you about it because I just didn't know what my role was there.

Supervisor: I felt really good. You saw my tears, you acknowledged them, you read behind my tears to my pain, and you refused to believe me. You called it the way it was. Part of me was scared to death, but part of me really liked it. I guess, up to now, you have also been avoiding.

Nancy: I think I have been.

Supervisor: You're avoiding like she's avoiding.

Nancy: I think I was, and I don't know what my role is, because I'm afraid I won't know what to do. I think I'd better clarify exactly what my role is and then I'll feel more comfortable.

Supervisor: That avoidance thing is deadly.

Nancy: Yeah, I really let it go this morning.

Supervisor: So, how did that feel, trying that out?

Nancy: It felt a lot better. It felt a lot more real to me, because I was beginning to feel like, like a visitor (laughs). Which is. . . .

Supervisor: I've been in that spot before, it's an easy spot to get into. When we're working with people and we're confronted with their problems, because their problems seem so overwhelming, it's easy for us to avoid them . . . because we feel inadequate. I don't know where to go with this girl. You know, obviously she has really deep problems. All these psychiatrists have been poking around at her, and nobody knows the answer.

This brief excerpt shows how Nancy began to face the issues of clarity of role, denial on the part of the client, and some of her own feelings which made it difficult for her to reach behind the facade of denial and to demand real work (see the following section). In a sense, the supervisor modeled the demand by reaching behind the general discussion of clients and the worker's own denial ("everything seems to be going all right") and getting into the specific details of the work. Thus, effective teaching by supervisors involves a continuous moving between specific analysis of the worker's practice and the generalizations which emerge from that practice.

If a supervisor senses resistance to such a discussion, the worker's feelings should be explored. The worker may be unsure of the supervisor's intent or may have had poor experiences with supervisors in the past who were punitive in their comments. As the purpose of the discussion becomes clear, and the supervisor is supportive rather than judgmental or harsh, the worker may be more open to this kind of help. If resistance is still present the supervisor must make a demand for work, since discussion of the specifics of the interview is critical if help is to be offered. A supervisor who feels comfortable about offering this kind of help will find it easier to make this demand.

Making a demand for work

Schwartz's notion of the demand for work (described in the super-visory context in Chapter 3) is based on the assumption that clients feel some ambivalence about the work to be done. In part the client is reaching out to solve problems and deal with life, to take responsi-bility for actions; in another part the client wants to avoid this necessity. A client may want to discuss painful feelings, for example, but at the same time may be afraid of them. This ambivalence results in both willingness to work and resistance.

There are many forms of resistance. Clients may not return to the agency or may miss an appointment following a particularly difficult session, refuse to be serious about the work, or avoid dealing with difficult areas and feelings. Workers may report sessions that appear to be an illusion of work, lacking in substance and feeling. Apathy, acting out, and passive resistance are other ways clients resist mov-ing into difficult areas. The important point for workers to under-stand is that resistance is often a sign that the work is going well, rather than a sign that it is going badly. When ambivalence is under-stood more clearly and resistance is seen as *part of the work,* they can recognize the importance of being prepared to make a demand for work on the client, rather than becoming discouraged and easing up.

When a positive relationship has been established within a clear contract, and the worker has demonstrated a capacity for empathy and understanding of a client's feelings, then it is possible for the worker to make clear demands on the client to act in his or her own interests. The client may initially get angry at the worker's demand, but that is exactly what is needed from the worker. In all life situa-tions, people who care about each other are willing to take risks by making demands on each other.

Specific skills workers can use in making a demand for work include partializing, holding to focus, challenging the illusion of work, and facilitative confrontation. *Partializing* is used to help clients who present numerous problems with which they are having difficulty. It is often a way of saying, "Look, there's nothing I can do." By breaking overwhelming problems into more manageable parts, the worker is, in effect, demanding work from the client. Then, when clients begin to work on one part of a problem, it is not unusual for them to switch from one concern to another as soon as the worker gets close. The skill of *holding to focus* entails asking clients to stay on a particular issue until it is resolved. The following example shows how a worker partialized a client's multiple problem and held the client to focus:

> It was our first session together. Mrs. C told me that her son (16) has been suspended from school and had gotten into a fight with a neighbor. The neighbor had complained to the landlord and now he was threatening to evict her. The neighbor had also come to see her and had been abusive and threatening. When she had talked to her son to try to get him to apologize, he had gotten angry and had stormed out of the house. She wasn't sure what to do about anything. I told her I could see it was an upsetting time for her. I pointed out she had to deal with the school, her landlord, her neighbor, and, most difficult of all, her son. I said I thought it would help if we could take things one at a time. Where would she like to start? She said the landlord's threats were most frightening to her. I asked her to tell me about the conversation with the landlord.

By partializing this problem, the worker made it more manageable. As the conversation continued, however, the client shifted back to the school suspension, and the worker needed to hold to focus:

> Mrs. C. said she couldn't promise the landlord her son would behave, since he was suspended from school, and hanging around the house all the time led to trouble. She went on to talk about the call from the school principal. I asked if we could stick to the landlord for a moment, and then discuss the call with the principal. I could see they were connected problems, but it would help if we stayed with one at a time.

Another form of making a demand for work is the skill of *challenging the illusion of work*. A worker who finds sessions with a client boring and lacking in substance and feeling, and who believes that the client feels the same way, may sense that they are getting nowhere. By challenging the illusion of work, the worker can call attention to the pattern. It is important to make it clear that the client is not being accused of having *created* the illusion of work and the worker is merely pointing it out to help both of them explore its meaning. The worker might say, for example, "I've been thinking about our last few sessions. It seems to me the discussion has been superficial. We haven't gotten our teeth into anything important. I wonder if you have any ideas why that's so." Opening up the discussion in this way can encourage the client to suggest a reason why the discussion is difficult; the work may have entered a taboo area, such as sexual relations, for example. As the client discusses the difficulty of talking to the worker about sex, the work will turn from illusion to substance.

The skill of facilitative confrontation is illustrated in an example in the next section which tells how a worker shared her anger in confronting Mark, a teenaged client who was making no effort on his own behalf at school. This was done effectively and in a facilitative manner because a good working relationship had been developed. Used prematurely, the skill could be experienced by the client as evidence of the worker's harshness and lack of understanding. The proper blend of caring and demand is subtle and difficult to achieve, as was noted in the supervision context in Chapter 3. Workers are often either demanding *or* empathic; usually, they find it difficult to make an empathic demand. Since this is a problem in all human relationships, it is no wonder that it is difficult in the helping professions. Workers who are empathic and understanding can develop a good relationship with clients but are not necessarily helpful. Workers who are just demanding are rejected by clients as being harsh. Workers who put the two together appear to be most effective.

Supervision Approaches. The supervisor's discussions of worker practice often uncover moments when workers felt like making a demand but were uncomfortable about it. They describe being bored in an interview or upset because a client keeps making commitments but never follows them through. They have moments when they feel angry at a client but are afraid to let the client know because, they say, they fear taking too much responsibility for their clients' lives.

By examining these moments and helping workers understand the interplay between demand and caring, the supervisor can help them to trust their own instincts in most situations. It is not unprofessional to care whether a client makes it or not, and the client needs to know that the worker cares. One does not take away the right to self-determination by demanding that people act in their own self-interest. In fact, the client often desperately needs just such a demand in order to take the next step.

In discussions of the demand for work, workers often reflect on the general difficulty of making demands in life situations, as with friends, children, or spouses. Such discussions can be helpful if they focus on how this difficulty affects their practice with clients. One reason workers may avoid making a demand is that they lack confidence in their ability to help. If a worker says, in effect: "If I make a demand on a client and he takes me up on it, then what will I do?" this is an indication to the supervisor of a need for help in developing and deepening the worker's own work phase skills. It is also often a cue that the worker is concerned about handling feelings.

As with the other practice skills, the supervisor's demonstration of the power of making a demand for work is helpful. Workers may be very resistant, for example, about sharing their material with supervisors and other colleagues by the use of process recordings or videotapes. Their negative reactions to being asked to use these techniques often serve as covers for their fears about the unknown. By their resistance they are waiting to see if the supervisor can be put off by their answer to the demand for work. The supervisor who recognizes this will empathize with the workers while making his or her expectations about the work clear.

One way supervisors can usefully apply their own work phase skills with workers in order to illustrate a practice skill is by demonstrating the power of the demand for work on job management. Supervisors who set clear expectations about how workers are to manage their agency responsibilities and who also are open to consideration of the realities of the job situation help workers become more responsible. Making a demand for work is also especially helpful when a worker is in personal trouble. Supervisors must be empathic about the strains faced by workers experiencing marital difficulties or other personal problems and the effects these can have on their work, and they can often be helpful in referring workers for outside help. However, it is not helpful to stop making expectations of workers or to try to cover for a worker who is having a hard time. It is better for the supervisor to maintain expectations about the work and thus help troubled workers to function effectively in the work place, which can in turn help them deal with their personal problems.

The following example, in which a supervisor requests a worker to share the details of his practice with process recordings, illustrates the demand for work coupled with empathy:

> I told Frank that I was expecting to get some of his material on his first interview so we could discuss how he began. I hadn't received it and wondered why. Frank said he'd been very busy that week. I told

him I realized the load was heavy, but I thought he would have had time to dictate some notes on that interview. He paused and then said that he wasn't sure why it was necessary to do that. Frank had stiffened and looked quite defensive at that point.

I told him that I had sensed that there might be some reluctance on his part to do it, and perhaps this would be a good time to discuss it. I asked why he felt it wasn't necessary. He said he couldn't see the purpose, and anyway he didn't think he could remember what went on at the sessions. I said that developing the skill of recall was a difficult one. I asked if he had ever written anything like this before. He said he had not. I told him perhaps part of the problem was that I could have been more helpful in describing what it was I was asking for. I asked if he understood. He said he wasn't clear, so I explained that I did not want the whole interview but rather just some brief comments about the conversation in the beginning, a summary of how the interview went, some more detail about any parts he was interested in discussing, and how it ended. I told him I thought it wasn't easy as a new worker to share his work with me, but I wanted to reassure him that I wasn't asking in order to just snoop, or to be critical. I felt that if I had some of the detail of what he was saying and doing with his clients I might be more helpful to him.

I asked him if it was true that he had been concerned about what I would do with the records. He said he was, and that he felt that the first interview hadn't gone very well at all. He was embarrassed to present it. I told him I didn't expect these interviews to go perfectly and that I thought by going over some of his work with clients I might be able to help him identify what he did that went well, as well as what he could do better. I then asked if he could recreate from memory some of the details of this first interview. I would try to show what I meant. I said I was willing to work from his memory of the experience, this time, but that the next time I would be expecting a written record.

It was important for the supervisor to explore the worker's feelings about using the record material, while at the same time making it quite clear that the material was expected.

There would be a slightly different problem in encouraging use of process recordings by experienced workers, who may not have had such experiences or training in their previous practice. Such workers may feel they are expected to know more than they really do, and they are embarrassed about sharing their uncertainties with their supervisors. A problem also arises if recordings have been used in a punitive manner. If they are used to draw mistakes to the workers' attention routinely, with no demonstration of empathy or support, they may give the idea that workers are expected to be perfect, and an experience such as this can become a block to any future use of the technique. A supervisor who uses recordings to explore past experiences with the workers and then tries to help them sort out how they could have done better frees the workers to take chances. In any case, they should be expected to meet the demand for work, in spite of their past experiences.

An important element in making the demand for work is that the helping person—worker or supervisor—is assuring the other person —client or worker—of faith in the ability to take the next step. People in general do not want others to give up on them. Even if workers appear to be asking a supervisor to back off, they will often be disappointed if the supervisor does so.

Some supervisors fear that if they ask workers to provide details or evidence of their work they will be expected to help with it, as we noted in Chapter 3. Since supervisors often are still learning with their right hands while they are teaching with their left, some uncertainty should be expected. When the supervisor's uncertainty is matched by the workers, however, the result can be an illusion of work.

Sharing own feelings

In their interactions with clients, workers experience many normal emotions. Nevertheless, in some models of the helping professions, expression of one's own feelings while working with clients is considered unprofessional. According to the practice theory developed by Schwartz, however, this forces an artificial dichotomy between the personal and the professional. Rather, he maintains, feelings can be used professionally, as long as they are related to the worker's function and the purpose of the encounter. A worker can —and should—spontaneously share such feelings as frustration, anger, and caring for clients. Clients find it easier to trust such a worker, who they describe as being "a real person."

Workers must seek to develop the same capacity to express feelings that they expect of their clients, as well as the ability to express their feelings spontaneously. As they deepen their understanding of their function they will learn to avoid making such mistakes as expressing feelings that are not helpful to clients. If a client comes on strong, for example, expressing concerns by making an angry attack on the worker, the worker needs to respond honestly at the moment, with real feelings. With experience, however, workers develop the ability to see past the anger and understand the hurt that is underneath, which makes them see that a better response might be to reach for that hurt. This ability will never be acquired, however, if workers are constantly monitoring their own feelings and are afraid to take risks. If they make mistakes, they can always apologize later. Clients are more accepting of workers who are honest and apologize when they make a mistake than they are of those who appear to be paragons of virtue, always cool, objective, and composed.

In the following example, the worker's expression of feeling was critical. The example is drawn from the ending phase of work with an adolescent teenager about to leave the care of the agency. Mary had known the worker for two years, and an intimate relationship had developed. During the conversation the worker revealed her feelings about Mary, saying:

> "I was beginning to think about the fact that we only have a couple of more sessions together. To be honest with you, although I'm glad you're going to be able to move out on your own now and start to be independent, I'm going to miss you." There was a long silence and I could sense that Mary was struggling for composure. She said, "You were the best worker I've ever had. I could always talk to you when I had things on my mind. I'm a little afraid about who I'm going to talk to now." I said, "Can you say some more about what it was about me that you thought made me the best worker?"

By asking the client for the specific qualities she found helpful, the worker can help her begin to think about the transition she will need to make to other support systems such as family or friends. If she is aware of the qualities she had found helpful in the worker, she may be able to find people with the same characteristics. An important conversation was taking place between the worker and the client about their parting; it might not have occurred if the worker had not honestly expressed her own feelings.

Being honest about feelings includes a willingness to share the anger and frustration workers often feel when they think a client is not trying. For example, after months of helping a client through a difficult school situation, a worker found out that Mark, the client, was again avoiding doing homework and was about to be suspended. The worker felt frustrated and angry at the waste of all of her efforts. She told Mark:

> I want you to know I'm really mad that you are just ready to blow everything at school. We've put a lot of time and effort into this, getting you back in, sorting out the problems you had with your teacher. Things were starting to straighten out, but now, you seem willing to just let your life get screwed up. Damn it all, that makes me frustrated and mad.

Mark responded with anger and said that it wasn't any of the worker's business. It was his own life and he would do with it as he wished. The interview ended on this note. At the next session, however, Mark reported he had seen the teacher, had gone over the missed assignments, and had worked out a plan for what he had to do to catch up. The demand, the anger, the frustration, all of which represented real caring on the part of the worker, were critical in helping this client take a next step on his own behalf.

Supervision Approaches. A review of client interviews is a helpful way to teach the skills of sharing feelings. Inquiring what workers felt at particular moments when the supervisor thinks they might have been upset or angry, for example, can encourage them to share these feelings. They may also share their thoughts about spontaneity and sharing feelings, not just in practice but in life generally. This provides an opportunity for the supervisor to empathize with the difficulty of sharing feelings, while pointing out how it might have helped in a particular instance. The supervisor might say, for example, "If you had leveled with the client right at that moment, how do you think she might have reacted?" In thinking about how the client would have responded, it often becomes clear that leveling could have brought a positive reaction.

Workers often respond to an exercise such as this with a comment like: "It seems so simple; I don't know why I don't do it." This opens up discussion of the difficulties of sharing feelings in our society and provides an opportunity to point out how the worker can be professional and personal simultaneously. Most important, the supervisor can use the exercise to give the worker permission to make mistakes. I often suggest to a worker who has made a mistake when being spontaneous with a client that it was "a good mistake." It was good because the worker was honest, and it was a mistake because it was not directly related to the current concerns of the client, or there was a better way of dealing with the client's problem. When the supervisor believes in the importance of spontaneity, learning is seen as a process in which the worker makes mistakes, analyzes them, learns from the analysis, goes back and corrects the mistake, and then makes more sophisticated mistakes. This provides a sense of freedom which allows workers to explore their own skills in this area.

The skills in sharing one's own feelings are easiest to teach when they are actively modeled. Anger, a common reaction in human relationships, is one of the feelings we are usually taught to suppress. When supervisors are angry with workers, it is a mistake to get angry "professionally" instead of being honest about it. Professional anger is usually less direct, colder, and more hurtful than real anger. Workers who find, perhaps after some time, that they can have a positive relationship with their supervisors which includes caring as well as anger, and that getting angry does not destroy a relationship, are freed to experiment in the same way with clients.

Sharing data

Another important skills factor for workers is the ability to share data with clients in a meaningful way. In this sense data (as noted in the supervision context, Chapter 3) includes information, facts, values, and beliefs held by the worker that may be relevant and helpful to the client in a particular instance. This is an area of much confusion in the helping professions; workers may consider it improper to provide data to clients because they should figure things out for themselves, and clients may want access to the worker's data but do not want it imposed on them as the "truth." Workers who realize that their knowledge, beliefs and values are only one part of reality are able to make them available to clients without feeling the need to convince them.

The notion of presenting ideas as open to challenge runs contrary to many views about how people help. Workers have become so used to being "sold" on ideas that they may believe they are only effective if they can sell their ideas to their clients. The opposite is true; they are more effective when they make their ideas available rather than trying to impose them. Clients will use information or values or beliefs only when they perceive their importance; in fact, they may reject ideas they feel are being sold to them by the worker. If information is shared at a time when it is not relevant to the client, it will not be used. Workers who suggest a client "needs to know" something in an area that is unrelated to the client's sense of urgency will be perceived as pursuing their own interests.

Workers should feel free to share their ideas directly. Trying to lead the client to answer, as by asking questions that will get the client to give the answer the worker wants, often shifts the work away from the client's task. Instead of working on the problem, the client attempts to figure out what it is the worker wants. Workers therefore should make their data available directly, making sure they are related to the client's urgency and leaving the client free to use the ideas or reject them.

The following excerpt is from the records of a worker who was asked for her opinion by a young unmarried mother faced with a decision whether or not to keep her child:

> I explained to Dora that she was asking a tough question. In the last analysis she was going to have to make that decision, and only she really knew whether she could keep the baby or not. I asked her why she was asking me at this point, what was troubling her. She went on to tell me that a part of her wanted to keep the baby but she was afraid that she was so young she would have nothing left of her life if she did. On the other hand, she kept thinking of what it would be like if she gave the baby up and felt guilty for not being more responsible.
>
> I acknowledged some of those feelings, telling her it was not unusual to feel both at exactly the same time. I told her it was a tough decision, because no matter which way she went it was going to hurt. I then went on to say that, from the agency's point of view, there was no indication that she would be an unfit mother. Therefore, the choice was really up to her. From getting to know her over these weeks, however, I had the sense that the biggest part of her really wanted to have more time to experience life. If this was true, she probably would be better off in the long run if she placed the child than if she tried to keep it because she felt guilty.
>
> I paused and there was silence. I said, "I've just told you how I felt, but I don't think that really helps very much. In the end, it still has to be your decision because you have to live with it." She nodded and said she knew that was true. She then went on to say it helped for her to take in other points of view and that she really had wanted to know how I saw things.

Supervision Approaches. By exploring workers' feelings of responsibility for providing information, the supervisor can be helpful in sorting out the differences between their opinions and reality. When the supervisor sees that they are trying to sell their ideas to clients, it is often possible to identify the clients' resistance and to demonstrate that clients cannot be easily "changed." When the supervisor senses that workers are holding back, it is helpful to explore their mixed feelings about giving advice and sharing their own views.

Practice research findings have indicated that better working relationships may be developed by workers who freely offer their own ideas to clients and leave the clients free to reject them (Shulman, 1978). Workers can be helped to understand this from their own experience with the supervisor. Asking how workers would feel if the supervisor had some information they needed but held it back so that they might learn it for themselves, for example, can help them understand clients' similar feelings.

Skills in sharing data are most closely related to the educational function, as noted in Chapter 3. The supervisor has to recognize that workers, like clients, must learn by themselves; they have to develop their own ideas and insights as they go along. Even ideas that most supervisors are very clear about have to be learned anew by workers, and time must be allowed for them to assimilate ideas that supervisors have developed over a period of years. Supervisors can be helpful as guides along the way, and if their views are qualified and shared in an undogmatic way, workers will find them helpful.

Sometimes a supervisor suspects that a worker accepts too easily whatever the supervisor says. In such a case discussion of the authority theme is in order. Helping workers to keep the supervisor in perspective and to use her or him as a resource for the workers' own learning is a part of the supervision process.

Monitoring Skills Development

Supervisors are most directly involved in monitoring the skill development of beginning workers, however some ongoing supervision must also be provided for those with experience. The process of examining skill development contributes to effective practice at any level of the worker's experience.

Beginning skill development

This section discusses the order and timing of skill development for beginning workers, to give supervisors a general standard against which workers' progress can be measured and evaluated. The description is based on workers' professional development during the first six months of practice. It assumes they have had a varied case load, a chance to discuss the work with a supervisor, and other training opportunities.

The following pattern can be expected in developing practice skills. At the end of six months workers should have some beginning skills at making clear statements of their purpose and role, and they should be making efforts to reach for client feedback. They should be somewhat tuned in to the client's feelings and concerns in first interviews. They should be beginning to reach for the issue of the authority theme as it emerges in the first sessions. It is probable that they will have difficulty with strong negative feelings from clients. They will need more experience to develop the confidence to handle really tough clients and to make demands for work in the face of strong client resistance.

Workers at this stage should be listening for indirect cues, but they find it hard to pick them up in the first sessions. In the first months workers should be able to show their interest and concern for clients. They should be listening and trying to understand the client's problems and points of view as well as learning to contain themselves until they are clear about the sessional contract. Their efforts at dealing with feelings will be apparent in tentative steps to reach for the client's affect or feelings and to articulate them. These skills should be strengthened during the first year. Efforts to deal with affect will often seem artificial as workers struggle to develop ways of putting feelings into their own words. Imitation of the supervisor may be a first step in this process.

The skill of reaching for negative feedback will not be evident until the worker develops greater confidence in the work. This often comes after the first year of practice. The ability to share new feelings spontaneously is a difficult skill to develop, but there should be evidence that it is being used with greater freedom during the second year.

The skill of sharing data *when relevant* should be evidenced, as well as a willingness to leave the client free to accept the worker's ideas, or not.

As this summary suggests, there should be limited expectations for skill development by beginning workers. Actual progress will vary, depending on what the worker brings to the situation and the success of the supervisory relationship. As noted in chapter 3, the supervisor must not forget how difficult the development of core skills can be or be too easily frustrated by the time required for workers to develop these skills. If contracting, listening, empathy, and evidence of honesty of feelings emerge in the first six months, the worker should be considered to be learning the skills satisfactorily.

Supervision of experienced workers

Practice supervision of new workers is the most critical period for supervisory effort. Nevertheless, skill development is continuous, and workers who have had some experience also need supervisory help. This may take the form of consultation or of group discussion in which staff members can provide mutual aid.

Limitations of time and other resources often make it difficult for supervisors to provide detailed help to workers on an ongoing basis. Some monitoring of skill development is important, however, because if workers do not continue to examine their own practices, they will lose the skills they have already developed. Tools that can help workers analyze their own work include tape recordings, client feedback instruments, and videotapes. Experienced workers need to be encouraged to utilize these techniques on an ongoing basis, even though supervisors may not be as intensively involved.

With experienced workers, supervisors must be sensitive to possible defensiveness caused by guilty feelings about past cases. Being asked to discuss a particular piece of work with a supervisor often recalls associations to other clients. In such a session the worker's eyes may take an a dazed expression as the worker appears to turn off. The supervisor who recognizes that the worker may be associating to past clients has an opportunity to explore the worker's feelings about unsatisfactory client experiences. Experienced workers who appear defensive on a particular issue are often sending a signal to the supervisor that the area is one where they have self-doubts. They need a great deal of support at this point to help them moderate their harsh views of themselves. The supervisor should point out that they have only been able to offer clients what they had at the time they worked with them, and they should not hold themselves responsible for more than that. They need to focus instead on what they will do for their present and future clients. Helping workers be less harsh on themselves and less judgmental is often the most important way a supervisor can help them open up their practice to a continuous process of learning from their experiences.

Research Findings

In our supervision study (Shulman, Robinson, and Luckyj, 1981), which has been described in the Research Findings sections of this book, workers were asked to identify what they would like to have discussed in their supervision contacts, as compared to the actual content of these contacts (see Table 1.2 in Chapter 1). Their first preference was that supervisors should devote more time to teaching practice skills, followed by more time on discussing research information and providing feedback on performance. Such supervision-consulting roles also were the favored tasks of supervisors queried in the study (see Table 1.1).

Other findings in respect to the content of supervision, contact frequency, and the educational role of the supervisor also were reported in some detail in Chapter 1, and the findings in relation to the sharing of data, largely a teaching function, were discussed in Chapter 3. Positive correlations were found, for example, between a supervisor's helpfulness and the percentage of time invested in the teaching role ($r = 0.32$), the sharing of research findings and child welfare theory ($r = 0.50$), the worker's perception of the supervisor as knowledgeable about policies and procedures ($r = 0.61$), and the supervisor's sharing of data ($r = 0.65$).

Other research has supported the idea that both supervisors and supervisees regard the educational function of supervision as important and a source of satisfaction. In the Kadushin (1973) study, two of the three strongest sources of supervisor satisfaction were found to be related to helping the supervisee grow and develop professionally and sharing social work knowledge and skill. In the same study, workers indicated that two of the three main sources of their satisfaction with supervision were receiving help in dealing with clients and in developing as professionals. In another study by Scott (1969), professionally oriented workers expressed a preference for supervisors who knew their theoretical fundamentals, were skilled in teaching, and were capable of offering professional assistance.

The idea of the parallel processes of work with clients and supervision of staff, which provides the basis for the relation of the skills of supervision to the skills of workers in this chapter, is based on the similarity of the dynamics of supervision and worker-client dynamics. Doehrman's (1972) study of eight sets of concurrent supervisor-supervisee relationships over a 20-week period indicated that patterns in the supervisor-worker interaction are similar to those in the worker-client engagement. A study by Arlow (1963) also supported this position.

The parallel processes idea also suggests that supervisors themselves need help and support if they are to provide these for their workers. Our own supervision study found that stress, for example, is not as strongly associated with being an effective supervisor as is access to ongoing emotional support.

Summary

The dynamics and skills of the educational function of supervision discussed in this chapter are based on underlying assumptions about teaching and learning. The supervisor's knowledge of the subject area and ability to transmit ideas clearly are central to teaching, but they are only part of the process. The task for supervisors is to mediate between the learner and the subject areas to be learned. In teaching core practice skills to workers, supervisors must demonstrate the same skills they teach. Modeling the use of these skills in supervision practice is an effective way of teaching their use in the worker-client context.

A basis for monitoring and evaluating the development of these skills can be found in a profile of the skill development pattern of the average new worker (or student) and the suggestions provided for dealing with the special problems of educational supervision of experienced workers.

Chapter 5

Supervision of Staff Groups

In the work of supervision which is done in the group context rather than on an individual basis, the supervisor deals with both formal and informal staff groups. The formal groups are easiest to conceptualize: staff meetings, group supervision, committee meetings, and other occasions for staff members to come together on a more or less formal basis. A good share of a supervisor's time, however, is devoted to dealing with the dynamics of the informal group, the unstructured collective of staff members which is in operation continually, not only during scheduled sessions. This informal group consists of all staff members who have ongoing interactions with one another as they carry out their tasks. Even though the professional staff may be the only group represented at staff meetings, for example, its informal group interactions with the clerical staff can powerfully affect the delivery of services. Indeed, in many supervisory situations the most important interactions take place in the informal group while the formal staff may take on the character of a charade in which the staff members and the supervisor merely go through the motions, creating what has been described as an illusion of work.

This chapter will look at how the supervisor can intervene to make formal group occasions such as meetings more effective, as well as how to deal with issues arising in the informal system. Since a single chapter cannot do justice to a subject as potentially rich as this one, it considers only those problems, dynamics, and examples that have been raised most often in my supervisors' workshops and that illustrate the most common concerns of supervisors. The group work aspects of this model are explored in more detail in my text on practice (Shulman, 1979), in which a major part (consisting of nine chapters) describes group work skills. The parallels between worker-client and supervisor-worker relationships which have been drawn in preceding chapters are evident again in the parallels between client groups and staff groups formed to work on the business of the agency or other institutional setting.

The focus of the chapter has also been limited to direct line supervision work, even though much of the content can easily be applied to middle- and upper-level administrators. One illustration deals with a nursing supervisor and her nursing staff, for example, but the head of a a nursing department could draw parallels to a group of nursing supervisors. In workshops I have conducted for administrators, many of their themes and concerns have proved to be similar to supervisors', only one or more levels removed from direct line practice. Whereas a social work supervisor might struggle to deal with the conflict between clerical and professional staff, a hospital administrator might have to tackle a conflict between the head of nursing and the chief of hospital maintenance, for example.

One aspect of group supervision discussed in the following chapter, is the part of the supervisory task involved in helping the staff to deal with the working environment, such as the work the supervisor must do when an administrative decision creates an angry backlash by workers demanding to know which side she or he is on. The dilemma of feeling caught in the middle is an important one in supervision work.

The chapter begins with some general comments about the dynamics of supervisory work with staff groups and the potential advantages of mutual aid groups. This is followed by a section on the beginning phase of work with a staff group that examines questions of group purpose and the supervisor's role. The section on work phase issues describes the development of a group culture, various roles of individuals in groups, and group conflict. The authority theme as related to group-supervisor relationships is examined in a separate section. Examples in these sections deal with both formal and informal groups. The section on endings and transitions focuses on the dynamics involved when a supervisor or staff member leaves a staff group and discusses some of the skills that can turn endings into productive experiences.

The Dynamics of Supervisory Work With Staff Groups

It is easy to see why the following question of usefulness of groups is often raised by supervisors: "Who needs them?" Most supervisors are even less well trained for their group leadership responsibilities than they are for their individual supervision tasks. Individual supervision can at least seem close to the work they are comfortable with, such as individual counseling, but supervisors often bring to their tasks a dread of group leadership derived from their own unsatisfactory experiences. Perhaps a group they led in the past went badly, leaving them feeling miserably responsible and incompetent. Every one has participated in groups of some sort, and, because there are so many ways groups can go wrong without effective leadership (and even at times, with effective leadership), poor experiences are more likely than positive ones. No wonder new supervisors face their first staff groups with less than total enthusiasm, sometimes, as one nursing supervisor told me, feeling "scared spitless."

Since minimal training in group processes is usually available and little can be expected in the way of ongoing assistance, some supervisors try to avoid group sessions completely or to have as few as possible. They use procedures for dealing with the sessions that they have derived from their experience as participants, because that is all they have to go on. All too often they adopt ineffective or boring practices which they know are unhelpful. Perhaps a worker has experienced staff meetings at which the supervisor read administrative directives with his or her face buried in the paper, looking up occasionally to ask if there were any questions and then quickly moving on to the next item on the agenda when the group responded with silence. Without other training or better examples to follow, this worker will do the same in a supervisory capacity, despite knowing exactly what the group participants are thinking and feeling about the meeting.

The strength in numbers represented by the staff group makes it a potent force for supervisors to deal with. If a supervisor senses negative feedback in the workers' comments or nonverbal expressions, it is easy to understand why he or she might not reach for it. Supervisors who feel overly responsible for a group's session often have difficulty tolerating silences and immediately assume that they are doing something wrong. Interestingly enough, these same supervisors may understand the meaning of silences in work with clients very well and recognize the need to deal with the underlying communications.

Because of their own powerful feelings of inadequacy and their fears of being disliked or of being judged incompetent, many supervisors seem to find that even their most elementary skills escape them when they must face a staff group. Their lack of confidence in themselves can lead them to adopt the strategy of leaving the difficult or most contentious items to the last on the agenda, knowing that they may not be reached or there will be so little time left to deal with them that the discussion will be superficial.

In spite of such difficulties, staff groups can be a potent force for carrying on the work of the agency or other setting. They cannot be positive forces, however, if they are simply left to themselves. Effective leadership is needed to help staff members release the potential for mutual aid and constructive work existing within each staff group, both formal and informal, and to learn to work together effectively. The obstacles that emerge in the normal course of events are not signals of the impossibility of working effectively as a group; rather they are agenda items for the group leader and the staff members to address.

If supervisors simply see a staff meeting as a convenient way of communicating directly to all staff members simultaneously, they might as well save their time and circulate a memo. They may fear that the staff will not read the memo, but what makes them think it will listen at a meeting? Whenever the staff is brought together for a committee meeting, an administrative session, or for group supervision, the supervisor must understand and facilitate the active role of all the participants. If group supervision is to be meaningful, for example, it is important to establish what other staff members are expected to do as a worker shares practice examples. Rather than sitting quietly as observers, patiently waiting their turn, they can be actively involved in the process if they are shown the ways they can be helpful. It is naive to assume that workers know how to participate, particularly in the beginning phase of a group's development, or to assume that they will do so easily if they do know how to get involved. They need some instruction and support as they try to get engaged, and regular demands for work must be placed on them by the supervisor.

The mutual aid process

The supervisor must risk and invest in an effort to make the staff group effective instead of an illusion, but the benefits can be immense. Positive group morale and a supportive atmosphere may be developed. Staff apathy, often the signal of underlying problems in the formal and informal systems, can be relieved, thus releasing the workers' potential to contribute to the service.

There are a number of specific ways in which an effective staff group can provide help to workers. One way is through the mutual sharing of data. The supervisor is not the only source of information; staff members can draw on their own life and work experiences and share facts, values, ideas, or beliefs that may be valuable to others.

A second form of mutual aid comes from the clash of ideas during debates as members share their views on a question under discussion. Group members can risk their tentative ideas and use the group as a sounding board—a place for their views to be challenged and possibly changed. In this kind of group culture, the argument between two or more members is dialectical: group members listen as one member presents the thesis and the other the antithesis. Then each member can use the discussion to develop a synthesis. It is not always easy to challenge ideas in a group, however, and a later section will describe how such a culture for work can be developed.

The section on developing a culture for work in the work phase in groups also discribes the third way in which mutual aid can operate: opening up discussion in a taboo area. Each staff member brings to the group the norms of behavior and implied taboos of our society's culture. The staff group, a microsociety, quickly recreates the rules of the larger culture. Workers thus may experience direct talk about certain subject areas, such as authority, sex, or dependency, as taboo. Each worker will feel power of the taboo differently. Some may be more ready than others to take a risk and move into the area of discussion. If staff members are upset with a supervisory decision, for example, they may act it out in the form of passive resistance. A staff member who either directly or indirectly expresses the real feeling, which has been blocked by taboos against challenging people in authority, can help lead the group into a crucial area of discussion. The group will watch what happens when the member ventures into frightening territory, and if the supervisor

handles it well, encouraging rather than discouraging honest feedback, she or he will be giving the staff permission to enter a formerly
taboo area. If the supervisor does not feel comfortable enough to be
able to hear what the staff has to say, intervening will reinforce the
taboo. Unfortunately, negative feelings never just go away: they
come back to haunt the supervisor in significant ways.

A fourth form of mutual aid comes from the "all in the same boat"
feeling. As staff members listen to others and discover emotions of
their own, some which they were aware of and others which surprise
them, they can experience the relief of knowing that others feel the
same way. Their feelings are less frightening and overwhelming if
shared by others. For example, nurses who find it difficult to deal
with the sexuality of patients who "come on" to them, particularly
those they find sexually attractive, will be relieved to know that
others share this difficulty. Child welfare workers who fear the potential violence of some of their clients are helped by knowing that
their fear is a natural one and not a sign of inadequacy. Staff members may joke about sexuality and violence, but they find it difficult
to discuss these feelings seriously.

Mutual support is another way group members help one another.
In a supportive group culture, the capacity for staff members to
empathize with one another is evident. The empathy must be genuine, however, workers must not feel they are being "social worked"
by their colleagues. Since staff members experience issues in an
individual way, often different from the way the supervisor understands them, they may be in the best position to provide meaningful
support in times of trouble.

Mutual demand is also important in a group helping relationship.
Mutual aid can be provided by expectation as well as caring; that is,
group members can confront each other within a context of support.
If the supervisor helps develop the proper conditions, they may be
able to make demands on each other better than the supervisor can
and respond more easily to a peer group's demands. When a worker
is presenting case material defensively, for example, it may be most
effective for a caring fellow worker to insist that the presenter lower
the barriers and let them all in.

Other sources of help in groups are individual problem solving
and rehearsal. When staff members present a particular concern to
the staff group for advice, as the others offer suggestions they can
help themselves with their similar concerns. And when faced with

a difficult task, like a troublesome encounter with a client or an important person in the system such as a judge or doctor, group members may welcome the opportunity to rehearse and get feedback from their peers.

The following sections examine how group dynamics operate in supervisory work with staff groups, illustrating how knowledgeable (and courageous) intervention of the supervisor and the hard work of the staff can achieve effective work in both formal and informal groups.

The Beginning Phase in Groups

As in all helping processes, the staff group has a beginning phase which lays the foundations on which the supervisor and staff members build the group's work phase. This discussion focuses on the beginning phase of work with a new staff group, such as a new staff grouping or a supervisor who joins an established group, but it is also relevant to existing groups and supervisory relationships. Contracting, the essential task in the beginning phase, must not be overlooked, or even long-standing groups will be troubled by lack of clarity of purpose or definition of the supervisor's role. It is always possible for the supervisor to recontract with the staff if such vagueness seems to be present in a group.

A formal staff group generally consists of a collection of staff members who come together specifically to work on the business of the agency. It is neither a social group nor a therapeutic group, although the staff may experience it as both.

It is not a social group because there is always business to be done, and it is not a therapeutic group because it would be inappropriate to deal with personal problems or even general interpersonal difficulties such as a member's inability to get along in the group. Just as the supervisor must guard the working contract to prevent supervision from becoming personal counseling, even when the supervisee asks for it, the same clarity of purpose is necessary in the group context. If a serious personal problem, perhaps illness or marital discord, is shared in a staff meeting, the support of the staff should be focused on how the problems will affect the *work* and on what staff members can do to help in the work context. A discussion about a conflict between staff members in the informal system, such as a social worker refusing to deal with a particular nurse on a case, should be focused on the problems of delivery of service to the patient, not the social worker's or the nurse's difficulties in interaction.

The proliferation of "sensitivity" or "growth" groups in our culture may cause some confusion about the purposes of staff work groups. It is important to discuss how effectively a group is working and to deal with patterns of interaction, such as defensiveness, which are blocking the work. The purpose of such a discussion, however, is simply to free the group for more effective work, or to uncover what the pattern of interactions may indicate as a form of indirect communication. A staff member who presents a case defensively may be signaling the insecurity all staff members feel about their level of practice and ability to trust one another, for example.

The discussion, therefore, should not be focused on helping the individual members to "grow." In fact, it is essential for staff members to feel free to share their thoughts and feelings spontaneously, knowing that they will be protected by a supervisor who is clear about purpose and function and will respect their right to privacy. There are those who claim that personal therapy is needed for workers to be able to function effectively with clients. I argue that such help should be sought in appropriate places such as other agencies or with private practitioners. If the staff group takes on such tasks, I have found, it soon ceases to deal with other tasks that are appropriate and necessary. Some more appropriate and more essential purposes for staff groups are described in the following section.

Purposes of staff groups

There are four major types of purposes in formal staff groups: (1) staff meetings, (2) case consultation, (3) group supervision, and (4) in-service training. Separate groups may exist for each of these purposes, or a single group may incorporate one or more of them. There could be a staff meeting one week followed by case consultation the next, for example, or different purposes can be served during a single meeting. Since the content and dynamics of the group and the focus of the group leader differ for each purpose, clarity about group purpose can make a major difference to the group's productivity, for both the leader and the members.

Staff Meetings. Staff meetings focus on the job management aspect of the work and issues of policy and program. For example, when work must be done in order to provide a service, an appropriate discussion for a staff meeting might be the division of labor—who is to cover what shifts or handle which aspects of the case load. Other appropriate group activities are evaluating overall performance of the unit, interpreting administration policies, eliciting reactions to policies and formulating feedback, and discussing innovative programs or special needs.

Although it is important for the supervisor to develop an agenda for discussion, the staff also must have some input into the agenda-building process. In some cases a preliminary agenda is circulated and staff members are asked to add their own items. It is always important to begin each staff meeting tentatively, utilizing the sessional contracting skill described in Chapter 3 in order to detect hidden agenda items, which can exert a powerful force on a staff meeting even though they are never openly discussed.

The following example is a hospital social work supervisor's report of how she opened a session by describing the agenda and reaching for other items:

> I told them I needed to discuss the new admissions policy and what it would mean to our staff. In particular, I was interested in their views as to the impact so I could share these at the next department directors' meetings. I also had a few brief announcements, which I would share at the beginning, but that was all on my agenda. I asked if they had anything they wanted on. There was no response, so I continued with the announcements. I felt I was getting very little reaction and that I was essentially speaking to blank faces. I decided to proceed with outlining the admissions policy.

In addition to sharing her own agenda, the supervisor described why she was bringing it up. All too often, there is little clarity as to the purpose of a group discussion. Is it for information only? Is there need for a response, and what will the supervisor do with the response? Supervisors need to be clear about what they expect from the staff and must guard against the temptation of creating an illusion of democracy. In this fairly common error, the supervisor raises an issue that has already been decided on by the administration, under the guise of gaining staff input into the decision-making process. When the staff does not provide the "right" input the supervisor is stuck, and the staff soon recognizes the attempt at manipulation. It is much better to be honest about the limits of the discussion, letting the staff know whether its input or just its reaction to an already firm decision is desired. The supervisor must clarify which decisions the staff can make on its own and over which ones he or she must retain a final veto.

In the excerpt above, the supervisor invited the addition of agenda items from the staff and received none. It would have been a mistake simply to assume there were indeed none and proceed to "cover the agenda," however. As the session proceeded, the supervisor sensed the apathy and dispirited involvement of the staff. Although she passed over the first cues, she couldn't ignore their lack of enthusiasm for the discussion of the new admissions policy. Her second effort at sessional contracting went as follows:

> I stopped my recitation of the new policy and asked if there were any questions or reactions. Frank asked for an interpretation on one point, and after [I provided] the answer, the group lapsed into silence. I pointed out their lack of enthusiasm and their apparent lethargy and asked what was really going on. More silence followed. I asked if they really had something else on their minds, since they were not getting into this question of the intake policy. I had thought they had a stake in it and was very surprised.
>
> Beth said, "It's hard to worry about intake of patients if you're not sure you're going to be around to deal with them." It suddenly hit me that they were probably still upset about my comments at the end of our last meeting that indicated budget cutbacks were possible which could affect our staff complement. I asked if that was what on all their minds. There was much nodding of heads. I said, "Perhaps we can spend some time on what I know about the cutbacks, even though I don't have any real facts yet, and then we can discuss how this is hitting you and affecting your work. I know it has me worried as well, and perhaps that's why I ended up ignoring it this week. After that we can get back to the admissions issue." The staff agreed, and their involvement picked up noticeably.

There are always important issues to be discussed at staff meetings. The reason so many meetings seem boring, even to the supervisor who is leading them, is that the real agendas often stay hidden just beneath the surface. For a staff meeting to be effective, staff members have to have a stake in the work, even if it is only partial, and some opportunity must be provided so their sense of urgency will be recognized. Once this is done, the staff often is content to wait until later in the meeting to deal with its items or can even put them off until another meeting if necessary.

The supervisor in this example utilized the skills of *monitoring the process* of the meeting and *reaching for the obstacle* when she sensed the work was not real. As is often the case, the attention to process led directly to work on the task. If the supervisor had simply accepted the tone of the meeting as "the way staff meetings usually go," she would have missed an important cue to an urgent issue affecting everyone's performance. The next chapter includes an example of how a supervisor would go further with the issue of helping workers provide services in a time of cutbacks.

Case Consultation. Case consultation is a type of staff meeting that is often confused with both group supervision and in-service training. The confusion stems from the fact that practice is the central subject in each type of session; it is the organizing principle that is different.

In case consultation, the focus of the discussion is the case itself. A worker is presenting a case in order to tap fellow workers and the supervisor as sources of help in thinking through his or her work with the case, as well as where to go next. In contrast, group supervision has as its organizing principle the worker's own practice skill development. Even though specific cases may be presented, the focus is on using fellow workers and the supervisor to consider the worker's skill development and to provide help in strengthening it. The same case could be discussed in both situations, but the way the group members and the supervisor respond would differ significantly. In case consultation, the focus remains on the case, with discussion of the worker's interventions designed to facilitate service delivery. In group supervision, the focus remains on the worker. To illustrate this difference, a case consultation session on work with a family in the child welfare context is presented in this section, and the next section considers how a similar situation would be handled in group supervision.

Louise, a young, inexperienced worker, had returned from a first home visit with a young mother of two children who had been the subject of a neglect complaint. At a group session she began her presentation of the case with some facts on the family situation and then indicated that she was concerned over the mother's handling of the child while she was there. The house was not clean, there were dirty dishes in the sink, and she felt the mother was quite defensive during the interview. She wanted help on the case because she was not sure this mother was doing an adequate job, and she felt the mother might not be "workable." The supervisor's summary of the case consultation process noted:

> I told Louise that it sounded like a tough case for her to be starting with. She acknowledged she was really concerned about what to do next. I asked if anyone could get us started. Fran asked some questions about the ex-spouse and family, trying to see if there were other resources available. I commented on that being a helpful start. Louise described what she already knew and indicated that she could have explored that a bit more with the client. Ted wanted to know if any other agencies were involved. Louise indicated that a public health nurse had made some contact after the client had visited a community health team. She said she intended to contact her but was not having much luck.

At this point in the discussion the supervisor made an extremely important demand for work. As other workers began to intervene with suggestions, comments about similar clients, and so on, the supervisor asked Louise to move the discussion into some of the details of the home interview. Thus far, the staff group had very little to go on in terms of what had happened during the interview. Often, case consultation only involves using the group members' opinions to come up with a group assessment of the client and a specific treatment plan. The model behind this process is for the worker to provide the facts (study), the group to make an assessment (diagnosis), and then for the group and worker to develop an idea for next steps (treatment plan). The difficulty in this process is that the staff group finds itself trying to assess the client as if she were a discrete entity, rather than seeing her in dynamic interaction with the worker. This is a crucial distinction, since it is impossible to understand the behavior of the client unless it is considered in terms of the worker's behavior: The client is continually acting and reacting, and the worker's input may have an important impact on the proceedings. The danger is that if the staff group decides the client is "resistant" and develops a treatment plan (which may even involve eventual apprehension of the child), it will be doing so with insufficient information.

The next excerpt reports what happened when the supervisor asked Louise to do some "memory work" to recall a bit of the detail of the interaction. What did she say to the client, and what did the client say back to her? This process makes the client seem less one-dimensional; in fact, it begins to open up possibilities for her to be very "workable" indeed, if the worker handles the interview differently. The supervisor's report continued:

> I asked Louise if she could take us back a bit to the interview and share how it began. What did she say to the client, and how did the client respond? She provided some of the details, indicating she had followed through on some of the preparatory role-playing we had done and [had begun] with an honest statement of why she was there, which at the same time tried to put the client at ease. I complimented her on her opening and asked at what point in the interview she really started to worry. She described how the mother had been sitting tensely during the discussion and had shaken her four-year-old and scolded her when the child hit the two-year-old. I asked how Louise felt when that happened, and she replied, "I felt tense myself, because I began to think this might not be a good mother and I could end up in court."
>
> Phil said he could understand that, because you know it will not be pleasant down the line. Carol said it's really tough with a young mother who looks so vulnerable herself. I agreed and asked if Louise could return to the interview. What had she said to the mother? Louise described how she had suggested that the client might handle her four-year-old differently, perhaps explaining to her why she shouldn't hit the two-year-old. I asked what the client's response was, and Louise said she seemed to freeze up. According to Louise, that was when she began to feel she would not get anywhere with this client.
>
> I asked the other workers to put themselves in the client's shoes and try to tune in to how she must have been feeling. I thought this might help Louise. There was nice work on how defensive [the client] must have felt, and afraid of the worker's judgment of her; she must have worried that her children would be taken away. Phil pointed out how oppressed she must feel being at home with those two kids, no husband, no family, in fact not much of anything for herself. I wondered if this could explain part of the defensiveness that had led Louise to feel it might be hopeless to try to work with her. Louise said she had not seen the mother that way because she was too upset herself.
>
> I asked if we could consider what Louise might be able to say to this mother at her next interview which might start to help the client

lower her defenses and begin to trust Louise a bit more. Perhaps nothing would help, since the client has a part in this, but was there any way Louise could try to engage her more? The workers began to try out some opening lines, most of which focused on how uncomfortable the client must have felt when the worker last visited.

Clearly, those few minutes of effort on the supervisor's part to obtain some of the details of the interaction deepened the case consultation process in very important ways. It is the lack of *moving from the general to the specific* which often results in group desicions based on the worker's subjective feelings rather than the actual details of the interaction. The worker wanted some help on next steps (the treatment plan) which might allow work with this client. It would not have been helpful to simply agree on the client's lack of "motivation" and then begin to devise structural plans for handling the problem, such as arranging temporary foster care. These steps may be necessary at some point in the future, but certainly not at this time.

The key difference between this process, in which the worker presented details of her practice and the discussion dealt with her skills, and group supervision is the focus on the case rather than the worker. As case consultation, the process called for the supervisor to keep the group focused on the case and the next steps involved. In group supervision, the same discussion might move more deeply into the worker's struggle to find a way to establish a working relationship, while simultaneously carrying a mandated responsibility for the protection of children. Group members would be expected to harness their efforts to help the worker think through this skill development problem.

Group Supervision. Group supervision is a variation of individual supervision which is often used as a supplement to work with individual staff members. A central consideration is the professional development of the workers being supervised. All of the learning subject areas of supervision specified in Figure 4.1 in the preceding chapter—job management skills and professional practice skills, impact skills, and learning skills—may be appropriately addressed in group supervision. The supervisor uses the group to serve this purpose because of a judgment that the other staff members can make important contributions to the worker's development, not because it saves time to approach all the workers together in a group. It is important for group members to understand their role in the proceedings and to know that they will be actively involved in providing support and making demands when appropriate.

In the following example of the process, the setting is a hospital social service department. As in the excerpt above, the worker was fairly new and inexperienced. In this case, the worker, Lou, had presented the case of a family with whom he felt he was not getting anywhere. A teenaged daughter had been committed to the psychiatric ward of the hospital, and he was attempting to engage the parents but was running into resistance. The supervisor made a demand for work, encouraging Lou to present some of the details of the interaction. At the point where he reported feeling the resistance from the father, it was obvious that Lou was identifying with the daughter and missing the father's feelings. The supervisor's report of the group supervision process notes how the discussion was moved away from the case to focus on the worker, and the case example was used to provide an illustration of a learning problem:

> Lou described how he had reached for the daughter's feelings when her father [told her] he had given up hope and didn't care if she didn't come home when she left the hospital. He described how the daughter had lowered her head and started to cry softly at this point. I said I thought it must have hit him very hard. I asked where his feelings were at that moment and he said, "I was really with Lois (the daughter)." I asked what he did, and he described how he tried to get the father to understand his daughter's hurt at this comment, but that he didn't feel he had gotten too far. I said I thought that must have been very frustrating for him. I asked if anyone had any ideas which might help.
>
> Phyllis said it was tough when you saw a father hurting his daughter that way. It would make her very angry. Jane wondered whether Lou had been so mad at the father, and so identified with the daughter, that he couldn't sense the father's hurt. I noticed Lou's reflective expression and asked if he understood what Jane was saying. He said a bit. I asked Jane if she could elaborate. She went on to describe how upset the father must have been and that he was probably hiding his hurt behind a mask of indifference. He probably wouldn't want to admit he was so vulnerable. John said that it's tougher for a man, who thinks he should have these things under control.
>
> I asked if we could focus on Lou here. I enquired if Lou, or anyone else, had any idea why it was so hard to stay with Dad. Lou said it was probably the same thing that happened when he identified with that

husband last week and ended up putting the wife down—and she didn't return to the interview. I said we should stay with this: "What goes on in your feelings, Lou, what makes it so tough?" Lou said that he gets lost when people act in ways which make him mad. I said that it seemed he wanted the father to feel for the daughter, and the wife to feel for the husband, at precisely the same time he was having trouble empathizing with them.

John said, "Don't feel too bad, Lou, we are describing my problem exactly. It's so bloody hard to identify with these people." I asked Lou if this could be described as countertransference, the placing of feelings onto clients which don't necessarily belong there. He asked what I meant, and we discussed this for a while.

Some important work was taking place as the group helped Lou examine the problem of countertransference in his work—not just his work with the original family members, but his practice in general. Before the session was over, the supervisor returned to the original case to ask the group to help Lou think through how to handle the next interview with the father, and they role-played some examples. Clearly, although the content of the work was similar to that in the example of case consultation, it was the worker's development that was the central and organizing factor.

In-Service Training. Just as the case is central to case consultation and the worker is central in group supervision, it is the ideas that are central in in-service training. Countertransference, for example, might be a subject for discussion by an in-service training group. The worker just discussed, Lou, might even present the same case example, but if this were an in-service training session on the concept of countertransference, his example would be used as an illustration of the practice construct under discussion, not as a means of furthering his skills development. Other staff members would be encouraged to share their own experiences and example in the discussion, rather than having to set aside their sense of urgency about their own cases and concentrate instead on the work of the presenter. In addition, the supervisor or some of the workers might be prepared to present some background on the subject under discussion, or outside resource people might contribute ideas. The purpose of such in-service training is to deepen everyone's understanding of the subject.

Fulfilling Staff Group Purposes. Whichever purposes are adopted for a staff group, and in whatever format they are presented, the supervisor needs to clarify for the staff the general purposes of group sessions, as well as to obtain feedback on the staff's investment in those purposes. When mutual agreement on purpose has been reached and the supervisor's role has been defined (the subject of the next section) the group will have a tentative working contract. The supervisor's work will then focus on guarding that contract and helping staff members to work effectively together to serve the group's purposes.

If a supervisor has neglected to clarify the group purpose or the supervisor's role, it is always possible to recontract, even in groups which have met for years. The supervisor can offer this possibility with a comment such as: "I was thinking about our understanding of the purpose of these sessions and my role in them, and I don't think I ever made clear what my ideas where about those two issues. Perhaps, because I don't think I was always clear myself, we should start again. . . ."

Later sections in this chapter focus on a number of the problems which make it difficult for staff groups to work together. It is not unusual for members to resist fulfilling the various purposes for staff meetings. The reasons for this resistance often have a great deal to do with the group's culture for work, which is examined in some detail in the section on the work phase in groups.

The supervisor's role

Because there is confusion about the role of the supervisor in group practice, defining and clarifying this role should be undertaken directly in an early session with the staff. Nevertheless, it will take time for the role to be clearly understood and tested by staff members. The first meetings will be the testing ground, in which the staff will watch to see if the supervisor really means the role definition that has been worked out. When negative feedback on the first session is offered, often very tentatively and cautiously, the staff will watch to see how it is handled. The supervisor's true leadership style will emerge in the day-to-day operations of the staff.

Leadership Styles. Most people have had many conflicting models of group leaders in their experiences. They may have known autocratic leaders, who attempt to dominate the work using their authority; laissez-faire leaders, who pretend they have no authority, often while dominating the work in more subtle ways; and democratic leaders, whose authority emerges from the group. None of these models makes exact sense in the supervision context, but they are characteristic of the major modes of group leadership practice.

The autocratic leader who takes responsibility for the group may turn staff members into submissive group participants who act out their feelings through passive resistance (long silences) or who sabotage group decisions by such techniques as failing to implement policies. This type of leadership often provides such a tight structure that there is no freedom for innovation, no provision for group members to play constructive roles, and no room on the agenda for issues of concern to the staff. Workers clearly perceive this type of group as "owned" by the supervisor. They will take little or no responsibility for making it work effectively.

The laissez-faire approach, in contrast, makes it seem that the leader is taking no responsibility for the group. Sessions often begin with the classic: "So what do you want to talk about?" Because no structure is provided, group members may be overwhelmed and, in fact, have as little freedom as their colleagues in groups with autocratic leaders. The laissez-faire supervisor allows discussion to ramble, providing little direction and rarely, if ever, making a demand for work. In practice, while appearing to relinquish control, a leader who operates in this manner often exercises control in more subtle ways. If a staff group does not work effectively, it seems, the supervisor must make all the decisions. When the structure is so loose that group productivity is low, the real decisions on important issues will be made away from the group. Such groups may suffer from depression or else express anger toward their passive leaders. If they demand that their leaders become more autocratic, they merely substitute a different leadership problem.

The laissez-faire approach has even been institutionalized in some settings. Certain agencies, for example, have established "team approaches" in which "colleagualism" is the key word, with each participant, including the supervisor, having an equal say in the operation. These "leaderless" groups often try to solve the problem of autocratic leadership by doing away with the idea of a leader. This ultimate overthrow of authority arises from a misunderstanding of the nature of group leadership and the key functional role of the leader, without whom most groups cannot operate effectively.

Another variation on this theme of diminishing the supervisor's authority is to assign staff members the responsibility for chairing meetings in rotation. This often frustrates members, and when the problems get tough they naturally turn to the supervisor, thereby indicating that they have never really lost sight of where the authority is vested. Staff members who are asked to take on the role of leader for a session report that they can do a number of things quite well in terms of leading a group discussion, but when it comes to making a demand for work, which must be rooted in a clear sense of function, they find themselves unable to act.

Democratic leadership comes closest to the functioning of the supervisor–group leader role, but it lacks the element of external authority. In any group an internal leader may be elected or assigned the role of group leader; that is, one of the members may be asked to take on the role of helping the group operate effectively. This member's authority is derived from the group members, and when the members no longer support this leader, effective operation in the role comes to an end.

Practical experiences as well as the research on group leadership have indicated that when the democratic leadership role is well implemented, it offers the best possibilities for involving group members actively in the work of the group. It provides members with a sense of achievement, enhances group morale, and even, in the long run, gets things done effectively. I say *in the long run,* because more efficient short-term effectiveness is often possible with other forms of leadership.

The major difficulty with this type of leadership for supervision is that supervisors do not derive their authority from their workers. Rather, their authority comes from the agency or institutions which hires and fires them, holding them accountable. Supervisors are not internal leaders; they are external leaders with external authority which can both help and hinder their effectiveness. In fact, in every supervisory group an internal leader or leaders, with functions slightly different from those of the supervisor, will emerge. Thus, although in the last analysis the *ability* of supervisors to lead is derived from their workers, their *authority* to lead is externally derived.

It is important to recognize this difference openly with the staff and to clarify the role boundaries as quickly as possible. On some issues the supervisor may be responsible only for helping the staff come to a decision which concerns them. On other questions, the staff may only provide input into the deliberation process, which eventually must be resolved by the supervisor. The staff should know which situation is the case before they undertake consideration of a problem. Supervisors who cloud this issue, in the name of democratic leadership, will pay for it when the staff comes up with the "wrong" decision.

The Mediation Role. In the following simple statement of role, a new social work supervisor attempted to clarify how he saw his part of the proceedings. He had already described the staff meeting and case consultation purposes for the social work staff group and had received positive responses from its members.

> Let me take a minute and spell out how I see my role in these meetings. I see myself as bringing issues to your attention which emerge from the administration, or my own observations of what we are doing, as well as helping you to raise things on your mind. Once we decide on our agenda, I'm going to try to hold us to the discussion, as well as help you all talk to and to listen to each other. In effect, I'm going to try to help us have an effective staff group. I can't do it alone, so I'm going to ask all of you to take some responsibility for making things work well. That's why, if you don't like what's happening at a meeting, let me hear about it right away—not a couple of days later. I think you all have a lot to contribute to these meetings. I think you can give each other a lot of good ideas, as well as some real support when you need it. I'm going to try to help you do that. Any questions?

In part, the role described by this supervisor could be conceptualized as mediating between each staff member and the group as a whole. This special case of the mediation function of the supervision model described in Chapter 1 is illustrated in Figure 5.1. The similarity to the mediating roles prescribed in preceding chapters for the parallel processes of supervisor-worker and worker-client relationships in their relevant systems is readily apparent. Many of the same principles apply in the implementation of this role in the day-to-day problems of supervision with staff. The supervisor's role as mediator between the staff group and the system (the agency or other institution) is discussed in Chapter 6.

The Work Phase in Groups

Work phase issues in respect to staff groups are related to developing a positive group culture, dealing with individual-group issues, and handling conflict in the group. The relationship between the

FIGURE 5.1
Mediation Role of the Supervisor in Staff Groups

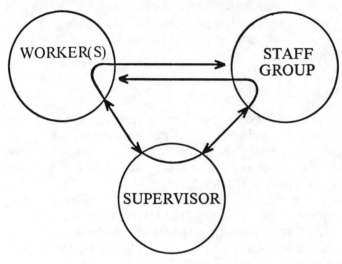

group and the supervisor, which can be a part of contracting in the beginning phase or a part of the work phase, is discussed in the next main section.

Work in groups is conducted in both formal and informal settings. Various forms of formal staff groups were described above in relation to group purpose: staff meetings, case consultation, group supervision, and in-service training. Some of the most significant encounters between staff members, however—encounters which can profoundly affect the delivery of services to clients—take place in the informal groups which consist of the staff members whose normal activities cause them to interact with one another on a regular basis. The informal group or system on a hospital ward may consist of all the nurses, aides, and clerical staff who work together on a regular shift. The interactions of these staff members may be a source of great aid and emotional support to the ward staff or, conversely, they can generate serious obstacles which make it difficult for an interdependent staff to offer a sound service to clients.

The examples in this section, drawn from both formal and informal groups, highlight the similarities in the dynamics involved, the functional role of the supervisor, and the skills required in the two settings. The boundaries between the formal and informal groups in a system are not clearly defined, since the activities of one often affect the other.

Developing a group culture

When a group of staff members comes together, formally or informally, something is created which is greater than simply the sum of the parts. This "something" is the group, and its properties are observable in that they can be inferred by group actions. The group members, therefore, act as if these group properties exist.

One of the strong norms of behavior in our society (as noted in preceding chapters) is the requirement that anger is not to be expressed directly. Politeness requires that it be suppressed, or, if it is expressed, that this be done indirectly and according to certain generally acceptable rules. As staff members join a staff group, they bring a number of cultural ideas, such as this norm against the strong expression of angry feelings, with them. In effect, there is a taboo, a social prohibition resulting from convention or tradition, which forbids direct discussion of anger. When all members share this norm of behavior and respect anger as a taboo subject for discussion, the group culture is said to have a property, called a norm, and a taboo subject area related to the expression of anger.

The existence of these properties can be inferred by the behavior of group members. If expression of anger is suppressed, group members who violate the norm may find themselves subject to group sanctions, or punishments, such as the silent treatment in the coffee room, which are used to enforce the group's rules of behavior. Although the rules are not formally codified, that is, written down for all to see, the power of these informal norms of behavior can nonetheless be immense. The problems they can cause may also be potent. In any close relationship, it must be expected that frictions will generate anger. If the anger is suppressed, so will other important emotions such as caring. It is not possible to be selective about which feelings will be experienced. Unexpressed negative feelings will go under the surface and emerge in indirect forms of all kinds, including apathy and the burnout syndrome.

The examination of group culture in this section focuses on norms, rules of behaviors, and taboos. Another aspect of group culture, the development of roles, has already been touched on in the discussion of the role of the group leader. In the next section role is considered in a different manner, in the context of the roles played by group members: internal leaders, scapegoats, deviant members, and so on.

One function of a group culture is to provide some certainty about how people will behave. For example the norm that our personal concerns should not be shared with every acquaintance, but rather reserved for more intimate friends, serves to protect us from inappropriate intimacy. The norm against unhindered expression of negative feelings helps to keep the social interaction reasonably lubricated. Group norms may be quite positive and supportive, such as those that rally support from colleagues experiencing traumatic personal difficulties.

The difficulty with group norms occurs when they block productive cooperation. In such a situation, the norm does not contribute to the development of a culture for work; rather, it generates obstacles to oppose effective collaboration. All staff groups have group norms that reflect the general societal norms, and problems will inevitably occur. It is the supervisor's job to identify these obstacles and bring them to the attention of staff members and then to help them develop new norms or rules that are more conducive to effective work.

Thus, as has been noted above, the supervisor is responsible for monitoring not only the content of the work in the group but also the process, the way of working. This role of the supervisor, described in Chapter 4 as the educational function, involves an ongoing attempt to train the staff group in order to help it develop a more functional group culture. Supervisors often find this a difficult role. Their first line of defense is to point out that it is time-consuming, and they are always hard pressed simply to get through the day's business. Closer examination of this rationale indicates that even though most of them really are hard pressed, some of the pressures they undergo result from work they have to do in response to the strains created by a poor culture for work. They spend a good deal of their time intervening to straighten out conflicts between staff members, each of whom may have come to the supervisor upset and angry but refusing to speak about the problem with the other antagonist. Instead of moving into conflict after conflict, wouldn't the supervisor save time by trying to change the group culture which causes all conflicts to end up on his or her desk? (This process will be illustrated later, in the section on conflicts.)

Most supervisors agree that much of their energy goes into dealing with problems which might not occur or could be handled by the staff members themselves if the group culture were different. The real reason why this work is difficult for them may be that they are also products of the general societal culture, and the norms and taboos are just as powerful for them as for their staffs. It's not that they can't see the negative impact of the culture on their staff's work; it's just that they are afraid of what might happen if they open up the question. The current problems and the illusion of work, while frustrating, are safe. Once supervisors recognize that they have a stake in maintaining the current culture, they make a first step in taking a risk and trying for something better. The following example illustrates how a supervisor challenged the illusion of work in order to improve the work group culture.

The Boring Staff Meeting. One of the most common complaints of supervisors is that they get bored at staff meetings, even meetings they are chairing. They can see that the workers are bored, too, so they may simply lower their heads and try to plow through their agendas quickly. A boring staff meeting is always a signal, even though the communication is indirect. It may be that the topic for discussion is not relevant to the workers, or the topic may be so relevant that it is hitting staff members hard in an area they find difficult to discuss.

In the following excerpt from a record of a staff meeting of nurses, the apparently simple discussion of time tables and division of labor took too long and kept getting interrupted:

> Sue felt the evening shift should not have to pull so many weekend duties. Jill disagreed and felt they should all pull equal weekend duty. I pointed out that was the fourth time we had gone around this, and we didn't seem to be getting any closer to consensus. I asked if anyone had any ideas. Chris said we should really tie down the training program for next week, since there was not much time left. A number of the group members nodded in agreement. Alice started to make a long, rambling statement about training philosophy and goals, and I

could see people looking as if they were thinking "Here she goes again." After five minutes of this I felt as bored and frustrated as they looked.

I finally decided to challenge them. I said: "This meeting is getting boring, and I don't think we are getting anywhere!" People looked up at my comment and a number of heads were shaking. I continued: "It started to get boring when we were going around in circles on the weekend issue, and then the subject was changed. Can we get back to the weekend issue? How come we weren't getting anywhere and no one seemed ready to budge?"

There was a silence, and Jill said, with feeling, that she was sick and tired of evening staff asking for more privileges. As far as she was concerned, they had it cushy as it was. There was a stunned silence. I said (feeling considerably less confident than I projected): "Good! Now it's out in the open, let's deal with it." The argument began with Jill leading one side and Sue the other. Each group of staff members thought the other had it easier. Evening staff felt the day staff had time when the patients were being tested or attending the rehab programs and could therefore take care of things that they often left for the evening staff to pick up on. The reverse feeling was true, with day staff figuring it was a breeze to handle patients at night—they just watched TV and then went to sleep. These feelings had been festering for a while without being openly revealed. As I thought back, there had been hints at meetings, sarcastic cracks or jokes, and certain important tasks consistently falling between the cracks, with neither doing a thing.

I listened for a while, intervening if it got too hot, to say things like, "I know you're angry, but can you say it in a way the others can hear?" After some ventilation, I pointed out that there were two distinct camps in the group, and that each seemed to feel the other did not understand how tough their part of the work was. I wondered if we might break the log jam by talking about this a bit: could the evening and the day staff educate the others a bit? Each group began to identify their special problems as I tried to help the others listen.

I pointed out after it was over that they all appeared to have a tough job, and that might be why they end up getting mad at the others. There was some agreement with this. I asked if there were any reasonable steps we could take to make everyone's job a bit easier. I recognized that I had my work to do as well, in getting administration to understand their pressures more clearly. A number of staff members started to come up with suggestions for minor yet important changes.

The evasion of work evident in the boredom that characterized this group was a signal to the supervisor that a tough issue was at hand. The norm against direct confrontation of people who had to work together with was very strong for these members. They could not make progress on the scheduling question because the real issue was lurking just beneath the surface.

When group members are close to an important issue, they may choose to avoid discussing it by employing the mechanisms decribed in psychoanalytic terms as *fight/flight* (Bion, 1961). In this example, flight behavior involved a group member taking the role of leading the group into *flight* from the real, but frightening, discussion. In other situations, discussion of emotional matters may lead a group to avoid the pain through the mechanism of *fight:* Two or more group members will confront each other and argue rather than face the strong emotions they have in common.

By challenging the illusion of work, the supervisor signaled that she wanted "real talk." When one of the members accepted the invitation the supervisor quickly credited her, sending another message to the rest of the group. The culture of work is undergoing a change here by the very process of ignoring the taboo and entering the formerly prohibited area. After the discussion was over, the supervisor moved to deal directly with the question of the culture of work.

I asked them if we could spend a few minutes talking about what had happened at this meeting. I pointed out that we were afraid to deal with an issue that involved angry feelings and that, as a result, we were going around in circles. When we finally had the courage to get it out in the open, it turned out to be very helpful, and we made some good steps.

I asked them what they thought about what I had just said. Leslie said she had had these feelings for a long time and was afraid to say anything. I asked why, and she told us she didn't want to make things worse between the two shifts; it was bad enough already. I asked if others felt the same way, and there was some discussion of fear of confrontation. I told them I could understand their fears, because I had them as well. In addition, I did not think we needed to confront each other all the time—I wasn't sure I could take it. They all laughed in agreement.

I went on to say that this was a good example of something that had to be dealt with, and I hoped that next time they had an issue like this, they would raise it directly. I would be glad to help them if they felt uncertain about bringing it out in the open themselves. I thought we could handle it, and it was the responsibility of all of them to get these issues on the table where we could handle them, rather than simply complaining in the coffee room all the time. There was general agreement with my comments.

Throughout the life of this staff group there would be many times when they could not be honest. While feelings of anger were one taboo, an even stronger taboo prevented sharing of some of the stronger feelings of depression related to their particular area of work (they had to deal often with death and dying). When the supervisor pointed this out, another discussion was necessary.

In effect, the supervisor helps the staff group to learn how it operates in its unique milieu. Both the general group themes, such as the difficulties of confronting members or of staying related to the topic and not wandering, as well as the specific group themes, or problems related to their particular work, are explored. The example described here is just the beginning of the educational process as staff members are taught how to take responsibility for their group activities.

The individual in the group

While the group culture effects the functioning of particular work groups, the individual members also help determine how the group operates by bringing their personalities to bear in their group interactions. The concept of role helps demonstrate how individual personality is translated into group interaction. Various individuals in the group may take the roles of deviant member, internal leader, quiet member, or scapegoat, for example. This section examines the roles of these individual members, while stressing that it is often impossible to understand them without considering them in the context of group interaction.

The concept of *role in a dynamic system* which is utilized in this section draws from the work of Nathan Ackerman for a definition of role and Kurt Lewin for a conception of the group as a dynamic system. Ackerman defines social role as "synonymous with the operations of the 'social self' or social identity of the person in the context of a defined life situation" (1958, p. 53). He suggests that individuals have a private inner self and a social outer self which emphasize the aspects of their personalities that are externally oriented. For purposes of this discussion, the crucial idea is that each individual will bring to the staff group a particular pattern of social activity, the outer self, which may differ in part from her or his real inner self.

Lewin, often referred to as the father of group dynamics, established the need to consider the activities of each member of a dynamic group in terms of his or her reactions to the activities of other members. It is not possible to understand the activity of a part of a group without seeing it in the context of the activity of the whole.

In synthesizing these ideas, the behavior of any member of a dynamic group must be seen as, at least in part, the expression of the individual's social role in relation to the activities of others. This principle applies in the following examples of a deviant group member, an internal leader, a quiet member, and a scapegoat.

The Deviant Member. The term *deviant* is not used here in a narrow, pathological sense but to refer to any group member who exhibits a pattern of deviating sharply from the normal group behavior. The example cited most often in workshops for supervisors is the one staff member who is always griping and complaining, who constantly takes pot shots at the supervisor and seems to lack enthusiasm and commitment. The supervisor may lament, "If I only didn't have X in my staff group, it would be very cooperative." This deviant member is experienced as an "enemy."

If such staff members were not seen as discrete entities, separate from the interactive process in the group, they would be regarded in quite a different light. When staff members feel negatively about issues in the system, for example, but do not feel completely free to share their feelings, they may elect a deviant member to play the role of expressing the feelings of the group as a whole. The election is not formal: more often than not, after a session where a member has pressed a point which the supervisor may not have wanted to hear or deal with, another staff member privately expresses support, perhaps by saying, "Nice going, it needed to be said." In a subtle, even unconscious way, the group is cultivating one of its members to play an important functional role.

The staff member who accepts the assignment of deviant member is usually one who plays this role in other situations as well, fitting Ackerman's notion of a social role. For a number of reasons, the deviant member feels the urgency of the concern strongly. Thus the deviant member's behavior is in part a function of his or her social role, and in part a response to the dynamics of the group.

Deviant behavior can be considered a communication in which the deviant member is speaking to the supervisor for the staff group. If the supervisor really wants honest communications from the group, therefore, the deviant member can be considered the supervisor's ally instead of the enemy. Striking evidence of this role-playing process may be observed if the deviant staff member leaves the group (quits or is fired). Almost instantly, a formerly quiet, cooperative member will assume the role of deviant member. The role thus is a functional necessity, and someone must fill it. If the supervisor could allow the staff to raise all issues directly, even controversial ones, the group would have no more need for the deviant member.

The following report illustrates a common response to a deviant group member. The supervisor reacted defensively and attempted to use the group to suppress the deviant:

> I had explained the meaning of the cutbacks, why our department had to take its share, and had asked the staff if they could come up with some ideas of how to make do with less and still maintain our service. I pointed out I knew it would not be easy. During my explanation, Frank had sat with a smirk on his face, as if to say, "Here it comes." I knew he was angry, so I just avoided his look.
>
> A few people asked some questions, there was some silence, then Lou made a suggestion for a minor cutback in his area. I said I thought that was a helpful start. Frank jumped in and said he thought the discussion was a waste of time. I was angry at his cutting off what I thought was a beginning at a hard job. I said: "I'm sorry you feel that way, Frank. It's not a very constructive attitude. I don't think you are being helpful, and I am sure the others in the department feel the same way." Lou said: "I don't like this either, Frank, but we are just going to have to live with it." Frank was quiet for the remainder of the discussion which, while lethargic, did produce some suggestions.

By cutting off the discussion in response to Frank's comment, the supervisor prevented the staff group from expressing their real feelings about the cutback. They would have to wait until they were in the coffee room, when the supervisor was not present, to let Frank know that they really agreed with him. Contrast this with a follow-up meeting in which the supervisor tried to catch his mistake and pick up on the meaning of Frank's outburst:

I began by saying: "I don't think we really leveled at the last meeting. When Frank said the discussion was a waste of time, I felt on the spot, so I put him off. I didn't admit how uncomfortable the whole idea of talking to you about the cuts had made me. I suspect many of you probably agreed with Frank. Is that true?"

Lorraine said she thought across-the-board cuts were unfair. The fact is, many other departments had fat in them, we all knew it, and yet each department was being treated equally in the cuts. I was surprised by how strongly she said this, obviously very upset.

Joan jumped in and said she thought they were being penalized for having done a good job of cutting to the bone last year. There was no recognition of the particular impact an across-the-board impact would have on us, as compared to other departments. If the administrator had any guts, he would set a procedure for evaluating exactly where the cuts should go, instead of this across-the-board bullshit.

As Joan was speaking, I was beginning to wonder what I had opened up and how I was going to deal with it. I shared that with staff, and Lou suggested that we might be able to make a case, if given the chance, that this cut was unfair. He asked if I would consider setting up a meeting with the administrator. I told him I could do that, although I didn't know if it would help. After all, we had to realize he was also under pressure from other departments. Frank said: "That's what he gets paid for!" We all laughed, and I said, "And I guess that goes for me too."

Not only did this second session allow the staff members to vent their feelings, it also let them see that there was something they could do about the problem. The strength of the staff members strengthened the supervisor to pursue this issue further, particularly since he fully agreed with them. The next chapter discusses the strategies and skills involved in attempting to negotiate between a staff and the administration.

Another common example of the deviant as an ally is given in the following excerpt. The supervisor reached for the indirect cues of a staff member who had missed staff meetings, usually came late, and often sat in the corner, staring out the window or pointedly reading his mail. The supervisor's first reaction was to want to give the staff member a boot in the derriere. Instead, he attempted to reach for the message behind the deviant behavior, using a staff meeting to start to deal with it:

About halfway through the meeting, I said I wanted to talk about Terry's participation in the meeting. I did not want to put him on the spot, but I did feel his continual lateness, lack of interest, and involvement was probably saying something to me about his feelings about the meeting. I asked if I was right. He paused, then said he frankly found the meetings a waste of his time. I told him that as the person responsible for our staff meetings, I did not like to hear that—but that I could see how it might be a waste for him and others as well. There were times I didn't find it useful and felt like I would read my mail too, only I had to chair the damn thing. The group members laughed. I asked if others felt the same as Terry, because then maybe we should discuss what's wrong with the meetings and how to improve them.

The rest of the discussion revolved around their lack of interest in many of the agenda items, their feeling that the discussion was often superficial and they did not get into their practice enough. Terry, who was very much involved in this discussion, revealed that he was having a tough time with a particular case and needed some help. As is often the case, the group member who seems most unhappy about the meetings may be sitting there with an urgent problem to be addressed. Rather than wanting the meetings eliminated, this member desperately needs to have them enhanced.

Another common example of a deviant member raising issues for the group comes from the context of a nursing group on a ward. The staff compliment was short, the beds were full, and the pressure on all staff members was heavy. One fairly recent nursing school graduate was having tremendous difficulty handling her responsibilities and was beginning to disappear for a time when things got rough on the ward. This made the other staff members angry, and a staff discussion resulted. The supervisor was able to help the new nurse share how overwhelmed she was (she cried as she spoke) and then to help the other members express their sense of being overly burdened. In addition to providing a catharsis for all staff members, the discussion turned to how they could help each other in time of stress as well as how to communicate the problems to administration. The deviant member in the informal system was playing a functional role for the group as a whole.

In large, complex systems such as hospitals, entire departments may play the deviant role for the system as a whole. For example, nursing staffs in surgery, emergency, and intensive care, because of the special stresses of their jobs, often become the first departments to signal to the whole hospital the extent of a problem.

The Internal Leader. The supervisor is the external leader of the group because he or she carries the authority that comes with the role and is granted by the system. In contrast, the internal leader is a staff member (or several members) who emerges through the group process and who helps the group to tackle important developmental tasks as well as to deal with its business. When the group tackles the supervisor, the internal leader may be experienced by the supervisor as a deviant member. This internal leader–deviant member can be an important ally for the supervisor. (Authority issues will be discussed in a later section.)

When supervisors feel insecure in their role, they often see the internal leader as challenging their leadership. This is a misunderstanding of the ways in which groups naturally work. All groups develop internal leaders, no matter how effective the external leader may be. They are functionally necessary; they help to develop the emotional function of the group (e.g., expressions of group caring for members under stress) as well as the task completion functions (e.g., getting jobs organized). Although the supervisor may provide an external demand and be a source of real support, in a well-functioning staff group, peer support and peer demand are crucial elements. Rather than seeing internal leaders as competitors, supervisors should be grateful for all the help they can get.

The Quiet Group Member. Supervisors often express concern about members who never or rarely speak in group meetings, even if it is obvious that such a member is listening and involved in the transactions. The usual techniques for involving quiet members often end up making things worse. Examples include going around the table, asking everyone for their opinions, just to get the quiet member to speak; or turning to the quiet member and directly asking for his or her opinion; or, even worse, asking the quiet member to chair a portion of the meeting. Most of the procedures are easily recognized by both the quiet member and the rest of the staff, and they often result in acute embarrassment. As one quiet member said, "When I'm put on the spot that way, even if I do have something to say, it flies right out of my mind."

It's important to recognize that there is nothing wrong with some staff members participating more than others in group discussions. A member can be actively involved without saying much at all. On the other hand, those who are always silent, and perhaps have been silent in group meetings all their lives, may begin to feel embarrassed about not contributing. In addition, those who speak a great deal may begin to wonder if they are being judged for what they say or if the others would like them to simply keep quiet.

A supervisor can be helpful to both groups, but the help has to be direct and supportive. An example is the following discussion between a supervisor and a new staff member who has not said anything at all while attending four staff meetings in a row. The supervisor stopped this member, Mary, in the hall after the fourth meeting, and this private discussion took place:

Supervisor: I just wanted to check to see how you have been finding the staff meetings. I noticed you haven't said very much, but you are obviously interested. I thought I'd see how it was going.

Mary: I know I should be speaking up more, but, frankly, I feel a bit intimidated since I'm so new.

Supervisor: I think we all know how that feels.

Worker: Actually, I don't speak too much in groups anyway. I just finished two years at social work school, and I don't think I said a word unless asked. By the time I was in my second year, I was afraid to say anything. I thought all of the other students would fall out of their seats if they heard my voice.

Supervisor (laughing): Seriously, though, are you feeling a bit of that here, too? (Worker nods.) Look, you can take your time getting into the discussion, but obviously, after a while, if you don't speak at all it will make others uncomfortable. They may feel they are risking their ideas while you're just sitting back in judgment. If you like, I can help by watching for you, and if you want to get into the discussion but the action is going too fast, or you're a bit unsure, just give me a signal and I'll help you in. I won't do it, unless you give me the signal. How does that sound?

Mary: Thanks, I may take you up on that.

During the next staff meeting, the worker sat absolutely still, obviously taking great pains to make sure she did not accidentally give a signal. At the next session, midway through a heated discussion on an issue that Mary had some special knowledge of, she nodded to the supervisor, who interrupted the flow of discussion and said: "Did you have something to say, Mary?" and the ice was broken. While Mary did not become the most vocal member of the discussion, she did enter it more frequently, sometimes using the supervisor's help, at other times on her own.

In situations where those who speak a great deal are concerned about talking too much, the supervisor can be helpful by opening up a discussion of how the staff group operates. In the following example, the supervisor picked up on the hint and reached for the real feelings behind it:

Louise: Well, I've been talking enough about this, let someone else speak for a while.

Supervisor: Louise, are you really feeling you talk too much in this group? Because if you are, let's talk about that for a moment. (Louise nods.) What are you worried about?

Louise: Well, a lot of people sit around saying nothing at these meetings, and I figure they must be thinking, "Why doesn't she shut up?" or maybe they are thinking I'm just running off at the mouth and sounding dumb. Last week I decided to just keep quiet for a whole meeting, but I couldn't make it.

Supervisor: How about it, you quieter members, how do you feel about Louise's participation. (Silence.)

Terry: Frankly, Louise, I'm glad you have the guts to get into the discussion. I'm often sitting here thinking similar things, but I'm afraid to say them. I kind of figure it's easier to keep quiet.

Supervisor: ... and let Louise say it? (Terry nods.)

Sam: I'm one of the quiet ones. It's not that I'm not interested, or think you guys are saying dumb things—actually, you're often right on. I have always had a hard time speaking in groups, since I was a kid, and this one is no different.

Supervisor: Even speaking right now was tough for you? (Sam nods.) Look, I think people participate differently in groups, depending on their own patterns. I don't believe others resent your participation, Louise; I think most envy you. On the other hand, if the same people always have to carry the ball, then we only get input from a part of the group, and I think that deprives us of a source of help. After a while, I bet people like Louise will feel a bit used by the group, and want something in return. (Louise nods vigorously.) Can we agree to allow some to speak more than others, but that everyone takes some responsibility to contribute in some way? (All group members are nodding at this comment.) Actually, I think you have all made a great start by being so honest about your feelings.

The Scapegoat. To understand the dynamics of the scapegoating process, it is helpful to consider the origin of the idea. The scapegoat is derived from an ancient Hebrew ritual each year, when on the Day of Atonement the chief priest would symbolically lay the sins of the people on the back of a goat (the scape) and then drive the goat into the wilderness. This symbolized the ritual cleansing of the sins of the people. In a like manner, when a group scapegoats one of its members, the members usually attack the aspect of the scapegoat that they most dislike in themselves. The supervisor can consider this a form of communication of the group members' feelings about themselves.

This process is a familiar one to those who work with families. The child in the family who is in the most trouble often turns out to be a family scapegoat, signaling to the community a problem in the family. If this child is seen as the problem and perhaps placed in a residence or foster home, another child may assume the role. This will continue until the real problems in the family dynamics are addressed.

Understanding scapegoating as a dynamic process can help supervisors avoid a common mistake—identifying with either the staff against the scapegoat or the scapegoat against the staff. Either position cuts the supervisor off from being able to help in the dynamic interaction between the two. If the mediating function (see Figure 5.1 above) is truly integrated by the supervisor, it is possible to identify with both the individual scapegoat and the group at the same time. Then the supervisor can pay attention to what Schwartz calls, in the practice context, the *two clients*—the individual and the group.

In the following example from my own teaching practice, a group discussion was taking place on a sensitive topic. This particular student group had been together the previous year in a two-year program. As the students explored the feelings involved, Len began to theorize about practice in an abstract manner; he appeared to be trying to impress the group with his understanding of different points of view. This group had been meeting under other leadership for a time, and this pattern was a long-standing one. Whenever Len began to intellectualize and theorize, the group members sent out all sorts of nonverbal cues of displeasure, as if to say: "Here he goes again." I had noticed the pattern in my first few weeks with the group and had simply passed it by, but I had decided that this week, if it happened again, I would challenge it. My process recording noted:

> I stopped the discussion and pointed out what had just happened—Len started to theorize just as we got to the emotions, and the group was obviously displeased by this, but not saying so directly. I said it seemed to be a pattern in this group, and I felt we should get it out in the open. I asked what was going on. There was a long silence, which I waited out. Then Ian said, with much feeling, that Len always did this, all last year; he always intellectualized instead of dealing with feelings. Len looked taken aback by the comment, so I offered some support. I said, "I know it's tough to hear this, Len, but try to stay with it for a minute or two; I think it can be important." Others joined the discussion,

starting to list all of Len's faults. He was intellectual, cold, clinical, etc., a typical "professional." The affect was anger and the word *professional* was uttered almost as a curse.

After listening for a while, monitoring Len, who seemed to be painfully taking things in, I asked the group members why they were so angry at Len. I said: "So he intellectualizes, theorizes, seems to be cold, and so on. Why are you so mad at him for that? Maybe that's just Len." There was a period of silence, and then Theresa said: "You know, all those things you just described, that's what I'm worried my training here at school is doing to me. I'm beginning to worry if I'm also becoming *professional.*"

I said that was honest, and hard to say, and asked if anyone else worried about that at times. A dam seemed to burst loose as they entered the discussion about their previous experiences, how they had come to school feeling good about some of their natural talents and then started to wonder, as they read all the theories, if they had just been naive. Others commented how they were finding themselves analyzing everyone, their clients, their friends, even their families. They were getting the feeling other people were not really enjoying hearing all of their insights. The core of the discussion was that they were troubled about how to integrate personal self and professional self, especially when so many of the theories seemed to split the two.

I enquired how Len was doing during the discussion, and he nodded and indicated they should continue. I tried to take some time to put their concerns into perspective, to normalize them as appropriate for this stage in their development. After further discussion, I complimented them on what I thought was a crucial piece of work which, if they noticed, we would never have discussed if we kept simply being angry at Len for the very qualities we didn't like in ourselves.

In this part of the discussion I had been able to uncover the group's real feelings communicated to me through the attacks on Len. I was not sure what they might mean when I started the process, which is why I was nervous about opening things up, but, with my help, the strength of the group came through beautifully. There was more work to come, however, since we still had Len sitting there through all of this. The group needed a scapegoat because they had trouble handling difficult feelings directly. But why had Len volunteered to play the role? I turned to Len at this point.

I asked Len how all of this discussion had been hitting him. I said it probably was not easy to hear some of the things they said about him, even though they admitted they had the same problems. Len sighed, and then he said they were right in accusing him of being intellectual and not dealing with emotion. He said he had discovered that being too emotional wasn't always such a good idea.

I asked if he could share why that was so with the class. After another long pause, he described a 16-year-old boy he had been working with during his last practicum, a boy who had been on the street for a while after being kicked out of his own home and every residential center in town. Len described how he had befriended the boy, gotten really close to him, and even thought he was getting somewhere. He continued, with some bitterness in his voice: "Sure I dealt with his feelings, I helped him to open up, he even cried one night with me. But two weeks later he killed himself."

The group and I sat in shocked silence as Len started to cry. I said I thought they probably wanted to reach out to Len. Rose crossed the room and sat next to Len, putting her arm around him. Others in the room, including myself, were showing the emotions we felt at the moment. After a while I said I thought Len had just shared a big hurt with us, one he had kept inside all of last year. It would help a lot to understand why it might be easier for him to equate professional with intellectual. I wondered if there was any help they could give Len on this, in addition to the obvious support they were expressing.

A number of students revealed similar experiences with clients, describing how they felt as Len did, responsible and guilty, and how they had to work those feelings through to get things into perspective. The theme of the discussion was that one always wonders if one could have done more, but that one tends to be too hard on oneself. As they were talking to Len I felt they were all talking to themselves as well, and said this to them. I pointed out how easy it would be to close up our feelings when faced with such hard emotions.

The session was over by that time, and I congratulated the group and Len on some very hard work. I suggested we continue on this discussion of professional and personal and their sense of responsibility next time.

The key to being able to help effectively in all of the individual-group situations described here—with the deviant, quiet, or scapegoat member or the internal leader—is in being able to search out the connection between the individual (the one) and the group (the many). This is what Schwartz described in his theory as *searching out the common ground* (Schwartz, 1979). In the example above, while the differences between Len and the group appeared obvious, with a little faith (perhaps I should say a *lot* of faith) and some willingness to take a risk, I was able to identify the more powerful areas of common ground. This is not so different from the practice skill of learning to find areas of mutuality when clients often only see the obstacles which keep them apart. This same task for the supervisor, to search out the common ground, is crucial in dealing with conflicts, which is the topic of the next section, and in negotiating the system, the topic of Chapter 6.

Conflict in the group

One of the most difficult developments for supervisors to handle in the formal or informal group is conflict. In the typical example, one worker approaches the supervisor with a complaint about another: "He doesn't pull his share of the load," or "She just sits and drinks coffee all the time," or "I know my staff are only clerical workers, and he's professional staff, but that doesn't give him the right to treat us like dirt!" These are the moments that most supervisors dread, particularly when their suggestion that the staff member talk directly to the other person meets with a response like "I couldn't do that," or "I've already tried, but he just won't listen," or "That's what *you* get paid for!" The problem is compounded when the supervisor agrees to talk to the offender to see what can be done, and the worker says, "But don't tell him I said anything." When the supervisor inquires why not, the response is often: "I'm not a squealer," or "I have to have coffee with her every day." The supervisor is thus being asked to accept the task of speaking to an offending staff member without divulging where the information was obtained, and then to "straighten out" that member.

It is not so surprising that staff members ask supervisors to do this as it is that so many supervisors agree to try. In terms of the functional role of the supervisor as a mediator which has been developed in this book, particularly as it applies to creating a culture for work, it is possible to redefine the supervisor's tasks at a point of conflict and make them more manageable. In addition, the supervisor can place responsibility for helping them deal with problems more firmly with the staff. In arriving at these solutions, however, a number of principles must be followed.

First, the personal relations between staff members are their own business. Whether or not members of a staff group choose to become friends is completely up to them, although working in close proximity with people who share problems, tasks, and feelings often leads to the deepest friendships. Many workers look forward to Friday afternoon sessions with co-workers at the pub when they wrap up their week and prepare for the weekend. However, it is not necessary to be friends in order to work effectively together. Constructive communal work can be done by people whose relationships to one another range on a continuum from strong friendship to complete antipathy. It is not the supervisor's business to deal with the staff's friendship patterns, but it is very much the supervisor's role to deal with interpersonal relationships as they affect the delivery of service to clients. Thus, dealing with staff conflict in the informal system is a crucial part of the job.

Second, the supervisor makes a mistake by taking on the role of judge, arbitrator, confidant, or ally in conflicts between staff. There are times a supervisor may have to play such roles, as when there is no way for the staff to resolve strong differences and, for the sake of continuity of service, the supervisor must take a stand. But if the supervisor accepts responsibility for "solving" all the group's problems, even if the staff asks for this, a good deal of the supervisor's energies will be spent in this area of work, often leaving little time for other crucial tasks.

Instead of defining their role as solving problems, supervisors define it as helping staff members develop the abilities to solve their own problems. Thus they will be building into the group culture the crucial self-correcting mechanisms which will help the staff to work effectively together, particularly at points of conflict, in mature and responsible ways. In this sense, each conflict becomes not only an instance of substantive work but also an opportunity to develop staff skills and a sense of responsibility. When supervisors invest time in this role, it can pay off in big ways by decreasing the number of problems that are "dumped" in their laps.

A third principle is that the supervisor should not get lost in dealing with the *content* of a complaint (although it may be important in its own right), and instead should pay close attention to the *process* of the encounter. All efforts should be made to bring the conflicting parties together, eventually at least, so they can work on the problems themselves.

The following example suggests a technique for implementing these principles. The setting is the emergency room in a medium-size hospital in a rural area. A new nurse was needed for a particular role in the emergency room, and Marie was hired from outside the hospital. She had strong general training, but though she had recently taken a refresher course in emergency room work, she had little actual experience there. Two current staff members had coveted the job and had more experience, but because of their level of training they had lost out. They had feelings about the matter. In addition, Marie was French Canadian, and she was coming to an area of Canada where everyone did not welcome Quebecers. After her arrival it was also clear that she had something of a language problem and spoke only halting English.

The first weeks were predictably difficult, and many of the staff came to the supervisor with complaints. After a number of these, the supervisor spoke to Marie:

Supervisor: I was wondering how things were going now that you have been here for a while.

Nurse (Marie): There are no problems. I still have a lot to learn, but I'll get there.

Supervisor: Don't you think that being so new to the job, and having so little experience, there might be some ways I could help you—some techniques you could brush up on—you know what I mean?

Marie: Why are you asking? Have I made some mistakes? I thought I was doing okay.

Supervisor: Well, there are a few things we can work on when I get some time. (The nurse nods in agreement and the conversation is over.)

When this supervisor brought up this example at a supervisory workshop, she admitted she had not leveled about the problems the staff was bringing her because she was too embarrassed. In the discussion it became clear that instead she was trying to lead Marie to accept that there *were* problems. The supervisor had not leveled about the problems, brought up the feelings of the other staff, or mentioned the language problems. When the consultant noted that Marie must have been feeling pretty lousy about how things had gone, the supervisor said she had sensed that but had not acknowledged Marie's feelings because, she said, "I guess I'm really angry at her myself." Her honesty was credited when she pointed out she had really wanted one of the other staff members who had been turned down for the job. When the consultant pointed out that in part she would probably be just as happy if Marie failed, she agreed and then said: "But I would feel lousy if she did, because I know it's my job to try to help."

The fact that this supervisor brought up the example probably meant she really wanted to help. It was a good example of a supervisor identifying with one side in a problem and not being able to help with the interaction. If Marie was going to be able to make it in the job, given her inexperience and language problems, she would need all the help she could get from the supervisor and the other nurses. The task might be too great, and she might not be able to meet the requirements, but at least all of them would know that she had had a good shot at it. The supervisor agreed that, in spite of her feelings, she wanted to do her job properly

The workshop group then did some preparation on how to deal with first the staff and then the nurse in this conflict. They began by role-playing how she would handle the staff members' next complaint. The focus was on being supportive to the staff, but at the same time making a demand for them to take some responsibility in the process. In the role play, Lillian took the part of the next nurse to voice a complaint:

Nurse (Lillian): Look, something has to be done about Marie. We had a man in this morning, and when I tried to get her to help she just froze. (Fran, another nurse, agrees.)

Supervisor: Can you describe what happened?

Lillian: Well, I shouted to her to get five things I needed immediately, and she hesitated and seemed to go blank.

Supervisor: What did you do then?

Lillian: Well, I blew my top and told her she was next to useless.

Supervisor: You must have been feeling under pressure to get so upset. Probably, when you shouted at her that way, she got more frozen.

Lillian: That's what happened! I'm afraid it could lead to a serious problem if she stays around here.

Supervisor: Look, we know she may not be up to snuff, and perhaps she will have to leave eventually, but frankly, we probably haven't given her a fair chance. We were really against her from the start, and she must have sensed that. Most of us didn't want her, and I'm sure she has gotten that message from us. No wonder she freezes up.

Fran: Maybe that's true, but now we can't do anything about that—and she is just not working out.

Supervisor: I think it's time we had this out in the open. All of you come to me with your complaints and won't share them directly with Marie. She knows you're upset with her, but it's all under the surface. Maybe if we could discuss it honestly, it might clear the air. I could try to be more helpful in getting you to level with her about your expectations, and, perhaps, she could let us know what it's been like for her starting here. Maybe it won't help, but at least it's worth a try.

When a supervisor begins to make demands on the staff to play an honest and responsible role, as in this example, he or she must stay sensitive to the feelings of the staff. It is at precisely this point that resistance to the idea will emerge. Instead of ignoring the resistance, it is important for the supervisor to explore why it would be hard for the staff members to confront the isolated nurse.

In the supervisory workshop, the role play continued:

Lillian: Maybe you're right about her tough start here, but I think [since] you're the supervisor, you should talk to her.

Supervisor: Sounds like you're not too anxious to talk to her directly. Why not? Are you feeling uncomfortable about it?

Fran: Of course we are; I don't know about you, but that kind of directness scares me. If I say what's on my mind I might get angry at her, she could get angry back, and who needs a blowup? *You* talk to her!

Supervisor: I'm going to have to speak to her, to get things started, because I think I have to clear the air with how I started with her. But after that, I'm going to get us all together and ask all of you to start leveling. I think that's part of our responsibility, as hard as it is, as professional nurses, and I can't do it alone.

Lillian and Fran, who were role-playing the other two nurses, did not look too happy about the decision, but they agreed they would have to follow up if the supervisor insisted. If a supervisor wants to help a staff member to talk directly to another, it sometimes helps to role-play, asking what the staff member might say. A little practice, some support, and a push often make staff members more willing to take the next step of being honest. The crucial idea is that staff members should receive support and help when they are asked to do something that is known to be difficult, such as negotiating a confrontation with a person in authority (see Chapter 6).

In this example, preparatory work also needed to be done in the workshop sessions to help the supervisor work with Marie, the outcast. In the role-play preparation, the supervisor practiced leveling with Marie about her feelings at the start, how she had felt she had not really been as helpful as she should have been, and how she wanted to try to make it up now. She role-played listening to Marie's side of the story, trying to understand and to express her empathy, and then making a demand on Marie to deal with the conflict openly with the staff.

When the workshop group tried to prepare for the eventual meeting between Marie and the staff group, it became apparent how fearful all the supervisors were about confrontation. They were afraid that anger might be unleashed, that people would say hurtful things they might later regret, and, most important, that they would not know what to do. As one put it: "It's really opening a can of worms!" Another responded: "I wonder what's more painful for everyone involved, having the can of worms open or just leaving the lid on. I don't know how much worse things could get."

The group speculated on how to introduce the session. Perhaps the supervisor could say:

> We know there have been many strains between Marie and the rest of you, and these first few weeks have been uncomfortable for everyone, myself included. However, I thought if we could get some of the problems out in the open, in a constructive manner, maybe we could find ways we can be supportive of each other and make this place easier to work in for all of us. We all know it's no picnic in the best of times, and with these added pressures, it's even rougher. I'm going to try to help you talk to—and, most important—listen to each other. I'll put my own two cents in as we go along. Who wants to start?

The group agreed there would be a silence, and the supervisor would need to wait for some moments, perhaps acknowledging that it was tough, but then continue the demand. As the discussion began, it would be important not to stifle it (e.g., "I wish you could say that without sounding so angry,") since the feelings were real and would be part of the work. The supervisor would concentrate on the process (e.g., "How are you doing, Marie? Is this getting tough to hear?" or "It seems all of you are feeling the emergency room pressure so much yourselves, you hardly have room for anyone else's feelings of pressure.")

It would be important for the supervisor to help Marie convey the hurt, fear, and loneliness she must have felt as she started, an outsider in the hospital and probably also in the community. The other staff members needed to convey their real sense of disappointment at having been passed over for the job, perhaps their anger at the administration for not appreciating them. The supervisor agreed it was helpful to think it through in advance, but she figured there were going to be times when she just didn't know what to do. If she told the group members at that point that she did not know what to do, perhaps one of them could help.

The workshop group also anticipated that all might not work out well, particularly in this first session. Contrary to the usual Grade B movie scenario, the whole staff might not ride off into the sunset together singing "Happy Trails to You." In fact, the real impact of such a session might take some days as the thoughts and feelings worked their way through. The supervisor had to prepare for some ambiguity at the end of the session—a sense of unfinished business would probably be more like it. However, a start would have been made.

While the particular examples may differ, the general model is the same: helping the night shift at a residential treatment center begin to level with the day shift; opening up communications between the clerical staff and professional social workers; helping those who crossed the picket lines and worked during a strike talk to those who didn't; helping the registered nurses talk to the licensed practical nurses; and on, and on, and on. A good deal of a supervisor's energy must be invested in helping staff members relate to each other effectively. Courage is needed to take the risk, skills to help it work well, and most of all, faith in the capacity of the staff to deal with hard problems if given enough support and demand. In any staff system, the supervisor will find that as in any intimate relationship (like marriage or parenting), conflict and caring go hand in hand.

The Authority Theme: Group-Supervisor Relationships

While much of the preceding discussion has dealt with group-member interactions there is another major dynamic in staff groups. This involves the sensitive relationship between the supervisor and the group as a whole. Supervisors are very conscious of being judged by their staff groups, although as a result of a norm that issues of dependency and authority should not be openly discussed, much of the communication in this area is indirect. Most supervisors have themselves been members of supervisory groups and they are keenly aware that their strengths and weaknesses, particularly their weaknesses, are common topics of informal group discussion.

A myth persists that good supervisors always have a positive relationship with their staff groups. Supervisors are told: if you are effective, you will have no problems; if you have problems, you are ineffective. When the taboo on open communications by staff to the supervisor is combined with the myth of the perfect supervisor, powerful forces are at work which can easily block honest communications.

In essence effective supervision, like effective practice, involves catching one's mistakes as quickly as possible. The skillful supervisor is not the one who has no problems but the one who can get the inevitable problems out in the open. The relationship between the supervisor and the staff, what Schwartz has referred to as the *authority theme,* is one that requires constant attention. This theme has a number of subthemes, as was noted in the example in Chapter 3 of the child care supervisor who decided to do some "maintenance work" on his relations with his staff. These subthemes are: (1) the question of control and power; (2) the supervisor as an outsider; (3) the supervisor as a source of supports; (4) the limitations of the supervisor and; (5) the supervisor as a source of demands. The examples selected to illustrate a number of these subthemes in this section use excerpts from group discussions between supervisors and staff groups.

Control and power

The authority theme in supervision can be discussed in terms of specific issues of group leadership. One of the crucial questions on the minds of staff members is who "owns" the staff group. Most of their experiences with group leaders have led them to see the staff group as an instrument for the use of the supervisor. The selection of agenda items, the flow of group discussion, and the conclusions all appear to be in the hands of the supervisor. As a result, staff participation is often reactive, with staff members taking little responsibility for the effectiveness of the meetings. It's as if the staff were saying: "If the supervisor owns the group, he can be responsible for how it works."

A number of ways for the supervisor to help the staff make the group their own have been suggested in preceding chapters. Sessional contracting at the start of each session is a skill which allows meetings to be used to explore the staff's sense of urgency as well as the supervisor's agenda. The supervisor also can indicate willingness to change the agenda and move into new areas if the needs of the staff shift during a session, or can ask the staff to take responsibility for the way the members work together.

The following excerpt shows how the supervisor of a child care staff group directly addressed the issue of responsibility for the group process:

> I explained that I had been unhappy at the way our last meeting had gone. I said that we were often getting off the track and that I, and everyone else, just let it happen. I told them I thought that this happened a lot in meetings and wondered if they felt the same way.
>
> Chris agreed that we rambled a lot and at times it was boring. I asked if others felt the same way, and they nodded. I asked why they didn't say anything when it happened. Terry said that I was leading the group, so why didn't I speak up? I admitted that it was my responsibility, and I guessed I just felt uncomfortable about interrupting, or at times I felt that we might finally get back to our discussion. By the time I realized we were getting nowhere, the meeting was almost over.
>
> Terry said that I should say something when this happened. I agreed, but asked why it had to be just me. I asked why they couldn't say something as well. 'I could use all the help I could get, since sometimes I was confused and lost as well. Jean said she always thought that that was the leader's job. She said she would usually sit there wondering if I were ever going to intervene. I said that I could understand that, since I too had always said: "Let the leader do it." I told them that now that I was the leader, I realized it was important to have everyone take some responsibility for our sessions, not just me.
>
> I asked them if they could agree to be more active and responsible for how things went in the group sessions, and that I would try as well. The group members nodded in agreement. Terry smiled, and said:

"Don't you think we have discussed this long enough and should move on?" We all laughed in acknowledgment of his quick acceptance of the new role.

The supervisor as an outsider

One of the most difficult feelings a supervisor must come to grips with is the role of an outsider. Having come up through the ranks, perhaps in the same agency, and having experienced what the staff has gone through in his or her own practice, the supervisor may *feel* like an insider. In reality, however, a supervisor will never be an insider again. Once the supervisor moves one step beyond direct practice, the workers perceive her or him as different. A supervisor can partially overcome that feeling by using past experiences to tune in to the staff and to demonstrate a capacity for empathy. In the end, however, the supervisor remains the perpetual outsider.

The following excerpt is a segment of dialogue from a videotaped recording of a supervisor's staff group meeting that he had called to ask the staff to discuss his role with them. At the start of the meeting he contracted clearly, pointing out he had been hearing many hints about his way of relating to them. After giving examples of what made him feel the discussion was necessary, he sat back to listen. The first staff responses evaded his question and instead focused on the practice issues embedded in his examples. After a few moments of listening, he made a demand for work by acknowledging their concerns on the practice issues, but stressing that what he wanted to talk about was how he related to them when they brought those concerns to him. The staff then understood that he meant his invitation to talk directly about him and began to respond:

Supervisor: For example, John, you came to me with a kid you couldn't place after you had tried all the resources, and I tried to come up with other resources and, failing that, told you not to feel so bad because others were having the same problem. I didn't get the feeling I really helped.

John: You know, you're sitting there at the end of the day with this kid in your hands and no place to go. People say have you tried specialized resources, but you've already done that. The fact is, it's 5 P. M., you have the kid, there is no place to put him, and you're really all alone.

Supervisor: And my trying to tell you not to feel so bad really doesn't help.

John: You try hard to understand, and I know you were a worker too, but nobody, not even the supervisor, can understand what it feels like when you're stuck like that and all alone.

Supervisor: I think I do sense your pain, but instead of just sharing it with you, I probably try to cheer you up, which is next to useless.

The supervisor as a source of support

Even though the supervisor is an outsider, the staff wants and needs him or her to be a source of support when necessary. The ability of the supervisor to feel and express empathy is a crucial variable in determining whether supervision will be effective. The supervisor who genuinely empathizes with the worker provides a helping model of how to relate to clients. The following excerpt is from the same group:

James: Sometimes, when I come to you with a big problem, I really don't want to hear solutions, I just want to get the shit cleared up in my head.

Supervisor: And that's when I usually start to try and give you answers to the problem—ideas, things you should try.

James: I'm going to need those ideas, and they are probably good ones, but right then I can't hear them. I know, as you're talking, I'm thinking: "Run those by me once again, maybe I'll understand this time." But it doesn't work, because I'm sitting there too upset. Maybe it's my fault, because if I come to you and ask for a solution, that's what I'll get.

Supervisor: It sure doesn't help if all you hear are answers when you're sitting there all upset with your feelings.

James: Don't get me wrong, you have changed a lot over the last three years—you're much better now on letting us know you feel for us. I guess I don't come right out and ask for your support because I'm not sure that's what supervision is all about. I mean, somewhere back there I heard you say that you weren't our counselor for personal problems, so when I'm feeling overwhelmed I'm not sure if that's personal and if I should bring it to you. I think that I should have that all together before I come to see you, that it's my job to work that stuff out and come in ready to work.

The discussion of the supervisor as a source of support leads indirectly into unresolved contract issues, providing the supervisor with an opportunity to clarify for the whole group that their feelings are part of the work. Though their feelings are personal, they are relevant to the supervision process. It is interesting that the worker, James, is struggling with the problem of a split between what he thinks he should feel (in control) and what he actually does feel (overwhelmed).

The supervisor's limitations

The next excerpt, dealing with the supervisor's limitations, shows how the unresolved issue raised by James—the dichotomy between how we really feel and how we think we should feel—parallels the difficulty faced by the supervisor. So often, when staff members are having trouble doing something, it's the supervisor's problem as well:

Louise (speaking to the supervisor): How must you be feeling about all this? We seem to be putting a lot of responsibility on you to be there for us. Maybe there are times you wish we would just go away.

Supervisor: To be honest, there are times at the end of the day when I'm sitting there listening to you and feeling that I really don't have anything to offer you.

James: Do you ever say that?

Supervisor: Probably not.

John: But I can always tell. (Group members laugh.)

Louise: I guess we always expect you to have everything together, because you're the supervisor. You're not supposed to feel as overwhelmed as we do. You're supposed to come in always ready for work. We really do put a lot on you.

Supervisor: And I think I haven't been honest enough with you. I should just level when I don't have it for you; it would be better than just pretending.

John: I think we could appreciate that.

Simply discussing this problem in a nondefensive way will make a profound change in the culture of the group. The supervisor and the workers find that they can talk about a formerly tabooo subject, be honest with each other, and thereby strengthen the relationship. The discussion is not over yet, however, since the supervisor will have to build in continued structures for maintaining the relationship. Staff members never "work through" the authority theme, never resolve it; they simply learn how to address a subject which will be with them, in one form or another, throughout their relationships.

This conversation between the supervisor and his staff went well because he already had a good relationship with the workers. It would have sounded very different if they did not trust him. However, his being "pretty good the last three years" had built up a fund of positive relationships on which he could draw. Fortunately, it does not take three years to do this.

The supervisor as a source of demand

All through this chapter the need for supervisors to make demands on their staff groups has been emphasized. They must push them to talk about uncomfortable subjects. They must dig for lurking negatives when the entire group conspires to evade honest discussion. They must insist that staff members take an active responsibility for group operations. After a while, all this pushing, digging, and insisting is bound to generate some hostility. Even if the supervisor has combined these demands with the kind of caring and support which builds a sound relationship, and the staff members understand that the demands are in their own interests, they naturally respond angrily. In fact, as has been noted, if staff groups never get angry at a supervisor, it is usually because that supervisor has not made enough demands.

This anger is hard for a supervisor, particularly a new supervisor, to take, because the myth calls for a perpetually positive relationship: Anger seems a sign of poor supervision. While it can be that in some situations, in other cases it may simply be a reaction to effective supervision. The supervisor thus has to guard against letting staff reaction touch his or her own understandable self-doubts too deeply, so as not to put off. In tough situations such as these, it helps to have colleagues or other supervisors to talk with as a source of emotional support, as well as a sounding board for one's perceptions. As the supervisor's confidence increases it is a bit easier to hold the fort, and, in the end, the staff will appreciate it. They may also gain the confidence to do the same with their own clients.

The Ending Phase in Groups

The departure of a supervisor or a worker from a staff group is an ending, as was noted in respect to sessional ending skills in Chapter 3. General ending issues and evaluations are discussed in some detail in Chapter 7, which describes endings when a worker leaves a job and when a supervisor terminates a staff relationship.

There are stories of staff members or supervisors quietly cleaning out their desks a week before their last day, and then taking vacation days to avoid the last week and the need to say goodbye. The dynamics of endings with clients (Shulman, 1979) parallel the ending processes with a staff, but staff members often have an even greater reluctance to discuss them. Still, a close observer can see the various stages of the ending process: denial, anger, mourning, and learning to live with the idea.

It is helpful if the supervisor calls the ending process to everyone's attention early enough so that some discussion can take place. If a staff member is leaving, allowing some group time to discuss his or her involvement, perhaps to provide some feedback for the agency, and, most importantly, to examine the feelings associated with the leaving, can turn the ending phase of work into one of the most productive. And after all the work has been done, everyone can go for the farewell party.

Research Findings

The findings of our supervision study (Shulman, Robinson, and Luckyj, 1981) in relation to group sessions were presented in Chapter 1, in the discussion of the context of supervision. When workers were asked if their supervisors set regularly scheduled time for group supervision, the average response was "sometimes." When asked to approximate how often these sessions were held, the average score indicated twice a month. Holding regularly scheduled group sessions correlated positively with a good working relationship ($r = 0.34$), the supervisor playing the role of teacher (0.36), the supervisor helping the worker to deal with taboo subjects (0.29), and the ability of the supervisor to clarify his or her role (0.30). The frequency of group supervision also positively correlated with the supervisor's role as teacher (0.30).

In another study of group supervision, Sales and Navarre (1970) compared students who experienced group supervision versus individual supervision. When their instructors' ratings of them were compared, both groups of students performed equally well in the field work. However, supervisors reported saving time when they used group supervision. In additional support of the "strength in numbers" phenomenon, students in group supervision indicated they felt a greater freedom to disagree with the instructor and to express dissatisfaction with the agency. They also indicated that they liked the varying ideas and experiences to which they were exposed as they listened to cases presented by other students. Students receiving individual supervision liked the specific help they received most.

Summary

Supervision in the helping professions is concerned with the dynamics of both formal and informal staff groups. There are different purposes and procedures for the different types of formal staff groups: staff meetings, group consultation, group supervision, and in-service training. In addition, informal staff groups comprised of all staff members who interact together can powerfully affect the delivery of services.

Work with groups can be examined in relation to the phases of work. In the beginning phase, the role of the group leader and the contract process are highlighted. The work phase focuses on helping a staff group develop a culture for work, the individual in the staff group, and conflict in the group. In addition, the authority theme is related to the group leader–group member relationship. The importance of dealing with the ending dynamics is also stressed.

Chapter 6

Working with the System

The feeling of being caught in the middle is one of the most difficult problems faced by supervisors in the helping professions. On the one side is the staff, with whom the supervisor often identifies strongly. On the other side is the administration, with which the supervisor may feel some sense of shared identity. In all settings— large or small, social work, medical, or child care—a pervasive "us versus them" attitude is common. This is the one problem that is raised most often and in every one of my workshops for supervisors.

The Supervisor's Role in Mediating Conflict With the System

Conflicts between staff members and the administration are the rule rather than the exception, and they make up a large part of the interaction in the formal and informal systems of various settings in the helping professions. Unworkable policies are sometimes set by administrators, who may be too far removed from the realities of practice to understand their effect on services. New programs or procedures may be developed by study groups or outside consultants with little understanding of the actual nature of the practice. Competition for funds is fierce at all times, and particularly in times of cutbacks, when too many services must fight for a share of inadequate resources.

At the same time, staff members may resist changes that are threatening to the status quo or require sacrifices such as weekend work. They may be unwilling to consider the requirements of the entire institutional setting and instead stubbornly dig in their heels, remaining untouched by pleas for flexibility or consideration.

The causes of staff-administration friction vary, but in numerous situations friction exists, and it poses a difficult dilemma for supervisors. From the administration's point of view, a supervisor who identifies with the staff becomes a "traitor"; from the staff's point of view, a supervisor who sides with the administration becomes one of "them." As a result, many supervisors respond with apathy echoing their staffs' position that "You can't fight city hall," and following a policy William Schwartz described as letting sleeping dogs lie. This acceptance of the impossibility of change causes negative feelings to go underground, to emerge in many indirect ways which affect ongoing services. A staff that feels impotent in the agency system cannot easily help clients who feel just as impotent in dealing with society's systems.

The functional mediation role for the supervisor which has been developed in this book provides a framework in which the need to make a choice of identifying with either the staff or the administration can be avoided. In most cases, rather than taking sides with one over the other, the supervisor can take a stand on the side of the process. In fact, being "caught in the middle" can be a most effective position for stimulating change.

This role for the supervisor, however, is not one where the supervisor never takes a position or is neutral on every issue. In fact, honest expression of their own points of view by supervisors is an important part of the supervision process, though their personal points of view do not determine which part they will play. If the role of supervisor is dictated by personal views, a supervisor who agrees with an administrative change might try to "cool out" the staff so that they will accept it more easily, in spite of their reservations. Alternatively, a supervisor who disagrees with a policy might identify with staff in an attempt to subvert or sabotage the administration. In the mediation role, however, the supervisor is a "third force" or buffer in the complex hierarchy of bureaucratic systems, as was illustrated in Figure 1.2 in Chapter 1. Whether or not supervisors agree with a policy is not crucial in determining their actions. Rather, the job requires them to open up areas of differences so that both parties in a conflict can deal with them honestly. It is with this open process that the mediation role of the supervisor can be identified.

The mediation role does not mean the supervisor will shy away from conflict in attempts to smooth over real differences of interest between workers and the administration. Just the opposite is true. Effective implementation of this role requires that conflicts smoldering beneath the surface be brought to light. There will be times when advocacy of a staff position and confrontation of the administration are essential tools for the supervisor, although careful thought must be given to how these tools are used. Even in the role of advocate, the supervisor must not lose sight of the essential common ground between the staff and the administration.

To implement the mediation role, the supervisor must maintain a vision of this common ground even when all others—workers and administrators—have lost sight of it. Schwartz (1968) addressed this issue in a report of his work with supervisors and middle-level administrators in a large child welfare system:

> ... one had to believe that staff and administration could find some common ground on which to develop strategies of service that both could own and act upon. Was there a real relationship between the stake of the agency and that of its workers? Was it always a "versus" or could the administrator find the common interest between them— not in broad, philosophical terms, but on a given problem of service? Much of the we-they feeling is certainly inevitable in any worker-employer relationship, and particularly in a large bureaucracy. But in every meeting record we examined, on every specific practice question, the motives of staff and administration could be harnessed so that the job that brought them together could be done more effectively. Both had a stake in solving the problem—because it would make their jobs easier and more enjoyable, because they wanted a better service to people and because their own performance would look better in the process. And the administrator's skill lay in finding the way—often tangled and obscure—to this common ground. Where he could not find it, all the exhorting, persuading and cajoling he could muster would not produce the action he needed on any important problem. But where he could, he was able to precipitate an open and dignified problem-solving process that had at least the ring of reality, however difficult the issue. (p. 360)

In my own efforts to help supervisors examine ways to play this mediating role—by searching out and implementing the common ground, by challenging obstacles that make it difficult for both staff and administration to see their mutual interests, by reaching for strength in both their staffs and their administrators—one of the most serious barriers has been their despair of the possibility of change. They may have tried, sometimes skillfully, other times crudely, and met with resistance. Or they may have developed a stereotype of administrators which made it difficult for them to deal effectively with the resistance and ambivalence that can occur in administrators as easily as in workers. Their attitude is: "These administrators, they should be different."

I have found that, in most cases, when the details of an interaction are closely examined, a next step or a new approach or another way of seeing a problem is discovered which can provide help and hope to the supervisor. In some cases, since effective implementation of this role requires harnessing the energies of workers as well as administrators, change may not be possible. An administration may be so defensive, or frightened, or closed to change, or in an environmental bind it cannot escape (e.g., slashing budget cuts) that it is not possible to have any impact on it. In such circumstances, there is still work to be done (as will be described later in this chapter), while waiting for change in the administration or a change of administrators. The important point is that such dead-end situations are the exception rather than the rule.

In the supervisor's work with the system, the mediation role serves two principal functions: helping individual staff members deal with other parts of the system and the administration, and acting as a third force in relations between the staff group and the administration. This chapter examines these functions with examples from my supervision workshops, which have provided a means for supervisors to examine their crucial role in mediating between staff members and administrators. While no simple solutions are provided, a next step is always apparent. The principle of looking for the next step is a fundamental one in this type of work.

Helping the Staff Negotiate the System

Professional impact is one of the learning subject areas of skill development identified in Figure 4.1 in Chapter 4, which deals with the educational function of supervision. Professional impact skills are used by staff members in their day-to-day interactions with other professionals within their own agency, with professionals in other agencies, and with their own agency administration. Some of the problems of colleagual interaction were described in the discussion of supervision of staff groups in Chapter 5. Here the focus is on the particular problems involved in staff members' relations with others in their own system who have either implied or direct authority. The first example describes a supervisor's efforts to help a ward nurse who had to work with a rude doctor. The second concerns a supervisor's work with a staff member's conflicts with an agency administrator over her career development.

Further discussion and examples in this area of practice can be found in Program 3, "Working with the System," of *The Skills of Helping,* a videotape series in which helping professionals in a number of settings illustrate the dynamics of professional impact.[1] (See Appendix B for a complete description of the three programs in this series.)

Staff-authority conflict

Nurse-doctor conflict, which is common in hospital settings, provides a good illustration of the dynamics involved when the staff must deal with those who have authority in the system. In a supervisors' workshop, an experienced nursing supervisor who was new to the service described the doctor serving as the chief of service as one who frequently spoke harshly to nursing staff members about patient care which failed to meet his expectations. The relationship between this doctor and the nurses on the ward was strained, as was the relationship between the nursing supervisor and the doctor. The supervisor described in detail a conversation with a nurse who had reported a particular incident which greatly upset her. The record of my consultation work with the nursing supervisor follows:

> I asked the supervisor how she had felt when the nurse was describing the incident. She replied that she had been upset and angry and had felt that this problem had to be dealt with. I asked her what she said to the nurse, and she replied that she had comforted her and told her she would speak to the doctor. I told her it would be interesting to see how she handled the conversation with the doctor, but before that I wondered whether there might have been some ways she could help the nurse figure out what to do in such situations.

---

[1]Produced by Lawrence Shulman and available from the Instructional Communications Centre, McGill University, Montreal, Canada (1980).

The other workshop participants joined in as we discussed some strategies for dealing with the nurse. I pointed out that the supervisor did not want to be always called in to deal with these conflicts, and some time invested when a conflict arose might be worthwhile in the long run. In this way, the staff might feel more comfortable dealing with such problems, wherever they came from. We role-played some alternatives, and I (playing the supervisor's role) encouraged the supervisor (role-playing the nurse) to describe her feelings in the encounter and what she had said back to the doctor. As the role play proceeded, it became clear that the nurse had not said a thing, feeling too embarrassed and afraid. The problem involved had not really been her fault, but she had failed to share that with the doctor.

As the role play proceeded, I (as the supervisor) explored the nurse's feelings and why it was hard for her to confront the doctor and to be honest with how she felt when he dealt with her that way. I pointed out that if everyone simply rolled over and took it, how would the doctor ever get an idea of his effect on staff nurses? I suggested we role-play how she might have handled the confrontation differently, and could still handle it if it came up again. At the end of the conversation, I then said I, as supervisor, would also be speaking to the doctor about the impact he had on the staff, and that might make him more receptive to her. I said I would suggest that he speak to her about the incident, to clear the air, and she agreed that that would help.

In the discussion, the supervisors revealed how hard it was for them to help their staffs be more honest and assertive, partly because they themselves were not. One long-term nursing administrator, about to retire, brought gales of laughter to the group when she commented that she had been trained to "wear her little white hat, sit on a pink cushion, be ladylike, and take whatever crap was handed to her." It became clear that there was much confusion and mixed feeling about authority issues and how to deal with them. Most of the participants admitted that they had had trouble dealing with people with authority in the system, even other nursing administrators.

When I explored the conversation the nursing supervisor in this example had had with the doctor, it became clear that she had burst in on him and exploded. All of her pent-up feelings came out as she unloaded her frustrations with the way he was relating to her staff. His response, she said, was to listen impassively and then say: "I guess it's true, what they say about you; what you need is a good man!" When she reported his comment, the consultation group erupted in expressions of anger and recognition. I asked the supervisor how she had felt, and she replied "speechless with anger." When I asked what she said, she replied: "Nothing! I just stood there and started to cry."

As the supervisor reported this incident in the workshop, she began to cry again. I pointed out how embarrassed she must have felt about her response and asked others in the workshop if they could offer some support. They were quick to do so, with one supervisor putting her arm around her, and others agreeing how hard it was to deal with both the implied and direct examples of sexism they experienced. They reported numerous incidents of a similar nature, when male authority figures had made such comments as: "Must be that time of the month again," or "Does menopause really have to be that stressful?" It quickly became apparent that in this field authority and gender issues are closely related, since most administrators and doctors are male and most nursing supervisors are female.

As the workshop continued, it became obvious that before the supervisors could help their own staffs learn ways of being more direct with this system's representatives with authority, they needed to be able to do the same themselves. The workshop group went back to the original presenter and tuned in to what might have been going on for the doctor, why he reacted the way he did, and how the supervisor might go back and reopen the question directly, in such a way that he could not simply dismiss it with a sexist stereotype. I pointed out that although being honest about her feelings might make the supervisor feel vulnerable, it might also be the way to break a vicious cycle. Some participants were skeptical about the doctor's ability to change, and while I agreed that they might be right, I said I thought that simply giving up without some direct attempt at dealing with the problem could be an illustration of sexist stereotyping on their part: "He's a man, so what can you expect?" I pointed out that there would still be time to raise the issue with the hospital administration if the supervisor could not get anywhere with him.

In case after case, I have observed that direct and honest confrontation, if handled constructively, can force the authority person to respond differently and become less of a one-dimensional stereotype. In one case, direct discussion between a nurse on a neurosurgery ward and her chief surgeon over her anger at his implied orders to withhold life support systems to a dying patient led to a remarkable discussion of the difficulties faced by a surgeon who finds himself unable to help a patient. In that example all the staff, doctors and nurses, were operating under considerable stress, but rarely did they share their similar feelings. Lack of openness led to abruptness and apparent lack of caring, which was far from the truth.

In another case, a supervisor confronting an administrator with her unhappiness over a budget decision was able to listen to his problems with some genuine empathy, and she soon discovered how much pressure he was experiencing. She reported obtaining a greater understanding of the demands and the loneliness of his job. It was still necessary for her to press for her own department's budgetary needs, but at least she could do so with an understanding of some of the binds he was experiencing, a fact not lost on the administrator.

The examples in this chapter demonstrate that the combination of empathy and demand, so crucial to every supervision process described thus far, is equally important when dealing with the system's representatives of authority. Nevertheless, supervisors or staff members who have developed skill in tolerating and understanding deviant behavior by worker or clients appear to have little ability to understand the same behavior when it is demonstrated by people with authority in the system. When workshop participants say: "They (the administrators, etc.) should be different," I can only respond: "But they're not! Now, do you want to deal with the way they should be, or the way they are?" This comment usually meets with a reflective silence.

Career planning

A second example of helping staff members deal with the system involves a problem experienced by a staff member who had been following a particular career line in the agency which had led her to a dead end. She was interested in receiving agency support for training which would allow her to move into another career line with more room for development and promotion. While training opportunities did exist in the agency, policy had excluded staff members in her particular category of employment from access to such support. As a result, she felt frustrated and hopeless about her future at the agency. When this example of a particular staff member's problem was presented in a supervision workshop, it became clear it was a problem throughout the system. At the time the policy had been set, the administration had failed to take into account its full effects on the morale of the staff.

The supervisor in this case arranged to meet with the regional administrator, the area administrator (a member of the administrative group which set policy), and the worker. His plan was to bring the problem directly to their attention, rather than using a memo that could get lost in the system. This bold step had been a waste of time, however, because the area administrator simply commiserated with the worker but indicated that there was nothing he could do about the policy. The supervisor felt the meeting had simply increased both his and the worker's frustration.

When asked for details of this meeting, the supervisor made it clear that, once the issue had been stated, his approach had been passive. He described how he felt and how the staff member looked as the area administrator spelled out the policy, but, as I pointed out, he did not help the staff member share her real feelings about the situation, and he did not share his. The group decided to role-play the conference, with the supervisor taking the role of mediator between the staff member and the administrator and concentrating on trying to keep the communications honest and to be supportive of both parties. After a brief silence following the explanation by the administrator, who was role-played by an actual administrator on this level who was attending the workshop, the supervisor turned to the worker and said:

Supervisor: I have a feeling Sam's explanation hasn't helped. Am I right?

Worker: I already know the policy. What I don't understand is why they stick to it when it makes so many problems.

Supervisor: Perhaps you could explain to Sam what it means to you, in particular—how it feels to you.

Worker: I feel I'm in a dead end with no place to go. I'm only 30, and it already looks like I have no future at this agency. I like working with the agency, but frankly, I don't see staying on if I'm not challenged by my work —and yet I can't seem to get anywhere within the system. It feels like the agency just doesn't care a damn about staff, and this is supposed to be a helping profession.

Supervisor: I know that sounds a bit strong, Sam, but I have heard it from others in the system as well—and I think it's important for you to hear it directly. I know you do give a damn.

Administrator: Look, I don't agree with the policy, either. You think we are all the same at the central office, but the fact is we have many differences of opinion up there as well. There were pressures on us from a number of regional administrators and the civil service people to set the policy up that way.

Supervisor: I can understand how it came about, but now that we have had two years' experience with it, is it possible that the central office might reconsider? Perhaps you can use this example, or if it would help, I would be glad to document the problem. I could probably get other supervisors to provide documentation as well.

Administrator: I guess we have to face this sometime or another. You are not the only one we have been hearing from. Why don't you put together some documentation? I will get it on the agenda at the central office.

Calling the meeting was just the start of the process; the supervisor had to be prepared for the hard part: making the meeting meaningful. By concentrating on bringing out the real feelings, he was able to turn an illusion of work into a meaningful discussion. In addition, he treated the administrator as someone who did care, refusing to accept the stereotype of an unfeeling bureaucrat, even when the administrator appeared to be acting like one. He reached for the strength in the administrator, in the worker, and in himself.

As an interesting side note, the participant who role-played the administrator, and who was actually part of the central office planning group, used the experience as a basis for raising the issue, with some success, at a policy meeting held later that month. All such interventions will not be so successful, since, obviously, other factors will be involved. Nonetheless, the supervisor who plays his or her part effectively may help others be more effective in their own roles.

The Third-Force Function

Three areas of work are crucial in the third-force function of the supervisor: working with the staff group, working with the administration, and working with the two together.

Work with the staff group involves helping staff members to be honest about their thoughts and feelings on agency policies and procedures. They need help in developing a sense of responsibility for impact on the system and the skill required to have such an impact, and, most important, in overcoming the apathy and sense of hopelessness that are common in complicated systems. In addition, it may be necessary to help staff members identify elements of their reactions to policy and procedures which may, in truth, be signs of their fears and insecurity. An example is an automatic negative reaction to a policy change which would require the staff to develop new skills.

Work with the administration requires the supervisor to accurately communicate the staff's thoughts and feelings in a way that minimizes an administration response of defensiveness or evasive tactics. It also requires skill in developing a working relationship with the administrator that involves many of the supervisory skills identified in Chapter 3, such as empathy and demand. In general, the goal is to turn the administrator toward the staff, helping to identify and strengthen the areas of common ground, even when the differences are most strong. I have seen effective work done in preparing an administrator for a meeting with staff, for example, by anticipating some of the anger and helping develop a strategy for dealing with it.

At times work in this area requires confrontation and advocacy as a staff representative, when the system does not respond to the supervisor's efforts to "speak softly." Such confrontations must be handled skillfully, and supervisors are well advised to develop skills in mobilizing the informal group system in support of their efforts. The development of allies in the system, such as other supervisors or department heads, can significantly strengthen a presentation and prevent a supervisor from being isolated as the deviant member (see Chapter 5). Ongoing work by a supervisor in building up credits in the system, by offering support, cooperation, and so on, is important when it is time to "call in the tabs" and ask others in key positions to provide needed support.

At a large residential institution where I worked, there was a daily lunchtime ping pong game in the staff recreation room in which many of the key department heads were avid players. As a fan of the game, I joined in and was pleased to discover that I very quickly developed working relationships with key actors in the system. These relationships were extremely helpful to me later when I became involved in a major effort at systems impact (for a discussion of this process see Shulman, 1969a, 1969c, 1970). And I developed an extremely effective backhand slam as well.

When administrators and staff members are brought directly together, the supervisor needs to work on helping them talk to and listen to each other, keeping the talk honest and invested with real feelings, and overcoming the barriers on both sides that may be obscuring their common ground. In some cases, it is necessary to help both sides figure out how to keep their working relationship going when understanding or agreement in some specific area continues to elude them.

The following sections present examples from my records of supervision workshops dealing with the three areas of the supervisor's third-force function.

Work with the staff group

One workshop example concerned a change in government policy that required child welfare social workers to explore the possibility of financial support by natural parents when children were placed in alternate care facilities. A sliding scale was developed, and parents who could not afford to make payments did not have to do so. The argument advanced by the government officials was that making support payments was one important way for natural parents to continue their connection with their children. The change would also help save money which could be available for other children.

Many of the workers and supervisors believed, however, that this was a return to a means test and a disguised way of cutting services. They were furious, worried that their relationship with clients, already tenuous at best, would be destroyed. They did not want to become financial investigators. At the workshop, the supervisor revealed that he had heard out their complaints, had agreed with them, but then had said: "We can't fight city hall." The staff had reluctantly accepted the new policy, but the supervisor knew they were not happy.

In the discussion there was some disagreement among the supervisors. Some accepted that there might indeed be an advantage in involving natural parents in supporting their children. Some had had experiences in other agencies using a sliding scale for services, and they felt clients appreciated being able to pay something for what they were getting. When I asked these supervisors how they handled the reaction of staff members, they indicated that they had tried to "sell" the idea by pointing out all the possible advantages and had just pushed the objections under the table. They admitted their staff members were still upset.

Both the supervisors who agreed with the policy and those who did not suffered from what Schwartz called *functional diffusion:* they were unclear about their functions as supervisors in such conflicts and so had missed an opportunity to be helpful. I assured participants that functional diffusion was not a terminal illness, and with a bit of clarification they could recover quite easily.

The group began by tuning in to the feelings of the workers: why did they react so strongly? One of the supervisors reflected on his earlier experiences in assessing client fees, suggesting it might be because they were uncomfortable with talking about income and setting fees, which can be a taboo topic. Many of the workers may have simply felt uncomfortable not knowing how to handle it in an interview. One of the supervisors who had tried to sell the idea said this was where he had gone wrong; he had missed the underlying concerns and had only seen the resistance. The supervisor who had presented the example opposed the fees, and he said he felt that he had been so quick to agree with his workers that he had ignored this issue.

In the workshop work that followed (role play and discussion), the group developed an approach that both supervisors who opposed the new rule and those who had accepted it could use to open up the question, be honest about their own points of view, and try to understand the objections of the staff. All these were essential because there is usually some truth to the immediate concerns, and the supervisor who simply reaches for the underlying issues, while ignoring the objections, will be resented. They also practised how to reach for the hidden issues.

Here is the report of an encounter with his staff that one supervisor presented at a follow-up session:

> I began by telling them I wanted to discuss the support payment issue again. I told them I was not satisfied with how I had handled it before, in that I had agreed with the policy change and had simply tried to sell it. They had some important objections, and I wanted to go over them again. Frank (the internal leader) began to raise the problems he could see in terms of client resistance. He felt they would resent

having to make payments, and it would just be another barrier. I told them I could appreciate that the job was hard enough already, and they probably were not too happy about it being made harder in their view.

Theresa agreed with Frank, but then went on to say she didn't believe it would do any good to argue, since the decision had already been made. I agreed that they had to follow the policy, but that did not mean we could not raise our concerns with the administration, and if we felt strongly enough, perhaps we could keep some documentation on how this was received by clients, and then report back to the administration. I told them I was not sure it would help, but if they felt strongly enough, we should give it a try.

Frank wanted to know if I had changed my mind and was no longer supporting the policy. I told him I still held the same views on the matter, but I was open to examining the experience to see what came of it. I went on to say that in the last analysis, what really mattered was how they felt about this policy, because unless they could see some benefit, they would not be able to implement it with enthusiasm, and that would guarantee its failure. Most of the staff group nodded in agreement.

I asked if a subcommittee of staff could be set up to discuss ways of monitoring the experience, gathering data, and preparing to feed it back to the administration. There were three volunteers, including Frank. I then said I had been thinking about their reactions, and wondered if in part they were also worried about how to handle that part of the interview with the parents. I said I could see how they would be worried about the problems it could create. Minnie said she dreaded the first one she had to deal with, and it was coming up that afternoon. I asked what she was worried about, and that began a discussion on the technical aspect of conducting the interview: how they would feel, how the client might feel, and how they would introduce the idea. The discussion was a good one, with most staff joining in. We role-played Minnie's interview that afternoon, trying to help her (and all of us) find the right words.

In another example of working with the staff group, a supervisor was helping the staff get ready to meet with an administrator to discuss their reactions to a policy change. The group consisted of members of a nursing staff who were upset at a change in shift hours that had been implemented in what they felt was an arbitrary manner by the administrator. The staff had developed a system of working longer hours a number of days in a row, and then taking a sizable block of time off. This routine had been tried for a number of months, but the administration had decided it was not working well, and staff efficiency was falling after too many working hours on consecutive days. The administration had issued a memo requiring a return to the old system, and the staff was furious as much at the way it was announced as at the change itself.

The nursing supervisor had already met with the administrator to prepare her for the session. The following excerpt is her report of how she prepared the staff to make their argument. After helping them set down their views in point-by-point fashion, with their supporting data, she focused on the process of the encounter:

> I asked who would make the presentation. Louise said she would start it off, but wouldn't mind others helping as well—so she wouldn't feel alone. I wondered if they were worried about Miss Pomeroy's reaction. Carol felt we had to make the case, and make it strongly, and if that made her upset, there was nothing we could do. I reminded them that I had already spoken to her, so that what they said would not come as too much of a surprise. I had also let her know they were angry, and my guess was that she was as worried about speaking to them as they were about speaking to her. They laughed at this, and then went on to select a few more people to make the case.
>
> Tess wondered if we should be careful not to get too angry during the discussion, so angry that Miss Pomeroy might just storm out. I said it was a tough balance. On the one hand, they needed to let her know how they really felt, and they couldn't do that without getting angry. On the other, they did not want to back her in a corner so that she got too upset to hear anything. I told them I had told Miss Pomeroy that I would try to stay in the middle during the discussion, helping her make her points and them to make theirs. I would also get my own views in there, because, as they already knew, I had my own reservations about the long hours. However, I was much more concerned about how they and Miss Pomeroy handled this meeting, so I would concentrate on that part of it. They agreed that this would be helpful.

It was important that the supervisor clarify her sense of her role in the meeting so that the staff understood her interventions. By reaching for their fears about the confrontation, she helped to keep the discussion real. If a supervisor does not bring these issues out into the open, they often appear at the meeting itself in the form of long silences and evasions, as everyone waits for the supervisor to take the lead in the attack while they hold his or her coat. The record of the supervisor's preparatory work with the administrator for the joint meeting is presented in the next section.

Another example of the supervisor's work with a staff group illustrates the problems involved in helping staff members deal with a situation they cannot immediately influence. In this case, government reductions in a social agency budget had led to reclassifications and cutbacks in a large number of positions. Additional cutbacks were threatened but had been delayed, and the agency administration was carrying out a campaign against the budget. As a result, a number of workers without seniority were on temporary contracts, living from month to month without knowing what would happen next. The cutbacks and delays had been going on for months, causing a general malaise and widespread poor morale among all the workers and supervisors.

When the problem was presented in a workshop I could sense the depression felt by the supervisors under their expressions of anger. I reached for those feelings and tried to empathize with the difficulties they faced. We discussed social action steps which could be taken on a political level, as individual citizens, and as members of professional organizations. Many of these were already in progress, with only little hope of effect. As the examples were presented, all of us, including myself, felt a deepening despair and sense of hopelessness and helplessness.

As is often the case in workshops, the participants let me know what they were up against by their behavior in the session. This is an example of the parallel processes between supervisor with workers and worker with clients which has been described in preceding chapters. It was important to model an approach that demonstrated the principle that there always is a next step. I acknowledged their feelings and shared my own as follows:

Consultant: It's obvious to me that under all of this anger, you are all feeling a lot of frustration and depression. It's not hard to understand that, because after listening to you for the past little while I'm feeling it as well —and I go home tomorrow. You have to live with this problem.

Supervisor: It wasn't easy before, but now it seems to be hopeless. You have to wonder what the use is of trying anything. (Others in the group nod in agreement.)

Consultant: You know, you didn't bring me all the way here just so I could listen and feel what you're going through, and then agree with you that it's hopeless. It may be that you can't immediately influence these cutbacks, although you all seem to be making the right efforts to do so. If that's true, then we can look at how you can try to provide services within the context of the cutbacks. It might help to examine what the impacts of the cutbacks are and how to deal with them best. I don't mean administratively, that's not appropriate in my workshop, but in terms of your supervision of staff and, in turn, their provision of service to clients. What are some of the effects on staff members, and how have you been handling them?

One common problem arose from an example presented of a temporary worker whose work was seriously slacking off. He was obviously depressed about his job uncertainty. It became clear that the supervisor had felt so guilty that she had not discussed his work with him. We did some work on how she could overcome her apathy and begin to help him deal with his. She might, for example, confront him with the problem and examine how it was affecting his work with clients. I pointed out that his clients might sense the problem of his impermanence, and that would affect their response to him. The change in atmosphere in the consulting group was noticeable as the members harnessed their energies to efforts to understand the impact of these cutbacks on their supervision, their workers, and the staff's service to clients. This was one next step they could take. As one supervisor pointed out in the evaluation, I had modeled what they had to do with their workers—being supportive but at the same time demanding.

Work with the administration

There is little question that effective work with the administration is one of the most difficult aspects of the supervisor's job. The concept of transference which has been so helpful to an understanding of both client-worker relationship and worker-supervisor relationships is just as useful at the supervisor-administrator level. Supervisors have a long history of dealing with people in authority —family members, teachers, previous administrators—and feelings and patterns of interaction from all those relationships can be easily transferred to current authority symbols. Past experiences with other agencies, the current agency, and other large bureaucracies also contribute to the attitudes supervisors have developed over the years.

Difficulties in Supervisor-Administrator Relationships. Numerous factors make it difficult for supervisors to affect their own administrations. First, there are usually so many issues in any setting that even considering an attempt to have an impact on all of them is a bit overwhelming. As a result, supervisors may decide that nothing can be done about any of them. It's a bit like having a long list of chores to do on the weekend, so long that it becomes easy to decide not even to start. When we are serious about dealing with our chores, or the agency issues affecting practice, our first step is to use the skill of *partializing,* breaking big problems into smaller components and then focusing on one issue at a time.

In addition to the scope and extent of the problems, supervisors have to deal with their own feelings about change. They may bring to their work situation an apathetic attitude that reflects their view of themselves as incapable of exerting meaningful influence. This is a product of our socialization experiences which generally have encouraged us to conform to the existing social structure. Families, schools, peer groups, and work settings often do not encourage individual initiative. All systems have a profound stake in encouraging members to differentiate among themselves and make personal contributions by challenging the system and asserting their individuality. But all systems have not been aware of this need and acted upon it.

All too often, in fact, the system achieves the integration of its members at the expense of individual initiative. As a result of efforts to integrate individuals, system norms that encourage conformity may be developed. The life experiences of many supervisors produce a viewpoint which sees taking responsibility for professional impact as a major change in their relationship to systems in general and to people in authority in particular. Even if they are willing to take risks and involve themselves in attempts to impact on the administration, their experiences often discourage any further efforts. When they encounter resistance to their first attempts, they may fail to recognize the agency's potential for change. The potential is there, but change efforts probably require persistence. If supervisors regard agencies as dynamic systems, open to change but simultaneously resistant, then an initial rebuff does not necessarily mean failure. The timing of the change effort is also important. Supervisors are mistaken if they think their agencies are static and unchanging. An attempt to deal with a problem at one point in an agency's life may be blocked, while at a later stage in the agency's development the same effort would be welcome.

Many supervisors are simply afraid to assert themselves. If the agency culture has discouraged previous efforts, if supervisors regarded as troublemakers suspect that their jobs will be placed on the line, they will regard raising questions about services or policies as a risky business. Certainly there are times when, for a number of reasons, such as the extreme defensiveness of administrators or political pressures on an agency, these fears are well founded. Supervisors in such situations have to decide for themselves, in light of their personal situations and their feelings about the professional and ethical issues involved in the problem, whether they feel they can take the risk.

Other supervisors do not get involved because of stereotyped attitudes about an administration that they have never tested, rather than any actual experience in the agency that has led them to fear reprisals. In either case, the courage needed for making attempts at change should not be minimized. When the effort is risky, the supervisor would be wise to be sure of the presence of allies before trying.

Lack of time is also a serious factor. If supervisory loads are maintained at very high levels, the idea of becoming involved in an effort at agency or social change can seem completely unrealistic. In such settings, the first efforts might deal with the working situation itself. Often outside organizations such as professional associations or unions are the best media for effecting such changes.

The complex magnitude of administration-related issues thus tends to discourage supervisors' attempts at professional impact. Their personal feelings about asserting themselves, as well as specific experiences in agencies, may deter them. Fear of losing their jobs or other retribution may be an obstacle, and insufficient time can discourage such attempts. In spite of all of these obstacles, supervisors do attempt to influence their administrators and the agency system, and sometimes they even succeed.

Examples of Work with the Administration. The first example returns to the supervisor in setting up the meeting of nurses with Miss Pomeroy, the nursing administrator. When the nurses' first strong reaction to the decision changing the hours was evident, the supervisor went to see the administrator. This first excerpt illustrates how the initial resistance of Miss Pomeroy, which confirmed the supervisor's stereotype of the administrator, resulted in a nonproductive exchange.

> I told Miss Pomeroy that the nursing staff were very upset at the change, and in particular, at the way the change was announced. I said that she knew I had some reservations about how the longer shifts had been working, but, in spite of these, I could appreciate how the staff were feeling. I asked her what she would do about this. She was silent for a moment and then said that this would pass. The staff often get upset about policy changes such as these, but they cool down later. She told me there had been a great deal of discussion about this at the upper administrative levels, and she was under some pressure to straighten out the situation as quickly as possible.
>
> I was feeling a bit frustrated, and I told her I didn't think she understood just how strongly this had hit them. She told me that she had been a supervisor for a long time, and after I had more experience I would realize that you couldn't please the staff all of the time. I felt really put down and angry at the comment, but I said nothing, just thanked her for her time (probably sounding bitter) and left.

The supervisor had started the session expecting trouble, and she found it. In discussing the encounter retrospectively, she could see how her own feelings of having been put on the spot by her staff had dominated her, so that she had not bothered to tune in to what the administrator might feel when hearing of the angry reaction. The administrator's denial of the difficulty could instead have been interpreted as signaling her difficulty with the problem.

In this case, the administrator began to share some of the problem as she spoke of the pressures she was under from other administrators. The supervisor, instead of jumping back in with her argument, could have simply asked the administrator: "What kinds of pressures have you been under?" Of course, it is easy to propose this alternative after the fact, in the comfort of a workshop setting. It was understandable why the supervisor had responded as she did at the time, but she had to face the fact that at precisely the moment she was asking the administrator to understand how her staff felt, she was unable to empathize with the administrator's bind. With a bit of support and understanding, she might have been able to work with the administrator on how to handle the problem more effectively. As it was, she came across as all demand and no support, and this could partly explain why the administrator got back at her with the comment about her experience.

After she had tuned in, the supervisor tried again. Note the skills of *clarifying purpose, containment, elaboration, empathy, sharing own feelings,* and *the demand for work* in this second effort:

> I told Miss Pomeroy I was glad she could see me again, since I knew this was a busy time. I told her I did not think I had handled our last conversation about the hours problem as well as I could and that I wanted to try again. I had been upset by the pressure I was feeling from the staff, and I simply dumped it in her lap, when she obviously had pressures as well. She nodded but remained silent. I said I wasn't asking for a change in policy, but rather wanted to discuss ways I and she might be able to deal with the staff's reaction. I wasn't sure anything would help, and she might have been right; it may just have to go away by itself. But I wanted to at least try, if there were any ways to facilitate it. I would like her reactions to some of the thinking I had done about the problem.
>
> She said she would be glad to discuss it, but that she didn't think she could offer any answers, since top-level administration felt the experiment had been tried and had failed. I asked her if she had run into a rough time defending this new policy, and she went on at some length to describe how it had been attacked at an executive-level meeting. Other departments were afraid it might be demanded by their staffs as well. She told me she had tried to defend the nurses' right to experiment but had found it difficult, because she was not convinced it was such a great idea. I told her I knew what she meant, because I felt the same way, and it was easier to fight for something you really supported.
>
> She continued to talk about the communication problems on the executive level, and I listened, since it was obvious she needed someone to talk with. As I listened, I had some clearer insights into the difficulties she faced when she tried to protect the interests of the nursing staff. I shared this with her. I then tried to bring her back to the present problem by telling her I thought it might help a lot if the nursing staff knew about her efforts on their behalf. Also, she could have their direct feedback about this decision, which might be helpful to her in dealing with the executive committee. We might not resolve anything, but at least the staff would feel they had been heard, and they might appreciate hearing that she did fight for their interests. I said they have a distorted view of what goes on in administration, with all administrators simply lumped together as "them."

She said she wasn't sure a meeting would help. I asked her why, and she told me she didn't know how much she could share with the staff, since she did not want it to seem that she was separating herself from the rest of the administration. I told her I could appreciate the dilemma, since I felt the same way, caught between her and the staff. I told her I had found it helpful to level with staff and that they seemed to be able to understand that I could be with administration and, at the same time, try to be helpful to them. I pointed out that my talking to her right now was an example of what I meant, since they know I support the decision to change the policy. She nodded in agreement.

I then asked if she was also worried about what kind of encounter it would be. The staff were angry, and I wouldn't blame her for not wanting to face a bunch of angry staff. She said the worst problem with meetings like this is that nobody says anything; they just sit and glare at you. I told her that I had planned to meet with them before the meeting to help them prepare to share their reactions constructively. I thought they might be honest with her if they felt she really wanted to hear. I would be glad to concentrate on helping them level with her, as well as helping her to get her ideas across to them. I thought they would very much appreciate her making the effort to meet with them, especially if they could get a better idea of her binds. She said she would give it some thought and get back to me. I told her I appreciated her time, and the meeting ended.

The record of the encounter between the staff and the nursing administrator is given as an example in the next section. All supervisors' conversations with administrators do not go as well as the one above, however, even when they are handled skillfully. Some administrators resist so strongly that they cannot respond to the supervisor's reaching out. Even in such cases, the supervisor who does not lose hope immediately and instead allows some time to pass may find a greater responsiveness a few days later or the next week. Often it takes the administrator some time to reflect on the discussion and be ready to respond. The supervisor must respect the process involved and not be immediately disappointed at meeting resistance in difficult areas.

Other situations clearly call for advocacy and taking a stand by the supervisor. In one example, a supervisor of the dietician service at a large institution was faced with an edict that her service must cut back its budget by 10%, as part of an across-the-board cut for all departments. When we discussed this example in a workshop, another dietician suggested she take the cut out of the administrator's entertainment budget, a suggestion received with great delight by the group. This supervisor's style and her security in her job dictated her response: to empathize with the administrator's probems and then refuse to cut her budget. She had argued at a department head meeting that across-the-board cuts simply penalized departments that had already effectively economized and had not padded their budgets. Since she felt this was true in her case, she demanded, and got, an agreement to have audits of all budgets so that cuts would be based on service-related decisions. All workshop participants did not believe they would be able to make such a strong stand, but for this supervisor it made sense.

When Schwartz describes the worker's professional impact on systems on behalf of clients in a videotape program entitled "Private Troubles and Public Issues: One Job or Two?"[2] he says at one point: "There is a time to speak softly and a time to speak loudly." The same is true of the supervisor's relations with the administration on behalf of the staff. In many examples, I have found that supervisors have either confronted before they have spoken softly, or they have been too understanding when they needed to confront. Understanding which time is which is difficult in supervision, as it is in life.

Mediating the staff-administrator encounter

Although a supervisor can be extremely effective as a conduit of communications between staff and administration, it is helpful to bring the two together whenever possible. Administrators become less of a stereotype to workers if both groups can communicate directly, and the feelings of the staff have greater effect when they are experienced at first hand by administrators. It is useful to build in such contacts on a regular basis in order to develop a working relationship over time. When such encounters only take place at times of stress, they are usually more difficult for all parties involved. Because our society has developed norms which restrict open communication of negative feedback and anger, most people have had very little experience with such sessions, and they regard them with a great deal of fear.

---

[2]Program 2 in a videotape series produced by Lawrence Shulman, *The Helping Process in Social Work: Theory, Practice and Research* (Montreal: Instructional Communications Centre, McGill University, 1976).

The example of the planned meeting between the nursing administrator, Miss Pomeroy, and the nursing staff illustrates this process. This problem was presented at a workshop for nursing supervisors which met biweekly for two months, so the supervisor was able to draw on the help of colleagues and the consultant in her preparation for each step of the process.

The group first used tuning in to sensitize the supervisor to potential themes of concern and the indirect ways in which they might arise. For example, silence early in the session might be a cue of the staff's anxiety, so the supervisor developed a strategy for reaching inside the silence if it occurred (e.g., "I know it's not easy to begin, especially when there are some hot issues involved . . .").

It was also important to develop a simple contracting statement to start the session, so all the participants would begin with a clear sense of purpose and acquainted with the supervisor's role (e.g., "The purpose of this session is to discuss both the change in policy on shifts as well as the way in which the changes took place. Since we know there are some strong feelings about this, I thought it best if I concentrated on helping everyone talk to and listen to each other. Is that okay with all of you?").

Most important was the supervisor's tuning in to her own concerns and feelings about the session. It was clear that she was anxious, and she said that she was afraid things could get worse. Further discussion revealed that all the participants were worried that the real feelings would come out in the open, and they might not be up to handling them because they had had as much difficulty with anger and negative feelings as the staff. Perhaps, they thought, it was better to let sleeping dogs lie. When I asked what the worst problems they could imagine might be, the participants suggested that people might get into a shouting match, or they might cry. The meeting might fall flat and everyone would be silent, or the staff might open up and Miss Pomeroy would shut them down, all of which would make things worse.

As the group took up these points and developed some idea of what the supervisor could do in each instance, the "worst" problems began to seem less threatening. If the staff members did lose their tempers, the supervisor could step in and point out how angry they felt, but also how hard the anger was making it for them to hear each other. She could offer to act as a "traffic cop," keeping some sense of order. Most participants felt it would not come to that; in fact, the problem might be to get them to admit the anger. This has been my experience: our behavior has been so conditioned against expressing angry feelings directly that sarcasm, passive resistance, and other more indirect means of communication are likely in sessions such as these.

During a mini role play of what might happen if people cried at the meeting, the supervisor became so full of emotion herself that she was at a loss as to how to help. I suggested she could begin by being honest about her own feelings at the moment. Such directness often frees a person's energy, allowing greater regard for the feelings of others. As for the possibility of silences, the group explored their meaning, and the supervisor practised how she might ask the staff and Miss Pomeroy to discuss how difficult the session was—what it was that made it hard for them to talk together. Often a few minutes of such discussion reveals that both the administrator and the staff have the same fears and reluctance to open up. Recognition of this obstacle may be all that is needed to overcome it. If Miss Pomeroy should have a defensive reaction, the supervisor practised how she might reach for the staff's reaction to the defensiveness, while at the same time recognizing how hard such a meeting might be for the administrator (e.g., "You know, I think with everyone coming on so strong it must be putting Miss Pomeroy on the spot; she's really caught in the middle on this issue.").

After reviewing each of the "worst fears" and developing some strategy for responding to them, the group considered the possibility that none of the anticipated problems would occur. I suggested that it was crucial for the supervisor to have some faith in both her staff members and Miss Pomeroy; with her help in leading the discussion, they could find the strength to handle their parts. She replied that the preparation had helped somewhat, but she was still scared. The workshop participants agreed that it would be a bit frightening, no matter how prepared they felt.

The following is a summary report of the meeting which the supervisor presented at the next workshop session:

> On the morning of the meeting at least three or four of my staff members made joking comments about the session (e.g., "Well, are you ready for the showdown?"). Each time I laughed, and then acknowledged their concern, just as we had practised in the workshop. This helped steady my nerves a bit, because I felt I was starting to work as

planned. In fact, I was pleased with myself. When Miss Pomeroy
arrived, the staff all sat on one side of the conference room table and
she sat on the other side, with me at the head. I realized this was a
first signal, but I simply passed it over. I made my opening statement,
just as I had practised it, and when I asked for their comments, there
was a brief silence. I was ready to "reach inside" when Louise began
listing some of their points, as we had planned. Miss Pomeroy sat tense
and quiet, listening to their concerns and arguments. Most were already familiar to her, as I had shared them in our conference.

When she finished, I said it might help if we took up the issues one
at a time. I wondered where Miss Pomeroy might want to start. She
began by explaining the thinking in relation to the policy, why they
felt the system had not worked, and why she had to make the change.
To each of her points, different staff members countered with their
views, and I began to feel like we were going around in circles.

It is common for the discussion to begin on the substantive issue
—here, the question of shifts and hours—but there are often other
issues related to the process that can make it difficult for the two
sides to understand each other, reach a compromise, or change their
positions. In this case, the staff members' feelings about how the
change was made and their feelings that the administration did not
really value them were all part of the mixture in the meeting. In
turn, Miss Pomeroy felt concerns about service to patients. She was
caught in the middle between the nurses and the hospital, and yet
she understood some of the reasons the staff wanted the changes to
be made.

In order to break the deadlock, it was important for the supervisor
to share her sense of "going in circles" and to reach for some of the
other issues affecting the discussion. The group had anticipated this
problem, and the supervisor was prepared to try to break the cycle.
This skill could be called *calling attention to the process.*

I interrupted at this point and told them what I saw happening. I said
I thought there were other concerns which were not being shared. For
example, I knew that the staff felt the change in policy was just
another example of the administration not caring—but this was not
being said. I also knew that Miss Pomeroy had worked hard to defend
the experiment, to stick up for her nurses, but this was also not being
discussed. Carol asked if it was true that Miss Pomeroy had stuck up
for them. Miss Pomeroy shared some of the process which went into

the decision. She was very clear about saying that she had reservations about the new shift system, but that she had fought for the staff to have a chance to experiment. She tried to explain some of the problems in the system which created immense pressures when one area of the hospital tried to innovate. The staff was listening intently, obviously interested in this description of how the hospital administration actually ran.

In response, some of the staff members opened up about how upset they were about the fact that they were not consulted when the policy was changed. They felt left out and took this process as an indication that nobody cared about them. Miss Pomeroy said she had to own up to the blame for that, since she knew they would be upset about the change, but, also, that there was nothing that could be done. She went on to say that she really had felt the new shifts had led to serious problems in patient care, and she asked if they hadn't also noticed some of the difficulty. Ann said that there were some problems for some of the staff who were stretched pretty thin at the end of so many straight days on. She, and others, often had to cover for such staff. However, she didn't feel the whole idea needed to be abandoned, that it could work with some modifications. I remained quiet as Miss Pomeroy and the staff began to work out what compromises might be possible.

This meeting did not solve the problem of the shifts, nor did it solve the general morale problem. However, Miss Pomeroy was able to raise the question at an administrative meeting, and an agreement was reached for a modified version of the new plan to be implemented on a three-month trial basis. The nursing staff was still unhappy with some aspects of the modified plan but felt a start had been made in dealing with their problems. The supervisor was encouraged because she felt this had been a helpful first step in opening up direct communications between staff and administration.

In my opinion, this was a positive start largely because of the preparatory work that had been done by the supervisor and because of her skill and courage in the actual sessions. In large dynamic systems, such as a hospital or an agency, once any change is made in the system, even a small one, the old quasi equilibrium is upset (see Chapter 3), and the impact is usually felt in the system as a whole. Thus, while an incident such as this one does not solve all of the system's problems, it can be an important first step.

Research Findings

The item on the workers' questionnaire in our study of supervision skill (Shulman, Robinson, and Luckyj, 1981) that dealt with the supervisor's third-force role was stated as follows: "My supervisor will communicate my views to the administration about policy and procedures." The average score for the supervisors in the study was close to "a good part of the time." There was a significant positive correlation between this variable and supervisor helpfulness ($r = 0.65$).

Both supervisors and workers provided written comments on this issue. Some examples from the supervisors included the following:

> I feel frustrated as a supervisor because I feel powerless to stop the loss of good staff or to prevent burnout.

> One gets nervous and at times quite paranoid when one doesn't know what to expect.

> It's been a lonely experience—with being in the middle—I don't truly feel a part of the overall agency.

> A major concern for supervisors is handling of three forces which dictate his actions—client needs, staff needs, and the needs of senior management.

One supervisor summed up many comments by saying that "middle management provides opportunities for either satisfaction or ulcers." Workers also commented in writing on this issue:

> I feel my supervisor is very much a "company man."

> My supervisor supports and represents his staff and departmental issues exceptionally well.

Other research on supervision has consistently identified this area of a supervisor's task as crucial. For example, in the Olmstead and Christenson (1973) study, worker satisfaction was associated positively with adequate and effective communications in the agency. In the Kadushin (1973) study, the most frequently cited source of strong dissatisfaction with supervision, as indicated by 35% of the 384 social workers responding, was the supervisor's hesitancy to confront the administration. As for the supervisors in the same study, having to get workers to adhere to agency policies they disagreed with was cited by 41% as a strong source of dissatisfaction. In contrast, one of the strong sources of satisfaction for 45% of the supervisors surveyed was the greater opportunity the supervisory job provided for obtaining leverage to influence agency change.

Summary

In working with the system, the supervisor acts as a third force between staff members and the agency administration system. This mediating role allows the supervisor to help both the staff and the administration find their areas of common ground, even as they openly explore their areas of real difference.

Supervisors help individual staff members deal with people in the system who carry authority (e.g., doctors, administrators). They also help staff groups deal with the administration at points of conflict on policy and procedures. The tasks of working with the staff group and the administrator and overseeing the encounter between the two make up the supervisor's mediating role in the area of working with the system.

Chapter 7

Supervisory Evaluations and Endings

Evaluations and endings are closely related, and many supervisors find them equally difficult. In each of these situations, the positive and negative feelings of both the supervisor and the staff member may be heightened. Both often experience some guilt, wondering if they could have done more or played their parts better. The doorknob therapy phenomenon described in preceding chapters is also noticeable in these procedures, as the supervisor and the staff try to come to grips with issues and concerns they may have been reluctant to share directly in their work together.

Despite these obstacles, both evaluations and endings offer the supervisor and the staff opportunities for powerful and productive work if they will seize them. Given the difficulties, however, the opportunities are all too often lost.

Evaluations

An evaluation is an objective appraisal of a worker's performance. One kind of evaluation is *formative* in nature; it provides ongoing feedback to workers on their activity, to help form or shape their job performance. Such evaluations may be made on an ongoing basis in supervision contacts, as the supervisor provides immediate assessments of the work of the staff, and there may also be occasional more formal evaluations when performance in a wide range of areas, such as job management, and direct practice skills, is assessed. Another type of evaluation procedure combines formative purposes with agency assessment functions. In addition to providing feedback for the staff's development, this evaluation process may be used as a basis for career decisions about an employee, such as passing a probation period, promotion, or firing.

The supervisor's viewpoint

Most supervisors dislike the evaluation process, but most workers want more feedback on their work, though they may be somewhat uncertain and fearful of the outcomes. As Alfred Kadushin (1976) pointed out, evaluations call attention to the status differences between supervisor and worker and provide a sharp reminder that they are not peers. When the power of the supervisor has been muted during the supervisory process, both parties may feel discomfort at its sudden reassertion. He also points out that a negative assessment of a worker may cause the supervisor to feel guilty because he or she "has not taught the worker what he needs to know, has not given the worker the help he had the right to expect" (p. 277). One supervisor who had to provide a negative evaluation of a staff member on areas she had not discussed with him during his three-month probation period expressed this concern: "It was easy to avoid each of the individual problems since they were not by themselves serious enough to force me to respond. Every time I thought about doing something, he seemed to sense it and improve. So I took the easy way out, and now when I add it all up and see what has to be said in the evaluation, I feel sick about what I didn't do."

Another difficulty from the supervisor's viewpoint is the possibility that the worker may react angrily to an evaluation. Supervisors are not sure they want to face all the feelings which may be directed at them even if they feel justified in their judgments. If the relationship is generally a good one, they are afraid that they may upset the apple cart and it will become more strained. This is especially true for a new supervisor who has moved into an established unit or has been promoted from the ranks. One supervisor found herself in a difficult position: "I was shocked when I realized that every member of the unit had received all 'superbs' on their evaluations for the past three years. My predecessor had treated it as a joke, and now I was stuck having to be honest."

When she brought this up at a supervision workshop, the members reassured her that even though the going might be rough at the start, the staff would appreciate some honest feedback, since deep inside they must know that the evaluations had been meaningless. We all need critical feedback to improve our performance, as well as credit for what we are doing well. If the only feedback we receive is uniformly positive, it is meaningless and useless.

Another major problem is posed by the need for a negative evaluation that may threaten a worker's career. The power of being able to recommend whether a worker becomes a permanent staff member, gets a raise or promotion, or is fired can weigh heavily on a supervisor. One supervisor described how bad he felt when he had to give a negative evaluation to a probationary worker who was pleasant but incompetent. The young man had a family to support, and jobs in this field were in short supply. The supervisor said he lost sleep over the problem until finally he decided that it would be unethical not to be honest, both for the sake of the clients and for the long-term interest of the worker, who, he felt, should seriously consider another line of work. Even then, knowing that he had provided as much help as possible, the supervisor still said he felt like a "louse."

There is also the possibility that a negative evaluation will be contested. With the growth of public employee unions among social and health services, supervisors must be prepared to defend their opinions and actions at appeal hearings, under extreme pressure. Workers do need protection for their basic rights, so they need not fear losing their jobs because of vague charges against them or a confrontation with the supervisor or the administration. Safety measures such as appeal procedures are necessary to protect against such abuses.

While such procedures are necessary, they also place a premium on the ability of supervisors to justify an evaluation. In a job management issue, the supervisor may have had to deal with a host of complaints from colleagues of a worker, but the other workers will all suddenly lose their memories of the incidents if they are asked to testify against one of "their own." With direct practice problems, the supervisor may have documented complaints from consumers of the service, but even these can be interpreted away. Most difficult to prove without documentation is a charge of lack of skill. Since most case recording does not include process descriptions of the practice and most supervisors do not employ audiotape or videotape recordings of interviews in supervision conferences, this charge is particularly hard to document. (See the Coda section following this chapter for some observations on this issue.)

A supervisor who expects a problem to develop and foresees the need for a negative evaluation would be wise to document all records, communications, and contacts with the staff on the matter, starting as soon as possible. The material must be explicit, with a minimum of euphemisms or fudged statements. For example, take the case of a probationary worker who repeatedly ignores a supervisor's complaints about lateness and absenteeism and disregards all efforts to help. A memo from the supervisor which states "If this pattern is continued I shall have to recommend that you not be kept on at the end of your probation." will have a much better chance of standing up at an appeal hearing than one which states "Your continued pattern of lateness and absence causes great concern on my part."

If the recorded material is not needed, all the better. If it is, the supervisor will be ready to make a case and stick to it, even under great pressure. There is no easy way for a supervisor to take part in such grievance procedures; when under attack, even the most competent feel tremendous strain. However, the supervisor can be secure in the knowledge that he or she is doing the right thing for clients, the worker involved, other workers, and his or her own personal integrity. At times such as these the supervisor needs all the emotional support possible from administrators, colleagues, workers, friends, and family. It is one of the moments they may wish they hadn't taken the job, and, at the same time, it is one of the opportunities to do the most effective work.

Evaluation content and process

The importance and difficulty of evaluation for supervisors were indicated in a report based on a study of field work instruction in a school of social work (Gitterman and Gitterman, 1979). Supervisors surveyed reported various sources of strain inherent in the process, including "defining criteria, writing the formal document, assessing student practice, and engaging the student in the evaluation process." Similar procedures can cause difficulties for supervisors evaluating the performance of staff members.

The evaluation process has been made more difficult in the helping professions by vagueness about the skills to be evaluated. Getting statistics in on time is fairly easy to assess for example, but "providing support to clients" is quite a different matter. Gitterman and Gitterman describe the general content areas of evaluation in terms similar to the four learning subject matter areas identified in Chapter 4: (1) professional practice skill; (2) use of learning opportunities; (3) work management; and (4) professional influence. Kadushin (1976) provides a sample of an evaluation from and scales which can be employed in the process (pp. 297–311). The content of evaluation is also explored in Appendix C at the back of the book, which provides a sample of an evaluation guide from the University of British Columbia School of Social Work. This guide, developed by a number of contributors whose work was coordinated by the director of field instruction, Kloh-ann Amacher, specifies practice skills and indicates the desired level of performance on each one for the various levels of students. Supervisors concerned about how their students rate in comparison to others have found it particularly useful.

Steps in the Evaluation Process.   The process of evaluation in the helping professions varies according to the situation, but a number of general principles, can be incorporated in seven specific steps that usually can be followed. First, whenever possible, an evaluation guide should be presented to staff members at the beginning of the working relationship. They should know what areas will be assessed and from where the evidence of work will be drawn. For a new worker, in particular, such reassurance is helpful so the amount of work to be mastered does not seem overwhelming.

Second, items in the guide should be periodically referred to in the supervision process. They should become a natural part of the context of supervision.

Third, periods of assessment prior to the formal evaluation should be built into the supervision process, so that both supervisor and worker are aware of progress or lack of it and of areas that need concentration. One of the most positive uses of an evaluation guide is in helping to identify the learning agenda on an ongoing basis. In addition, periodic assessments (or checklists) help to assure that important areas are not being missed and that the worker is systematically informed of progress. The general goal is to avoid surprises in the final evaluation. There may be differences of opinion, and these should be clearly identified and noted, but no surprises.

Fourth, both the supervisor and the worker should take some responsibility for reviewing the evaluation guide and preparing a preliminary assessment. A supervisor who asks the worker to fill in the form, and then simply starts from there, will not seem to be serious about the process (as well as a bit lazy). But a supervisor who takes the whole responsibility, without asking the worker to also make a first assessment, is letting the worker off the hook. If a worker shows resistance to filling out the form, the supervisor should explore this in some detail. The worker may have had some bad prior experiences with such evaluations, may be afraid to commit his or her ideas to paper, or may be unsure of the standards or unaware of the process involved. Time spent in this way will be worthwhile in assuring that the evaluation is experienced as a joint process, and not simply as something the supervisor does to the supervisee.

Fifth, in preparing the draft versions of the evaluations, both the supervisor and the worker should provide some documentation of their views. For example, a supervisor who suggests that a worker "has developed appropriate skills for dealing with client feelings but is having some difficulty in reaching for negative client reactions, particularly with hostile clients" should try to mention particular cases that demonstrate both the skills gained and the need for more skill. The same would be true with comments on job management; particular details should be provided to illustrate strengths and weaknesses. This task of documenting the evaluation can be an onerous one if left until it is time to write the evaluation. If the supervisor has maintained some records of the supervision with the evaluation in mind, the writing is much simpler.

Many supervisors think that agency evaluation forms stifle their ability to express meaningful opinions, especially when they use standardized checklists that ask for overall or global ratings in order to produce a computerized score. As one supervisor put it after using such instruments, "My ability to write is gone, but I'm one hell of a computer card coder." When pressed, however, supervisors often admit that there is really nothing to keep them from expanding the evaluation into any format they wish—except their own discomfort with the process and the hard work it requires.

Sixth, a joint meeting to discuss the two versions of the preliminary evaluation (which both supervisor and worker have had an opportunity to review) is the crucial working time in the evaluation process. This provides the opportunity for both to expand on their comments, make their cases if there are differences, identify areas of agreement, and so on. It is often helpful to go through the form, section by section, and then devote some time to areas where differences are evident. These areas should be identified early in the conference, so the interaction does not take on a "waiting for the other shoe to drop" tone, as happens in the commonly used procedure where the supervisor identifies all the workers' strengths as a means of massaging their egos a bit and then hits them with all their weaknesses. In reality, the workers probably hear very little of the positive points while waiting to get to the trouble spots. A brief introduction which identifies both strengths and weaknesses often relieves the waiting pressure.

Finally, when agreements have been reached or disagreements identified, it is up to the supervisor to make a final decision about the content of the evaluation. If persuaded by the worker's arguments, the supervisor should change the tone or content of some passages. If not, it is important that the worker's disagreement be noted in the final form.

Considering the difficulties involved in these seven steps in the evaluation process, it is little wonder that supervisors experience evaluations as hard work; they *are* hard work! Although there are many variations in the content and process, and agencies and supervisors must develop their own styles, proper attention at these crucial times in the supervisory process will pay important dividends to the worker, the supervisor, and, ultimately, to the service.

Endings

The ending phase of the supervisory relationship includes two types of endings. In the first, the staff member leaves the job (or the student ends the year), and the supervisor must pay attention to three areas of work: the ending of the supervisory relationship, the ending of the worker-client relationships, and the ending of the worker-colleague relationships. All of these are important, and they are often intertwined. In the second type of ending, it is the supervisor who is leaving and must say goodbye to the staff while aiding the transition to a new supervisor.

The worker's ending experience

The dynamics of the ending of the supervisor-worker relationship are quite similar to those of the worker-client ending, a process discussed in some detail elsewhere (Shulman, 1979). The parallel nature of these processes can provide the supervisor with an opportunity to demonstrate the very skills the worker needs to employ with his or her clients.

The context of the ending will, of course, vary considerably. The staff member may be leaving voluntarily or involuntarily, or the supervisor may feel a great loss or a sense of relief when a particular worker leaves. Still, some common themes persist, such as denial of the feelings associated with the staff member's leaving. As the date approaches, very little discussion of the event takes place. Those who are leaving may come in on weekends to clean out their desks, and then take their accumulated vacation time so that they never actually have to say goodbye. They do this not because they don't care about the supervisor or other staff members, but because they care too much.

A sense of urgency about unfinished business is also characteristic. Both the staff member and the supervisor have much to say to each other, sharing positive feelings, or negative feelings, or both. Even if the relationship has been a poor one, a constructive discussion of the reasons why the supervisor and the worker had difficulty dealing with each other can be extremely helpful. In the "farewell bouquet" ending, staff members have some final thought about the experience they would like to share. The "bouquets" may be positive, or alternatively, all of the previously unstated negatives may finally emerge. Many agencies require final interviews (sometimes called *exit interviews*) in which staff members can share thoughts and feelings which may have been difficult to express while they were employed.

Feelings of guilt may also be characteristic of staff members' ending experiences. Could the worker have put more into the experience and gotten more out of it? Should the supervisor have been more available? It is not uncommon to detect a period of mourning as the ending approaches; apathy in conferences, for example, may signal strong feelings about leaving. At the same time there may be very positive feelings about making a new beginning. Students, for example, may be starting their professional careers, ready to test themselves in the real world. The supervisor may be able to help them with any feelings of ambivalence they have about facing the challenge.

Both the supervisor and the staff member may be inclined to be overly positive about the ending experience. If they give in to the temptation to deal only with the positives, however, they will cut off an opportunity to use the ending phase effectively. Negatives such as anger and regression are also common in this phase; workers may return to patterns of work or relationships which marked their early days at the agency. If they have become close to other staff members, and if the atmosphere has been supportive and intimate, their colleagues also may experience some real sense of rejection, coupled with feelings of loss.

Procedures for Easing Workers' Endings. One of the crucial reasons supervisors must devote careful attention to the worker's ending experiences is that a worker who is leaving a position is probably having similar experiences with clients. If the worker's feelings about the endings are not dealt with, they can adversely affect the effectiveness of agency services. A number of procedures can be used by supervisors to make an ending a helpful experience for the worker.

First, the supervisor can call attention to the approach of an ending by noting the date at a conference or a staff meeting. This sets the ending phase in motion.

Second, the supervisor can call attention to the dynamics of the ending as they emerge. If the supervisor notices apathy in conferences, for example, a direct question can be used to examine whether it has something to do with the worker's ending experiences.

Third (and most important), the supervisor can level with his or her own feelings about the worker's departure. Since it is hard to express feelings of warmth and closeness in any situation, the supervisor must take the first step in this. When these feelings are shared honestly, they often provide the catalyst needed to help the worker discuss similar emotions.

Fourth, the supervisor can structure an ending evaluation period which includes systematic attention to the supervision experience. The strengths of the relationship as well as the weaknesses should be specifically identified. A summary of the learning that has occurred and identification of a future learning agenda can help. Because of the tendency to be overly positive about the experience, the supervisor will have to reach hard for negatives and be honest in sharing them with the worker.

Fifth, attention to the ending between the worker and other staff members is often appreciated. It is as important for the supervisor to pay attention to the separation process when a staff member leaves as it is to deal with the engagement process when a member joins the staff. Making announcements at staff meetings, briefly discussing the worker's contributions, and reaching for the feelings of other staff members as well as sharing one's own feelings can all go far to help the staff deal directly with the loss of a colleague. If the members are not assisted in this way, the ending is often no more than a "farewell party," where little of real meaning is said and the staff is left with the feeling of unfinished business.

Finally, the supervisor can use the experience to help the worker focus on the specific skills of dealing with client endings. By identifying what is happening in their own relationship, as well as the parallel process with the client, the supervisor can contribute to the worker's ability to deal with the often neglected termination phase of practice.

Example of a Worker's Ending Experience. The following student supervisor's report of how he dealt with a student's ending of her experience at a family agency illustrates a number of the dynamics of workers' endings. The supervisor and the student had been together for one year, and the beginning of their work on endings was intermingled with his efforts to help her deal with termination with clients. The supervisor's report began:

Preparatory work: In working with Fran (the student) on her practice with Terry (the client), it was apparent that she was most concerned about the coming ending. Fran had only three weeks left on her placement, and I felt it was time to focus on her ending work with Terry. Fran had been working with Terry for five months, and it was not certain whether Terry would want to continue counseling with another worker or whether she would terminate with the agency when Fran left.

In a conference during which we discussed Terry, we did not go into great detail in discussing the skills needed to make the endings a useful piece of work. Fran, on her own, had made a list of the issues that she and Terry had tackled together that she wanted to review with her. I mentioned that she and Terry had developed a relationship over time and that there would be some feelings about the coming ending. I suggested that perhaps Terry might feel mad or sad about the ending and that Fran should try to pull for these feelings in the session. Fran agreed that this would be important. I also stated that endings can be a difficult piece of work, since the therapist often has strong feelings about the endings as well. I pointed out that you are in a session dealing with your own feelings as well as the clients'. Fran thought this might be true. She agreed to tape the session for our discussion at our next conference.

In this case, as all too often happens, the supervisor discussed the ending in relation to the client but ignored it in relation to the worker. The discussion of the dynamics of the worker-client process will remain lifeless as long as the dynamics of the supervisor-worker relationship are ignored. After studying endings, Fran could agree intellectually about what needs to be done, but emotionally she was not in touch with what was happening. Even though the supervisor described what it would be like for the worker to deal with her own feelings and the client's, unless he modeled how to do this in their session, the worker would respond to his actions, not his words. In the supervision conference which followed, the supervisor caught this mistake nicely and moved into both endings with feelings.

Supervision session: I asked her how it went. Fran said that it was OK, and then, immediately, that it was terrible. She was obviously upset. Fran then proceeded to summarize her session with Terry. They had talked about the various areas of Terry's life that had improved since coming for counseling. Terry summed up the improvement by saying that she felt a lot more confident and under a lot less pressure. She attributed this to the fact that she and Fran had done a lot of work on her self-esteem, and it had really improved. Terry said she was able to break her high-low cycle and live a more even life.

Fran said it was at this point that she raised the issue of ending the counseling with Terry, since Terry was doing so well. Fran said she tried to reach for Terry's feelings about the ending but simply could not do it. She found it to be very hard and pulled back. Fran began to cry when describing the process. The end result had been an agreement for Terry to call Fran when she returned from a short trip to discuss whether she needed another session.

I empathized with Fran, saying this was the hard part of the work, especially since she was feeling sad about ending, as sad as Terry. Fran said that she did not want to cry with Terry. I asked her what held her back. She said that she did not like people seeing her cry. I asked if she felt that being a worker made it more difficult for her to cry. Fran felt there was some of that happening, but mostly, it was that she did not like to cry in front of people. I then talked about a theme we had discussed before, that a counselor was both a counselor and a real person when working with a client, and at times it was very appropriate to react from your feelings about the work and the person. I continued that with Terry, it would have been fine to tell her how much you would miss her and that you were feeling sad, and that the two of you could have cried together. Fran agreed that it would not have been so terrible.

At this point I picked up the theme of endings for Fran. I said that she was not only ending with her clients, which was hard, but also that she was ending her stay at the agency. She had made a lot of friends here, and soon she would be ending with each of them. I told her I thought that must be hard for her. She agreed and began to cry. I then said that our relationship was also ending soon and that I would miss her. She agreed and said that she had had a fine time here. At this point there was a lovely, quiet pause.

We then returned to talk about Terry. Fran wondered if she could do something more, like call her back, because she would have liked to have said more to her. She said she regretted not saying some of the things we talked about. I asked some more questions about how close she felt to Terry and suggested she could say some of what she felt about the endings when Terry called her. She agreed.

I suggested we listen to the tape. Fran resisted a bit, saying it was painful to listen to the session. What emerged from the tape was that Fran did a fine job with summarizing her work, and it was clear that Terry was ready to end the counseling relationship. It was also clear that Fran had had many openings to talk about their feelings in relation to ending but had passed them up.

I talked about some of the endings skills, suggesting that one way to pull for feelings was to talk about her own first. We also discussed Fran's other clients who may feel somewhat differently about ending. For Terry, it was a natural ending of counseling, but others might want to continue and feel a bit angry at Fran's leaving in the middle. We did some tuning in about her other cases.

Fran felt that Jake (another client) was mad, and in fact, had been coming late to their appointments. Jake and his wife had been more aggressive in the last few sessions, for example, questioning closely what happened when I listened to Fran's audiotapes of their sessions with them. I suggested that perhaps Fran's hunch was right, and that some of their behavior was related to the ending dynamics. She thought she should confront them directly. I agreed, and we role-played a number of ways she might get into this discussion. I suggested that there would be some sadness as well as anger, and Fran asked if I had any ideas about how to reach for it. I role-played as follows: "I know you're feeling kind of frustrated with this situation about me leaving and your having to be transferred, but, you know, I'm also feeling sad about it. I'll miss you both, and I was wondering if you might be feeling some of the same." I asked how it sounded to her, and she said fine. I said it was going to be hard. She agreed, but felt it would probably be easier than ending with Terry.

We then went on to discuss our coming evaluation and how we would handle supervision in the next few weeks.

The Supervisor's Ending Experience

In large part, the dynamics and processes involved in the worker's endings which have been described in the preceding section are equally relevant to a supervisor's departure from a staff or an agency or other institutional setting. Again, the particulars will vary, depending on the situation. In some cases, both staff and supervisor will be pleased to say goodbye; in others, the leaving of a supervisor will have a profound, perhaps surprising, impact on all concerned. The process of transference and countertransference can lead to the development of relationships of unexpected intensity. Supervisors are as likely as workers to underplay their impact on the staff and the intensity of the feelings associated with leaving.

All the skills described above—pointing out the ending early, sharing feelings about endings, evaluating the working relationship —are useful when the supervisor leaves a setting. In the interests of agency effectiveness, special attention should be paid to the issues of transition: What are the staff members' thoughts and feelings about the new supervisor? How can the staff work to expedite a positive relationship with the new supervisor? If there are angry feelings about the supervisor leaving, can they be openly expressed so they will not be transferred to the new supervisor? If the new supervisor is known, can he or she sit in on the last staff meetings to get a feel for the ending?

In all working relationships, a new beginning is inherent in each ending. Supervisors who approach endings as a learning experience can use them to enhance their own personal and professional development. By focusing on the content of their work with the staff as well as the process of ending, they can use feedback from the staff to discover their own strengths and weaknesses, examine their behavior under pressure, and evaluate their ability to handle problems. Such an assessment can provide invaluable guidelines for future relationships.

In the following example, a supervisor of a hospital social service department invited her replacement to her last staff meeting to participate in her endings as a way of easing the new supervisor's beginning.

> After introducing Karen (the new supervisor) to the staff group, I explained that I had felt it would be helpful to her and to them if she could sit in on our last session together. I told them that even though we had talked about my leaving before, now that I was at the last day it was really hitting me. I had enjoyed my four years as their supervisor, and had gotten a great deal from them. I told them I would miss them in my new job, and hoped that we could keep some of our contacts alive. I had the sense from the looks on their faces that they were both pleased to hear what I had to say, as well as a bit embarrassed to talk about it. I asked if we could use the time to talk about what went well with my supervision as well as how I could have been more helpful. I said this would help me on my new job, as well as help Karen to connect up with them. Karen told the staff that she appreciated being in on this last session and would find the discussion helpful.
>
> Ron began by saying that he had always appreciated how I had been there for them, how I had kept my door open for them, and the support they could get from me. He said the job was often tough, like the time he felt overwhelmed when he had to deal with the family of dying child. It had been helpful to unload and to have me listen. I told him I had also gotten a great deal from that incident—understanding better how to help staff when the going got rough. Sandy said she appreciated my respecting their autonomy and professionalism. When I asked her what she meant, she went on to describe the way I offered supervision of her cases—providing help where needed but also allowing her to develop the agenda.
>
> I said it felt really good to hear the positives, since I cared what they thought about me. I went on to point out that it was also important to discuss the negatives. Ted said: "Well that's what I do most of the time anyway, so I might as well offer some of them today." I joined in the laughter and said that I did not always enjoy hearing what Ted

said, but that I very much appreciated his honesty and took it as a sign of caring about me and how we worked together. Ted described my tendency to keep my own problems to myself, always open to their concerns, but rarely sharing my own. I asked if others felt that way, and they did, indicating they could often sense when I was in trouble or upset, but had the message that they should not deal with that. I told them it was something I needed to work on, since I carried the image of a good supervisor having things worked out, and always being available for the workers. Ted said that was the opposite of what I suggested they do with clients. I agreed it was probably easier to preach than to practice. I would try to keep that in mind in my new job.

There was further discussion about the specific ways we handled supervision sessions, our staff meetings, and the problems in the hospital. In each case, I had them expand on the specifics of what they found helpful and what was not so helpful. As we reached the end of the meeting time, I asked Karen for her reactions to the discussion. She said that she was impressed with the relationship between the staff and myself, but a bit awed by it. She thought it would be a tough act to follow. She said she hoped that the staff would grow to trust her and to be just as honest with her. It was clear from the reactions on their faces that the staff group appreciated her remarks.

As she was speaking I found myself trying to hold back my tears —feeling very choked up. I finally blurted out that they had all been special to me, and that I would really miss them. Ron said the feeling was quite mutual.

We sat silent for a while, and then Ted suggested it was time for our farewell lunch. We left quietly, had a nice lunch and I saved my individual goodbyes for the afternoon.

Research Findings

In our study of supervision skill (Shulman, Robinson, and Luckyj, 1981), an item on the workers' questionnaire which dealt with evaluation asked the worker to indicate the percentage of time actually spent on discussing ongoing job performance in supervisory conferences, compared to the percentage of time the worker would like this topic to be discussed. The responses indicated that 11.5% of the total time in supervisory conferences was devoted to ongoing job performance, while workers would have preferred it to take 13.6% of the total.

Correlations between these variables and other items on the supervisors' and workers' questionnaires provide interesting insights into factors which may affect the actual and desired proportion of time devoted to evaluation. The supervisors' questionnaire indicated area of work was important (r = 0.33), with supervisors involved in child welfare being less active in evaluating ongoing job performance ($r = -0.29$). This fit another finding which indicated that the larger the number of staff members other than social workers a supervisor supervised, the less involved the supervisor was in evaluation. These correlations were - 0.24 for clerical and administrative workers, - 0.27 for financial aid workers, and - 0.35 for family support workers. In addition, the larger the "other" staff supervised, the more positive was the correlation with actual discussions in this area (0.46). One interpretation is that the larger supervisory load for many of the supervisors in child welfare, particularly supervision of non-social work staff, substantially cuts into the time available for evaluation feedback. This would fit with many of the comments of the supervisors and workers.

Items on the workers' questionnaire which were associated with these variables had the following correlations: area of work (0.38); actual time spent on individual case planning (- .60); preference for social work skill training (0.27). The first of these findings (area of work) reflects the impact of less evaluation feedback by the child welfare supervisors. The negative correlation with case planning provides some idea of what is discussed in place of ongoing feedback (case planning). The preference for social work skill training is also logically associated with a desire for more feedback. Of additional interest was the strong association between the actual time spent on such feedback and the worker's desire for such feedback (r = 0.64). It is understandable that it would be easier for a supervisor to provide ongoing evaluation to a worker who was eager to receive it.

Findings from the Kadushin (1973) study indicated that for workers, supervisors who were not sufficiently critical of their work were the second strongest source of their dissatisfaction with supervision (26%). Conversely, supervisors who provided critical feedback so that workers would know how they were doing were a strong source of satisfaction for 24% of the sample. The dilemma experienced by supervisors in this respect was reflected in the findings that for 26% of the supervisors, conflict between the educational aspects of their work and the evaluative aspects was a strong source of dissatisfaction. Moreover, 21% of the supervisors identified the evaluation responsibility as a strong source of dissatisfaction for them.

Summary

Evaluation is an objective appraisal of a worker's performance, whether ongoing formative evaluations as work is reviewed, systematic evaluations, or evaluations used by the agency to make career judgments such as firing or promotion. The number of difficulties in the evaluation process explains why supervisors often resist making them: a heightened sense of the supervisor's authority, guilt over unfinished business, anticipation of the worker's anger, the requirement for documentation in the event of appeals, and so on. The content and process of evaluation are concerned with definition of the skills and behaviors to be assessed and an effort to involve the worker as an active participant.

In the ending phase there are similarities between supervisor-worker endings and worker-client endings. The dynamics of the ending process suggest procedures the supervisor can use to help the worker end relationships with the supervisor, with clients, and with colleagues. Supervisors also must deal with their own leaving, when they depart from a staff or an agency setting, and the transition to a new supervisor.

Coda: Recording Procedures and Professional Competence

This book has drawn on the practice illustrations of many supervisors. I have used process recordings, transcripts of audiotapes and videotapes, summary devices, and examples recalled from memory by workshop participants. These examples have provided insights into the moment-by-moment activities of supervisors in interaction with individual workers, staff groups, and representatives of the system. This book could not have been written without these examples.

Unfortunately, the idea of paying attention to the details of work in the helping professions through the use of some form of process or audiovideo recording has been losing favor. A number of years ago, the writing of process records was considered students' work, a task which was quickly dropped after graduation. New workers who requested help from supervisors with such recordings were often told to realize they were in the "real world" where such devices were luxuries, or, even more devastatingly, they were accused of being "overly dependent." More recently, the trend has been to abandon the use of recording even in the professional school experience. Many graduates comment in my workshops that they did not write a single process recording in their two years of training.

This state of affairs is both ironic and alarming. It is ironic because recording and attention to detail were very much a part of early professional practices at a time when the ability to conceptualize practice skills was still at an infant stage. While practice was being examined in detail, often it was without the analytical tools required for the job. Now that many middle-range models of practice from a number of theoretical frameworks are available, the tendency seems to be to move away from examining practice. The trend is alarming, I believe, because it is not possible to develop practice skills in working with clients or supervision of staff without some ongoing means of examining the details of one's practice efforts.

One event which ran contrary to the tide was the publication in 1976 of a book on guidelines for recording by Suanna J. Wilson (2nd ed., 1980). This excellent addition to the literature examines a number of types of recording in some detail and provides many illustrations which can be useful for supervisors who want to strengthen their workers' recording efforts. The book also provides a model supervisors can adapt for recording their own supervision practice.

When I discuss the recording issue with supervisors in my workshops, their first response is usually to raise the time problem. The argument is that neither workers nor supervisors have time to record all of their work in such detail. I agree with the point but suggest that selecting cases or supervision interviews for periodic recording is practicable. Most supervisors agree, but then they point out how time-consuming writing and reading full process recordings can be. This is also true, so I offer a shortened version of the process recording, described by Williams Schwartz as accordion style, in which the beginning, middle, and the ending of a session are written in detailed process, with summary descriptions providing the links. The term *accordion* describes the expansion and contraction of the detailed portions of the record. The total writing might be less than two pages. Most agree this would be a more manageable device.

The next problem with recording that supervisors raise is often worker resistance. This initiates a discussion of the meaning of such resistance and how to handle it (this topic is discussed in some detail, with examples, in Chapters 3 and 4). Many supervisors admit they have had bad experiences themselves with recording—submitting records the supervisor never read, or having detailed supervisory comments that were critical or punitive added to the margins of their recordings. One supervisor said she had learned quickly not to write down what she had really said in an encounter but what she thought the supervisor would have wanted her to say. Certainly, such experiences cause ambivalent feelings about the procedure when the supervisor is faced with resistance to it from staff members.

One of the most serious concerns about introducing recording into the supervisory process was put this way by one supervisor: "If I ask my workers to write records, I'm going to have to come through and offer them help." This fear of not being up to the task is common with supervisors who feel they must provide "answers" to their workers rather than suggesting a way of working. I try to reassure them that it is all right to be teaching and learning at the same time, and workers will still respect them when they honestly share their own struggles with recording events. One supervisor described how he was process recording his own conferences with workers so he could become comfortable with the tool in his own work, before he set expectations for recording on his workers. He had shared this with his workers, even showing them his beginning efforts. They were impressed with his willingness to risk himself.

In training workshops for field instructors I have provided at the School of Social Work at the University of British Columbia, each supervisor takes a turn at videotaping a conference with a student for presentation. Unless there are severe problems with the student, he or she is invited to sit in on the session and be a resource for our discussions. For example, we might inquire what the students were really feeling at points in their conferences. They quickly relax when they realize we are analyzing the supervisor's activities, and they are not on the spot.

These sessions are always powerful learning devices for all concerned. When students are asked for their reactions at the end of the sessions, they invariably mention their surprise at discovering that their supervisors were still learning. They point out how much it relieves them to feel they do not have to have all the answers before they graduate. Field instructors also report that the experience has a marked impact on their supervision, usually opening up communications dramatically. Many report they continue to use discussions of audiotaped or videotaped conferences with their students for their own learning.

While it is often painful for supervisors to allow colleagues to view tapes of their supervision (an issue which must be discussed at the start of each workshop), they should find that the benefits of mutual aid and support make it worthwhile. Professional practice at any level is difficult, and supervisors can use all the help they can get. Overcoming the fear of risking oneself with colleagues is a first step in gaining access to this support. It is also hard to ask the worker to make this effort unless the supervisor does it as well.

In addition to process recordings and audiotape or videotape analysis, supervisors can make use of feedback questionnaires to provide information on how their workers view their supervision. The supervisors in the study reported in the research findings sections of this book (Shulman, Robinson, and Luckyj, 1981) received confidential reports with their average scores for every item. For comparison purposes, they also were provided with the averages for the overall study and for their professional groups (e.g., social workers, child care workers), as well as the averages for their agencies. With the use of a computer, larger agencies could build in such a feedback process as an aid to supervisory development.

Supervisors who adopt some forms of recording will probably find themselves going against the trend in the profession. At a time when supervisors are being described in many settings as *managers,* with a decreased emphasis on direct teaching and practice supervision, attention to the details of the work is not always encouraged. It is easier to look for structural solutions such as changing agency practices or staffing patterns, or social policy solutions. Structural and policy changes can have an important impact on client service, however, in the last analysis, practice competence must also be addressed.

As one example, when I discussed my research findings on supervision with an administrator, his first question was: "Can you tell me from your findings who to hire?" The implication was that if he could only find the right people for the staff, the positive results would follow. In reality, although selection can have an important impact on the quality of supervision in an agency, if my research and practice experience have taught me anything, it is that the hard part comes after selection.

I had a recent personal discussion with William Schwartz on ways to develop higher levels of interest in practice and supervision competency in the profession. We agreed that this was difficult in a society which did not place great value on attention to method, and in fact was somewhat ambivalent on the whole question of services to people in need. He made an observation that I found helpful, and which may also be helpful to a supervisor who feels he or she is swimming against the stream. While in the last analysis major changes in our service systems will depend on changes in our society's attitudes and values, it is important that professionals, even if in a minority, keep alive their interest in the details of how they do their work. I support this perspective. Not only will it help many workers and, in turn, their clients, but it provides a means professionals can use to continue developing their understanding of the art and science of the practice as they work to create a climate in which it can flourish.

Appendix A

Notes on Research Methodology

This appendix describes the research methodology I employed, with my colleagues Elizabeth Robinson and Anna Luckyj, in the study reported in the Research Findings sections of each chapter in this book. The findings of this research must be viewed with consideration for the methodology employed and the study's limitations, as noted in the final section of this appendix. A more detailed discussion can be found in the research report (Shulman, Robinson, and Luckyj, 1981).

The central line of the inquiry was an examination of the communication, relationship, and problem-solving skills of supervisors. We were interested in the associations between the use of the various skills and supervisor's development of a positive working relationship with workers or the supervisor's helpfulness. This aspect of the study, with its focus on the process of supervision, paralleled an earlier study of similar skills in social work practice with clients (Shulman, 1978), which was the basis for my book on direct practice skills (Shulman, 1979).

In addition to examining the process of supervision, we were also interested in exploring the context in which supervision is set, such as individual or group sessions, the frequency of sessions, and the content of supervision encounters, such as case consultation, job management, or practice skills teaching. Among the variables included in the analysis were demographic factors for both the supervisors and the workers, such as training, age, and experience, and their diverse perceptions of the supervisor's time investment in various roles (e.g., manager, case consultant, teacher). Attempts were also made to measure the supervisor's satisfaction with role demands, sense of job stress and job manageability, and estimates of ongoing training and emotional support received.

Following established research procedures, we started with a number of hypotheses about the effects of these factors on the outcomes of supervision, as suggested by a theoretical model. Then we developed a research design to obtain empirical data for testing these hypotheses, using the findings to support, challenge, elaborate, or rethink some of the basic constructs. This in turn created a new set of theoretical generalizations which could provide hypotheses for further study. The research process thus is an ongoing one in which each step is preliminary to another step, and the findings are always tentative. Only when repeated research in a range of settings has replicated our findings could we move from tentative hypotheses to confirmed generalizations. It is important to understand this research stance in order to make a proper evaluation of the findings.

Our first step in this research process was to develop and test the survey instruments to be used in making the study: Supervision Questionnaire: Worker Version and Supervision Questionnaire: Supervisor's Version.

Supervision Questionnaire: Worker's Version

The worker's questionnaire was developed by Elizabeth Robinson as part of her major paper written under my supervision as a requirement for the master's of social work degree at the University of British Columbia (Robinson, 1980). The questionnaire instrument was part of a research course assignment for Dr. John Crane, of the social work faculty, who served as a consultant on the instrument methodology. Professor Anne Furness also served on the advisory committee for the major paper.

This questionnaire was designed to be completed by workers and to provide data on their perceptions of their supervision. For example, the supervisory skill of articulating the worker's feelings (or putting them into words) was phrased as: "My supervisor can sense my feelings without my having to put them into words." The worker chose a response from the following categories: "(1) None of the time: (2) A little of the time: (3) Sometimes; (4) A good part of the time; (5) Most or all of the time; (6) Undecided." The response scale for similar items was the same.

A number of items asked for percentage estimates, such as "Please indicate what percentage of time during supervisory sessions your supervisor spends on the following categories. This should add to 100%." Categories for this item included: "*(a)* Planning on individual cases; *(b)* Practice skills; *(c)* Discussion of information from research that may be helpful to you on the job; *(d)* Your ongoing job performance; *(e)* How to meet the administrative requirements of your job; *(f)* Other (specify)."

Items which were used as dependent (outcome) variables asked for the worker's perception of the working relationship with the supervisor ("In general, how satisfied are you with your working relationship with your supervisor?") and the helpfulness of the supervisor ("In general, how helpful is your supervisor?"). Four scale responses to the first question ranged from "not satisfied at all" to "very satisfied," and to the second from "not helpful" to "very helpful."

Demographic data were compiled on such variables as the worker's training, experience, age, and sex. In addition, scores from the nondemographic items on this questionnaire were combined into indexes, or scales, designed to measure various constructs. These were the worker's evaluation of (1) contact regularity with the supervisor, (2) the supervisor's availability, (3) level of trust in the supervisor, (4) the supervisor's empathic skills, and (5) the supervisor's problem-solving skills. Another index combined the supervisor's relationship and helpfulness scores. Items included in the trust, empathic skills, problem-solving skills, and relationship-helpfulness scales were drawn from a questionnnaire I had developed for my earlier social work skill study (Shulman, 1978, 1979, 1981). Additional items related specifically to agency practices in the child welfare area, such as actively involving natural parents whenever possible or the use of research knowledge and child development theory in supervision, were included for child welfare supervisors, but these results are not reported in the text. (See Table 1.)

Reliability and validity

A number of procedures were undertaken to determine the reliability and validity of the workers' questionnaire. Early drafts were considered by workers, supervisors, child welfare consultants, students, social work faculty, and individuals with no experience in social work. These key informants reported that the questionnaire

TABLE 1
WORKERS' QUESTIONNAIRE ITEMS CORRELATED WITH SUPERVISOR
HELPFULNESS

Factor	Item	Pearson r
Availability	My supervisor is available when I need him/her.	0.47*
Individual regularity	My supervisor sets aside regularly scheduled time with me for individual supervision sessions.	0.16
Individual frequency	Approximately how often?	−0.05
Group regularity	My supervisor sets aside regularly scheduled time for group supervision sessions.	0.26*
Group frequency	Approximately how often?	−0.10
Actual content	Please indicate what percentage of time during supervisory sessions your supervisor spends on the following categories. *This should add to 100%.*	
	a. Planning on individual cases	0.05
	b. Practice skills	0.10
	c. Discussion of information from research that may be helpful to you on the job.	0.17
	d. Your ongoing job performance	−0.05
	e. How to meet the administrative requirements of your job	−0.11
	f. Other (specify)	−0.13
Preferred content	Sometimes there may be a discrepancy between what you talk about and what you would like to talk about in supervision sessions. Please indicate what percentage of time *you would like* your supervisor to spend on the following areas. *This should add to 100%.*	
	a. Planning on individual cases	0.11
	b. Practice skills	−0.12
	c. Discussion of information from research that may be helpful to you on the job	−0.16
	d. Your ongoing job performance	−0.16
	e. How to meet the administrative requirements of your job	−0.06
	f. Other (specify)	0.31*

TABLE 1 (Continued)

Factor	Item	Pearson r
Clarifying roles	My supervisor has explained how we might work together, and has described the kind of help he/she can provide to me.	0.62*
Supporting worker in taboo areas	My supervisor helps me to talk about subjects that are not comfortable to discuss (e.g., my reactions to working with clients around sexual issues).	0.70*
Sharing thoughts and feelings	My supervisor shares his/her thoughts and feelings (e.g., sharing frustrations around a work situation).	0.53*
Understanding worker's feelings	When I tell my supervisor how I feel, she/he understands (e.g., my own frustrations with a client).	0.70*
Dealing with the theme of authority	When I am upset about something my supervisor says or does, he/she encourages me to talk about it.	0.75*
Putting worker's feelings into words	My supervisor can sense my feelings without my having to put them into words.	0.77*
Partializing worker's concern	My supervisor helps me sort out my concerns in a situation and look at them one at a time.	0.77*
Providing data	My supervisor shares his/her suggestions about the subjects we discuss for my consideration.	0.65*
Developing a supportive atmosphere	My supervisor creates the kind of emotional atmosphere in which I feel free to discuss my mistakes and failures as well as my successes.	0.74*
Permitting mistakes	My supervisor permits me to make my own mistakes (e.g., those areas where I have discretion within the boundaries of policies and procedures).	0.42*
Helping worker raise concerns openly with supervisor	I can talk openly to my supervisor about job-related concerns.	0.78*
Ability to raise concerns openly with colleagues	I can talk openly to my fellow workers about job-related concerns.	−0.08

TABLE 1 (Continued)

Factor	Item	Pearson r
Knowledge of policy and procedures	My supervisor has a detailed and accurate grasp of policy and procedures.	0.61*
Communicating workers' views	My supervisor will communicate my views to the administration about policy and procedures.	0.65*
Supervisor's helpfulness	In general, how helpful is your supervisor?	—
Supervisor's working relationship	In general, how satisfied are you with your working relationship with your supervisor?	0.89*
Supervisor's role	Approximately what percentage of his/her time do you see your supervisor actually allocating to each of these roles? *This should add to 100%.*	
	a. Manager	−0.37*
	b. Consultant	0.36*
	c. Teacher	0.32*
	d. Other (specify)	−0.26*

*$p \leq 0.05$.

appeared valid in terms of relevance and clarity of expression and instructions.

With this indication of face validity, a pretest which involved three workers and one supervisor was undertaken. This resulted in some scaling modifications, and a second test was then conducted with the revised questionnaire. The test used a sample of 37 workers reporting on four supervisors in a regional office of the British Columbia Ministry of Human Resources. Both workers and supervisors were guaranteed confidentiality.

Stability

In order to obtain information on the reliability of responses over time, questionnaires were distributed again one week later, as part of a test-retest design. Twenty-two workers mailed back the second questionnaire, and it is this sample on which the stability results are based.

All data analysis for this study used the computer software program Statistical Package for the Social Sciences (SPSS), Version 8 (Nie et al., 1975), on the University of British Columbia computer. Of the total of 43 items on the questionnaire, in 31 (72%) a significant correlation ($p \leq .05$) was obtained between the scores on the first and second administrations of the questionnaire. These correlations (Pearson r) were generally high, ranging from 0.45 to 0.91. The items with the lower correlations were related to the content and role of supervision, and the item asking for worker level of satisfaction with how he or she got along with the supervisor. Generally, items dealing with communications and relationship skills, the use of research-generated knowledge, the rating of the supervisor's helpfulness, and the context of supervision were judged to have positive results. It is the findings from these items which are reported in this book.

The test-retest scores of computed scales such as the one for empathic skills were also examined. Using more than one item to measure a variable increases the reliability of that measure. The test-retest correlations on the computed scales were as follows: contact regularity (0.76), supervisor availability (0.75), trust in supervisor (0.90), empathic skills (0.89), problem-solving skills (0.50), supervisor helpfulness and working relationship (0.63), agency practices (0.49), and the use of research and theory (0.77).

Internal consistency

In order to determine internal consistency of the computed scales, Cronbach's alpha (Cronbach, 1951) was computed as a measure of the interitem correlation on appropriate scales. The results were as follows: availability (0.47), trust (0.88), empathy (0.82), problem solving (0.78), relationship-helpfulness (0.94), agency practices (0.84), and the use of research and theory (0.77). Results of the analyses of both the stability and the internal consistency of the scales were judged to be at acceptable levels of reliability.

Construct validity

In addition to using a research design with face validity, as described above, other efforts were made to obtain validity data on this questionnaire. Construct validity was supported by analysis of correlations employing the constructs of the practice theory stated in the hypotheses. For example, a good working relationship between the supervisor and worker would be expected to have a strong association with supervisor helpfulness, which it did ($r = 0.89$). In addition, while content and context were considered important to supervision, the theoretical model guiding this research suggested that interactional skills would be central in determining a supervisor's effectiveness. It was expected that these skills would be the most highly correlated variables, as opposed to other factors such as supervisor stress, education, or experience. The findings in this study paralleled those in my practice study in that these variables were found to be most highly correlated with helpfulness.

Table 1 gives all of the nondemographic and non-child welfare items on the worker's questionnaire. Correlations with supervisor helpfulness are also reported using the Pearson r statistic. An asterisk is used on the Table to indicate which correlations were significant at $p \leq .05$.

The following items were found to be significantly correlated with supervisor helpfulness. An asterisk in the text indicates the item was also significantly correlated with helpfulness in my social work practice study. It should be noted that the wording on some of the social work practice items varied slightly from the supervision items, since that questionnaire was written for clients, not workers.

"I can talk openly to my supervisor about job-related concerns" (0.78); "My supervisor helps me sort out my concerns in a situation and look at them one at a time" (0.77)*; "My supervisor can sense my feelings without my having to put them into words" (0.77)*; "When I am upset about something my supervisor says or does, he/she encourages me to talk about it" (0.75)*; "My supervisor creates an atmosphere in which I feel free to discuss mistakes, failures, successes" (0.74); "When I tell my supervisor how I feel he/she understands" (0.70)*; "My supervisor helps me to talk about uncomfortable subjects (0.70)*; "My supervisor communicates my views to administration about policy and procedures" (0.65); "My supervisor shares suggestions for my consideration" (0.62)*; "My supervisor explains how we might work together and what kind of help is available" (0.62)*; "My supervisor has a good grasp of policy and procedures" (0.61); "My supervisor shares his/her thoughts and feelings about the work situation" (0.53)*; "My supervisor is available when I need him/her" (0.47); "My supervisor permits me to make my own mistakes" (0.42); "Percent of time my supervisor spends as a manager" (–0.37); "Percent of time my supervisor spends as a consultant" (0.36); "Percent of time my supervisor spends as a teacher" (0.32); "Percent of time my supervisor spends as an 'other' " (–0.26).

Note that 8 of these 18 skills have asterisks to indicate they were also associated with practice skill effectiveness in my social work practice study, although their correlations in the supervision study are all substantially stronger. Three other skills in the social work study identified as correlating with helpfulness were not included in the supervision questionnaire, and the ten additional variables with strong correlations with helpfulness in the supervision study were not part of the social work practice design. *Thus all eight variables that were common to both studies and were found to be correlated with helpfulness were so correlated in both studies.* In addition, as expected, consultation and teaching were positively associated with helpfulness, while managing and "other" supervision content were negatively correlated.

These findings offer evidence for construct validity of the workers' questionnaire, since the theoretical constructs supported in the study of social work practice were also supported in this second research design exploring similar constructs related to supervision practice. In addition to providing evidence of construct validity of the supervision questionnaire items, these findings also add support to the existence of a set of core skills which are important in a wide range of helping functions.

Predictive validity

Another form of validity, termed *predictive validity,* is one of the most important types, since it determines the ability of a variable to predict an outcome measure. To explore this avenue, we selected those supervisors, out of the total of 109 participants, who were in the top 25% and the bottom 25% on the computed scales. The theoretical model guiding this research would lead us to expect significant differences between the scores of these two groups on the relationship-helpfulness computed scale. Further, the model would suggest that the context and content scales should make some difference, although the process skills should be more important.

Our findings strongly supported predictive validity. Significant differences on the relationship-helpfulness scale between the two groups of supervisors were found for all scales, as follows: contact regularity ($F = 13.71$, $df = 51$, $p = .001$); availability ($F = 18.22$, $df = 51$, $p = .000$); content satisfaction ($F = 5.8$, $df = 52$, $p = .02$); trust ($F = 83.00$, $df = 51$, $p = .000$); empathic skills ($F = 68.43$, $df = 52$, $p = .000$); problem-solving skills ($F = 77.33$, $df = 54$, $p = .000$). When the trust, empathy, and problem-solving skills were combined into one score as an index of interactional skills, the difference in helpfulness was also found for the two groups ($F = 103.17$, $df = 51$, $p = .000$). As predicted, the context and content scales were important, but not as important as the process scales.

In summary, reliability and validity for the Supervision Questionnaire: Worker's Version were supported in terms of stability, internal consistency, face, construct, and predictive validity. While we see these findings as positive, it should be noted that this instrument is still in a developmental stage. Further work will add to our understanding of its levels of reliability and validity.

Supervision Questionnaire: Supervisor's Version

A separate questionnaire was developed to obtain information on supervision from the supervisors themselves (Supervision Questionnaire: Supervisor's Version). The procedures for developing the questionnaire were similar to those employed with the workers' version, including conversations with key informants (supervisors, workers, social work faculty, administrators, etc.) to determine items which might be relevant to this study.

In addition to demographic data (age, educational level, experience, sex, etc.), the questionnaire requested information on four major areas which were then computed into scales. One scale combined training and support; items for this scale measured level of education, preparation for the task ("I received adequate preparation for the tasks and problems I faced as a beginning supervisor"); ongoing training; emotional support ("I have access to ongoing emotional support from other staff in the agency which helps me to carry out my job as a supervisor"); and colleagual support ("I can talk to my fellow supervisors about job-related concerns"). The response scale to most items was: "(1) Strongly agree; (2) Agree; (3) Uncertain; (4) Disagree; (5) Strongly disagree."

Another scale was designed to measure the stress and manageability of the job. Items in this area ("My job as a supervisor is stressful" and "My job as a supervisor is manageable") had the following response categories: "(1) None of the time; (2) A little of the time; (3) Sometimes; (4) A good part of the time; (5) Most or all of the time; (6) Undecided." Since supervisors had indicated that it was possible to reply that their job was stressful but at the same time manageable, we computed a stress-manageability index by combining these variables in a manner which allowed respondents to be scored on a scale ranging from low stress–high manageability to high stress–low manageability.

An index of role satisfaction was computed by examining the supervisors' perceptions of the percentage of time they allocated to various tasks—supervision and consultation, management, personnel work, coordinating, and other—and what percentage of time the supervisor would *like* to allocate to these tasks. The index of role satisfaction was computed by subtracting the preferred from the actual percentages for each task and then adding the absolute values for a final score.

Child welfare supervisors were also asked to comment on their perceptions of their agency administration's emphasis on certain child welfare practices (e.g., developing a child in-care tracking system). The results of this aspect of the study were not reported in the text.

Table 2 gives all of the nondemographic and non-child welfare items on the supervisor's questionnaire. Correlations with supervisor helpfulness are also reported using the Pearson r statistic.

Reliability and validity

The design employed to obtain reliability and validity data for the supervisors' questionnaire was similar to the one used with the workers' version. Face validity was determined through a number of key-informant interviews with supervisors in the field, administrators, and social work faculty members. Forty-five of the supervisors participating in the main study were sent second copies of the questionnaire one week after they had completed the first one. Of this group, 41 responded, providing data for the test-retest analysis.

TABLE 2
SUPERVISORS' QUESTIONNAIRE ITEMS CORRELATED WITH SUPERVISOR HELPFULNESS (WORKERS' PERCEPTION)

Factor	Item	Pearson r
Preparation	I received adequate preparation for the tasks and problems I faced as a beginning supervisor.	−0.06
Ongoing training	I have opportunities for ongoing training to deal with the tasks and problems I face as a supervisor.	−0.01
Emotional support	I have access to ongoing emotional support from other staff in the agency which helps me to carry out my job as a supervisor.	0.15
Talk about concerns	I can talk to my fellow supervisors about job-related concerns.	0.08
Job stress	My job as a supervisor is stressful.	−0.06
Job manageability	My job as a supervisor is manageable.	0.07
Actual tasks	In your role as supervisor, approximately what percentage of your time do you allocate to each of the following tasks? *This should total 100%.*	
	a. Supervision and consultation	0.16
	b. Management (e.g., budgeting, planning, administration)	0.09
	c. Personnel work (e.g., evaluations, hiring staff, grievances)	0.10
	d. Coordinating (e.g., community liaison, team meetings, management meetings)	0.02
	e. Other (e.g., responsibilities above and beyond office tasks)	−0.03
Preferred tasks	Approximately what percentage of your time would you like to allocate to each of these tasks? *This should total 100%.*	
	a. Supervision and consultation	0.11
	b. Management (e.g., budgeting, planning, administration)	0.08
	c. Personnel work (e.g., evaluations, hiring staff, grievances)	0.05
	d. Coordinating (e.g., community liaison, team meetings, management meetings)	0.02
	e. Other (e.g., responsibilities above and beyond office tasks)	0.07

Note: No significant Pearson's r correlations were found at $p \leqslant 0.05$.

Stability

There were 21 items on the questionnaire, excluding demographic questions. Significant correlations were obtained for 19 of these at the $p \leq .05$ level, while 2 were significant at the .06 level. Correlations for the individual items reported on in this book ranged from 0.53 to 0.82 and were judged to be within acceptable limits.

Correlations for the four computed scales were as follows: supervisor support and training ($r = 0.78$, $p = .000$); supervisor job stress and manageability ($r = 0.53$, $p = .000$); supervisor role satisfaction ($r = 0.33$, $p = .02$), and agency child welfare practice ($r = 0.68$, $p = .000$). The levels for the first, second, and fourth scales were within acceptable limits, while the lower level for the role satisfaction scale suggests the need for caution in interpreting data involving this scale. Examination of the data on test-retest scores for each of the percentage categories (e.g., percent of time spent providing consultation and percent of time the supervisor would like to spend consulting) indicated high correlations on individual items (0.59 to 0.82). The lower correlation for the scale may mean that the gap between what supervisors do with their time and what they would like to do with their time may vary week to week, and this variation was picked up in the scores.

Internal consistency

Analysis of internal consistency of three of the computed scales, based on the returns of all 109 supervisors and employing Cronbach's alpha, revealed the following results: supervisor support and training ($a = 0.68$); job stress and manageability ($a = 0.50$); agency child welfare practices ($a = 0.81$). In general, the results supported the questionnaire's reliability.

Criterion and predictor validity

As for criterion and predictor validity, the theoretical model suggested that the individual variables which comprised the scales—support and training, stress and manageability, and role satisfaction—would not, by themselves, be major factors affecting outcome measures such as the supervisor's working relationship and helpfulness as perceived by workers. This was supported; none of these variables was significantly correlated with the outcome measures.

As a test of predictive validity, the procedure of selecting the top 25% and bottom 25% of the supervisors on each of the computed scales, and then comparing their scores on the relationship-helpfulness scale, was used. As expected, the contrasting groups of supervisors on the three scales of support and training, stress and manageability, and role satisfaction were not significantly different in their scores on the relationship-helpfulness scale. The data were: support and training ($F = 0.043$, $df = 42$, $p = .84$); stress and manageability ($F = 0.053$, $df = 48$, $p = .82$); role satisfaction ($F = 0.196$, $df = 38$, $p = .20$).

The significance of these possibly surprising findings are discussed in the text. They should be interpreted in the light of the limitations of the design described in the final section of this appendix. In particular, the self-selection of supervisors for participation may have made for a biased sample; those supervisors under greatest stress perhaps did not participate in the study. There is some evidence of this in the range of scores on the stress and manageability items. The mean score on the stress item was 3.53 on a 5-point scale, indicating the job was stressful "sometimes" to "a good part of the time" for the average supervisor (the standard deviation was 0.74). As for manageability, the mean score was 4.29 on the same scale, indicating the job was manageable "a good part of the time" to "most or all of the time" for the average supervisor (standard deviation was 0.72).

For the purpose of arguing for criterion and predictive validity, however, these results offer some supporting evidence.

Data-Gathering Procedures

The procedures employed to gather data for this study included mailing questionnaires to 120 supervisors and all of their professional (i.e., nonclerical) staff members. Although the study was originally designed to include only district office supervisors from the British Columbia Ministry of Human Resources, interest expressed by other supervisors led to its expansion.

Workers and supervisors were provided with stamped envelopes addressed to the research team at the University of British Columbia. The instructions were that each participant was to complete the questionnaire, seal the envelope, and mail it directly to the project. There were no worker identification codes on the questionnaires, and the participants were informed that supervisors would receive only average scores from their units, to protect individual worker confidentiality. While larger unit scores for regions, departments, or an agency were to be computed, these would also be provided in a way which maintained individual region, department, or agency confidentiality.

Study samples

Characteristics of the final samples of supervisors and workers are shown in Tables 3 and 4. Of the 120 supervisors who were mailed questionnaires, 109 (91%) responded. These supervisors all had volunteered to participate in this study, and many of them had been participants in one of my two-day workshops on the skills of supervision. Some had participated in longer-term supervision training projects which had been carried on over a number of years. The 55 participants from the British Columbia Ministry of Human Resources represented 46% of the total 120 potential supervisor participants in this agency. From the Ottawa Children's Aid Society, the 27 participating supervisors represented 84% of the 32 possibles in this agency. The largest group of nonreturns was from nursing supervisors who may have felt the questionnaire did not relate directly enough to their situation.

The final supervisor sample included 55 social work supervisors from child welfare settings in British Columbia (Ministry of Human Resources), 2 from Manitoba children's aid societies, and 14 from the Ottawa Children's Aid Society. Thus, as Table 3 shows, 71 (65%) of the participating supervisors were involved in child welfare or child welfare and financial aid practice. The remainder of the sample consisted of 15 participants (13.8%) who were nursing supervisors, 13 (11.9%) who were residential treatment center supervisors, and 10 (9.2%) who were social work supervisors from non-child welfare settings such as hospitals or schools.

The selection of supervisors to take part in the study from a number of areas of Canada and different locations (rural, urban, and suburban), from various settings and different agencies, and with a variety of functions (e.g., social workers, nurses) made it possible to generalize from the findings. But the factors of self-selection, prior training experiences with the researcher, and the heavy weighting

TABLE 3
CHARACTERISTICS OF SUPERVISOR SAMPLE (N = 109)

Variables	N	Percent
Age		
20–25	1	1
26–30	38	35
31–35	0	0
36–45	43	39
Over 46	27	25
Sex		
Male	66	61
Female	43	39
Education		
Community college or		
technical school	18	16
B.A.	16	15
B.S.W.	15	14
M.S.W.	36	33
Other	24	22
Supervisory experience		
2 years or less	31	28
3–5 years	22	20
6–10 years	34	31
More than 10 years	22	20
Area of majority of work		
Child welfare/financial		
aid	71	65
Nursing	15	14
Residential treatment	13	12
Other social work	10	9

given to child welfare supervision suggest that the sample should be viewed as biased, which has implications for external validity.

Table 3 also shows there were more men than women among the supervisors surveyed; 66 (60.6%) were male and 43 (39.4%) were female. Their educational background included 18 (16.5%) with community college degrees, 16 (14.7%) with bachelor of arts degrees, 15 (13.8%) with bachelor of social work degrees, 36 (33%) with master of social work degrees, and 24 (22%) with "other" degrees such as bachelor of science in nursing (B.S.N.). In terms of supervisory experience, 31 (28.4%) had 2 years or less, 22 (20.2%) had 3–5 years, 34 (31.2%) had 6–10 years, and 22 (20.2%) had been supervisors for more than 10 years.

Out of 1,078 workers who were sent questionnaires, 671 (62.2%) responded. Some of these worker responses, however, were associated with supervisors who did not return their questionnaires. These returns were not included in the findings because the unit of analysis was the supervisor.

In the final worker sample, as Table 4 shows, 270 (40.2%) of the workers identified themselves as in the child welfare field, 102 (15.-2%) as dealing with financial assistance, and 59 (8.8%) as residential treatment workers. In addition, 138 (20.6%) said they were in nursing, 98 (14.6%) indicated other social work settings, and 4 (0.6%) did not provide this information.

In the workers' group, 210 (31.3%) were male, 450 (67.1%) were female, and 11 (1.6%) did not provide gender data. Answers to the education question indicated 213 (31.7%) of the workers had had community college training, 143 (21.3%) had B. A. degrees, 119 (17.-7%) had B.S.W. degrees, 57 (8.5%) had M.S.W. degrees, and 135 (20.1%) had "other" degrees. Four others (0.61%) did not respond to the question.

Like the supervisor sample, the worker sample represented a diverse population in terms of training, job function, setting, geographic area, and agency. Nevertheless, self-selection must be taken into account, since the returns were from those workers who chose to respond. In a brief discussion with workers on factors which might influence nonresponse, it was clear that fear of being identified persisted with some workers, even though we attempted to provide reassurances of confidentiality. On a number of returns identifying data were not provided, probably due to this concern. It might be inferred that return rates were affected in situations where trust was low and fear of supervisor retaliation was high (perhaps against an entire staff group if individuals could not be identified), resulting in sample bias.

Data Analysis Procedures

All data were entered by trained coders on computer coding sheets designed for this study. Coding and key punch checks were

TABLE 4
CHARACTERISTICS OF WORKER SAMPLE (N = 671)

Variables	N	Percent
Age		
20–30	289	43
31–40	225	34
41–50	89	13
Over 50	63	9
No data	5	1
Sex		
Male	210	31
Female	450	67
No data	11	2
Education		
Community college or technical school	213	32
B.A.	143	21
B.S.W.	119	18
M.S.W.	57	8
Other	135	20
No data	4	1
Related work experience		
2 years or less	146	22
3–5 years	176	26
6–10 years	178	27
More than 10 years	170	25
No data	1	0
Area of majority of work		
Child welfare	270	40
Financial aid	102	15
Residential treatment	59	9
Nursing	138	20
Other	98	15
No data	4	1
Time in present setting		
2 years or less	345	51
3–5 years	187	28
6–10 years	104	16
More than 10 years	33	5
No data	2	0
Time under this supervisor		
2 years or less	470	70
3–5 years	137	20
6–10 years	53	8
More than 10 years	8	1
No data	3	1

made at regular intervals to keep the data as clean as possible and within acceptable limits.

Average scores for each supervisor were computed for each variable on the workers' questionnaires. These scores were then added to the supervisor's own returns in an SPSS system file with the supervisor as the unit of analysis. Thus all procedures were implemented with a sample of 109 supervisors.

A number of analyses were undertaken, including correlations, regression analysis, analysis of variance, and partial correlation. The results of these analyses and the researcher's interpretations are reported throughout the text, usually at the end of the relevant chapter. For a more technical report of the project, see the study report (Shulman, Robinson, and Luckyj, 1981).

Third-variable analysis

One of the analyses reported in the study involved examining the correlations between a number of supervision skills and the quality of the working relationship between the supervisor and the worker, as well as the help provided by the supervisor. This third-variable analysis, based on a technique described by Rosenberg (1968), makes use of the partial correlation procedure to examine what happens to the association between two variables if a third, supposedly related, variable is held constant.

In this analysis we examined the simple correlation between each skill and helpfulness and then observed the change (if any) in the correlation when relationship was held constant. If a correlation dropped significantly when controlling for relationship, then it might be inferred that the skill actually contributed to relationship (an intervening variable), which in turn was associated with being helpful. Each skill was also correlated with relationship, with helpfulness controlled, to see if the reverse might be true. Thus an effort was made to determine how a specific skill made its contribution to the process.

Table 5 provides the actual correlations. The simple correlations between the skills and helpfulness differ slightly from those reported in other places in the text (including Table 1 in this appendix). This is because the normal option for the computer program calculating partial correlations is to drop cases with missing data on any of the variables when computing the statistic. Thus, these sim-

TABLE 5
CORRELATIONS BETWEEN SUPERVISORS' SKILLS AND HELPFUL-
NESS WITH RELATIONSHIP CONTROLLED AND BETWEEN SKILLS
AND RELATIONSHIP WITH HELPFULNESS CONTROLLED

Supervisors' Skills	Helpfulness		Relationship	
	Pearson *r*	Relationship Controlled	Pearson *r*	Helpfulness Controlled
Putting the worker's feelings into words	0.76	0.42	0.70	0.06
Helping the worker raise concerns openly	0.79	0.07	0.86	0.56
Developing a supportive atmosphere	0.75	0.18	0.78	0.36
Permitting mistakes	0.43	0.13	0.42	0.08
Supporting worker in taboo areas	0.72	0.43	0.64	0.03
Understanding worker's feelings	0.72	0.16	0.75	0.34
Sharing thoughts and feelings	0.53	0.19	0.51	0.09
Partializing worker's concerns	0.77	0.42	0.72	0.07
Dealing with the theme of authority	0.76	0.34	0.73	0.17
Providing data	0.67	0.18	0.67	0.23
Knowledge of policy and procedures	0.61	0.29	0.56	0.38

ple correlations are based on a smaller sample of supervisors ($N = 101$). For each skill listed in the first column, the simple correlation with helpfulness is given in the second column, and that correlation with relationship controlled is given in the third column. The fourth column provides the simple correlation of the relevant skill with relationship, and the fifth gives the correlation with relationship with helpfulness controlled. Discussion of the inferences made from these findings can be found in the text.

Limitations of the Study

The findings in the supervision study must be considered in light of the limitations in its design. A large number of the participants were located in child welfare agencies, and the impact of setting can be serious. In an effort to explore this factor, returns from the various groups of professionals were compared. No significant differences on the crucial variables of the study were found, but the weight of this limitation is still a serious one, since effects which might not be easy to perceive may be at work.

Perhaps the most important limitation of this study is the self-selection factor for participants. In a follow-up discussion, a number of supervisors who chose not to participate gave various reasons, including lack of confidence in procedures for protecting confidentiality, anger at the agency, refusal to participate in an agency-sanctioned project, fear of an agency "hidden agenda" in the research, or reactions to recent policies of budget restraint. Others said they were so overwhelmed with the job that there was no time to participate, or, with great candor, "I'm afraid to have my staff fill those forms out on me." Whatever their reasons for not participating, we believe the nonrespondents as a group might have had some impact on certain aspects of the study, such as the stress and manageability findings. Nonetheless, their participation might have even heightened the importance of other findings, such as the impact of the supervisor's availability. In general, self-selection may have served to make the sample more mellow.

The research instruments must also be considered in reviewing limitations of the study. While supporting data were found for their reliability and validity, the workers' and supervisors' questionnaires need to be used in other settings and with further tests before there can be stong enough confidence in them to consider them more than developmental. The parallel findings of the importance of similar items in this study and my study of social work practice skills are a step in this direction.

Finally, the study is essentially one of supervisors' and workers' perceptions, and while they are the best judges, their perceptions must be considered somewhat subjective. Are supervisors who are described by their workers as helpful, a key outcome measure, really helpful? Can this be translated into objective, measurable factors, such as differences in worker behaviors and impact on services to clients? These are important questions which are unanswered in this study but which I have scheduled for exploration in my next projects.

With the groundwork laid by the studies of practice skill and supervision skill, one next step will be to examine the parallel process idea. The goal will be to see if supervisors who employ certain skills with workers (e.g., are more empathic) turn out to have workers who employ the same skills with clients. Another next step would be to see if this supervisor-worker complex influences specific outcomes of practice, such as helping to keep children with their natural parents or to return them from alternate care more quickly. While a client's or a worker's perception of helpfulness is an important outcome in itself, future work must move on to incorporate more "hard" outcome measures that are applicable in practice. For now, the use of subjective outcome measures has to be considered as one of the study's limitations.

Videotape Programs on Skills of Helping

The Skills of Helping is a series of three videotape programs produced by Lawrence Shulman which identifies and illustrates core practice skills for work with individuals, families, and groups, as well as with other professionals. A brochure is available from the Instructional Communications Centre, McGill University, 815 Sherbrooke St. W., Montreal, P.Q., H3A 2K6, 514-392-8031.

Program 1: Preliminary, beginning, and work phases (96 minutes)

Shulman presents a model of the dynamics involved in each of these phases of work and describes a number of specific core skills useful in work with individuals, groups, and families. The model draws on the work of William Schwartz. It is presented in the form of a discussion with a group of beginning social work students whose questions and reactions help to focus the presentation on issues that are central to their practice concerns. Each skill is illustrated with verbatim excerpts from practice. The skills described include tuning in, responding directly to indirect communication, contracting, dealing with the issue of authority, sessional contracting, elaborating, empathy, sharing workers' feelings, and demand-for-work skills.

Program 2: Leading a first group session (88 minutes)

Shulman discusses the core skills of the beginning phase in group work practice with social work students. The theory is illustrated with videotaped excerpts from an actual married couples' group led by Shulman. Skills described in the presentation include clarifying purpose and role for group members, reaching for group member feedback, encouraging group member interaction, developing a working consensus for next steps, evaluating the first session, and dealing with authority issues. The approach to group work presented is based on the mutual aid model developed by William Schwartz.

Excerpts from the group session provide striking illustrations of the initial defensiveness of group members, the importance of discussion of their fears and concerns about the power of group leaders, and group members' ability to begin to work quickly once they feel that they 'own' the group. Ages of the couples range from the mid-twenties to the seventies. The latter portion of the videotape consists of an example of internal leadership as a 70-year-old group member asks each couple how they handle anger in their relationships.

Program 3: Working with the system (93 minutes)

Shulman leads a discussion with a group of experienced practitioners on the dynamics and skills involved in working with other helping professionals, both within and outside one's own agency. The focus is on how the practitioner can have professional impact on system representatives who are important to clients (e.g., teachers, doctors, agency supervisors). Shulman presents a model of practice which encourages application of the core communication and relationship skills workers have developed in their work with clients to their efforts to impact on the system.

Appendix C

Standards and Expectations in Field Practice

Statements about expected student performance in the field on 24 core practice skills were developed by faculty and field instructors at the School of Social Work of the University of British Columbia. Under the direction of Dr. Kloh-Ann Amacher, coordinator of field instruction, a project was undertaken to describe these essential skills, to develop a rating instrument for the use of both students and field instructors, and to gather data which would provide a beginning statement of norms for each level of the undergraduate program.

This project was viewed as a first step in the difficult task of developing tools for making more specific student assessments. The instrument described should be regarded as embryonic and in need of testing for reliability and validity. The normative data on the different program levels should also be considered preliminary. This material is shared as work in progress.

The approach taken required a lengthy process and considerable time and patience on the part of field instructors and students. First, a draft of descriptive statements about skills was circulated to methods instructors, and they were asked for feedback on its relevance, clarity, and inclusiveness. The instructors were also asked if the wording was sufficiently "theory free" and if the skills were applicable to work with individuals, families, small groups, and communities. Based on this feedback, the form was revised and distributed to field instructors and students to be used in midyear progress reports. The objective was to seek profiles and norms of actual performance at various points in the educational process.

The tentative instrument provides average, or mean, scores for each skill for students in the school's three undergraduate programs. The undergraduate bachelor of social work (B.S.W.) degree is viewed as the first professional degree level. Third-year students in this program have completed two years of general arts. They undertake a mixed program of social work and arts electives which includes two days per week in a supervised field practicum. Upon completion of the third year, they continue the fourth-year program, which consists of mostly social work courses with some arts electives. There is also a weekly two-and-one-half-day supervised field practicum. Upon completion of the fourth year students are awarded a B.S.W. degree.

The third program for which scores are provided is called the concentrated bachelor of social work (C.B.S.W.) program. Students in this program have already obtained a bachelor's degree in some other area and have had a number of years of supervised social work or related experiences. The program consists of an extended school year (10 months) during which the students take their social work courses as well as a weekly two-and-one-half-day supervised field practicum. Upon completion of this program, students are awarded a B.S.W. degree.

In presenting the material on the project to field instructors and students, the University of British Columbia School of Social Work acknowledged their interest in clear statements about expected performance in the field. The project's developers noted that as educators they "share the view that clarity about objectives can promote learning and increase equity in the evaluation of performance."

Detailed reports on the progress of each student on each of the skills were not expected. Rather, the material was presented for teaching and learning purposes, as a basis for discussion between students and field instructors, and to identify areas of particular strength or weakness for a student or a program.

Scoring Procedures

The skills were individually coded by field instructors in conferences with the student, according to the following coding sheet:

0. The field instructor does not have evidence needed to make a judgment. The student may or may not have developed this skill. Not known.
1. The student has not yet developed this skill.
2. Grasps the idea and is beginning to recognize in hindsight how it might have been applied in a given practice situation.
3. Demonstrates the skill at a beginning level. Performance is uneven. Needs time and practice.
4. The skill is applied quite consistently but there are gaps, e.g., not used with some clients, or some feelings are avoided, etc.
5. The skill is an integrated part of the student's stance and style.

Average (mean) scores were computed for each class on each skill at midyear and the end of the year. Items coded 0 were excluded in the calculation. The average scores can be interpreted in terms of the coding sheet. For example, a 2.00 score would mean that the average student grasps the idea; a 2.50 would indicate that the average student grasps the idea and is beginning to demonstrate the skill in practice.

A total average on all skills also was computed for each class. The skills were rank ordered from highest level of achievement to lowest for the three classes combined, or the total B.S.W. program.

Mean Scores on Core Skills

Overall average scores on all skills for all students in the three B.S.W. programs at midyear and the end of the year were:

	Midyear Mean	End-of-Year Mean
Third-year B.S.W.	2.24	3.28
Fourth-year B.S.W.	3.70	4.53
C.B.S.W. (concentrated)	3.67	4.31

As these scores indicate, on the average, by midyear the third-year student was grasping the idea, seeing in hindsight what might have been done, and some students were beginning to apply some of the skills. Fourth-year and C.B.S.W. students were approaching a level of quite consistent application, with some gaps.

The following outline lists the core practice skills in rank order, from highest level of mastery to lowest, according to mean scores for the total group on each one.

1. *Ability to relate comfortably with clients who have different values or lifestyles, or who behave in ways that are labeled as "deviant" by the dominant society.*

   Students often struggle with value differences, at first not even recognizing their own values. Acceptance comes from self-awareness, understanding of the client, finding the areas of commonality as well as difference, and respecting the client's right to be different.

	Midyear Mean	End-of-Year Mean
Third-year	2.88	3.56
Fourth-year	4.11	4.80
C.B.S.W.	4.23	4.61

2. *Ability to recognize the feelings in the client's expression.*

   This skill involves picking up and emphathizing with expressed feelings, sensitivity to subtle or disguised expressions of feeling, perceptiveness about nonverbal clues, ability to tune in to probable feelings that are not quite expressed (e.g., the hurt beneath the anger), and perceptiveness about ambivalent feelings.

	Midyear Mean	End-of-Year Mean
Third-year	2.77	3.71
Fourth-year	4.00	4.63
C.B.S.W.	3.93	4.48

3. *Ability to clarify purposes, role, and agency function and to establish a mutual contract.*

   Initially students may offer a solution without exploring the problem and the client's perception of needs. They may jump too quickly to provide a concrete service or have difficulty in explaining purpose or role without jargon. Eventually they should develop a negotiating style, exploring the client's problems and wishes and explaining what the agency and worker can offer. Students should be able to make a tentative plan, consistently checking out, evaluating, and renegotiating the mutual understanding with the client of the goals and the process.

	Midyear Mean	End-of-Year Mean
Third-year	2.53	3.57
Fourth-year	3.89	4.81
C.B.S.W.	3.87	4.43

4. *Ability to recognize the range of factors which influence the client.*

These factors may be *(a)* biological (e.g., physical health); *(b)* social (e.g., peer group pressures); *(c)* psychological (e.g., vulnerability to separations); *(d)* cultural (e.g., values); or *(e)* political (e.g., legal recognition of rights). During the learning process there can be a tendency to emphasize one of these aspects to the exclusion of the others. Students should develop a perceptiveness of all the aspects and an understanding of which factors are most relevant to a particular situation.

	Midyear Mean	End-of-Year Mean
Third-year	2.76	3.52
Fourth-year	3.80	4.81
C.B.S.W.	3.93	4.65

5. *Ability to tune in, relate differently, and use the self in different ways, according to the fluctuating needs of various clients at various times.*

Initially students succeed in establishing warm, positive relationships; then they begin to tune in more sensitively to the client's mood, become comfortable with quietness, can join the client's moments of enthusiasm, and can understand and accept the client's distorted images and feelings toward the worker without premature explanations or defensiveness. Students learn to empathize with that part of the client which resists changes as well as that part which strives for growth and begin to see that working relationships are based on understanding and a shared sense of purpose and need not always be warm and friendly.

	Midyear Mean	End-of-Year Mean
Third-year	2.43	3.52
Fourth-year	3.83	4.63
C.B.S.W.	3.83	4.30

6. *Ability to explore, draw out, get the facts or the story.*

Students often begin by being hesitant and concerned about privacy and intrusion; they can be awkward about framing questions and fearful that the questions might sound accusatory. They may not explore because they are uncertain about how to respond or use the information gained. With time, they should be able to offer support and explanation about the purpose of the questions; they should be able to clarify the communication, realizing that the message sent is not necessarily the message received.

	Midyear Mean	End-of-Year Mean
Third-year	2.28	3.52
Fourth-year	3.80	4.50
C.B.S.W.	4.00	4.35

7. *Ability to question and think critically about programs, theories, the effectiveness of interventions, alternative approaches.*

This skill should be based on knowledge of policies, theories, and programs, their history and rationales. Critical thinking should lead to ideas about changes and strategies to bring about change.

	Midyear Mean	End-of-Year Mean
Third-year	2.00	3.15
Fourth-year	4.05	4.13
C.B.S.W.	3.87	4.77

8. *Ability to move back and forth across the objectivity-subjectivity line.*

This skill involves the capacity to empathize and feel with the client and the ability to step back and look objectively at the client, the self, and the interaction between them.

	Midyear Mean	*End-of-Year Mean*
Third-year	2.47	3.29
Fourth-year	3.84	4.50
C.B.S.W.	3.67	4.13

9. *Ability to formulate ideas about the process and the steps involved in moving from initial contracting through termination.*

   Initially students should question the purpose and the process and cannot be expected to have a clear view of what is helpful or why. They begin by seeing one useful step and move toward seeing a range of approaches.

	Midyear Mean	*End-of-Year Mean*
Third-year	2.45	3.33
Fourth-year	3.75	4.56
C.B.S.W.	3.80	4.30

10. *Ability to focus, maintain a sense of purpose and direction, and keep the client on the track.*

    Students may show a beginning awkwardness, a need to be friendly and establish a relationship before getting down to business. They may be more comfortable in the friend role. Eventually they may begin to bring the discussion back to a focus—if the client is uncomfortable or avoiding the issues, they have some ability to discuss the client's discomfort. A consistent sense of purpose should emerge.

	Midyear Mean	*End-of-Year Mean*
Third-year	2.41	3.57
Fourth-year	3.85	4.63
C.B.S.W.	3.71	4.43

11. *Ability to integrate acceptance and expectation of clients.*

Students must learn to accept the client, then begin to make some demands, providing support along with the demands. Some students will go through periods of being too heavy on the acceptance side or too heavy on the demand side, eventually achieving the integration with some clients, possibly not with others. Eventually they should develop a consistent style that incorporates both acceptance and expectation, with a sense of tact and appropriate timing.

	Midyear Mean	End-of-Year Mean
Third-year	2.52	3.29
Fourth-year	3.50	4.50
C.B.S.W.	3.80	4.23

12. *Ability to pick up themes, messages, and patterns underlying the client's presenting content.*

Students begin to see in hindsight the relevance of the client's comments or digressions. They may wonder during interviews "Why is the client saying this, to me, now?" and occasionally comment on the themes and connections, as they learn to discern the messages that are embedded in other contexts. In group meetings, students begin to comment on the themes, helping members connect with one another.

	Midyear Mean	End-of-Year Mean
Third-year	2.34	3.24
Fourth-year	3.85	4.31
C.B.S.W.	3.50	4.19

13. *Awareness of feelings toward the client and ability to sort out the realistic from the provoked, and to identify self-generated responses to the client.*

Awareness of one's own personal reactions can be a tool for understanding the client's interpersonal defenses. Students must first be aware of their feelings toward clients and then begin to question whether the feeling is realistic or part of the client's way of keeping distance, or if it stems from the worker's own unfinished business (e.g., an unrealistic need to mother, or resentment of domineering or ineffectual people).

	Midyear Mean	End-of-Year Mean
Third-year	1.96	2.89
Fourth-year	3.93	4.56
C.B.S.W.	3.64	4.09

14. *Ability to achieve an active-passive balance.*

This skill combines passivity in letting the client struggle, and activity in the ability to speak up, suggest, advise, confront or do for the client. Students may go through phases of being too active in giving suggestions, advice, or referrals and in doing for the client, or of being too passive, hesitant about making suggestions, and giving opinions or information but being unwilling to do some things for some clients at some times. Eventually they should be comfortable with both activity and passivity, and have a clear sense of the professional tasks.

	Midyear Mean	End-of-Year Mean
Third-year	2.38	3.25
Fourth-year	3.74	4.56
C.B.S.W.	3.60	4.04

15. *Ability to respond to feelings and facilitate their expression.*

Early in their learning students may tend to reassure clients prematurely or change the subject, because of their discomfort in experiencing too much of the client's pain, anger, or fearfulness or their uncertainty about how to respond. This moves toward the ability to express empathy, put unexpressed feelings into words, and explore both sides of ambivalence. The ability to accept and deal with hostility, to tolerate anxiety,

	Midyear Mean	End-of-Year Mean
Third-year	2.23	3.33
Fourth-year	3.53	4.31
C.B.S.W.	3.80	4.35

and, in group situations, to draw upon the cues or feelings of other group members also develops.

16. *Ability to respond to and accept both the rational and irrational components in the client's behavior.*

Students should relate to the rational components and learn to accept and not try to struggle against the inevitable irrational components by means of logic and debate. The irrational is purposive and rooted in fears and feelings which need to be addressed.

	Midyear Mean	End-of-Year Mean
Third-year	2.21	3.30
Fourth-year	3.59	4.63
C.B.S.W.	3.77	4.13

17. *Ability to understand, accept, and work with resistance.*

Some students will tend to give up when faced with resistance from a client; others will push, confront, exhort, advise, or get into a battle with the client. Eventually they should be able to discuss the client's resistance, the meaning to the client of being helped, and the fear and resentment inherent in change; they should recognize the need for defenses and for periodic avoidance of stressful content. Students should learn to respect the integrity of the human being and to see how resistance reflects the client's efforts to maintain self-esteem and is a patterned approach to interpersonal relationships and social demands.

	Midyear Mean	End-of-Year Mean
Third-year	2.07	3.05
Fourth-year	3.71	4.63
C.B.S.W.	3.71	4.19

18. *Ability to share personal thoughts and feelings about the client and the client's situation.*

Students' inhibition can move to spontaneity, so feelings are conveyed bodily and verbally—awkwardly at first. At times students will assume that the client would feel as they do without checking it out, or they will get into personal experiences that interrupt the flow and focus on the client's experience. This is followed by sensitivity to the client's reaction to their own feelings and the ability to sense when the client is embarrassed or fearful of the closeness, or resentful. Eventually the student can discuss the relationship.

	Midyear Mean	End-of-Year Mean
Third-year	2.30	3.25
Fourth-year	3.63	4.50
C.B.S.W.	3.54	4.52

19. *Ability to make referrals, helping the client identify needs and resources, exploring the client's feelings and expectations about the resources, giving clear information.*

    Students should check out a resource and know about eligibility, the services actually provided, and the clientele served. They should be able to discuss the client's previous experiences and feelings about similar resources. Referrals should be based on a discussion of the client's hopes and motivation and personal priorities. There should be follow-through feedback from the client about the experience and its usefulness, clearing up misunderstandings.

	Midyear Mean	End-of-Year Mean
Third-year	2.08	3.45
Fourth-year	3.81	4.33
C.B.S.W.	3.42	4.55

20. *Ability to accept the authority of the professional role and make difficult decisions without abusing power and control over the client.*

    Students can be very hesitant to use their authority, as in apprehending a child or in setting firm limits in situations where the client is a danger to himself or others. There can also be a tendency to use power to punish when a client has been frustratingly uncooperative.

	Midyear *Mean*	*End-of-Year* *Mean*
Third-year	1.76	2.78
Fourth-year	3.43	4.54
C.B.S.W.	3.79	4.27

21. *Ability to help the client select goals that maximize the client's motivation, capacity, and opportunity.*

Students may be too protective, not making demands. Or they may be too ambitious, imposing unreasonable expectations on the client, thinking only of long-range goals without being able to see the short-range, realizable steps toward longer-term goals. Students should work in partnership with the client in establishing clear goals, articulating first steps, and achieving goals. They should have a sense of consistently helping the client to do his/her work, achieve his/her goals.

	Midyear *Mean*	*End-of-Year* *Mean*
Third-year	2.00	3.38
Fourth-year	3.47	4.44
C.B.S.W.	3.53	4.33

22. *Ability to use programming, structured, and/or educative approaches.*

Over time students will become selective about the clients who may benefit from these approaches and clear about the relationship of the approach to the client's needs and goals. They will be able to explain the purpose with clarity and get feedback.

	Midyear *Mean*	*End-of-Year* *Mean*
Third-year	1.92	3.18
Fourth-year	3.38	4.64
C.B.S.W.	3.50	4.20

23. *Ability to articulate aspects of the assumptions, theories, and knowledge base that shape the understanding and the action.*

Students may be spontaneous and intuitive without understanding the "whys" and "hows". In the early stages they often need directions and prescriptions but move toward greater independence in thinking things through for themselves. Initial efforts to apply theory in practice situations can be awkward and self-conscious. Eventually the thinking process becomes integrated and natural and consistently guides the worker's activities without the loss of spontaneity, intuitiveness, and feeling.

	Midyear Mean	End-of-Year Mean
Third-year	1.93	3.05
Fourth-year	3.25	4.38
C.B.S.W.	3.21	4.23

24. *Ability to use research concepts in the analysis, planning, and evaluation of practice in routine work with any case, groups, or community assignment.*

This implies an appreciation of the relevance of research principles to practice, not just to empirical studies. This would include *(a)* knowledge of the range of possible data collection methods and the ability to make a well-reasoned selection of methods in a particular situation; *(b)* knowledge of the major types and sources of error in the social worker's use of data; *(c)* knowledge of and ability to use the criteria by which the adequacy of the data collected in practice situations may be assessed for its validity and usefulness in case planning; *(d)* ability to evaluate evidence relevant to the effectiveness of the student's intervention.

	Midyear Mean	End-of-Year Mean
Third-year	1.06	1.33
Fourth-year	3.13	3.90
C.B.S.W.	2.33	3.44

References

Abrahamson, Arthur C. *Group Methods in Supervision and Staff Development.* New York: Harper, 1959.

Ackerman, Nathan W. *Psychodynamics of Family Life.* New York: Basic Books, 1958.

Amacher, Kloh-Ann. "Explorations into the Dynamics of Learning in Field Work." D.S.W. dissertation, Smith College, School of Social Work, 1971.

Arlow, Jacob A. "The Supervisory Situation." *Journal of the American Psychoanalytic Association* 11 (1963): 574–94.

Austin, Lucille. "Supervision in Social Work." *Social Work Year Book,* 1960, pp. 579–86.

Bennis, Warren G., and Shepard, Herbert A. "A Theory of Group Development." *Human Relations* 9 (1956): 415–37.

Bion, William R. *Experiences in Groups.* New York: Basic Books, 1961.

Briar, Scott. "Family Services." In Henry Maas (ed.), *Five Fields of Social Services: Reviews of the Literature,* pp. 9–50. New York: National Association of Social Workers, 1966.

Briar, Scott. "Family Services and Casework." In Henry Maas (ed.), *Research in the Social Services: A Five Year Review,* pp. 108–25. New York: National Association of Social Workers, 1971.

Burns, Mary E. "The Historical Development of the Process of Casework Supervision." Ph.D. dissertation, School of Social Service Administration, University of Chicago, 1958.

Carkhuff, Robert R. *Helping and Human Relations: A Primer for Lay and Professional Helpers.* Vol. 1, *Selection and Training.* New York: Holt, Rinehart and Winston, 1969.

Charney, E. "How Well Do Patients Take Oral Penicillin? Collaborative Study in Private Practice." *Pediatrics* 40 (1967): 188–95.

Cronbach, L. J. "Coefficient Alpha and the Internal Structure of Tests." *Psychometrica* 16 (1951): 297–334.

Dawson, John B. "The Case Supervisor in a Family Agency." *Family* 6 (1967): 293–95

Dewey, John. *Democracy and Education; An Introduction to the Philosophy of Education.* New York: Free Press, 1916.

Doehrman, Marjery J. "Parallel Processes in Supervision and Psychotherapy." Ph.D. dissertation, University of Michigan, 1972.

Flanders, Ned A. *Analyzing Teaching Behaviors.* Reading, Mass.: Addison-Wesley Publishing Co., 1970.

Freud, Sigmund. "Freud's Psychoanalytic Method." In *Standard Edition,* Vol. 7. London: Hogarth Press, 1953.

Galm, Sharon. *Isssues in Welfare Administration: Welfare–An Administrative Nightmare.* U.S. Congress. Subcommittee on Fiscal Policy of the Joint Economic Committee. Washington, D.C.: U.S. Government Printing Office 1972.

Gitterman, Alex, and Gitterman, Naomi Pines. "Social Work Student Evaluation: Format and Method." *Journal of Education for Social Work* 15 (Fall 1979): 103–8.

Hollander, E. P. "Emergent Leadership and Social Influence." In Luigi Petrullo and Bernard M. Bass (eds.), *Leadership and Interpersonal Behavior,* pp. 30–47. New York: Holt, Rinehart and Winston, 1961.

Holt, John. *How Children Learn.* New York: Pitman Publishing Corp., 1969.

Holtzman, Reva Fine. "Major Teaching Methods in Field Instruction in Casework." D.S.W. dissertation, Columbia University, School of Social Work, 1966.

Kadushin, Alfred. *Supervisor-Supervisee: A Questionnaire Study.* Madison: School of Social Work, University of Wisconsin, 1973.

Kadushin, Alfred. "Supervisor-Supervisee: A Survey." *Social Work* 19 (1974): 288–98.

Kadushin, Alfred. *Supervision in Social Work.* New York: Columbia University Press, 1976.

Kaslow, Florence W. "Group Supervision." In Florence W. Kaslow and associates (eds.), *Issues in Human Services,* pp. 115–41. San Francisco: Jossey-Bass, 1972.

Kaslow, Florence Whiteman, and Associates. *Supervision, Consultation, and Staff Training in the Helping Professions.* San Francisco: Jossey-Bass, 1977.

Kettner, Peter M. "Some Factors Affecting Use of Professional Knowledge and Skill by the Social Worker in Public Welfare Agencies." D.S.W. dissertation, University of Southern California, School of Social Work, 1973.

Kledaras, Constantine G. "A Study of Role Conflict in Supervision." D.S.W. dissertation, Catholic University of America, 1971.

Kutzik, Alfred S. "The Social Work Field" and "The Medical Field." In Florence Whiteman Kaslow (ed.), *Supervision, Consultation, and Staff Development,* pp. 1–24 and 25–60. San Francisco: Jossey-Bass Publishers, 1977.

Lewin, Kurt. *A Dynamic Theory of Personality: Selected Papers of Kurt Lewin.* New York: McGraw-Hill Book Co., Inc., 1935.

Lewin, Kurt. "Field Theory in Social Science." In Dorwin Cartwright (ed.), *Frontiers in Group Dynamics,* pp. 221–33. New York: Harper and Row, 1951.

Marcus, Grace. "How Case Work Training May Be Adapted to Meet Workers' Personal Problems." In *Proceedings of the National Conference of Social Work,* pp. 127–39. Chicago: University of Chicago Press, 1927.

Mayer, John E., and Rosenblatt, Aaron. "Sources of Stress among Student Practitioners in Social Work: A Sociological View." *Journal of Education for Social Work* 10 (1974): 56–66.

Mayer, John E., and Rosenblatt, Aaron. "Objectionable Supervisory Styles: Student's Views." *Social Work* 20 (1975): 184–89.

Meyer, Carol H. *Staff Development in Public Welfare Agencies.* New York: Columbia University Press, 1966.

Munson, Carlton E. (ed.). *Social Work Supervision: Classic Statements and Critical Issues.* New York: Free Press, 1979.

Nie, Norman H., Hull, C. H., Jenkins, Jean G., Steinbrenner, Karin, and Bent, Dalett. *Statistical Package for the Social Sciences (SPSS), Version 8.* New York: McGraw-Hill Book Co., 1975.

Olmstead, Joseph, and Christenson, Harold E. "Effects of Agency Work Contexts: An Intensive Field Study." *Research Report No. 2.* Washington, D.C.: Department of Health, Education, and Welfare, Social Rehabilitation Service, 1973.

Olyan, Sidney D. "An Explanatory Study of Supervision in Jewish Community Centers as Compared to Other Welfare Settings." Ph.D. dissertation, University of Pittsburgh, 1972.

Reynolds, Bertha C. *Learning and Teaching in the Practice of Social Work.* New York: Farrar, 1942.

Robinson, Elizabeth. "Development of an Instrument to Measure the Skills and Knowledge of Child Welfare Supervisors." Unpublished paper, School of Social Work, University of British Columbia, Canada, 1980.

Robinson, Virginia. *Supervision in Social Casework.* Chapel Hill, N.C.: University of North Carolina Press, 1936.

Robinson, Virginia. *The Dynamics of Supervision under Functional Controls.* Philadelphia: University of Pennsylvania Press, 1949.

Rogers, Carl R. *On Becoming a Person.* Boston: Houghton Mifflin Co., 1961.

Rosenberg, Morris. *Logic of Survey Analysis.* New York: Basic Books, 1968.

Sales, Esther, and Navarre, Elizabeth. *Individual and Group Supervision in Field Instruction: A Research Report.* Ann Arbor: School of Social Work, University of Michigan, 1970.

Schwartz, William. "Content and Process in the Educative Experience." Doctoral dissertation, Teachers College, Columbia University, 1960.

Schwartz, William. "The Social Worker in the Group." In *New Perspectives on Services to Groups: Theory, Organization, Practice.* New York: National Association of Social Workers, 1961, pp. 7–34. Also published by The Social Welfare Forum, 1961, and Columbia University Press, New York, 1961, pp. 146–77.

Schwartz, William. "Toward a Strategy of Group Work Practice." *Social Service Review* 36 (September 1962): 268–79.

Schwartz, William. "The Classroom Teaching of Social Work with Groups." Paper presented at the annual meeting of the Council on Social Work Education, Toronto, January 28, 1964.

Schwartz, William. "Group Work in Public Welfare." *Public Welfare* 26 (October 1968): 322–68.

Schwartz, William. "Private Troubles and Public Issues: One Social Work Job or Two?" *The Social Welfare Forum, 1969,* pp. 22–43. New York: Columbia University Press, 1969.

Schwartz, William. "Between Client and System: The Mediating Function." In Robert W. Roberts and Helen Northern (eds.), *Theories of Social Work with Groups.* New York: Columbia University Press, 1976.

Schwartz, William. "Social Group Work: The Interactionist Approach." In John B. Turner (ed.), *Encyclopedia of Social Work,* Vol. II. New York: National Association of Social Workers, 1977.

Schwartz, William. "Education in the Classroom." Paper presented at the annual meeting of the Council on Social Work Education, Boston, Mass., March 5, 1979.

Schwartz, William, and Zalba, Serapio. *The Practice of Group Work.* New York: Columbia University Press, 1971.

Scott, W. Richard. "Professional Employees in the Bureaucratic Structure." In Etzioni Amitai (ed.), *The Semi-Professions and their Organizations,* pp. 82–140. New York: Free Press, 1969.

Shulman, Lawrence. "Scapegoats, Group Workers and Preemptive Intervention." *Social Work,* 12, No. 2 (1967): 37–43.

Shulman, Lawrence. *A Casebook of Social Work with Groups: The Mediating Model.* New York: Council on Social Work Education, 1969a.

Shulman, Lawrence. "Social Systems Theory in Field Instruction." In Gordon Hearn (ed.), *Social Systems Theory in Social Work Education.* New York: Council on Social Work Education, 1969b.

Shulman, Lawrence. "Social Work Skill: The Anatomy of a Helping Act." In *Social Work Practice,* pp. 29–48. New York: Columbia University Press, 1969c.

Shulman, Lawrence. "Client, Staff and the Social Agency." In *Social Work Practice,* pp. 21–40. New York: Columbia University Press, 1970.

Shulman, Lawrence. "Group Work and Effective College Teaching." Ed.D. dissertation, Temple University, 1972.

Shulman, Lawrence. *The Impact of Reduced Caseloads on Preventative Services.* Research report submitted to the Ontario Ministry of Community and Social Affairs, 1977.

Shulman, Lawrence. "A Study of Practice Skill." *Social Work* 23 (July 1978): 274–81.

Shulman, Lawrence. *The Skills of Helping Individuals and Groups.* Itasca, Ill.: F. E. Peacock Publishers, 1979.

Shulman, Lawrence. *Identifying, Measuring and Teaching the Helping Skills.* New York: Council on Social Work Education and the Canadian Association of Schools of Social Work, 1981.

Shulman, Lawrence, Robinson, Elizabeth, and Luckyj, Anna. *"A Study of Supervision Skill: Context, Content and Process."* Unpublished report. Vancouver, B.C.: University of British Columbia School of Social Work, 1981.

Strean, Herbert S. *Clinical Social Work Theory and Practice.* New York: Free Press, 1978.

Taft, Jessie. "Living and Feeling." *Child Study* 10 (1933): 100–12.

Taft, Jessie. "Time as the Medium of the Helping Process." *Jewish Social Service Quarterly* 26 (December 1949): 230–43.

Towle, Charlotte. *The Learner in Education for the Professions: As Seen in Education for Social Work.* Chicago: University of Chicago Press, 1954.

Truax, C. B. "Therapist Empathy, Warmth, and Genuineness, and Patient Personality Change in Group Psychotherapy: A Comparison Between Interaction Unit Measures, Time Sample Measures, and Patient Perception Measures." *Journal of Clinical Psychology* 71 (1966): 1–9.

Wilson, Suanna J. *Recording: Guidelines for Social Workers.* New York: Free Press, 1980.

Name Index

Subject Index

Index of Case Illustrations